PICK OF
PUNCH

"I've seen worse as far as puppet dictators go."

"Don't ask me – I thought they were yours."

PICK OF
PUNCH

EDITED BY DAVID TAYLOR

"Ever been on an elephant-hunt before, Witherton?"

A PUNCH BOOK

Published in association with **GRAFTON BOOKS**

"Dammit, Serjeant, pygmies are the least of our problems at the moment!"

Grafton Books
A Division of the Collins Publishing Group
8 Grafton Street, London W1X 3LA

Published by Grafton Books 1988

A CIP catalogue record for this book is available from the British Library

ISBN 0-246-13412-7

Designed by Sheena Boyd

Printed in Great Britain by
William Collins Sons Ltd, Westerhill, Glasgow

CONTENTS

IS SHE
LOSING HER BOTTLE?

Ding-dong. Pause. Click.

Milkman: Mornin', Mrs T. Milk. Sorry to have to bring this up, but you owe for three weeks.

PM: Oh dear, oh dear! How absurd, you don't take that seriously. In the eight years, nine months, three days, eleven hours and two-and-a-quarter minutes since we came through this door, we *have* paid every week, *and the Right Honourable Milkman knows that perfectly well.*

MM: Sorry, Mrs T., but it's right down here in black and white – three weeks; I've got the figures.

PM: Let me say this: we are watching very carefully what goes on, and we shall be looking at ways of dealing with the difficulties which do exist, *and we shall continue* to do so.

MM: Mrs T., I just want the money, I don't need a speech.

PM: *We have a bounden duty* to look at ways of remedying the situation, and *that is why* we have a specific programme, and *it is why we shall carry on* as we have been doing.

MM: You mean, you're not goin' to pay? You're makin' this very difficult, Mrs T.

PM: We *obviously* hear about the difficulties: we don't often hear the true facts. The story is often very different when we do get the facts. Let me give you an example –

MM: No examples, please, just the money, otherwise I'm afraid something'll 'ave to be done about this.

PM: But *more is being done*: increased resources are being made available –

MM: *When* – next time 'Alley's Comet comes round?

PM: *If I may continue, Mr Milkman:* that is *exactly why*, eight years after we came in through this front door, after eight years of enterprise, people *know* we have to pay our way in the world. People come *flooding* in to see us, and we are *delighted, absolutely delighted,* to see them –

MM: Does that include my firm's solicitors, 'cause that's what it'll come to, I'm afraid –

PM: We shall be looking very closely at ways of getting all the facts, and *we shall go on doing so* –

MM: Right, that's it. You'll be hearing from us. Good morning. *(Rattle of crate: fade.)*

Mrs Thatcher tries out her new
House of Commons TV act by busking in the Tube

OUT OF THE AIR
(Radio 3 Dept.)

CONTINUITY ANNOUNCER: That was the song-cycle *"Das verkaufte Flugzeug"* by Pimpelmann, played by the English Viola Consort under their conductor Nigel Mousecroft. The singers were Annamaria Sampdoria, soprano; Arturo Vespasiano, tenor; Rycroft Vesely, baritone; and Nurtti Strånggulä, bass. The harpsichord continuo was played by Victoria Flegg-Westeringholme.

(Long pause)

And as we have a few moments in hand, I can remind you that This Week's Composer is the eighteenth-century Hanoverian *kapellmeister* Dingbad von Nastisch, who died 150 years ago next Tuesday. At 7.45 tomorrow evening, in a concert broadcast live from the Free Trade Hall, Manchester, you can hear a Sesquicentennial Programme of von Nastisch's work, played by the Hallé Orchestra under its visiting conductor Sviatislav Poposnodko. The programme will include the popular overture to von Nastisch's opera *I Pisellini*, and his masterwork, the Symphony No. 12 in D major, "The Unlikely".

(Pause)

And now over to the Fairfield Halls, Croydon, where we are to hear a recital of vocal works, given by Clifford Richard. The recital is introduced by Cloudesley Quantock.

(Fade up background hum of audience)

QUANTOCK: Good evening, and welcome to the Fairfield Halls in Croydon, where, as you've heard, we're to hear a recital of vocal music, given by the internationally renowned English baritone Clifford Richard. Born Harry Roger Webb in Lucknow, India, in 1940, Clifford Richard came to prominence in the late 1950s with a remarkably successful series of studio recordings. His early manner clearly originated in the grand baroque of Presley, though it was charged with an anarchic energy more plainly redolent of Little Richard (to whom Richard is incidentally unrelated) and Wee Willie Harris. Since that time, Richard has maintained for thirty years a scarcely interrupted flow of popular performances, alternating artfully between the controlled savagery of rock and the elegiac balladeering of roll. He has also shown evidence of a devotional and even ecclesiastical bent not often encountered outside the realms of gospel music. He has consistently championed short forms, or "numbers", and it is a selection of these that we shall be hearing tonight.

(Applause)

QUANTOCK: And on to the stage now come the featured instrumentalists, Henry B. Marvin, guitar *obbligato*, and Ronald Verrell, percussion.

(Louder applause)

QUANTOCK: A lively greeting for our conductor, Flash Braunsberg.

(Hysterical applause)

QUANTOCK: And the audience rises to acclaim tonight's soloist, Clifford Richard. Excuse me. I think I'm going to scream.

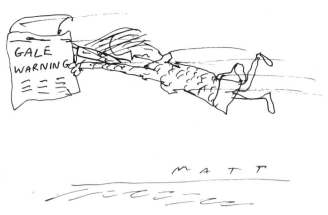

M A T T

NEVER A DULL MOMENT

A colourful, carnival atmosphere filled the streets of Panama this week as smiling troops drove gaily-painted water cannon through the bustling streets and fired festive pepper gas at passers-by. Bonfires on every corner added to the fun-filled atmosphere, as revellers torched overturned cars. Speaking about the jolly crack-crack of distant fireworks, the ever popular General Noriega explained to the fascist bourgeoisie of the world's press that it was a heart-warming demonstration of widespread support for his

bold, reforming budget which had taken a firm line on the money supply.

Meanwhile, just up the road in sunny Honduras, excitement mounted to fever pitch as preparations went into full swing for a "mardi gras" with their Nicaraguan neighbours. President Azcona would not comment on a rumour that he was arranging for an all-star American cabaret to be flown in to add to the revels, but already there was the crump-crump of sporadic calypso bands and next week's big programme of events is widely expected to be a real show-stopper.

"Do the Liberal MPs look a bit fuzzy to you?"

THIS WEEK'S LUCKY E-NUMBERS

E639 Emulsified pig's spleen extract (cheese & onion)
●The winner eats in a burger bar
E645 Butylated orthophospheric benzoate (crispy bacon)
E678 Conglomerated sheepshank sludge (Thousand Island)
E685 Permitted pulper (just pop under grill)
E699 Monolithic spigoted sardine substitute (for the way we live today)

SORRY ABOUT THAT

The BBC's first Head of Apologies is to be Mr Jeremy Blushe, a former station announcer at Liverpool Street. Details of the short-list from which Mr Blushe was chosen have not been released, but BBC sources have indicated that his performance in interview strongly swayed the Appointments Board. Blushe is said to have been the only candidate to turn up annoyingly late so as to have something serious to apologise for.

SORRY

Backing into the limelight at what the official invitation described as "a rather inadequate sort of stand-up buffet thing" held last night on the sixth floor of Television Centre, Mr Blushe, a balding middle-aged man who seemed constantly on the verge of tears, was described by the Corporation's Vice-Chairman, Sir Rockford Fildes, as "painful" in his awareness of his own limitations. "Yet we are dealing here," Sir Rockford went on, "with an exceptional communicator, a man whose first recorded words were an apology to his mother for the inconvenience caused. We think he is ideally placed, in these troubled times, to restore to the BBC's image some of the abject humility that government, press and public are so very properly demanding. He deeply believes, as we all do, in the BBC's propensity for getting things terribly, terribly wrong."

Accepting prolonged boos of welcome with bowed head, Mr Blushe pledged himself to uphold the traditional white feather at all times. "For too long," he said, "the BBC has ridden roughshod over the opinions of the man in the street, who in fact knows far better than we do what is going on. We have employed far too many correspondents who have assumed that just because they travel around the

world a lot, asking embarrassing questions and receiving inside information, their opinions on international affairs are worth hearing. We have handed over sums of money to so-called playwrights who have then gone away and thought up imaginary worlds of their own, where people's skin peels off and bare bottoms are seen bobbing up and down in fields. We know it will not do, but we are taking steps to change it. What the British people require is more Bob Monkhouse and Henry Kelly, and we are determined to give them those on a daily basis. All future single plays will be by J.B. Priestley, and Panorama will be presented by Mr Paul Daniels who will make unwanted topics disappear. In a great stride forward for both women and foreign reporting, Kate Adie will be the first BBC correspondent stationed on the moon. We realise this is only a drop in the ocean, but we've started so we'll finish."

TERRIBLY SORRY

Responding almost inaudibly to questions, Mr Blushe offered to commit suicide if viewing figures for Asian Music programmes did not improve. The BBC had approached Mr Jeremy Beadle, he revealed, with a view to presenting such items. He further undertook to set in train another series of *Dad's Army*. "I understand that most of the cast are dead, but of course that is no excuse," commented Mr Blushe. The BBC canteen, he added, was to be closed, since too many presenters were making tedious jokes about it. In conclusion, Mr Blushe apologised to the assembled company for taking so long to say so little, and amid a gentle rain of vegetables the meeting adjourned to the Tebbit Suite for buns and lemonade.

"I sentence you to whatever term turns out to be politically convenient."

The Sunday Times Literary Banquet

Kingsley Pinter, Harold Fraser, Lady Antonia Thubron and Melvyn Street-Porter will be among the distinguished guests at this scintillating, all-media occasion to be held at the sumptuous Wogan Hotel, Wapping, on March 28.

It will be the key literary, social, and artistic event of the last 100 years, overshadowing even the Sunday Times Fun Run, as hundreds of glittering names, known and loved by millions the world over through their appearances on TV and in the pages of The Sunday Times, *actually appear in the flesh*, and plough their way through 12 superb courses specially prepared by our Cook of the Month, Gary Blonk, chief *chef de salmonelle* at the Wogan Hotel.

At last year's banquet, over 7,000 privileged guests paid fabulous sums to stand and watch through bullet-proof smoked glass as a star-studded cast of authors, journalists and TV personalities sat down to a magnificent no-holds-barred champagne and quail dinner, their witty and memorable quips faithfully relayed by loudspeaker to the waiting crowds.

This year, an even larger space has been cleared in the car-park making room for up to 10,000 guests. So if you've ever dreamed of dining with Dickens, tucking in with Tolstoy, or cracking a couple of carafes in the company of Agatha Christie, why not do the next best thing, and Dine with the Stars on March 28?

MENU

Cold Cream of Cartland Soup
Poulet de Printemps Maschler Grillé sur le
Bonfeu des Vanités
Pommes de Terre Waldheim
Crisp Green Radice Salad (with Fiddicks)

Traditional Hunniford Cakes with Warm,
Thick Syrup

Fresh Chuck Berries

Please send me…**LITERARY BANQUET** tickets at £375.00 (food and wine extra). Guests will stand in groups of several hundred. Black tie and windbreaker.
I enclose my cheque for £...
I certify that I am over 18 and a complete bozo.

Thank you for not smoking in this advertisement

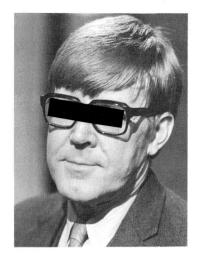

BANGING ON
A stoical monologue
by Alan B*nn*tt

"Ooh, I can't seem to get me bearings this morning, it's that fuss we had with the chewing-gum. We were on our way back from the Co-op, she was pushing the basket, like she does, she insists on that, although it can't be good for her sternum, and just as we were passing Clegg's she suddenly says, 'I think I've trodden in some chewing-gum, I think it's stuck to the bottom of me shoe, it's tilting me over.' Well, there's worse things to tread in, we all know that, but you have to humour her a bit Monday mornings, she's still depressed from the hymns. So I said well stop and lift your shoe up, I said, let's have a look at it, I'll prise it off or scrape it or something, I've probably got a lolly stick in this pocket somewhere (because I don't clean me raincoat pockets out enough, I know I don't, there's probably a ration-book in there getting hairy at the edges, I end up bulging out as if I had child-bearing hips, I expect it's a neurosis). But Mother wouldn't hear of stopping, she's like that Mangus Mangleson, she's started so she'll finish. So she kept plodding on, and she was right, she *was* tilting over and it didn't look safe to me, you can bang your head on a pillar-box or something and get no compensation whatsoever from the Post Office. So I said Mother are you sure it's chewing-gum, it could be a drawing-pin and you know what happens with them, they work their way through and before you know where you are you've got a pin sticking right through your in-sole. She hates injections. But no, silence. Like a breakdown on the Third Programme. All right, I said, mortify your flesh. Mortify your flesh for the sake of a few tins of Pedigree Chum, I said. Well, we got home, still not a word spoken by Mother, and of course we'd forgotten the Windolene, so I was spitting. Put your feet up, Mother, I said, wanting of course to have a little peek at the bottom of her shoe, she saw that one coming, she isn't daft isn't Mother, except about the royal family. So there she sits, feet planted right down in the uncut moquette, tatting away in front of that Asian programme, is it called 'Nai Zindagi Naya Jeevan', it certainly used to be, but ooh she can be difficult…"

(To be continued next week by another actor/actress)

"Would you mind if you passively smoked?"

"First it was homosexuals, now it's heterosexuals. When are they going to get around to us?"

"Come on, darling, there are thousands of flights every day. The chances of Ian Botham being on ours…"

ARTHURIAN LEGEND

It was morning and the sun sparkled gold across the south Derbyshire coalfields.

Way out alone, beyond the scabs, secret deals and all-chances-of-a-prompt-and-peaceful-settlement, Jonathan Livingston Scargill circled, whipping up support with his loud-hailer. His ears tightly streaked against his temples, he lowered his auburn-haired head and ran.

Two miles an hour, three and faster still. He couldn't stop. He wouldn't back down. Swept on by a fresh mandate and a draconian disciplinary code, he narrowed his eyes and harder and faster he ran. Smash the UDM, bring down Thatcher and destroy capitalism, he thought and the thought was power and power was joy and pure beauty and the industry itself was purely secondary.

"Is he mad?" asked a voice.

"Don't be hard on the lad," said another. "He deserves our understanding for few think as he thinks."

And Jonathan Livingston Scargill was indeed not ordinary, being a creature touching perfection in his own mind. "What's with you?" his mother had once asked of him and in reply he had said, "Let me make this point quite clear once and for all, Mr Snow. I just want to know what I can get away with. I don't care what the majority thinks."

For Jonathan believed the reason for living was touching perfection in the thing you most wanted to do in life and for him this was orchestrating ineffective industrial action.

And he helped others to discover his Valhalla, exalting them to come out and kick up a stink for in that, he believed, glory awaited them. He lightened their minds shouting special, gifted and divine things like, "Here we go! Here we go! Here we go!" and in all this he never once let anyone stand in his way or fell to wondering if there was any other life to be led than his – out on a wing.

DON'T WING US

Strong winds and unusually mild early-January temperatures have occasioned the arrival on our shores of several unusual birds of passage, some of them never seen in this country before. Ornithologists are currently enjoying a rare opportunity to observe the behaviour of the following migrant species:

LITTLE EARNER: Secretive bird in spite of garish pin-striped plumage. Usually winters in Spain, flying to Caribbean when bored. Obsessive collector of nest-eggs. Takes many mates in course of season, but devoted to mother. Flies by night, falls off lorries.

Recognised by bent beak.

RED-WINGED KINNOCK: Unmistakable pink-orange plumage where not entirely bald. Erratic seasonal behaviour, being sometimes the noisiest of songsters, sometimes silent but for low muttering call "Shuddup*ken*, shuddup*ken*". Breeding pair sighted, female the more spectacular of the two, lacks bald patches but not much else.

PLUNGING DOLLAR: Being by now virtually flightless, this tattered immigrant from America can only have hitched its way here on deck of a tramp-steamer. Once a bird of prey with worldwide distribution, now kept as a pet by Japanese. In Europe, many have

been bought in recent years, but bird attracts little interest and is usually disposed of quickly. Endangered species.

BEARDED WONDER: Seldom seen, though repetitive song known from Australia to West Indies. Makes noise like cricket. Builds huge nest of paper in old commentary-boxes. Large variety of seemingly random calls, often ignored or ridiculed by other birds.

PHILBY'S PLIGHT: Once a British resident, but exclusive to Russia in recent years. Mostly grey, with fading pink underparts, recognisable by guttural cry of "vod-ka, vod-ka", and habit of gazing longingly over any high wall. Similar plights observed all over East-

ern Europe. Unconfirmed sighting in Cambridge.

BUM TIT: While British tits display in the Sun, this Scandinavian relative nests in darkened cinemas with its legs crossed. Dark circles under eyes, low panting call. Keeps pecker up. Flies undone.

OLIVER REEDLING: Most conspicuous of all temporary residents, large colony has established territory on Isle of Dogs. Though both smaller and younger, this bird is hard to distinguish from the standard Red-Faced Boomer of the Channel Islands. Graceless, walks with difficulty, happiest when flying, the higher the better. Reliably found near watering-holes, lays eggs in public.

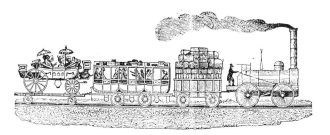

A STATION MOURNS

Angry commuters yesterday declared the 8.03 a.m. from Cambridge to Liverpool Street an Independent Islamic Republic. As the hour-late service stood awaiting the outcome of a signal failure in the Broxbourne area, twin task forces of fanatical office-workers staged lightning raids on both ends of the train, seizing the driver and guard and impounding their sandwiches. These were later pronounced inedible on religious, gastronomic and sanitary grounds.

In a brief ceremony, articled clerk Horace Wicksneed, 47, raised his season ticket in his right hand and declaimed a provisional constitution, pledging the Republic of Kapit-Al-Kahd to "a future of eternal progress, subject neither to unscheduled stops nor diversions". The Republic, he averred, would come to be known as "the land of adequate heating, enough seats, and the ever-open buffet car, featuring the Popular All-Day Breakfast that never shall run out." Whenever the Republic passed through a tunnel, he added, visitors would exclaim with surprise, because the lights would have been put on in time. Any guard failing to effect this requirement of the constitution would be sentenced to eat old lightbulbs for a month. A further pro-

vision of the penal code, he said, would condemn any guard uttering useless information over the Tannoy to having his voice-box ripped out and fed to whatever was in those baskets in the luggage van.

In adopting a Muslim system, emphasised Justice Minister Gail Waterworth, 25, a typist from Saffron Walden, the Republic of Kapit-Al-Kahd meant no disrespect to Her Majesty the Queen, it was just that they wanted to put the fear of God up British Rail, which appeared to be the last thing the Archbishop of Canterbury was interested in or capable of. President-elect Wicksneed insisted that the Republic now had no further territorial demands to make, outside of the 6.05 p.m. Liverpool Street-Cambridge, which it intended to annex in order to ensure the healthy oscillation and *perpetuum mobile* of its nomad peoples.

In the event, the 6.05 was cancelled. British rail apologised for any loss of impetus towards self-determination caused.

THOSE HISTORIC BRUSSELS ACCORDS

The newly-agreed Common Agricultural Eurosheep, now classified as a goat. Like the United Kingdom, it is to be phased out by 1st January 1991.

As more details have emerged from the Brussels Summit, many observers are now openly predicting that the harmonisation of peach-halves throughout the EEC could be a reality as early as 1991.

At the same time, the price of some staples (including paper-clips) may rise, but the effects should be more than offset by the negative-return stabilisers which will bring into line the ceiling on over-production of most pickled gherkins, certain non-patrial marzipan men (except Luxembourg) and the metrication of bottled fish extracts.

After more than 26 hours of tough talking, ministers agreed that important concessions had almost certainly been made on distorted olives, permitted agricultural hoists and participating poultry, excluding deceased geese (as defined by the Treaty of Utrecht). The date-stamping of consolidated ghee has now been made legally binding.

Such far-reaching measures have opened the way towards full chocolate monetary union and could soon permit the transfer of drained, or partially drained, fructose pastes without trade barriers or tariffs, at least not between Belgium and Denmark, Mondays to Thursdays, by barge.

The Easing of Restraints Upon (ERUs) comminuted cuttlefish derivatives (used as a marine varnish, to flavour margarines and to treat certain duodenal disorders) will nevertheless apply as outlined in Statutory Instrument 66543/0037/K, which now also deals with the changes relating to pressurised artificial mulches. The position of nougat is unchanged.

"I can't toot if I support strikers."

CUTTINGS

A peaceful Swansea Valley village could become a small Soho or seem like Swansea on a Saturday night if it has another hot-food takeaway, a councillor warned yesterday.

C. HARRIS (*South Wales Evening Post*)

The Office of
Dr Gordon Jaquith
Osteopath
will be closed until March
due to a wrist fracture

D. SMITH (*Kitchener-Waterloo Record*, Ontario)

Mandy has struck a deal with Conroy whereby she uses some of her earnings to buy him fuel and oil and, in return, he publicises her business. While other riders have names of oil multi-nationals plastered over their colours, Conroy has Mandy's name, address and telephone number.

T. STEEN (*Halifax Evening Courier*, New Orleans)

Mardi Gras is not a festival that sends us wild in this part of Gwynedd, but Shrove Tuesday next week will be marked by a pancake tea at the Old Vicarage from 3 p.m. to 4.30 p.m. next Tuesday.

W. LEWIS (*Liverpool Daily Post*)

Aucklander Alan Robert Stockhausen, officially listed among the dead in a train crash in China, is determined to continue his overland travels to England. "He's a determined guy," said his brother-in-law Corrigan, of Whangaparaoa.

G. SUTTON (*NZ News UK*)

Saturday, 6 Feb – 8 p.m. (Pavilion)
Humphrey Lyttleton and his band
A Special Threat For All Jazz Fans

I. HAMMOND (*Evening Argus*, Maidstone)

In this case we are hopeful that the lines will be installed anytime, which is much quicker than normal.

C. MADELEY (*Belper News*)

"Bloke outside wants us to take out a subscription to The Listener."

CUTTINGS

Birmingham's New Street Station is to be transformed into a seaside resort complete with its own beach, in a bid to promote its holiday services.

A British Rail spokesman said: "We want New Street to be transformed into a traditional resort with all the amenities of the old-style piers."

C. BEST (*Birmingham Daily News*)

On behalf of Shrewsbury County Court
AMSTRAD COMPUTER
comprising: visual display unit, printer
and keyboard, software for accounts, invoicing
management, and, for small businessman,
10 blank cassettes, two programme working
discs and 2,000 sheet computer paper
which
Davies White and Perry submit for sale by
Public Auction
Additional item – Chain Saw

K. BROAD (*The Newport Advertiser*)

The less said about the weather the better. One thing it does do, though, is to emphasise the importance of having cheerful-looking pants in the garden during the winter.

E. ALDRIDGE (*Star*, Herts)

Multi-millionaire sex king Paul Raymond wants to buy Watford, the English First Division's bottom club.

W. BOYLE (*Gulf Daily News*)

Four months ago, former carpenter Mike McGrath opened up Gino's Dial-a-Pizza business in Avon Road, Cannock. He got the idea of delivering hot pizzas quickly to customers who ring in their orders from Australia.

R. WOODALL (*Express and Star*, Halesowen)

Plans have been submitted to Rushcliffe Borough Council for a slaughterhouse in Sandy Lane, Redcliffe-on-Trent.

The Vicar, the Rev Robert Breckles, said the scheme began last November but they had received just one call for help.

J. PANKHURST (*South Notts Advertiser*)

"Dear Editor,
How are you?
I am fine…"

PUNCH

25TH MARCH 1988   £1

HERE IS THE NEWS FROM THE BBC

DOES THE LISTENER KNOW THERE'S A WAR ON AT BROADCASTING HOUSE?

A

BILL

TO

Abolish the British Broadcasting Corporation and To Restore the Air Over the British Isles to the People

EXPLANATORY MEMORANDUM:

The onset of Universal Enlightenment by way of satellite and cable transmission from all known lands has rendered the British Broadcasting Corporation obsolete and removed the last pretext for imposing licence fees on a resentful populace.

This Bill sets out to annihilate a corporate body with a record of insolence unmatched in modern times.

WHEREAS, in January 1923 and on succeeding dates, the body calling itself the British Broadcasting Company (later Corporation) did conspire with the Postmaster-General (deceased) to seize dominion over the air (or "ether") above and surrounding the British Isles, the said air (or "ether") being a natural commodity which the BBC did not provide,
5 regulate, purify or renew, and which had been used without let or hindrance by the population for the purpose of breathing and supporting balloons;

    And Whereas, notwithstanding the representations of the newspapers owned by the Baron Beaverbrook, the BBC and the Postmaster-General did falsely claim authority under the Wireless Telegraphy Act 1904 to levy financial charges on the population for the use of the air (or "ether"),
10 in so far as the said air (or "ether") might be used to transmit messages by electro-magnetic means, whether such messages were originated by the BBC or by broadcasting stations in Paris, Luxembourg, The Hague, Pittsburgh or Schenectady;

    And Whereas the BBC did wilfully and recklessly undertake to use the said air (or "ether") for the propagation of moral and spiritual uplift, well knowing that such ideals would be incapable of
15 fulfilment if television were to be invented, or even if it were not;

    And Whereas the BBC did actively seek to deny facilities to other broadcasters, whether based in the British Isles or on the waters surrounding them, and did collude in the dispatch of punitive expeditions against such operators, publicly rejoicing when the offenders were captured or shipwrecked;
20   And Whereas the BBC and the Postmaster-General did on numerous occasions send out waves of so-called detector vans to bluff and intimidate listeners into purchasing licences, and did foment hatred, ridicule and contempt for those who held out against their campaign of terror;

    And Whereas, following the introduction of Independent Television in 1955, the BBC did continue brazenly to demand licence fees from those who had no mind or stomach to watch its
25 programmes;

    And Whereas the BBC did, without any authority, ballot or referendum, take upon itself to construct innumerable new radio and television stations, for no other reason than to extend its tyrannical power and influence over the nation, and to serve as a further pretext for increasing its revenues;
30   And Whereas, since the days of its inception, the BBC did display at all times a studied hostility towards all governments and every form of established authority, whether of man or God;

BE IT THEREFORE ENACTED by the Queen's most Excellent Majesty, by and with the consent of the Lords Spiritual and Temporal, and Commons, in this present Parliament assembled, and by the authority of the same, as follows:
35 **1.** That the British Broadcasting Corporation be dissolved as from January 1, 198—;

    2. That its installations, equipment, buildings and publications be sold off to the highest bidder; or, failing that, that they be destroyed and the site sown with salt;

    3. That the collection of licence fees be instantly discontinued;

    4. That a free pardon be granted to all persons who, between 1923 and 198—, have been convicted
40   for not possessing a receiving licence.

This Bill may be cited as the BBC (Annihilation) Bill.

Marginal notes:

Conspiracy of British Broadcasting Corporation against natural freedoms and highest interests of Her Majesty's Subjects, etc

1904. c.13

1955. b.25

Dissolution and deregulation of Corporation with concomitant suspension of levies and penalties

> "NO OTHER PRIME MINISTER HAS EVER QUITE SO CLEARLY TAKEN THE VIEW THAT, AS THE LICENCE FEE IS AT GOVERNMENT DISPOSAL, THE BBC SHOULD SUPPORT THE GOVERNMENT."

AND NOW PERHAPS THEY'LL HAND US BACK TO THE STUDIO

Will the surprise appointment of Paul Fox to the Broadcasting House hierarchy stop what has been an embarrassingly public rot? Our BBC War Correspondent GILLIAN REYNOLDS reports from the front line at W1A 1AA

When the news broke within the BBC that Paul Fox was coming back people cheered. Who'd have thought it? The monarch of the ITV glen returning to be Number Three to a man who has never made a programme in his life and a bit of a lad with a few daft ideas. The very idea of it was staggering. But noble, too.

After a year of deep unease under the new management, after several years of siege and undermining by the Government, the news of Fox was like the relief of Mafeking.

That it came to most people as a complete surprise is significant. No one knew, not even Bill Cotton, whose job it is that Fox will step into next month. "Checkland played his cards so close to his chest the ink could have rubbed off on his jumper," said one of the rejoicing toilers in the vineyard, where estimation of the Director-General has gone up no end following the coup.

For coup it is, both in the sense of a blow for victory and a seizure of power. Michael Checkland, having brought in John Birt to be both his Deputy and Head of the huge new News Division, clearly had to do something about stopping the rot in morale which set in immediately afterwards and has been galloping onwards ever since. He also had to show that it is he who is, actually, the boss. With the appointment of Fox he has done both.

Forget for a moment the numbers of high-class journalists who have been lunching of late with old friends on newspapers and bemoaning their fate under the Birtian lash. Poor things. It must be hard, when you still think of yourself as a whizzkid, to have persons twenty years younger come in from regional ITV programmes and start giving you orders. Pride has been injured, prejudice against Birt and his hand-picked minions has been fed, and an awful lot of

stories have ended up in the press as a result.

Only the lone, craggy figure of John Lloyd stood up to be counted as a witness for the Birt defence. In the unlikely parallel pulpits of the *New Statesman* and *The Sunday Times* he said it might not be a bad idea to give him a bit of a chance, he hasn't been in the job that long, etc. Then up rose David Mills, formerly of the BBC,

THERE IS A WAR ON AND THE BBC IS IN THE THICK OF IT.

now of Granada TV where recently he made a *World in Action* which claimed the Government had tamed the BBC. How objective was Lloyd being, he asked? Wasn't he in line for a job offer from Birt?

Oh dear, to think it should come to this. Grown men bitching at each other in public, crocodile tears and snapping jaws. Still, it goes with the atmosphere inside Fort Apache, Portland Place.

"Psst – did you know that Birt is in with the Chairman every morning, a good half-hour before Checkland clocks on?" "Do you want a copy of the poem about Birt not watching the news?"

"Shh – don't say I showed it to you, but here's the memo…"

It would be easy to say that happy paranoid days are here again and leave it at that. There's nothing they like better at TV Centre or Broadcasting House (or Ford, or ICI, for that matter) than a big wave of scariness. It gets people talking to each other, just like the War.

But this time it really is serious. There *is* a war

15

on and the BBC is in the thick of it.

The Prime Minister thinks that broadcasting has been too tightly controlled by both its bureaucrats and its unions. By this she means all broadcasting, ITV and BBC, both sorts of radio. She intends to bring in more competition, new programme suppliers, new networks. ITV will have to push down payrolls and push up profits. The BBC will need to be acutely cost-conscious. In future ITV must pay for its franchises before it gets them, as well as while they are in business, and the BBC must learn to lick the hand which feeds it with taxpayers' money.

No other Prime Minister has ever quite so clearly taken the view that, as the licence fee is

THE NEWS OF FOX WAS LIKE THE RELIEF OF MAFEKING.

at Government disposal, the BBC should support the Government. It is a simple view but one which other leaders (de Gaulle, Duvalier, Nixon and Gaddafi, for example) have been known to share and it is one on which she has acted with characteristic force and consistency.

BBC programmes which overtly or implicitly criticise Government policy, whether *Real Lives* or the Duncan Campbell *Secret Society* series on TV or Radio 4's *My Country, Right or Wrong*, get pulled before transmission. Pressure has been placed on the BBC Governors; the Special Branch has been sent in to raid the offices in Glasgow; injunctions have been slapped on; and all so openly and so fast as to take the breath away.

When, as in the case of the Glasgow raid, not a single prosecution has come as a result, it is made to seem as if some good has been done after all, the equivalent of a school dental check-up which found nil caries and claims the credit. Perhaps it is the thought of having Norman Tebbit sent round to give them all a good telling off which keeps the BBC official response in these matters a touch muted.

"What's the point?" the thinking seems to run. "Who remembers what we said when we

"If we don't get some violence soon, I'm going to smash it up."

proved him wrong over Kate Adie and the way we reported the bombing of Libya? All anyone recalls is him going on about bias."

Come, come. Surely not. This is a free country. People can make their own minds up. We read more newspapers than any other country in the world. Yes, of course, most papers support the Government and the biggest ones are very keen to break up the BBC/ITV duopoly. But readers are bound to take account of that.

Yet even such sunny bursts of optimism fade when showers of BBC revisionism break out from within. The Chairman, Marmaduke Hussey, told the Institute of Directors how bad things had been until he got there to tidy them up. On Radio 4's *Analysis* Michael Checkland

confessed to Peter Hennessy assorted worries about journalistic standards in the recent past.

When the generals start slagging off the poor bloody infantry, it's no wonder the spirit in the trenches sinks even lower. At Television Centre, where they have been through a year and more of all change at the top, where decisions about programmes and policy and schedules have all, therefore, had to be taken on a more *ad hoc* basis than might have been wished, where nobody ever taps on a glass for attention since the day Milne was sacked and where Grade's defection to Channel 4 was the last straw, it is very hard indeed to feel loyalty towards a Chairman and a D-G who appear publicly to believe the Tebbit version of recent events rather than the facts.

The facts state quite clearly, to anyone who cares to examine them, that the BBC's record for journalistic accuracy and integrity is outstanding. It is not the reporter's fault that she sees what happens when American bombs fall on Libya. It is to her credit that she told the story so well its significance was understood. It is not the director's fault when the scenes he finds in a hospital reveal strains in the NHS rather than record investment. It is not, surely, a producer who is to blame for a story which shows that the Government may have misled Parliament.

It is the duty of a reporter to tell the truth. It is the duty of public service broadcasting to stay clear of a propaganda role. No broadcasting organisation should be allowed to be intimidated by a government which may find uncomfortable the verifiable stories told against it. That happens in dictatorships. It cannot be allowed to happen in a democracy. And to

"Can you ring back?
He's watching
'Play School'."

LISTEN TO THAT!
THEY'RE AT IT AGAIN

The Prime Minister finds time only to glance at the papers, but there's not much on radio or television news which escapes her interest. Has the whole nature of broadcast political coverage changed as a direct result? We hand you over now to JULIA LANGDON

There must have been some relief at the BBC when a satellite dish was hooked up to Number Ten to enable Mrs Thatcher to watch other people's television. The collective sigh was probably audible from Bush House to Shepherd's Bush. If there's one thing the Prime Minister likes getting stuck into, it's the broadcasters.

The Cabinet discuss matters each week under subject headings. Or at least they used to in the olden days when the Cabinet still discussed things. Departmental Ministers put their papers before their Cabinet colleagues and, where necessary, made verbal reports on particular issues. Willie Whitelaw, who was Mrs Thatcher's first Home Secretary, quickly learned, however, that it was always a mistake to mention anything to do with broadcasting. She was much too interested. Instead he used to keep mum and hope like hell.

The installation of cable TV at Number Ten took place a few months ago. It means that Mrs Thatcher can tune into programmes like the American twenty-four hour Cable News Network and can check up on what Ronnie's up to

at any time of the day or night. The hope at the BBC was, of course, that this might help take some of the heat off them. The hope was misplaced.

The Prime Minister does not read the newspapers. In this respect she has a huge advantage over Neil Kinnock, who pores over them all with mounting rage and resentment every day of the week. Mr Kinnock may indeed have some justification in his fury at the way British politics is reported in general – and his own doings in particular – in the vast majority of the British newspapers, but he is wrong to let it get to him.

This is where Mrs Thatcher scores. It is, of course, easier for her with a ludicrously idolatrous press behind her, but, if she looked, she would be able to find some pretty nasty personal comments hidden away among the praise and plaudits.

She doesn't need to read the newspapers, of course, because someone else does it for her and she reads a press summary drawn up for her daily by her press secretary, Bernard Ingham. In any case she has already heard quite a few of the main points from the papers because she has been tuned in to Radio Four since 6 a.m.

According to legend, however, the trouble really starts when Denis rolls over, wakes up and turns the radio on.

"Listen to that!" he says. "They're at it again! Margaret, you must do something!"

Denis is firmly convinced that the BBC is a hotbed of pinkoes, many of whom read *The Guardian* and most of whom vote Labour. He is moved to great indignation by what he hears on the *Today* programme if it is less than totally enthusiastic about the policies of his beloved. This may be commendable loyalty, but is it any way to run an "independent" national broadcasting service?

When she first took office, before the BBC had been put on a leash and brought rather firmly to heel, these early morning intimacies of the Thatcher household used to be translated into a telephone call from the Downing Street duty officer to the *Today* studios calling for a better balance. Then it all got much more serious.

think we have to say so!

The Government, interestingly, is also demonstrating its determination to put its own story across elsewhere. Channel 4's excellent *Media Show* revealed recently that Mrs Thatcher's chaps spend more on selling their product (BP shares, DTI schemes and so on) *than any other advertiser*. This is amazing news. Unilever, who used to be the biggest spender, have in the past year persuaded me to give up Persil and go over to Wisk, although as they make both I don't suppose it much matters in the end. But does this mean I will buy my children a new improved YTS scheme from Lord Young or a BUPA (now with added miracle ingredients) from John Moore?

The intriguing question is why Mrs Thatcher and the chaps need it, what with a whopping majority, three clear years of a third term still ahead, no effective Opposition, the press in her pocket and the broadcasters under her thumb. Maybe she suspects someone is still capable of making up his own mind, in spite of it all.

The three years which lie ahead of Paul Fox at the BBC are possibly the most crucial ones in its history. As the Government changes the domestic television system (and Fox has led the protests against some of the means proposed), so the technological future will arrive. The satellites will be up and running. The first operator who brings to market a package which costs the same for all those new channels of sport, film, rock and soft porn as a video does now, will have the whole audience in his hand. The champions of public service broadcasting will need to be bonny fighters. At least in Fox they have the best general.

"Remember the good old days when we were employed but didn't work!"

"First off, forget I'm a woman."

like broadcasting. They gave grand interviews, of course, from time to time and at their own convenience, but they didn't indulge in the vulgarity of rushing from one studio to the next in order to share their views with the waiting world. There was a rule, for example, that Cabinet Ministers did not accept invitations to appear on *Any Questions?*. It was, admittedly, an outdated point of view and misplaced politically in that it failed to recognise the importance of broadcasting on the dissemination of news and views.

It went very swiftly. Ministers were instructed to accept every invitation going and,

BROADCAST POLITICAL COVERAGE HAS CHANGED GREATLY UNDER THIS GOVERNMENT.

when necessary, to ring up themselves and request the right of reply. The radio car started buzzing around in the early morning to be outside the right Cabinet front door. Ministers with initiatives to unveil ensured that they were accorded appropriate publicity by fixing their television appearances long before they got round to bothering about press conferences. It has led, among other things, to an increasing tendency for reporters of the written word to record the broadcast views of individual politicians, often in preference to what they have told the House of Commons.

It has also, in at least one unfortunate and regrettable case, brought about the downfall of a Cabinet Minister. One of the prime slots, identified early under the new Thatcher broom, is the invitation to appear on the Sunday lunchtime political TV programmes. This is not because anyone is under the impression that anyone else, except other politicians and political journalists, watches political programmes at Sunday lunchtime. It is because precious little else happens in the political world on Sundays and therefore whatever you might have to say receives an extremely good show in the Monday morning newspapers. It was bad luck on poor John Biffen that his commendable honesty in observing, with his usual rigorous objectivity, that Mrs Thatcher needed to maintain a balance in her Cabinet had such a good play in the papers; she tipped him out of the Cabinet at the first opportunity.

The nature of broadcast political coverage has changed greatly under this Government. Much of it is highly visible and is now provoking some expressed concern – in, for example, the recent Granada *World in Action* report on "The Taming of the Beeb". Much of the rest is insidious.

"I think it might be better if you didn't say that," murmurs the timid producer to the programme presenter. "We don't want to cause any trouble, you know?"

The aggressive stance struck by Norman Tebbit is most commonly blamed, but he was doing no more than fulfilling the wishes of his Prime Minister.

Myself, I blame Denis.

For one thing Norman Tebbit became involved. As is well known and now a matter of historical record, the former Conservative Party chairman shares the prejudices of Denis Thatcher about BBC pinkoes. Mr Tebbit once revealed in all apparent seriousness that he had complained to the BBC about Brian Redhead's running jokes on the *Today* programme concerning the roadworks on the M6. His reason was that Redhead was using this as a subtly disguised and repeated reminder about the need for more public spending on the infrastructure and therefore about the shortcomings of the Government.

One of the things which changed was the orders to Ministers about appearing on radio and television. In the long gone days of the old Tory Party, its bigwigs were rather above things

"That's a lost deposit face if ever I saw one."

VOTE FOR

TRUMBLE.

"What exactly is a deep-pan pizza?"

Sorry, can't say how we came by these. Quite unaccountable.
Came out of the blue. No money changed hands, not a red cent.
Or a blue cent, or anything. Revealing stuff, though

If Memo Serves Me Right

BBC Memorandum

PRIVATE AND CONFIDENTIAL
Monday a.m.

FROM: Montague Shotfoot, Chairman of Governors

TO: M. D. Combined Ops. (Tel) (Acting)

Reggie, I've just come down from Tommy Manners's place after the weekend and I find the whole shop in an uproar. Apparently some fellow called Fox has warbled his way into a fairly senior post. Who is Fox? Is he related to the little singing popsy with the big chest? Would appreciate brief CV and advice. On Fox, I mean.

Monty

Broadcasting Ho., Wed.

Dear Reggie,
Personal note in haste. Sorry to hear your news. I think you'd better sit down as coolly as you can and write out what she said to you. She's always like that midweek, I should have warned you. M.

---

①

B. H., Wednesday p.m.

Reggie,

I7m typing this myself because I don7t want Beryl to do it. She's a faithful old Corporation warhorse but with retirement just six weeks off I can't help fearing she might be thinking in terms of going out with a bang by leaking something. Anyway, the thing is this, it7s as you were, don't bother to write. Phone rang this afternoon and I duly received what I'd be prepared to bet was the identical earful. Basically the gist was this. She feels that after spending ten years reducing Labour and the unions to rubble she's not going to stand by and let the BBC become the ''effective opposition''. I demurred quite huffily at that, making the point that this business of the programme-makers all being lefties is really a frightful canard, but she wasn't in a mood to be reasoned with. Kept on about being undermined. Govt couldn't be expected to govern if it kept on being undermined, BBC reporters asking awkward questions all the time, and so forth. I said look here, if <u>BBC reporters</u> don't ask awkward questions, who the devil's going to? <u>Precisely</u>, she said. Now you're catching on, she said. I was a bit taken aback quite frankly. Then she said, things are not happening quickly enough. And I said, what things. She said, well, things like that Kate ~~Axeley~~ Adeney girl in the news department, she should have moved on long ago. Now Reggie, I've come up against this

---

BBC Memorandum

PRIVATE AND CONFIDENTIAL
Tuesday a.m.

FROM: Montague Shotfoot, Chairman of Governors

TO: M. D. Combined Ops. (Tel) (Acting)

Reggie, you have a real gift for characterisation, should have been a novelist. As soon as you said "jug-eared element, looks like a wrestler", I knew I had the blighter Fox in my sights. Is he Jewish at all? I only ask because in the past we have had to make dietary provision for these bods at the inevitable lunches. Joel Barnett never will touch his Devils on Horseback. And is he going to give us trouble? Fox, I mean. Because I didn't take on this post so as to be a glorified baffle-board between Downing Street and some campaigning son of Abraham. I gather Fox made quite a success of Yorkshire. Well, that's more than God managed to do, so I suppose he deserves some credit. Fox, I mean.

Monty

Kate Adeney in the course of duty, I thought she was rather a sparky little damsel actually, and easily a match for that bullying oik Tebbit who is one of nature's deck-chair attendants if ever I saw one. So I said, no, no, we can't lose Kate Adeney, she's a good reporter, likes reporting and is good at it. Well, let her go and report elsewhere, says she. I said, what's the point of changing the BBC by weakening it? And then she puts on the very-weary-headmistress, last-day-of-term voice, and explains that by getting good people to leave the BBC, we eventually reduce it to a state where even the merest duffer perceives that it, the BBC, is every bit as bad as she's been saying it is. Now this was going a bit fast for me, but before I could put the logic into reverse and see if it stalled, the damn woman rang off. So there it is. How does that tally with your experience, Reggie old chum? I should be interested to hear, but not before a sizeable stiffy or two has gone down the red lane. Yours with a red ear (my God, perhaps I am turning red),
Monty

B. H., Friday

Reggie,

A quickie in haste, got to fire a few shots across a few bows after Govs' meeting this morning. Good news. Apparently a ''Panorama'' reporter chap called Cockerell has left this week. He seems to have been here some years so he was probably one of the arrogant set. Anyway that gives me something positive to report to The Management. In addition I have briefed Algy to keep me posted on anything regrettable perpetrated in news bulletins, e.g. earlier this week we had some poor sap actually thanking Col Gaddafi on the News for letting him out of a Libyan jail! Can't have that. I immediately fired off a few memos, including a pre-empter to Bernard Ingham et al agreeing in advance to what was going to be their very fair point that the BBC is not in the business of offering unsolicited testimonials to terrorist leaders and their ilk. By the by, did you know that a jazz band plays in the BBC Club on certain Fridays? I will eventually put a stop to this, but only after Beryl has gone. She is a Rosemary Cluny enthusiast.
Monty

BBC Memorandum

PRIVATE AND CONFIDENTIAL

FROM: Monty

TO: Reggie

Thursday

Excuse familiarity in office hours. Yes, she rang me back too. Same gen, same cracks, bit of a bad day, nothing that an early repeat of "Yes Prime Minister" won't put right. But on the other hand didn't take back a word of the policy part, and so forth. Complex woman. Not really my type. Look, are you going to be at this brain-bashing session over the weekend, out at the Nag's Bladder, Bloxwich, or wherever? Or is it just for deskbound theorists? I gather this Fox may be there, rather in advance of his membership card. At this stage, it would not distress me deeply if he stayed at home and fed his gerfilter fish, but there we are. My ear is on the mend, how's yours?
Monty

BBC Memorandum

PRIVATE AND CONFIDENTIAL

FROM: Montague Shotfoot MC, OBE, VHF, Chairman of Governors

TO: Reginald Wrackenstowe

Dear Reggie,

It was good to see you at the weekend and raise a glass to the old times. I'm sorry to say you're fired. Not strictly my place to let you know, of course, but I thought it might be better coming from me. I didn't know what it was, something to do with your piping up on behalf of the departed Cockchafer or whatever his name was, or maybe it was your rather extraordinary tirade against the "Horizon" programme that went behind the scenes with the fighting services. The man Naughton of "The Observer", whose opinion you quoted with approval, is an Irishman you know. It is very unwise, I have found, to agree with a Paddy's view of the British armed forces.
We'd all be obliged if you made the usual noises about desire for a change, fresh pastures, independent production company, Channel 4 and so forth. No doubt we shall meet again at one of those awards fiascos. Fear not for the future of the BBC, you have left it in excellent hands.
Monty

PS Would you drop your Entry Permit and Identity Card in the post to Beryl? Many thanks.

A MESSAGE FROM THE SECRETARY OF STATE FOR ENERGY

Hallo!

Many of you have written to me asking: *Just what is this energy we hear so much about, and why does it need its own secretary?*

It's all terribly straightforward, really. Energy is what makes things go, whether you happen to be a chap or a steelworks. Details may of course vary – a steelworks does not, for example, have to run upstairs two at a time, the way a chap might suddenly feel the urge to, a steelworks does not have to pound away half the night in one place and then rush across the country to start pounding the second half away in another – but the principle is the same. Energy is, quite simply, a property manufactured by fuel to be turned into power.

And power is what makes things happen.

Power is the best stuff there is.

Power is what makes the world go round.

So there is absolutely no point at all in having energy unless it gives you power at the end of it. That is why we must deploy energy to the best effect, and not misuse it. With, for example, the wrong techniques, or the wrong people; or, of course, the wrong tools. By the same token, everything could be chugging along tickety-boo, when, quite out of the blue, you experience a sudden and quite terrifying *loss* of power. Drops away completely. Phut!

The commonest technical explanation for this is that the energy has been misdirected.

But what, I hear you say, *is* energy, exactly? Energy is food. Think of energy as the staple diet of industry. We all know how the food we eat relates directly to the efficiency of what we do. To pluck an example at random, and a random pluck is as good as any, it is a well-known fact that a dozen oysters can give you up to 3.4 minutes more power.

Especially if you have large Whitstables.

But supposing you wash those oysters down with two bottles of Chablis – have you ever noticed how, despite the input of fuel, your power seems unaccountably to be diminished? Oh yes, you *want* to

do things, all right, it isn't as if the will isn't there, but somehow, when you get right down to it, when you get stuck in to the job in hand, nothing quite works the way it ought to. Well, that's because you were running on the wrong fuel, and a large part of my job, I might even say a part of my large job, is making sure that we have the right fuel to create the energy to drive the tools that give us the power we need to bring the particular job to a successful conclusion.

In, it goes without saying, the right amount of time.

Which may vary, depending on the circumstances. But since the important thing is to see that the job was done properly, by converting the energy available into the power required, to the satisfaction of everyone involved, then the amount of time it took is more or less *defined* as the right time, isn't it?

And this brings us naturally to the question of the secretary, and why energy needs one. The secretary is there to control energy, to be sensitive to its needs, and efficient in its deployment. Energy, of its very nature, is volatile and capricious, neither constant nor reliable, and, most disturbing of all, by no means inexhaustible: uncontrolled, unleashed, undisciplined, it is prone to expend itself in great surges that are of little benefit to anyone, leading, in a word, to waste.

The secretary's job is to use every morsel of skill, every smidgeon of inventiveness, every whit of experience, and every trick in the book to make the most of the *store* of energy available, and of the *potential* of energy as yet untapped. Give us the tools, cries the secretary, and we shall finish the job!

It is a daunting job, yes, and unquestionably a risky one! But it can also be the most rewarding and satisfying job there is, and I do not shrink from it. Shrinking is not my way. You may be confident that, as your secretary, I shall rise to the opportunity I have been so graciously offered and discharge my duties with all the rigour and commitment of my being. Thank you.

THE OLD BIZARRE IN CAIRO

*In a room
unswept for a century,
KEITH WATERHOUSE risks
the Curse of the Carnarvons
to bring to light an
astonishing hoard of ancient
English antiquities*

An astonishing hoard of English antiquities, hidden for over sixty years in the ancestral villa of an Egyptian boxed dates tycoon, has just been unearthed by an old retainer.

More than 300 objects, including celluloid collars, back numbers of *Country Life*, packets of De Reske cigarettes and Parson's Pleasure tobacco, jars of boiled sweets, bottles of Malvern water, whisky and brandy decanters, soda siphons, and a half-eaten tin of Bath Oliver biscuits, all in perfect condition and packed in fourteen cabin trunks, came to light when the old retainer was ordered to make a better job of the spring-cleaning this year than in previous years if she hoped to keep her position.

The important find, in a room previously unswept for half a century, can almost certainly be linked with the fifth Earl of Carnarvon who is believed to have stayed in the villa while supervising the search for Tutankhamun's tomb. While no tenancy agreement, rentbook or other documentation has survived to prove Lord Carnarvon's occupancy, the villa is indisputably very handy for the Valley of the Kings; thus, the Luxor Sheraton not having yet been built at that time, it has always seemed reasonable to suppose that he would have been accommodated there rather than in a tent. This new discovery, for all that none of the items so far examined bears the Carnarvon crest or any other proof of ownership, can only strengthen the theory. No one but an earl, the experts contend, would have troubled to hump a cricket bat and pads all that way when the possibility of getting a visiting side together was virtually nil.

The present owner of the villa, a Mr Hakim, recalls being shown the cache as a boy by his grandfather, who swore him to secrecy. It was feared in the family at that time that should their stewardship of the Carnarvon treasure come under public scrutiny, the revelation would bring them bad luck, in that they would be expected to finance the return of the fourteen bulky cabin trunks to their rightful ownership at Highclere Castle; also that they would be liable for the fine on a Boot's Circulating Library copy of Edgar Wallace's *Sanders of the River*, by then considerably overdue.

The villa's owner grew into manhood believing, nonetheless, that his late father had quietly disposed of the hoard to a Cairo junk dealer, after delicate but fruitless negotiations with the sixth Earl who refused to accept the return of the cabin trunks COD, or indeed at all, and with Boot's Circulating Library which firmly declined to waive the fine on the Edgar Wallace volume, by now running into tens of shillings. In the light of this week's remarkable discovery, Mr Hakim is now inclined to think that his father did have every intention of getting rid of the treasure, but that either he was scared off by the so-called curse of the Carnarvons or he could not get a good enough price for the stuff.

The curse of the Carnarvons, which according to legend visits all who tamper with the contents of the fourteen cabin trunks, has its roots in the grisly experience of an old retainer – not the present old retainer, but another old retainer, now dead – who attempted to give the room in which they have always been stored a bit of a sweep, back in 1914.

Or such was her story. In fact, it was to prove that at least one of the cabin trunks had been tampered with after she entered with her broom. Later that fateful day, the wretched old retainer was discovered in a distressed condition on the roof of the villa, gibbering to herself and throwing slats at imaginary creatures that were troubling her. A theory that she had been 'at the gin again has always been discounted. Mr Hakim agrees that a number of empty Booth's gin bottles were said to have been found in the vicinity of the desecrated trunk, but the family have always believed that the old retainer discovered them in that state, and that she was loading them into a raffia bag in the hope of getting something on them at the Valley of the Kings Discount Wine Warehouse when she was stricken by the curse of the Carnarvons. At all events, the old retainer was dismissed, the room was locked, and the legend of the curse has ever since persisted, to the extent that, convinced as Mr Hakim was that his father had disposed of the treasure, it therefore came as no surprise to him when Mr Hakim senior was run over by a Cairo tram less than ten years later.

As to how the Carnarvon find lay undisturbed all these years, Mr Hakim explains that he was not very often in that part of the house and in any case his father had the room bricked up and plastered over. To get into the sealed chamber, the old retainer – the present old retainer, that is, not the one who was found on the roof with a raffia bag full of gin bottles – was obliged, in her fear of dismissal if she didn't give the villa the spring-cleaning of its life this time round, to get in through the window, dragging the vacuum cleaner behind her. Her cries of sur-

"I understand you're a freedom fighter."

prise alerted several of her relatives, and the whole pack of them were engaged in man-handling the first of the cabin trunks out of the window with a view, as they explained, to giving it a really good clean, when Mr Hakim chanced by and sent them about their business.

Having unbricked the doorway, Mr Hakim made a thorough examination of the fourteen cabin trunks. The fact that the majority of them were labelled "Sir Eustace Ffarthing-Ffarthing (an obscure amateur archaeologist, 1846-1925), Not Wanted On Voyage" was enough to persuade him, initially, that they could not possibly be the legendary property of the fifth Lord Carnarvon but that they must be fourteen utterly different cabin trunks which for reasons unbeknown had been lying around the villa all this time.

It was with an easy mind, therefore, that Mr Hakim set about making a careful inventory of the extraordinary Aladdin's Cave his servant had stumbled upon. Opening trunk after trunk, he became absorbed in cataloguing an amazing cornucopia of British Empire artefacts – collapsible canvas stools, artist's watercolours, Bendick's Sporting and Military Chocolate, Bovril, tins of boot polish, silver powder and moustache wax, suits of pyjamas, spats, grapescissors, bottled cocktail cherries, Mazawattee tea, Eno's fruit salts, Colman's mustard, ink, gravy browning, light fiction – such as the world has never seen, or anyway not since the fifth Earl's valet packed what are believed to have been his weekend trunks so many years ago.

It was only when he badly broke a finger-nail on his pocket calculator while working out the accrued fine on the Boot's Circulating Library copy of *Sanders of the River* (now standing at some £66, not allowing for inflation), that Mr Hakim remembered the curse of the Carnarvons. Examining the treasure with a new eye, and now recognising a jar of humbugs uncannily like the one he recalls taking his fancy when his grandfather originally showed him the hoard as a boy, he became convinced that after all he had stumbled across the fourteen cabin trunks left behind by Lord Carnarvon when, for reasons known to no one but himself, he abruptly took his leave of the villa, only to die from an infected mosquito bite on altogether different premises. Mr Hakim dimly remembers a story still going the rounds in his boyhood, to the effect that the fifth Earl was the victim of his own curse as a consequence of dipping into one of his trunks for his shaving tackle, but little credence is placed on this nowadays.

What will happen to the priceless Carnarvon antiquities now? Mr Hakim is torn between offering them to the family in exchange for the Egyptian antiquities recently flushed out by the present Lord Carnarvon's former butler, and selling them off in a series of car boot sales. In the meantime, he is hoping to interest *Exchange & Mart* in this exciting find.

CLAP HANDS, HERE COMES FERGIE!

Feisty Fergie, the swashbuckling Duchess of York, is the target now for Fleet Street's snide, sanctimonious and sexist royalty-bashers. LIBBY PURVES says to hell with dainty femininity, let's hear it for extrovert gals! Wha-hay!

"**L**oud". "Rackety". "Brassy". "Coquettish". "Over the Top". The gentlemen of the press, so recently laid out in neat, adoring rows at the feet of the Duchess of York, are now turning nasty. Andy and Fergie's American tour, with its jolly banter, bottle-smashing and extrovert marital teasing, has caused a number of pallid, tight-buttocked Fleet Street commentators to deplore the happy yippee couple in print.

"*The Duke and Duchess of Yob*" (Craig Brown, *The Sunday Times*).

"*Her rather raunchy sense of humour... The Queen has had occasion to remind the Duchess of certain aspects of lèse-majesté, such as the fact that you don't wave when someone wolf-whistles at you*" (Anon-but-clearly-constipated profile writer, *The Observer*).

Oh yes, the knives are out, all right. They have even begun adding up how many days' holiday the Duchess takes, a trick rarely pulled on the rest of the royal family (perhaps for the simple reason that none of them ever seems to be enjoying themselves much. Fergie does, enormously, and the press can't bear it).

Even the tabloid columnists, not themselves notable for quiet good taste and restrained dignity of bearing, have begun to turn against her. It won't do. Someone must stand up for the magnificent red-headed aviatrix, and reveal the underlying motives of her critics as the sinister, boring, sexist rubbish that they are. Never mind the royal status – for what is the royal soap-opera but a handy magnifying-glass, through which our culture likes to focus and examine its own attitudes? The point is that Sarah Ferguson was, is now, and ever shall be a classic exemplar of a much-despised group: *the Swashbuckling Woman.*

She bounces with health. She slaps backs. She taps her foot in frustration when they don't let her defy g-forces in a jet. Pregnant or not, she skis. When she gets heckled, she answers back. When her husband makes a speech, she joshes him on. She has no interest in pretending to be a silent, blushing waif, in glancing up sweetly through her eyelashes, or in dieting herself into the semblance of a humble stick-insect. She does not listen to the advice of the myriad fashion-writers, mercenary obstetricians, or pale stylish young things who lecture her from the press benches on decorum, restraint, peplum jackets and Putting Your Feet Up for nine months. She dresses with a terrifyingly theatrical panache. She would go down a treat in pantomime, slapping her thigh and swishing

"Ha! You missed it again – do you want to keep this job or what?"

tecting her while he was away on his business trips and she was looking after four children, a seven-month bump, two houses and a job. What the eye doesn't see, the romantic heart doesn't grieve for.)

This desire for women to be quiet creatures has always been there, probably due to some peculiar Oedipal yearning for a lifetime of lullabies. Even the sanest of male writers have perpetuated it, in their weaker moments ("*Her voice was ever soft, Gentle and low, an excellent thing in woman*"). In the dark ages, there were drippy Madonnas and saints, clutching the spears to their bosoms with sweet-smiling rapture. There was the horrid tale of Patient Griselda, putting up with everything her bent, tyrannical old husband threw at her; there was the whole ghastly tradition of courtly love, in which the lover moans and sighs to a pale princess, never gets anywhere, and everyone ends up dead.

Then you get Dickens's Dora and Agnes, Thackeray's dismal Amelia Sedley and Lady Jane Crawley, and all those other Victorian ideals of womanhood: never mind that the Victorian facts were actually memsahibs, matriarchs, madams and Florence Nightingale – the ideal remained a bloodless, spiritually inspiring creature who didn't answer back, win races, or cause a chap to choke by clapping him on the back. (Mind you, Dickens I suspect had his lucid moments when he realised that Peggotty was the real heroine; and Thackeray secretly preferred Becky Sharp. They had an audience to pander to, that was all.)

When the two great wars in Europe came, a series of excruciating mental contortions and pretences had to be kept up in order that nobody should admit that without rather fierce, assertive women taking over at home, barking orders, driving trucks and bashing the innards of Ack-Ack guns with greasy spanners, the whole thing would have been impossible.

"*Keep beneath your dungaree, Dainty femininitee,*" pleaded the advertisers, merchants of

her sword. "Ha Ha! Abanazar! I have the Lamp!"

But women are not *supposed* to swashbuckle.

Exuberant women are loathed and feared by a race of men who have grown increasingly

SHE HAS NO INTEREST IN PRETENDING TO BE A SILENT, BLUSHING WAIF.

timid and staid. These poor aesthetes don't mind it if men are positive, even noisy (Cliff Morgan, the Duke of Edinburgh, Lt-Col Blashford-Snell…) but they like their women to be very thin, very weak-looking, rather pale and spiritual and quiet. They prefer Burne-Jones maidens to the awesome images of Beryl Cook. They accept women going out to work, but prefer them to wear nice tight business suits and high stilettos to stop them swinging breezily down the corporate corridors, taking up space. They don't mind their wives carrying three-stone toddlers up and down stairs all day, but can't abide them taking up hammer- (or even wellie-) throwing; they approve of females teaching huge classes of noisy schoolchildren, but abhor them making speeches.

Granted, the men who actually marry the noisy sort of woman seem, in the main, to be quite content and secure in the knowledge that someone else will take a turn at carrying in the coal without flinching. Yet even so, one such husband once told me in his cups that his happiest months were during the pregnancies of his very jolly, kids-and-career-no-problems wife. "She's always at home, nice and quiet," he said wistfully. "I can protect her." (He admitted, under questioning, that he didn't mind not pro-

dreams: and when the War was over, most of the women sank defensively back into that dear old sweet placidity.

At least, they did in public. The public profile is the acid test of a truly gung-ho, swashbuckling woman: I speak as one who, for some freak reason, was born with a tendency to ham it up after dinner and shout down hecklers with, "Shurrup or I'll show you my war wound!" or some such crude witticism. Being such a cheery, stout ham myself, and knowing the fun it can be, I have frequently been saddened by the sight of experienced, even brilliant ladies addressing audiences in a terrified, note-clutching, humble,

LET'S HEAR IT FOR BET LYNCH, MAE WEST, VICTORIA WOOD AND LUCINDA LAMBTON.

eyelash-glancing style which would have done little credit to a meek sixteen-year-old Vestal Virgin.

As ever, women collaborate in their own oppression: they don't want anyone to think they're *loud* or *vulgar*, or *aggressive*, or just rather *peculiar*. They want, God help them in their iron-grey hair and sensible suits, to be Princess Di.

So for heaven's sake let's hear it for the Few: for the rackety girls with the belly-laughs, the ones who roar out sea-shanties in the pub, who tell the jokes. Let's hear it for Bet Lynch and Mae West, for Victoria Wood doing a strip-tease dressed as Bessie Bunter, for Lucinda Lambton, for our friend Cheryl who breaks Shire Horses to harness before breakfast, for The Roly Polies. Hooray for Head Prefects and Gym Mistresses. Clap your hands, please, for Claire Rayner, who once yelled at me across the floor at London Weekend Television: "The secret of breastfeeding is to *get high on your own hormones!*"

Give a cheer for my own baby girl, Rose, who intends to continue the family tradition: faced with her first pantomime demon, she did not flinch, but stood up on her seat and roared, "*Piss off, demon!*" Give a small cheer, even, for Ruby Wax. She may not be to everyone's taste, but at least she's not refined.

And all you poor constipated fellows who pretend to worry about members of the royal family as a disguise for your own private terror of big tough women, I have bad news for you. You can stop hoping that motherhood will tone Fergie down. It won't. It will actually tune her *up*. The British athletics coach, Frank Dick, has revealed some utterly delightful research by a Bulgarian professor proving that after having a child, women become stronger mentally and physically and show "a steeper improvement gradient".

The Duchess will have lots more lovely energy to get rid of. *Yippee! Wha-hay!* I am sure she will think of some good ways to express it, in jet aeroplanes and corny jokes and huge, mad, exuberant dresses. If not, I could send her the words of some sea-shanties.

Gilbert White IV's Natural History of Selborne

LETTER VIII

Happening to look out of my big window at the first gleam of day, I observed the vicar traversing the common. What a curious creature! & how wonderful he looks in his double-breasted full-skirted winter frockcoat! His face gives off a rosy glow & he travels along with a limp-wristed air & pronounced, slightly poncey lope. His daily proceedings are an unending source of interest to me. He seems independent of sexual attachment &, through long & assiduous investigation, I am confirmed in my opinion that he's as queer as a coot. Only last week I got a sight (in the mirror which helps me reverse safely into the main road) of him & the mobile librarian, Mr Craig, chasing each other through the long grass. I know a bunch of pansies when I see one!

LETTER XV

The air is strongly scented & impregnated with a most heady stench. My senses inform me that either my humus toilet's on the blink or those bloody gyppos are back again. Hordes of them are spoiling the village's truly rural charm & that they dump their detritus everywhere & let their filthy Alsatians pee all over my melon beds makes me most Melancholy. Dryads & Fawns (The Estate Agents) are putting up For Sale signs all over the place. Even next door. In a country so diversified, it would be just my luck for some Hell's Angels or a family of Pakis to fix residence as neighbours.

LETTER XXI

What beguiling & fascinating creatures surround me! Miss Hewitt has just tried to commit suicide. She was depressed that nobody bought any of her quince marmalade at the annual fête. They managed to cut her down from her heated towel-rail just in time. Mr Barrington's healthfood store burned down yesterday. The fire service say the explosion was caused by a build-up of soya beans. Mr Tyson had a nasty accident with his chainsaw. He's recovered well but is only a sawlog length of his former self.

Such occasions & incidents, furnished by an over-indulgent Providence, make me feel singularly blessed to be the monographer of this, my native place. Nothing could ever persuade me to quit it.

LETTER XXXIII

I saw a most unusual sight today. No, alas, not a bus (they are a rarity) but a pair of surveyors. What a delight & inspiration they are with their ambitious beautifying road-widening schemes! They have the brains of a field carrot & the sensitivity of a five-pound sack of tats. To the thinking mind nothing is so despicable as developers. They are the lowliest link in the chain of human nature. I can see a time when the only listed building will be a big plastic Old Mother Hubbard shoe in the village pub's back garden.

LETTER XXXIX

Rose before daybreak to the most stridulous clatter. Pneumatic drills are indelicate songsters. I much prefer the soft churring of the woodchat & the drowsy cooing of the common pigeon to that of workmen shovelling & a generator humming. How can a field naturalist marvel at birdsong – a robin, for instance, whistling in the plum trees – when the road is being dug up all round him? How can one enjoy the true rapture of Wordsworth's "The Green Linnet" & meditate on the lyrical beauties of the Odes of Gray & Collins, the majesty of the mature broadleaf & the grandeur of Natural Creation itself with roadworks right outside your sodding doorstep? It causes no small dissatisfaction to me that it is becoming increasingly impossible, in this age & day, to be an appreciative countryman. I want a new Arcadia. Not a new Waitrose.

LETTER XL

Seldom are we assailed by ungenial weather but, when we do, my boiler gets blown out & I lose lots of tiles off the roof. My television reception becomes lousy & it's just Bills, Bills & Bills.

I have been active & inquisitive of late. I have completed my ornithological studies. I can now recognise any species of bird just by examining the marks it leaves on people's thornproof Barbours.

Hay Fever greatly displeases me. Your eyes get all sore & itchy & you sneeze so much you don't have to water your house plants for weeks.

Making no pretence to any other skill, I do subscribe to country lore. Spring can properly be said to have arrived with the first appearance of the Wood Flasher & the Window Washer. The Plumber, too, being largely torpid in the winter months, a shy & cautious animal of whom it is very difficult to get sight, also becomes a common visitor during the months of March & April. Vast flocks of Caravanners & Picnickers, frequent inundations of long-haired Hippies following their migratory ley lines to their breeding-ground Pop Festivals; all these shall test the patience of the most hardy of naturalists; who, in turn, shall become better informed with regard to the rich & inexhaustible analysis of human nature.

WHERE THERE'S NO WILL, THERE'S NO WAY

HUNTER DAVIES looks round his mother's estate

I came out of Charing Cross Tube station, clutching the official form. "The interview will be informal and held in private," so it read. That could be interesting. "I am unable to tell you exactly how much the fee will be until your interview." Hmm, that's not so interesting. Dying can prove an expensive business.

I had to find a building called Golden Cross House in a street called Duncannon Street. I had ruined my eyes on the *A-Z* trying to find it, having first ruined my temper trying to find an *A-Z*. Gawd knows what they do with them in our house. Someone's eating them. I found one eventually, hidden in the Old Trout's secret drawer, the one where she hides her personal and private possessions which no one is allowed to know about, far less touch. It's the place where she keeps her Sellotape. Oh no, I've let it out of the bag. I'll be for it.

The street is directly off Trafalgar Square – no wonder the name was vaguely familiar – but it's so short and the only office block in it so anonymous that you could pass it every day, yet never see it. Very MI5. This is the sort of building they always used in the old days, before MI5 became part of show business. Now all Top Secret places practically do guided tours: see our spies at work, that's where M used to sit, books and postcards on sale in the spy souvenir shop, please use the dead-letter box.

Golden Cross House, once I'd found the hidden away main door, still retains its mystery, with a faceless entrance, no obvious directions, no clue to what might go on inside. My letter instructed me to proceed to Room 526 on the fifth floor, and wait. I also had to bring the death certificate, if not already sent. The Chief Clerk had signed the letter with his big toe, by the look of his illegible squiggle.

The official address was clear enough and must keep an army of printers in work, every time they re-do the letter-heads. "Principal Registry of the Family Division of the High Court, Probate Personal Application Dept." What a mouthful. No chance of the trippers flocking to that. MI5 or even MI6 sounds so much zippier, don't you think.

My mother died six weeks ago. I was away at the time, in deepest Venezuela, around the Ori-noco Delta, not my fault, some of us have to work. The OT, bless her fashion sox, did all the arrangements for the funeral. Since my return, I've been trying to put the rest of the affairs in order. Let me see, where's my check-list. I've informed the DHSS at Archway that she won't need her pension book any more. I've told the Clydesdale Bank in Carlisle and asked for the meagre amount she had in there to be sent to me, but they said hard cheddar, they need proof that I'm the executor. The National Savings

DON'T SIGN IT. DON'T DO ANYTHING WITH IT. JUST SIT THERE AND READ IT.

people said no problem, and sent me her massive savings by return, £13.10p to be precise. Much more than I expected. Turns out that last year they credited her with interest of 36p, and for the previous three years, jolly generous of them, but in 1984 they paid her only 33p. Thin year that, for capitalist pigs like my poor mother.

I also told the tax people in Cardiff; always wondered why the folks in Cardiff kept tabs on my mum, but now it's too late. And I told the Postmaster General in Crawley, Sussex, what on earth is he doing down there. My mother has had a Civil Service widow's pension since my father died in 1958, so that's got to stop, thanks all the same, PMG.

Ditto her interest on the 3½% War Stock. She inherited this from my father and it's brought in, wait for it, interest of £5.08. Every year I've had to declare it on her tax returns and all the other complicated dopey forms I've been ploughing through these last six weeks, yet this War Stock is a nonsense. It was a Government con during the War, dunno which one, all wars probably. They dropped leaflets from planes urging suckers to help finance new Spitfires by taking out War Stock. My Dad had £290.50 worth. Goodness knows where he got that sort of money. Perhaps he inherited them from his Dad. I remember when he died I found they could not be cashed, it's all a mirage, this £290.50, practically worthless. But we're lumbered with them. When I go, Caitlin, Jake or Flora will have to declare them. Let's hope they're in the Orinoco, or orbiting.

My mother left no will, not that we can find, and why should she have done, having no wordly possessions. They always lived in council or RAF houses, my dear parents. No money for holidays when I was at home, far less savings; please don't cry, this new lay-out does not absorb emotion like the Coren pages did. Absence of a will meant that I had to apply for Probate. I'm not letting those buggers at the Clydesdale hang on to her loot.

The corridors on the fifth floor stretched for miles and I realised at once what it reminded me of. The BBC, any BBC block, but Bush House particularly. It was only slowly, when I got to the officials themselves, hidden away in their vast barren rooms, that I realised what it was really like – Russia. They could shoot the next Le Carré film here. No need for elderly young girls to be dressed up in 1950s clothes, trudging

"Barry's out-of-body experiences have been particularly boring lately."

27

"Oh, stop worrying – I told you, he's promised to bring you his best friend."

THAT'S NEARLY AN ARMFUL

Fearless of the industrial action, heebie-jeebies or the spectre of you-know-what, TIM HEALD and PAUL COX roll up sleeves at a blood transfusion centre

silently down endless, soulless corridors. They're all here. I don't think I've seen so many women wearing shapeless cardigans, certainly not in Central London, heart of the Empire, heart of the world's street fashion.

Actually, they're better dressed in Central Moscow, he added quickly, before the complaints come in. And just joking about the Probate gels. All groovy. Why ever did they start a letters pages. When we were in Moscow the summer before last, we met a Russian Sloane, secretary to the OT's Moscow publisher. I have a snap of her somewhere. Tossing her headscarf.

"Read this, Mr Davies," said a clerk at a desk, taking a form from an old box of rolled-up documents tied with what looked like dusty ribbons. "Don't sign it. Don't do anything with it. Just sit there, and read it."

WHO'S PINCHED £564?

Yes, sir, three bags full, sir. There was an elderly couple, already seated, already confused, who went back with their form, to be told to sit down and wait. You'll be called.

The room was enormous and completely sterile, institutionally barren. On a board on a far wall I could see a London Flood notice, what to do, and a Police Bomb Alert notice, also what to do. They looked as useless as my mother's War Stock, and probably as old.

Behind a grille I could see a woman clerk, slowly counting kopeks, I mean coppers. I wasn't sure if she was alive at first, or left over from a wartime display, till she suddenly shouted to the male clerk, what about lunch then, what was he going to do about it, then. It was 10.13 in the morning. Two minutes to go till my private interview.

When my call came, I was taken down another corridor by another ageless female clerk and into a room marked Commissioner. I read it first as Commissar.

I now had to sign the form I'd been given, agreeing that I was my mother's lawful son and

agreeing that "When required by court, I will exhibit in court a full inventory of the said estate." I was assured that was a formality, and I should never be called.

I then had to swear on the Bible to Almighty God that "This is my handwriting." That was tough. It's so awful I often can't even read it, never mind identify it. And swear "that the contents of the affidavits are true". Hmm, another toughie. In those millions of forms I'd filled in for Probate I'd put the Nat Savings at £10.36, not knowing about the 33p interest which later turned up. Could I be sent to prison. Not to worry, she said, it's what the deceased is worth at the time of death.

They had calculated that my mother's estate, counting everything, even those joke War Stocks, came to £862 gross, or £296 net. Heh up, who's pinched £564. You can't surely be taxing the poor old soul, even when she's gone.

No, it's because they allow the funeral bill. It would have cost more, £594.61, so I was warned on the bill, unless I'd settled it by January 18. It was the cheapest, simplest possible funeral. How can the really poor manage. No wonder my father-in-law, aged 88 this year, has been saving pennies a week all his life, just so he'll leave enough to pay his final bill.

She said it was always a bit sad, dealing with probate. It was the end of the line for the relatives concerned, the last formality. Yes, but what a lot of palaver, what a lot of bother you make us go to, in this case just for £296.

"Oh, might as well spend it while you have it," she said, half smiling, only half listening.

Listen, babooshka, she never had nothing to spend. That was it. That's the puny miserable sum she'd acquired, after a lifetime of hard work, love and diligence.

They're not totally heartless. The final fee came to only £1, the very minimum charge.

We've had a family conference. We're going to split the estate between the seven grandchildren. They're going to be given a volume of Burns each. My mother would have liked that.

There was blood everywhere.

Of 129 people who passed through the doors of an unremarkable building in St George's Road, Wimbledon, that afternoon, only sixteen emerged unscathed. Outside, the inhabitants of this most prosperous, respectable and bourgeois of suburbs went about their daily business without an apparent care. Meanwhile, only yards away, 113 of their fellow countrymen were bleeding terribly. On average each person lost an appalling three-quarters of a pint before the flow could be stopped. Not a word of this appeared in the nation's press and yet official sources estimated that on that one day alone no less than twelve gallons were spilt.

Well, "spilt" isn't quite the right word. The stuff was pumped with great precision into carefully labelled plastic bags under the expert supervision of Dr Jane McCulloch, the Head Vampire of the Wimbledon Community Centre. After they'd been bled, the bleeders were led away by the nice nurses – every one of whom could have come from the cast of one of Richard Gordon's *Doctor* films – for a bit of a lie down, followed by a cup of coffee and a biccy.

The National Blood Transfusion Service has been in the wars recently. First it was Aids, which panicked those donors who envisaged people like Doctor McCulloch running amok with a rusty needle and spreading the virus among the innocent. More recently, there has been a dispute about pay and subsistence

ON AVERAGE EACH PERSON LOST AN APPALLING THREE-QUARTERS OF A PINT BEFORE THE FLOW COULD BE STOPPED.

allowances for the blood collectors. Getting money out of the authorities proved more like getting blood out of a stone than a donor. When miserliness is compounded by pettifogging, it's small wonder that even nurses take umbrage.

There is something very reassuring about life turning out to be just as Tony Hancock described it. In the entrance hall of the Community Centre, there was a notice-board with

the week's activities chalked in: "Rambling, Whist Drive, Bridge, Blood Transfusion". Inside Dr McCulloch was sitting in the middle of the hall having a seethe. She had just been given a parking ticket. There was a large red triangle in her windscreen saying, "Doctor on Blood Transfusion", but pettifoggery had struck again. Two policemen had just come in to give blood and had said sorry luv there was nothing they could do about it. The good doctor was wondering whether or not to allow them their local anaesthetic.

I asked her if she had seen my friend, the illustrator. "He's over there on the far bed," she said. They had moved pretty fast. No sooner was Cox in the door than they'd been pricking his thumb to see what group he was and whether his iron level was okay. Now he was flat on his back smiling up at an exceptionally pretty nurse while inky red liquid seeped out of a tube in his left elbow.

The drill starts with the – necessary – bureaucracy. A jovial New Zealander with a beard and a red sweater sat doing the paperwork, while a slightly less jovial Asian in a white coat took blood samples, plopping some droplets in copper sulphate to determine iron level

29

and swirling other droplets round a sort of white palette to determine the grouping.

"Ah, a new victim … er … donor," said the New Zealander cheerily to an anxious thirty-year-old male in an anorak. The new victim looked distinctly unamused. In front of him was a dreadful notice warning certain people not to give blood. No prostitutes. No men who've had sex with other men since 1977. No one who's had sex with anyone living in Africa unless it's on the Mediterranean.

"I've been to Madeira," said the next applicant.

"Ah," said the New Zealander, "make cake there, don't they?"

An executive type in a grey suit said, rather grandly, that he had recently been in China and would be going again next month. He was politely told to keep his blood to himself.

"I had two aspirins this morning," said a

rather frantic woman who'd woken up with a headache. "Does that preclude me?"

"You'd better go and see the lady in the white coat," he said, pointing at Dr McCulloch who

THE BEDS LOOKED AS IF THEY MIGHT HAVE SEEN SERVICE AT SCUTARI.

was jabbing a needle into one of the policemen. The woman did and was duly precluded.

After the form-filling and testing, the donors sat in a queue of elderly canvas and tubular steel chairs facing the wall and away from the horrors of the actual blood-letting. Once or twice, said Dr McCulloch, a potential donor will get halfway down the queue, turn surreptitiously to see what is going on and flee from the room green and trembling. "They're usually the ones who didn't really want to be there in the first place but have been shamed into it by wives or girl-friends." It's the males who behave in the most extreme fashion. The women just get on with it. "It's always the men who ask for it to be done without anaesthetic," said the doctor. "I suppose they think it's macho."

The 113 people blooded in Wimbledon that day seemed to me to be as near as dammit to that elusive phenomenon, "a representative cross-section". One man, an engineer from the City, said that he guessed a very high proportion would have voted Liberal. I think I know what he meant but I have a hunch that, even if it were true, it told you as much about Wimbledon as it did about blood. Most people were casually dressed, though there was one man in an MCC tie. The age-span was from late teens to fifties, with a majority in their twenties and thirties. Both sexes were well represented. Most were white, though by no means all. A larky Trinida-

dian said he liked to give regularly because he thought he'd got too much of the stuff and getting rid of it made him feel better. Several people I asked about their motives in coming said "Guilt", though Dr McCulloch said that when they move further into the city they do get the odd meths drinker in for tea and company.

It takes about eight minutes to get three quarters of a pint out of the average person. Because my team were a nurse short they were operating on five beds. The queue moved slowly and apprehensively with a corporate, nervous grin every time a new victim was summoned and everyone moved up one seat.

Over by the beds, which looked as if they might have seen service at Scutari, the nurses kept up a steady flow of bedside mannerisms to keep the donors' minds off the steady flow into the plastic bag. No matter how nonchalant they tried to appear (one poseur read his evening paper with great ostentation throughout his transfusion), I didn't see one person actually watch the needle go in.

Dr McCulloch flitted from bed to bed like a darts player in a white coat and the new Oscar Wilde biography on her table remained unopened. A busy day in the office, but fairly routine. The worst that happened was a faulty bag ("Don't worry, the lab will use what we've got") and one woman who didn't confess that she'd been on holiday in Turkey till she'd had half a pint removed. "Mark it T.A.," said a technician. T.A. is "Tropical Area".

They advise a ten-minute lie down afterwards, fifteen for beginners, and then say a cold drink is better than a hot one. Seasoned donors make rather a play of spending a mere two or three minutes on the bed, quick cup of tea and off. One or two people looked decidedly wobbly when three-quarters of a pint light. But by the time they got to the tea table most of them seemed quite euphoric and chattery. "Ever so nice to meet you," I heard one couple say to another. "Hope we'll see you in six months' time." Maybe blood doning's proper place *is* alongside whist and rambling.

Doctor McCulloch stuck a label on the illustrator's chest saying, "Be nice to me, I've given blood today." One of the technicians ("You won't catch me giving any, can't stand needles") looked at his watch and said, "It was 8.20 last night when the last needle went in. It'll be nearer 9.00 tonight."

They were all looking pretty weary by closing time but the humour stayed good. The doctor said it nearly always did. One or two people gave her a hard time when she asked about Aids – they took it personally. But the worst was when she had to turn away a long-standing donor because they'd been somewhere dodgy, or taken an aspirin. "It's a very personal thing for some people," she said, "and they don't like being rejected." Some people cry.

My session at Wimbledon made me think it brought the best out of people. Metaphorically too.

LATEST AUTUMN ON RECORD SHOCK

By our Scandals Staff

London's brand-new Weather Centre, a high-tech complex situated in the heart of the Cornish countryside, raced into top gear ahead of schedule this week with a promise to locate the winter.

"We know it's out there somewhere," gritted Weather Centre supremo Alec Pottle, formerly Head of Hail at the Meteorological Office Computer Centre, Bracknell. "So all of us here at the new W.C. will be bending our efforts to the task of rounding it up. It is most important that we do get our winter back, because what we have on our hands here at the moment is an exhausted autumn. Exhausted and confused. You cannot expect things to keep on dropping off other things in a mellow and fruitful fashion for ever and ever. After a while, everything starts to give up and fall over completely. Trees in particular are beginning to feel that this is their role in life."

Evidence so far collected as to the whereabouts of the British winter is inconclusive. It took its continental holiday a little late this year, and was briefly sighted in Albania. "But it is much too early," Mr Pottle assured me, "to talk in terms of defection. Our winter has nothing to teach the Soviets that they don't know already." He dismissed as "Scotch mist" a suggestion that the British winter was taking secret instruction from its Russian counterpart, with a view to initiating disruptive action in the run-up to next Christmas.

WEATHER NOTE: Temperatures on the Met Office roof reached an all-time late-February high of 72°F last night when somebody left the deep-fat fryer on. A cleaner, Mrs Daisy Mullery, 58, was admitted to hospital suffering from spits and spots and more general precipitation.

THE EYE OF THE STORM

Men and machines go hand in hand to follow the trail of Britain's savage showers and intimidating breezes.

Only a matter of hours after an erroneous forecast of high winds has been broadcast, the Met Office's hurricane machine swings into action to restore public confidence

Effect of hurricane machine registers hundreds of miles away at Stirling Castle, Scotland

As reports come in of a cloud approaching the Scilly Isles, Bracknell's top brains commence an intensive radar scrutiny of the southwestern approaches

The recently-completed New London Weather Centre, situated somewhere in Cornwall. Warm weather: right-hand dome. Cold weather: left-hand dome. The entrance ladder enables forecasters to feel in their bones whether it's going to be wet

WHAT'S IN LAWSON'S BOX?

Gentleman's gentleman Walter Whibley has packed the Budget boxes of upwards of a dozen Chancellors. Now for the first time he tells the story of what goes into Britain's most important item of hand luggage

"That Mr Lawson," says Walter Whibley with a twinkle, "he's a one. Always insists on having a plane ticket put in his box. Ticket to anywhere, just so long as he could make a quick getaway. 'Course, he hasn't had to, not yet. Not so far." And Walter crosses his gnarled old fingers, as a small tear of mirth splashes down on to his starched apron. He cries rather easily, Walter does. It's a legacy of wartime, when he served as an RAF batman, and pilots maddened with beer, fear and fatigue used to beat him up. "But I always maintained my standards. I used to polish those flying jackets with neatsfoot oil, polish 'em till they squeaked. In fact we were known as the Squeaking Squadron. I was proud of that." And Walter's shining eyes confirm that it is so.

It's a long way from the dandelion-strewn runways of Biggin Hill to the heavy-duty Axminsters of Downing Street, but Walter made the transition with scarcely a stumble. "I was a tram-driver for a while," he recalls, "but there's no scope for neatness in it. It's all done for you by the rails and that. Had I gone for a trolley-bus things might have been different. But I resigned, and went into ironing newspapers for the Savile Club, and from there it was a short step to my present employment. I'm officially Keeper of Cuff-Links In Ordinary to the Treasury, that's my title."

And are there cuff-links to keep? "Well, there are," Walter confides, "but you wouldn't wear 'em, not the actual links, they're covered with lions and unicorns and that, you'd have your jacket sleeves in ribbons. So I just put them in the case for luck. In the Budget box, that is, but I call it a case because that's how I think of it when I'm packing it. It's a kind of voyage, isn't it, going out and giving the Budget, you need your things with you."

So what things will actually be in the Chancellor's box this Budget Day? "Well," reveals Walter, "there are certain things that are traditional. Clean socks and underpants, you have to have those, I don't suppose there's been a case packed in the history of the world that hasn't had clean socks and underpants in. I certainly hope not. And a toothbrush of course. A bottle of Aspirins. A pair of pyjamas, just in case. I always put the *Concise Oxford Dictionary* in as well, just for checking the speech. I don't want my gentlemen committing solipsisms over the wireless."

What about sustenance, I asked him, do

The Chancellor gives his friends in the City a hint

Chancellors go in for that? "Ooh yes, sir, they do, well, they all have your basic tomato sandwiches, which I do up nicely in House of Commons crested greaseproof. And Mr Lawson, being a Jewish gentleman, he likes his chicken soup. Mind, I can't give it him in the Silver Thermos, because that's the Prime Minister's, and she is the First Lord of the Treasury you know, not everybody knows that. So I lend him a flask of my own, it's got Noddy on, I'm afraid; I couldn't get the Kermit the Frog, they were out of stock. And I always put a Mars bar in the box. I started that with Mr Butler away back in the rationing time. He was delighted when a Mars bar fell out of his box because you couldn't get them, of course, them days. Not legally.

"Superstitious? Ooh, they're all superstitious. That Mr Heathcoat Amory, he was a bachelor like me, he always had to have a bit of lemon peel in his box. Lemon peel, and a ping-pong ball. Puzzled me too, sir. And

there was one Chancellor, I won't say which, he used to go out for that photo, you know the one, where they hold the box up for the cameras? Well, he used to have a picture of a naked lady stuck to the backside of that box, nobody ever saw it let alone took a picture of it, oh he used to get a great kick out of that. I didn't hold with it myself."

Surely, over the years, one or two of these distinguished men have let slip the odd advance detail of their proposed new measures? "No, sir, and I never asked. It's always been my opinion that people who know about money are a race apart, sir, I really do feel that, these are men with wonderful minds, sir, they can make money out of nothing. Thin air. So it's always been more of a pleasure than a duty to serve them in any way I can. And they've been good to me in return. Now I've got my grace-and-favour barrel to live in, down in Barking, I'm fixed for life, sir. Fixed." And Walter burst into tears.

PUNCH

18TH MARCH 1988   £1

CUT!

NIGEL
THE SIMPLIFIER
IS UNLEASHED

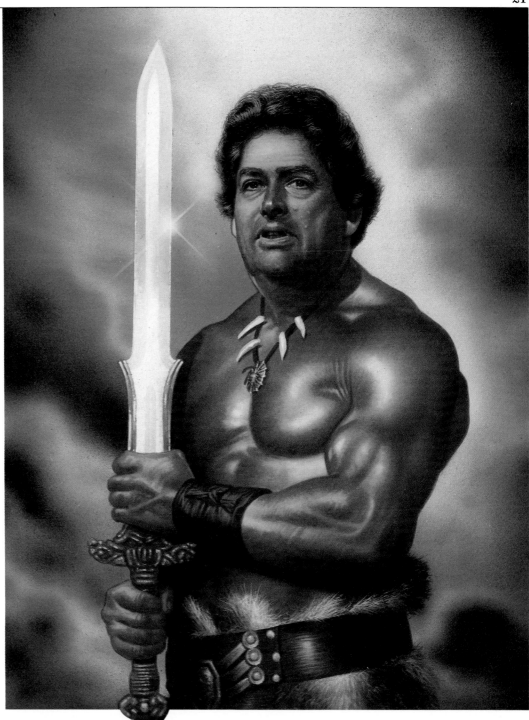

DAVID TAYLOR TALKS TO

LORD DENNING

THE door's open. Propped open with a deck-chair, do you see, and the sun streaming in as it generally does. But bless my soul, there's not a soul about. So there we are. Thirty-five acres with no one in. Ring the blessed bell again, but still not a sound. Except, of course, for the bell and quite a few bees, as there generally are. I telephone from the car. Who? Oh, yes, yes, well I'd better come in. Door's open. One is a bit deaf, do I see, as old 19th-century gentlemen generally are. Oh, indeed he is. Was born in 1899 as a matter of fact. So there we are, anyway. *Punch*? Oh yes, well I'd better come in. Door's open. I'd better make my way to the library. That is where he generally is. House is called The Lawn. Near the church, you can't miss it. Door's open.

Ah, there I am. Telephoning from the motor-car, indeed. Now there's an extraordinary thing. This is the Regency bit. The plasterwork is rather good. They had the other bit added on. Now look here, that's old Sir Nicholas Bacon over there, Francis's father, Lord Keeper, and quite a decent painting. Oh, and this is amusing: a door set into the book-case, with dummy

> **"He will bring on the halt and the lame as witnesses. There is a nice old blind chap who will testify. His Lordship can't get about like he used to, though he is ever so much better since he had his hip done."**

books set into it, so that at a glance you might think the whole wall was a book-case, do you see? He always shows visitors that, because he doubts there's another quite like it, except there's one in the Athenaeum. There's a copy of Magna Carta and Nelson's will on the table, which people generally like to see. And so there we are. I shall have to speak up, because he's a bit deaf these days. Can't hear the bell.

Oh goodness him, yes, he is ever so busy. The Lords for one thing, and the local goings-on for another. They do take up time, especially the footpath. The Highways Department is not doing its job there. The footpath is all rutted, and the old folk can't get through, the children get their boots all muddy and so forth. It ought to be maintained. The case was set for August 17th, but the County Council's witness can't be there, so it seems he'll have to wait until September. So long as it gets done before the winter, that's the thing.

Oh yes, he's rather looking forward to it. It'll be his first presentation of a court case since, when, 1943 it was, when he ceased to be a King's Counsel and became a judge. He will bring on the halt and the lame as witnesses. There is a nice old blind chap who will testify. And of course he can't get about himself, not like he used to, though he is ever so much better since he had his hip done. Oh, that made all the difference, having that done. He can get into the garden and about as far as the plantation. They keep bees, by the way. His Lordship was stung twenty times the other week. So there we are.

The last case was over the bench, by the way. There has been an old bench here in Whitchurch, out on the London Road it has stood, for 80 years. He used to use it as a young lad and nobody has any right to interfere with it. But a builder chap wanted to do away with it, so now the council is taking up the case and a good thing, too. So there we are. It was a wrought-iron bench.

You have to be vigilant. He was born here, of course, a Hampshire lad. The Americans put up a plaque on the old shop his father kept, a draper's shop, oh and the Lord Chancellor came down, they made quite a to-do. In the old church across the road, Dennings have sat for a hundred years, always the same pew, and everyone brought up to say their prayers every day, which they don't do nowadays. In the old days, you were made to do it. She (Lady Denning) still kneels down properly by the bed, but his hip won't bend any more so there we are.

The Lords still do. The bishops start proceedings with a prayer. In the Commons, they have the chaplain, but there he looks at the assembly and prays for the nation. Goodness, what a rough and ready lot. In the Upper House, do you see, they mostly know what they're talking about. You can find an expert on every conceivable subject in the Lords, whether it is the City or salmon-fishing. Particularly salmon-fishing.

They're televised now, do I know, which is a good thing on the whole. It wouldn't be in the Commons. They would show themselves up. And God forbid in a court of law. You'd have playing to the gallery and goodness knows what. Do I know there's an old water-driven silk mill in the garden? It has been there since Domesday. They ought to get it restored.

Goodness him, just imagine the Jeffrey Archer case, on the television. Of course, the judge there took a view very much against the newspaper, oh very much against. He had a similar situation when he presided over the Profumo scandal. The misbehaviour of the press is always a tricky one, but on the other hand they are the watchdogs of justice, as he said in that little book of his, *Freedom Under The Law*, that was in 1949 as he recalls. But good gracious him, it was quite a summing-up. Goodness, yes. So there we are.

Well now, what are we going to talk about for *Punch* did I say? Oh, there's visitors here all the time. Well, there's the garden to see, Charlie does that, and there's the River Test running through, so the judges like to come down and do some fishing and he stands on the old stone (from Lincoln's Inn) bridge and does a recitation of Tennyson's *The Brook*. Then there's the cricket matches and the garden parties and the fêtes and he does not know what else, a chap came from India just the other day. Law student, he said. Lord Denning showed him the book-case.

He's kept his books. Old judges often get rid of their old books, but he has kept his and found them no end useful. There's this business of the European Court getting ever so high-handed for one thing. He sent in a piece to *The Times*

about that. They're doing the letters now, then he'll have his say again. So there we are. He is a bit forgetful, now and again. He'll go up to London (they have a place in Old Square in Lincoln's Inn, mostly for grand-daughters now) and he'll forget to take his train fare and she (Lady Denning) has to go down later and pay the chap. He put two socks on the same foot, once. Goodness him, he is 88 and been retired five years. But he never forgets the clocks. He winds them up after breakfast. The grandfather clock here in the study belonged to his first wife's father, who was the vicar here.

Then there's this business with the "poll tax", have I seen that? Well now, look here, what's going to happen over that? What's to stop people thinking they don't take much interest in politics and all that lark, so they won't bother going on the electoral register, if you please, then they'll not be bothered with the tax? Mmm? And, do I see, there is the business of finding juries. In the old days, you always had middle-class, middle-aged men, reasonably well-educated, and jolly good they were, too. Well now, just look at what happens now. They get every Tom, Dick and Harry, picked at random off the register and look at the juries we get. Oh, goodness him. Lord Roskill has been saying for ages that in difficult cases, like City frauds and so on, where there has to be specialised knowledge, it's no good at all having a jury which hasn't the faintest what is going on, there ought instead to be a tribunal, and he's quite right, of course, but the Government won't do

anything about it. So there we are. When he goes to London, he wears his bowler hat. People still recognise that, and he'd dare say it's the only one in London nowadays. He was around for a long time, to be sure, on the bench from 1944 to 1982 and 20 years Master of the Rolls, so he does get recognised, still. Well.

There's a pickle now over this Peter Wright business. He would think that the House of Lords will over-rule the Court of Appeal, but goodness gracious, things should never have come to this over that awful man. On the other hand, it is high time, of course, that Section 2 of the Official Secrets Act was done away with.

Of course, there has been a tremendous change during his lifetime over relationships between the judiciary and the executive, governments, departments of state and so on. This business of judicial review is a tremendous advance, do you see. By the way, that big bowl on the wall comes all the way from Fiji. They used to go all over the world. Now they are old and people come to them. It's best when some judges come over, because legal people are the best gossips and the best story-tellers that ever there were.

Anyhow, here she (Lady Denning) is and it'll shortly be time for tea. The sun is still shining and it is to be hoped it does on Sunday, the first Sunday in August, when The Lawn always has a cricket match, but it generally rains. Everyone will just have to come inside if it does. They could admire the book-case.

So there we are.

"We're in the mood for a little entertainment. Send in The Supremes."

BETWEEN THE DEVIL AND THE SDP

*The crunch. A fiasco. A shambles. And other matters arising
from the Liberal assembly. JULIA LANGDON reports*

The rain sweeps in sheets down the deserted sands. The donkeys have long since departed for their winter sanctuary. The plastic decorations slap in the wind along the mile of closed pleasure arcades. The "No Vacancy" notices hang in every other window while the landladies are off living it up in Tenerife.

But where does anyone go from Blackpool – apart from Tenerife, that is? Where, above all, does David Steel go? Here at the end of the M55 he has reached the end of his political road and after twelve years at the top it turns out that he might just as well have been building sandcastles on the beach all this time. All those years of looking like the hope for the future, of looking, anyway, like a figure off a Fifties knitting-pattern, are over. The Boy David's boyhood is gone and even David Owen never succeeded in making a man of him.

He tried. They will have to put that on his political epitaph. He did try. The trouble is that the extent to which David Steel has perpetually been out of sync with his own party has always been underestimated. He has always felt that he was in sufficient control of the whole machine to be able to command it; sometimes it was true but more often other people had to keep him under control. The proof of that comes from the Social Democrats, the old Social Democrats. The only way they kept the Alliance on the road, they will tell you, was by working out, on Steel's behalf, what the Liberal Party would be prepared to wear. When he was, in the end, let out on his own – or, at least with Bob Maclennan, which comes to much the same thing – he blew it.

Blackpool in January! What better location to make anyone – even a Liberal – feel better just for the sight of the dismal desolation on every side! Why, even Bob Maclennan seems colourful and charismatic in contrast to the average Blackpudlian battling down the prom in search of an open chip shop.

The illuminations have been taken down and sold, as ever, to the Middle East to lighten some Arabian nights, but it doesn't matter. The Liberals didn't come here to see the light. They came, rather, every one of them, on a personal pilgrimage to save the Liberal Party, for themselves,

THEY CAME ON A PERSONAL PILGRIMAGE TO SAVE THE LIBERAL PARTY FROM ITSELF.

from itself. After what David's done – well, it had to be up to them, didn't it?

They've done this before and, come to that, so have I. The last time I was in Blackpool in January was ten years ago this week. And what was I doing here then? Why, I came to see David Steel roasted and eaten alive by a special Liberal Assembly. The only thing was it didn't happen then.

As it turned out, the pigeon fanciers' annual show on the other side of the Winter Gardens was a great deal more lively than the debate on the future of the Lib-Lab Pact, threatened as it was by the failure of the British Parliament to accept proportional representation for the forthcoming European elections. And who remembers that now?

David Steel probably, for one. He was no doubt musing about his last outing to Blackpool as he journeyed here again to face the beards, fewer of them these days, and the sandals, worn of course with socks in January. It was just about ten years ago that he was writing in *The Times*: "Few people join the Liberal Party in expectation of any reward or any power. That is partly its attraction…I do not despise this role. It is an honourable one, and a useful one to be such a pressure group in the body politic and one which the Liberal Party has very effectively fulfilled for twenty years. But is that all we want to be? I thought not." Depending upon whether you happen to be David Steel or not, ten years is either an extremely long time in politics or seems like just the other day.

There is a difference this time. For a start, they decided to try to escape all the jokes about the pigeon fanciers and the other highlights of downtown Blackpool in the off season by avoiding the Winter Gardens altogether. This is probably not wise, or not if the alternative was the Norbreck Castle. Unless you happen to be some kind of a masochist with highly dubious tastes, you have probably never heard of the Norbreck Castle. Take a tip from an old-timer: keep it like that. The Norbreck Castle is famed in the annals of political and journalistic experience. If Blackpool is the last resort, it was the Norbreck which provided the crowning qualifications.

It used to be called the Norbreck Hydro, but then one of the many owners who bought it in yet another unsuccessful attempt to turn it into a money-making con-

cern, put some fortifications on the outside and called it a Castle instead. Colditz was probably more homely. Colditz was certainly easier to get out of, as any of the generations of escape committees, formed for as long as political parties have been meeting in Blackpool, will tell you.

There are several problems. The Norbreck is miles from anywhere, including Blackpool, but you don't need to worry about that unless you manage to make it out of the door. This is difficult enough because the original architect designed it so that the door would not open in anything more than a dancing breeze. This was then exacerbated by the addition of another door which doubled the difficulty and enhanced the excitement – as the draught thus created produces a constant howling moan which can be heard throughout the hotel.

A great deal of care had to be taken last weekend to distinguish this noise from the keening of the dissatisfied guests coupled with the public agonising of the Liberal Party. But at least the knowledge of the entrance and exit

THEY THINK IT IS DAVID STEEL WHO OUGHT TO BE BREAKING DOWN IN TEARS.

problems prevented the more emotional among the conference delegates from rushing out and hurling themselves lemming-like into the Irish Sea.

The uninitiated who have only recently started taking note of the carnage on the centre ground of British politics – since, in fact, it started getting interesting – might have thought that this conference was arranged to enable us all to share their public breast-beating. In fact it was organised months ago and should have been a mere formality to endorse the terms of the merger with the Social Democrats.

Back in Harrogate in September, most of the Liberals were quite happy with the way things were going, not least because they were getting rid of David Owen, and Maclennan looked like a pushover. In those days he was being compared to Neville Chamberlain – by Roy Hattersley, because he carries a rolled umbrella everywhere he goes, and by the Liberals because it was clear that he was heavily into appeasement.

The fact that he sees himself as rather more of a "Churchillian" figure has not gone down quite so well with the Liberal Party. For one thing, they think it is David Steel who ought to be breaking down in tears. And in private he probably was. For this was his swansong and although the rest of them left Blackpool to return to whatever represents normal life for a Liberal, he knew that things would never be quite the same for him again. Probably the most hurtful thing was the knowledge that in ten years' time he could reprint that *Times* article of ten years ago and it would still be true.

I DID HOPE I COULD COUNT ON YOUR VOTE

Always a merger man, ALISTAIR SAMPSON was one of the SDP's first candidates. His disenchantment shows

You want to know what it was like? All right, I will tell you. The heady days when it all began. The Limehouse Declaration. The flocking to the colours of centrists like Camilla and me and the children. They were twelve and eight then; they did not actually flock to the colours; we flocked them.

Setting up the St Marylebone – as it then was – SDP. There were fourteen of us the first week. I made do with Deputy Chairman.

Then I remember wandering into Lords to see a cricket match. The headline in the *Evening Standard* was "Alliance leads with 52%". That was our high point.

The amazing first conference in Perth. I spoke. By that time, I had a constituency. I was, I may say, the third SDP candidate to be chosen. Put that in your meerschaum and smoke it. I said, if memory serves me right, that amongst the hedgerows of Honiton I had come across the odd Tory; that all Tories were odd, but none more odd than the Tories of Honiton. I went on to say that when we found Tories in the hedgerows we should spray them with SDP. I was after the ecology vote.

Then we were down in Honiton, SDP and Liberals working together to rid the constituency of its sitting member. Tramping the street, rain or shine. "I do hope I can count on your vote."

"You could tie a blue ribbon to a shih-tzu and they'd elect it down here." They were more or

THE TRAGEDY IS THAT BOB MACLENNAN IS NO DAVID OWEN.

less right. I failed to do the Conservative Party a service by unseating the sitting member, but we gave him a fright. Nearly halved his majority.

It was a beginning. The dream that this country could be turned into one nation by a party attaining power (a party that was not – because it represented one section of the community – divisive) remained in existence.

You cannot, denied PR, beat the system overnight. Yet even after the '83 election, we felt we could see the light at the end of the tunnel. Especially when the dishy, charismatic Owen took over from Roy Jenkins. Jenkins in his Dimbleby lecture had shown the way. Jenkins had been the best Chancellor and the most imaginative Home Secretary since the war. But he was not the man to lead us, as I had found out on the

"Acknowledging your mistakes is all part of becoming a Liberal."

doorsteps of my constituency.

And then we went into the last election, with a fudged, wishy-washy Alliance manifesto and exposed ourselves to Tweedledum-Tweedledee taunts. Personally I had always been a merger man. I was a signatory to Dick Taverne's "Victory '88" movement, which was a coming-together of those who believed that a mere alliance was not credible in the long term. We felt that SDP and Liberal had enough in common to merge. We also felt that, should merger take place, David Owen, by sheer force of personality, would emerge as leader.

We had reckoned without the destructive force of David Steel. Steel should never have led the Liberal Party. He is a schemer. To attain the leadership, he out-manoeuvred Pardoe, a man of infinitely greater capacity who would have worked harmoniously with Owen. Now he has out-manoeuvred Owen also – or has he?

I voted for merger. I even sent £25 to the merger campaign. I wanted merger. The tragedy is that Bob Maclennan is no Owen. And that Owen was a large part of the magic of the Alliance. So here I am, an ex-candidate, a devout believer that this country needs a middle way, watching these chaotic negotiations much as a white hunter might watch the writhings of the body of a snake after he had cut off its head. I do not care which party governs us if its policies make sense. The Alliance at the moment of writing appears to have committed suicide. We can now only hope either that Bryan Gould takes over the Labour Party or that Margaret Hilda succumbs to the lure of Dulwich and is succeeded, not by someone who wishes to chastise us with scorpions, but by a healer.

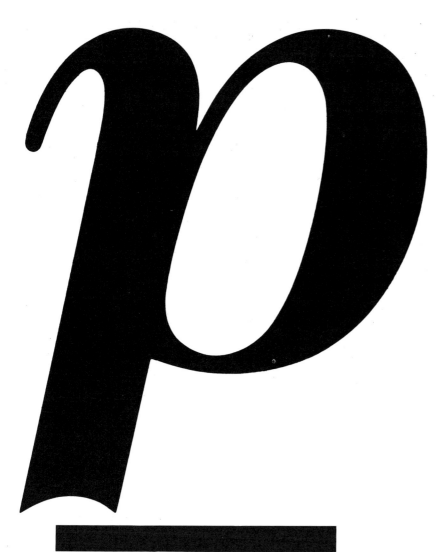

p

The exciting new mag-in-a-mag concept for the way we read today

In today's busy and exciting world, successful decision-makers like Donald Trelford, Gayle Hunnicut, Peter Hillmore and Jasper Conran spend a lot of time in Paris, New York, Los Angeles and Metropolitan Wigan.

They live life to the full, in the exuberant company of power people like Peter Langan, Jack Nicholson, Ena Kendall or the fabulous Fergie.

They're pushing their bodies to the limit, right around the clock in a dozen different time zones, pausing only for a bite of avocado, papaya and rocket salad or a jeroboam of Sainsbury's excitingly fresh Manzanilla sherry.

Today's international scene-stealers have no time to spare, not even to experience hair-loss. No window of opportunity exists for them to uptake all of today's exciting new media.

In reading a magazine, as in choosing a personal deodorant, they exercise choice and exclusivity. They pipeline their information input with the same targeted commitment they bring to choosing their brain food, entering into a relationship, or buying into BP.

p **magazine was conceptualised for them.**

p **stands for** *p***eople.**

For *p***ower.**

For *p***ertinence.**

For *p***errier.**

And for *p***omegranate.**

p is for people who must live tomorrow today.

Donald Trelford

People who know instinctively that there's never been better time to insulate a loft, bring Andrew Lloyd Webber into their home on CD, to collect beautifully hand-crafted enamel pendant miniatures of the world's favourite dogs in a style that would have delighted George III, or to take a fresh look at an elegant, Regency-style sofa-bed with sturdy oak-look frame and floral bolster.

p is for *P*ositioning.
For *P*erfect-Binding. For *P*ackaging.
For *P*rofile. And for *P*iffle.

Inside This Week's Perfectly Packaged *p*

Entre Nous *Between you and me and these four walls...* the latest buzz on how a 17-stone housewife's friends just could not believe their eyes when they saw how much weight she'd lost... why today's exciting new shoppers-by-post are all talking about the new designer bonk bag in soft, supple, elegant Neoprene with the accent on style and practicality... plus the insider low-down on an exciting new retailing and leisure project that's taking the West Midlands by storm.

Just Jasper – His eclectically stunning designs are engagingly open, but the young master himself remains an enigma, as EVE ARNOLD found out as she photographed his new fitted kitchen wall units and practically vibrationless extractor fan.

Today's Woman
Men talk frankly to *p* about the women in their lives, and what they'd like for Christmas.

Men Today
Women confess to *p* about what kind of things make a man and where they send off for them.

Bolthole Today's top writing talent tells why it can make sound sense to drop a line to The Guernsey Tourist Board, Dept 29 (P), PO Box 23, White Rock, Guernsey, CI (Ref P).

The Menace In Our Taps We take water for granted. It is the very essence of a simple drink, or a piping bubble bath. Yet it might contain contaminants, fluoride, chloro-organics, or even diluted E-numbers. BARTY JOFFE looked at designer water-filtration systems for *p* and asked: Can I pay by credit card?

The World's Super Rich At the end of the day, even mega-millionaires like nothing better than to snuggle down in front of the cosy log effect of one of today's exciting new range of living flame gas fires, many of which, reveals PATRICK MALONE, now feature a built-in back boiler.

DunSellin
Our exciting new back of the mag-in-a-mag concept page finds an excitingly new twist on the old chestnut of *A Life In The Day Of.*

Me And My Durable Spring-Steel Stomach Trimmer Which Keeps Me In Great Shape All The Year Round Yet Folds Down Under A Bed

This Week: **Quintin Hogg**

RUSSELL ASH

THE EVEN MORE COMPACT DICTIONARY OF NATIONAL BIOGRAPHY

Wonderful book, the 63-volume
Dictionary of National Biography (1885-1900).
They're all there – the heroes and villains,
the famous and the totally forgotten, the towering
giants and the pathetic prats. Just the other day,
I was looking for the entry on Thomas Carlyle
in Vol. 9, when I noticed that on the spine was
inscribed "Canute Chaloner". I took these to be
the names of the first and last entries in
that particular volume – until I looked a little closer

Vol. 1 ABBADIE ANNE (1910-72)

A distant cousin of Raggedy Ann, heroine of Johnny Gruell's *Raggedy Ann Stories* (1918), Abbadie Anne aspired to become an equally famous children's character, largely to cash in on the associated merchandise. She first adopted the persona of a mouse with large feet and a squeaky voice, only to find herself at the receiving end of a writ from Walt Disney. Her attempts to imitate a dog she called "Sloopy" and to take up residence in a burrow on Wimbledon Common were similarly thwarted. Her later years spent living in Paddington, dressed as a Peruvian bear wearing a duffel-coat and Wellington boots, went largely unremarked. After her death, the Swedish pop group, Abba, was named after her.

Vol. 9 CANUTE CHALONER (1843-96)

Major-General Canute Chaloner was one of the colonial administrators who put the "Great" into Great Britain (or possibly the "Berk" into Berkshire). His early career was devoted to the quest for the source of the Nile, which he was convinced arose near Esher. He went in search

of Livingstone sixteen years after Stanley had found him, thought the Mad Mahdi only mildly eccentric and, like his regal namesake, attempted to impress a group of ignorant savages by making the waters recede – but unfortunately chose the Victoria Falls and was swept away, amid much giggling among the ignorant savages.

Vol. 12 CONDOR CRAGIE (1860-1910)

Condor "Birdman" Cragie, Laird of Invergrubby, pioneer aviator, succeeded to the title after his father, Hamish "The Loon" Cragie, met an untimely end when he "got in a wee bit of a muddle" in a sword dance and was diced to death. Hearing a Highland seer's enigmatic (and appallingly scanning) prophecy ("Tartan-clad Caledonians shall one day fly/In the sky"), Condor became obsessed with man-powered flight. His early attempts with turbo-charged bagpipes were unsuccessful and left him totally deaf, but after consuming a few drams and remarking "Dinna talk tae me aboot the Wright Brothers!" he hurled himself from the battlements of his ancestral home wearing his remarkable winged sporran. His kilt billowed upwards and momentarily he resembled an airborne flasher; a split second later he resembled a haggis that's been through a mangle.

Vol. 15 DIAMOND DRAKE (1858-1945)

Diamond "James" Drake (curiously, Diamond was his real name,

"James" his nickname) was a larger-than-life prospector, famed throughout the veldt (which he insisted on mispronouncing in order to annoy Boers). Rider Haggard might have modelled Allan Quatermain on him – but fortunately found someone more suitable. At one time it was touch and go whether he or Cecil Rhodes would found a new colony, but the thought of living in a country called "Drakesia" finally tipped the balance in Rhodes's favour. Drake once stumbled on the Cullinan Diamond, thought it was "a bit of old glass", and cast it aside. He then found and attempted to remove the Kohinoor – but as he found it in the Jewel House of the Tower of London, he spent the rest of his days in prison.

[Rather uninterestingly, the reprint of Vol. 5 is about his brother, Craik Drake, the noted duck impersonator.]

Vol. 25 HARRIS HENRY I (1855-1921)

Josiah Henry was too idle to think of new names for all his twelve sons and simply gave them all the same name and numbered them. Harris Henry I went into partnership with his younger brothers, Harris Henry VI and Harris Henry IX, forming a music hall juggling act called "The Three Henries", specialising in juggling objects that no performer had ever before attempted – lemon meringues, live hand-grenades and rabid fruit bats. More or less single-handedly – or maybe six-handedly – they caused the death of the music hall.

Vol. 51 SCOFFIN SHEARES (dates withheld until relatives have been informed)

Scoffin Sheares was but one of several aliases used by the hell-raising Australian, Dingo Castlemaine, who was also known as Crocodile Billabong and Kangaroo Jumbuck, depending on how the

"The committee on women's rights will now come to order."

mood took him. He was among the very few Australian convicts transported *to* England (for his own safety, after describing the inmates of Botany Bay penal colony as "a bunch of poofters"). He became an itinerant sheep-shearer who, as his principal ill-spelt pseudonym implies, scoffed at the use of shears in favour of giving sheep a shampoo, light trim and blow-dry. He was drowned after being butted into a trough of sheep-dip by a dissatisfied ewe.

Vol. 58 UBALDINI WAKEFIELD (c.1343-1372)

Correctly Saint Ubaldini of Wakefield, he was a wandering monk of the Middle Ages who after a few bottles of Valpolicella somehow wandered from Siena to Yorkshire. Carrying the culinary skills of his native Italy with him, he tried to make pasta, but was disappointed to find fourteenth-century Yorkshire poorly served by delicatessens. Making do with local ingredients, he succeeded instead in inventing the Yorkshire pudding. He then wandered across the Pennines and attempted to invent the Lancashire Hotpot, but, while stirring his cauldron and muttering in Latin, was stoned to death as a witch.

[Since the first publication of the *Dictionary of National Biography*, Ubaldini has been canonised. On his saint's day (31 June, alternate millennia), the chefs and vicars of Wakefield play a boisterous game of 47-a-side rugby with a giant Yorkshire pudding.]

Vol. 63 WORDSWORTH ZUYLESTEIN (1822-1904)

Wordsworth Zuylestein was the son of an East End immigrant Jewish tailor. His mother, Ruth, had poetic aspirations and dreamed of referring to "My son, the poet ..." Parental pressure and limited horizons drove him to write *Ode on a Three-Piece Suit* and such immortal lines as "I wandered lonely as a yard of worsted." Later, following a dramatic mid-life career move, he became a successful lawyer, and broke his mother's heart. His less well-known brothers, Keats and Coleridge Zuylestein, were entertainers. Both were successful mime artists and consequently never spoke to each other.

A R T S

C O U N S E L

JOHN MORTIMER
. . . .

VISITING a university, it was reported, our Prime Minister asked an undergraduate what he was studying. When he answered "history", she said, "What a luxury!" and passed on, presumably, to the department of business studies. In the Americanisation of Britain, the land of "media presentation" and "market share", in the fast food, fast buck (now fast-disappearing buck) economy, our history, like that of Henry Ford's own land, has now apparently also become bunk and, worse still, a luxurious and self-indulgent type of bunk.

Nobody, of course, expects much love of learning and the arts from politicians, although the much derided Neville Chamberlain carried a pocket edition of Shakespeare and could quote *Henry IV, Part 1* at historical moments. However, the curt dismissal of one of the Muses is combined with a steady onslaught on the other eight. The new Education Bill seems calculated to turn out succeeding generations of computer programmers, hairdressers and estate agents. The insistence on privatisation means that the arts are no longer to be regarded as the birthright of those born in this country, as essential to the preservation of a civilised community as an army or the police, but as another sort of luxury for which we should be grateful to the *noblesse oblige* of Barclays Bank or Marks & Spencer. Of course, governments down the ages have shown themselves more or less indifferent to the arts, but this is a government which is in fashion and one whose attitudes are adopted by a number of writers and journalists who should know better. They, perhaps, and our practically minded masters, are presiding over the collapse of our culture.

What was that culture when it was at home? It certainly had its roots in Latin and Greek, although the defence of Latin has been made more difficult by the extraordinary failure of generations of schoolmasters to teach it imaginatively or with any degree of success. For ninety per cent of public schoolboys to emerge from years of Latin lessons with no real ability to read the language is evidence only of the dogged inefficiency of their form masters. However, the faded photographs of the Parthenon on the sixth form wall, the chipped Hermes in the art room and some half-understood but deeply recognisable lines of Catullus still tied us to the Mediterranean source of our civilisation. Now, when even the most expensive private schools don't undertake Greek O-levels and classics departments are threatened, the thread is almost cut.

Our other cultural basis is Christianity. The devout, the agnostic, even the atheist, are the products of a Christian culture. The Christian tradition not only provides the moral framework for Shakespeare's plays and Dickens's novels, the agnostic George Eliot was as conscious as anyone of Christian ethics. But now the moral attitudes which produced our greatest literature are under attack. The Bishops are regarded as impractical "do-gooders" (as though it were better, from time to time, for a Bishop to "do bad"). Anger at the cruelties and injustices produced by unrestrained money grubbing, the basis of Dickens's best writing, is now considered no more than the whingeing of a wet. So both the classics and Christianity are undermined, greatly assisting our cultural collapse.

But what did we have knocking about in our minds half a century ago

THE NEW EDUCATION BILL SEEMS CALCULATED TO TURN OUT SUCCEEDING GENERATIONS OF COMPUTER PROGRAMMERS, HAIRDRESSERS AND ESTATE AGENTS.

that was so valuable anyway? I speak, I have to admit, from a position of privilege and as the child of a professional family, but first of all I had quantities of the *Oxford Book Of English Verse* and Shakespeare by heart. The decline, rather the full stop, in learning poetry is something that, with the best will in the world, can't be blamed on the present government. Why, or exactly when, it ceased I have no idea. One of the few great advantages of being a child is that it is an easy time to slip verses into your mind, to the infinite

"Bad news, Cromwell – you're being replaced by a machine!"

chase

solace of your future years. I suppose school teachers now are also of the sad generation that has no poetry by heart. It is difficult to know what to do in a National Health waiting-room if you can't recite "Earth hath not anything to show more fair" to yourself, accompanied, perhaps, by Milton on the late massacre in Piedmont.

Avenge O Lord they slaughtered Saints,
whose bones,
Lie scattered on the Alpine mountains
cold…

You could, I suppose, read the torn copy of the *Sunday Express* magazine or play with the Lego, but it's not the same. Children are now set to writing poetry, at which they are not usually very good, indulging in large Whitman-like generalisations instead of accurate descriptions, and not put to learning it, at which they are superb. Their reading also seems to be restricted to Philip Larkin and Seamus Heaney, admirable writers but no substitute for the great romantics. In this way, Wordsworth and Tennyson seem about to fall off our cultural precipice; Browning, Shelley and Byron having

long since slid into the sea of the respected and the unread.

What is also sad is the books that have been chosen in schools in place of the great masterpieces, for they are, on the whole, a joyless collection. School teachers seem to take a grim delight in

ANGER AT THE CRUELTIES AND INJUSTICES PRODUCED BY UNRESTRAINED MONEY GRUBBING, THE BASIS OF DICKENS'S BEST WRITING, IS NOW CONSIDERED NO MORE THAN THE WHINGEING OF A WET.

George Orwell, an author who misinformed us about the future, and *Lord Of The Flies*, a work which takes a glum view of human nature. The novels of D. H. Lawrence are considered somehow more relevant to our daily lives than the novels of Dickens. We are no longer encouraged to travel to past glories to discover our culture, perhaps because to do so is too much like history and history, as we all know, is something that we are now not able to afford.

I have, in all this, had good words to say for the Church and its political attitude; but the literary influence of modern Christianity has been an unqualified disaster and contributed much to our cultural collapse. I must ask you, distasteful as it must be to many, to glance at the Good News Bible in what is called "Today's English" version. There you may read, "The Lord is my Shepherd if I have everything I need, He lets me rest in fields of green grass and leads me to quiet pools of fresh water. He gives me new strength…" This is no more or less understandable than, "The Lord is my Shepherd; I shall not want. He maketh me to lie down in green pastures; he leadeth me beside the still waters. He restoreth my soul." It is just worse, uglier, clumsier and far less memorable.

Whoever said that the great advantage of the Bible is that it was translated by a panel of Elizabethan Bishops spoke the truth if not the whole truth. Widely read and no doubt understood, it became the basis for the language of oratory and Parliament and the law courts echoed

to its magnificent rhythms. There is a story of an Irish barrister who saw his opponent end his speech to the jury in tears. He began his reply by saying, "Never, since Moses smote the rock in the desert, has water been seen to flow from such an improbable source as the eyes of my learned friend." Such a speech could only come from someone brought up on the sonorities of the Authorised Version. The translation into so-called "Today's English" seems only to have influenced the colourless utterances to tax counsel and junior ministers for Trade and Industry.

Of course, the idea of a collective culture may, in itself, be outdated. Our culture is something we each have to grow for ourselves, and the sonnets of Shakespeare, Don Juan and the Sherlock Holmes stories are still available at the best garden centres. This is, however, a cold and windy season when the lifelines of our past need holding on to. May the time come when an undergraduate confesses that he is majoring in computer technology and a Prime Minister replies, "What an extraordinarily flippant thing to do!"

H A N D E L S M A N ' S HARD · CASE · HISTORY

BLOOD AND IRON The true account of a militaristic herring's namesake

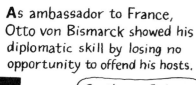

THE YELLOW PERIL

MR BOTTOMLEY'S LITTLE RACKET

He's Minister for Roads and Traffic, so it's down to him.
It's supposed to speed the roar of London's traffic.
It's a necessary sanction – had to be done, by Jove.
It's also a pain in the neck and an infringement of liberties.
MICHAEL BYWATER gets to grips with THE CLAMP

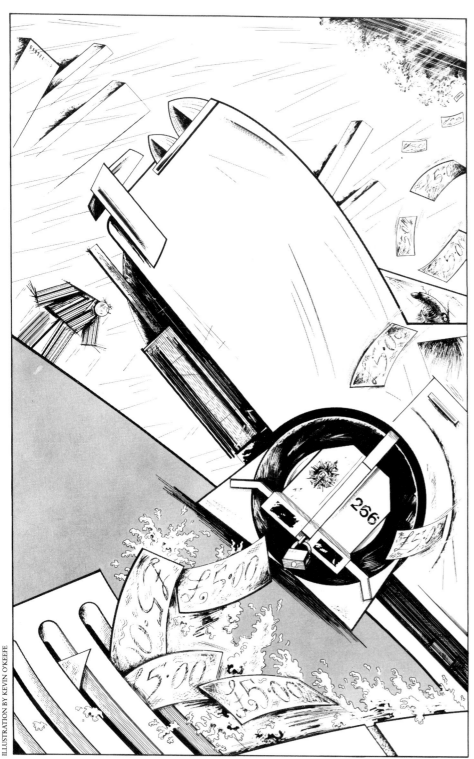

"This £25: what exactly is it?"

The man behind the counter was trying to be courteous, but it was an effort. Too many late nights, too many angry people, too much stewed tea and too many ill-written, sullen little notices tacked to the wall with yellowing Sellotape had defeated him; he was damp and grey and tired; perhaps he realised to what his life had come. He looked at me dully.

"A payment, sir. It's a payment."

"What for, precisely?"

"A payment for the van."

"The van?"

"The van. To release you, sir."

Further along the cheap, shabby counter, two women were complaining. "Do you think it's clever," said one, "or sensible, to force two women to hang around the West End in the middle of the night? We've already been propositioned twice."

The tensely-cheerful Asian girl dealing with them tried to make a little joke, but nobody laughed.

"So it's not a fine. It's a payment for something I do not require and did not ask for."

"It's not a fine, no, sir. The fine is on the ticket."

"Why do I have to pay it?"

"Because you have committed an offence."

"An alleged offence."

"Alleged, yes."

"Therefore I am entitled to dispute it."

"Yes."

"Yet having committed this alleged offence, you sequester my property and force me, without any form of legal process, to pay £25, not by way of a fine, but as a payment to have my property returned to me."

The man did not say he was only doing his job. Perhaps he didn't think he *was* doing his job. Do young men become coppers to stand in a dank and inhospitable subterranean oubliette below Hyde Park, writing out receipts? What do they feel when they watch police dramas on the television?

If he had said he was only doing his job, I would have punched him. Then I would have leapt over the counter, ravished the Asian girl, beaten the fat man to death, stolen the money and, rushing out of the little wicket gate, torched the petrol station at the bottom of the ramp and watched joyfully as Hyde Park bellied out and belched itself forth in yellow flame, and stench, and clamps, and anoraks, and mud.

But he did not say he was only doing his job. He walked away.

"Pathetic," said the Belgian next to me, "but predictable. Your country has no pride any more, and so will permit these offences against liberty. You dare not complain or resist because you are ashamed of yourselves."

If I were a politician I would like best to be one in England. The Belgian was right. We will tolerate anything, and the bossy inadequates and the petty commissionaires who seek preferment in politics must find great joy in our acquiescence. What fun to govern this rain-

It's still the same old story, a fight for love & glory, a case of do or die...

"Course, he hasn't got a clue what he's singing about..."

soaked, nipped, pinched, blue-nosed, chip-stuffed, docile cinema-queue of a nation! And how much nicer than having to deal with Americans, who demand democracy and accept corruption as the price; or the Italians, who, if a law is manifestly spiteful, or petty, or absurd, ignore it conscientiously or rise up baying for the blood of its perpetrators, and presently, armed with little knives, obtain it in profusion!

The wheel clamp was introduced in London

a little over a year ago, without anything which could, even charitably, be called a "democratic process" (charity being a necessity when considering many of the processes of this Government in terms of their adherence to democratic principles). Everyone involved tried to deny their involvement, and even Mr Nicholas Ridley, the then Minister of Transport, tried to worm out of responsibility. It was being introduced on a temporary experimental basis, he

announced, and who was to say for certain that Mr Nicholas Ridley's nose grew as he spoke? He personally detested the idea, he muttered, but something had to be *done*, by Jove, by Jove; and having said his say, sat down, and was returned to store again until required.

Commander Neil Dickens, of Territorial Operations' Crime and Traffic Branch, New Scotland Yard, said: "There will be many benefits for drivers in central London through the Metropolitan Police substantially increasing the enforcement of parking regulations. A reduction of illegal parking would improve traffic flow, enabling faster journey times and an increased availability of parking meters," and who is to say that nobody believed him? Who, too, can say for certain that Mr Peter Bottomley, Her Majesty's Minister of State for Roads and Traffic, was merely drivelling sycophantically when, last June, he told the British Road Federation that clamping was speeding the flow of traffic and saving motorists £18 million in petrol a year? These are important men, although there may be some cynical enough to believe that the *authentic* rationale behind the scheme is best heard in the tones of WPC Laraine Burnett: "It's quite funny how everyone disappears when we arrive in the street and they hear those casters rattling along."

Well, now. Let's look at some figures, before we get all over-excited. First of all, this "charge" – about as justifiable as the crooks on Petticoat Lane, who steal your umbrella at one end to resell it to you at the other – of £25. We have to understand that this is not a fine. The fine is the £12 on the parking-ticket which you also have to pay. The £25 is a charge payable to the people who have clamped you, so that they will unclamp you again. And the reason they clamped you was so that you would pay the £25 charge so that they would unclamp you again. Clear? There is no pretence that it is anything else than what I would suspect is probably

EVERYONE INVOLVED TRIED TO DENY THEIR INVOLVEMENT.

extortion with menaces, a rather seedy protection racket.

First of all, where does this money go? "Off-street parking" is, of course, the wholly satisfactory answer of Mr Peter Bottomley's Department (while denying that it was really Mr Peter Bottomley's pigeon, although Mr Peter Bottomley is Minister, after all, of Roads and Traffic, and speaks at length about Roads and Traffic, and is reported at length as doing so; possibly his Department knows something which we do not know, but until they tell us that Mr Peter Bottomley isn't *really* Roads and Traffic Minister, we ought to go on, for the sake of good form, assuming that he is). Is this the same off-street parking as was going to be provided with the money from parking meters, and, indeed, the same off-street parking as was going to be provided from the fraudulent sale of non-existent residents' parking spaces by the London boroughs? (A separate matter, of course, but surely a man who sells eight fish

IT'S QUITE FUNNY HOW EVERYONE DISAPPEARS WHEN WE ARRIVE IN THE STREET.

when he owns only five fish is trading fraudulently; unless, of course, he is trading in the City, when he is a commodity broker.) We will be investigating the firm plans for all these off-street parking places next week, but, for the moment, let us see how much money Mr Peter Bottomley and his friends will have to spend.

Last year, around 100,000 cars were clamped. Each car generated £25 in blackmail money, a total of £2.5 million. The private firms who do the clamping – Mr Barry Hancock's Vehicle Parking Protection Services, and Highway Maintenance Services – will not tell us what sort of fee they get per car, but it can hardly be economical for Mr Barry Hancock and his competitors to do it for less than £13 a go; after all, that is what you would pay for, say, fifteen minutes with one of the lower class of London prostitutes, and they do not have the overheads of Mr Barry Hancock or his competitors.

So that leaves £12 a car, a revenue of £1.2 million for the "authorities". But the "authorities" have to pay for the grey, tired man, and the tensely cheerful Asian girl, and the fat man, and their colleagues, and the policemen who ride in the vans, and we had better allow £325,000 for their salaries and £150,000 a year establishment

"I'm sorry but Mr Goddard can't be disturbed just now. He's due considering prior to arriving at following conclusions."

costs, which leaves us a gross revenue of £725,000. A man in London has just paid £20,000 for a parking space, suggesting that even allowing for bulk discount, Mr Peter Bottomley's Department would be unable to purchase more than forty spaces with the revenue from their protection racket; hardly worth the trouble, one would have thought (though it may simply be that Mr Peter Bottomley's

Department will not be *taking* the trouble, a not-unlikely course of events, given our experience of earlier off-street parking initiatives).

Perhaps, in order to work out for ourselves the true value of Mr Peter Bottomley's protection racket, we should consider the other costs involved. Let us say that the average motorist in London is earning £16,000 a year. Let us forget what he may be doing in London (or trying to

"Don't play the innocent with me – I've read your horoscope!"

do, despite the efforts of Mr Peter Bottomley to thwart him, Mr Peter Bottomley being one of those people, one instinctively feels, who would be happier if we were all at home, and preferably in bed, where we could do no harm and cause no nuisance to interfere with the proper business of the country, which is, of course, government and the making of rules) and simply value his time.

Allowing that our average motorist works forty hours a week for his money, and has four weeks' holiday a year, his time works out at £8.30 an hour. Let us also suppose that it takes around five hours for him to deal with the unclamping of his car. The cost in total of the 100,000 average men, over a year, in their lost time alone, is thus £4,165,000. But, of course, they are not alone. Let us be generous, and

THE PROTECTION MONEY PAYABLE TO MR PETER BOTTOMLEY'S FRIENDS IS AROUND 25 PER CENT OF THE AVERAGE AFTER-TAX WEEKLY WAGE.

assume that only half of these people are keeping someone else waiting, and we may increase the value of wasted time to £6,250,000 a year. And let us not forget the establishment costs incurred by every employee, and let us average these out at £3,000 a year, and we can come to a grand (or, rather, reasonably modestly-assumed) total of around £7.5 million a year wasted by Mr Peter Bottomley and his fellow-supporters of the clamp in London alone.

Finally, let's just notice, as we pass by, that the protection money payable to Mr Peter Bottomley's friends is around 25 per cent of the average after-tax weekly wage; or, to put it another way, were all the victims Members of Parliament, a proportional sum would be £166.50; or, to put it yet another way, were all the victims to be of similar financial standing to Mr Peter Bottomley MP and his wife, Mrs Peter Bottomley MP, who, between them, must enjoy an income of not less than £70,000, a proportional sum would be £282.50. But, of course, one must not doubt that neither Mr Peter Bottomley nor Mrs Peter Bottomley would balk at all at paying £282.50 for an alleged parking-offence, because the law must be obeyed, and the traffic eased, and the off-street parking paid for; nor must we doubt that any of the worthy Members of the House of Commons would fail to support such a level of extortion, always presuming the matter were to be brought before the House of Commons, which, it seems, is unlikely.

So there we are. Mr Peter Bottomley, as Minister of Roads and Traffic, is giving continued and indeed enthusiastic support to a strange sort of protection racket, whereby money is demanded for the relief of a deliberate inconvenience; which nets the price of forty parking spaces a year, yet costs the economy a minimum of £7.5 million a year. Is Mr Peter Bottomley entirely happy with this state of affairs? Perhaps so. Is everyone? Perhaps not.

If Only We'd

Keep this handy pull-out guide for next time wintry weather strikes

During a hurricane or sudden flash flood, close doors and windows securely and unplug TV sets fitted with an external or "outdoor" aerial. Any exposed drains, outlets or sockets should be rinsed in mild detergent, then isolated with Fuller's Earth. Secure loose-fitting inspection chambers with epoxy resin and clout nails or a quick-curing waterproof paste.

Household pets should be clearly marked and fitted with a flotation collar. Senior citizens are best removed to a place of safety or positioned beside a reflective triangle. Keep a record of the serial numbers of other valuable property, such as log-effect fires, digital barometers, or portable cam-corders, and lightly grease any exposed parts with a mineral-based silicone preservative such as *Cascomite* or smear with an acrylic bath-stain remover. In hard water areas, open all vents.

Water cascading through a ceiling, or a tree trunk poking through a cornice, may be tell-tale indications of roof trouble caused by wind. Often birds or certain types of bat are present in upstairs rooms.

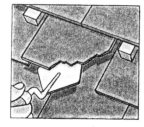

Had More Warning

Where a brick chimney stack has penetrated the structure, draughts can occur. If you suspect that more than two-thirds of your home (based on the floor area as at 1 January 1948) may have collapsed altogether, the Salvation Army runs a number of useful schemes. It is advisable to book.

Make a visual check for any unexpected occurrences. If an unusual tree is found in a bedroom or loft space, note what type it is. In cases where you are in doubt, a local radio station can often be of assistance with advice from a "phone-in". Their numbers are listed in *Yellow Pages*, under "Radio Stations, Local". It is important to remember to dial "01" when calling London numbers from outside the London area. Alternatively you may seek clarification from the emergency services or from your local arboretum. At busy times, such as can often occur during a hurricane, you may have to make several attempts to get through, but it pays to be patient. As a precaution, you should cover exposed or damaged branches with PVC sheeting. Fallen trees should not be fed, "pollarded" or mulched without professional advice.

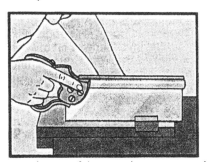

It is quite normal for a few cracks to appear as a house "settles" during a hurricane, but keep an eye on brickwork fissures more than a few inches wide and note the location of any missing gable ends. A useful tip is to keep a tarpaulin handy in a bedside cupboard and to have sheets of hardboad to hand, pre-cut and trimmed to your window sizes. Be sure to ensure there is adequate ventilation when boarding up missing patio doors and watch out for condensation problems when sandbagging loose-fitting doors.

Hurricanes can occur at night as well as during the daylight hours, so it pays to keep a torch at the ready, fitted with the correct size and type of battery. Do not neglect to check the bulb for satisfactory operation. In the event of an electrical failure, caused by damage to the "national grid", a torch can be a boon when using a ripper to re-seat loose shingles or raking foliage from cladding, downspouts, air bricks, damaged flashing, etc etc.

Where a smell or stain occurs, dampness may be present as a result of penetration by rain. Make a visual check to ensure that roofs, walls, windows and the like are securely in position, then note the presence of any mould, efflorescence or pest infestation. Green or greenish-brown streaking on a wall may indicate the passage of a tree or large shrub. If there are skid marks or greasy patches present, ensure that no motor vehicles have been dislodged and got trapped in guttering.

Silverfish are sometimes a nuisance around crevices or basins, where they feed during the hours of darkness. They should be sprayed with a proprietary solution such as *Kybosh*. Care must be taken not to allow seepage on to any nearby acrylics or certain types of laminated cedar cladding. In constricted places, it may be preferable to bait a trap with a small piece of military chocolate or processed cheese.

Don't tackle a job like removing telegraph poles from a loft unless you are experienced in D-I-Y repair work. Unless you have a "head for heights" even a straightforward job like demolishing a storm-damaged garage or using a chainsaw to fell and log a stricken oak can cause headaches. Do not hesitate to seek professional advice where large sections of your home, for example an outhouse or utility room, have been blown over and do be extra wary of "cowboys" who may knock at your door and offer to put your roof back with materials "left over from the last job".

Where a chimney stack or section of roof has been dislodged into a downstairs living area, it may prove tricky to remove without special lifting equipment. A temporary solution can be to turn it into a decorative feature, perhaps enhancing its appearance with mirror tiles or one of the many coloured grouts now on the market. Ask friends or local builders' merchants for their advice.

Before removing trees from a living area, take a moment to consider whether they, too, might not make an unusual decorative feature. Most deciduous woods can be treated with a wax sealant requiring only an occasional wipe over with a lint-free cloth or length of mercerised scrim to keep them in tip-top condition. You may be able to use lights to create an accent. Many softwoods, such as pine, larch, fir or spruce, can be treated with a preservative gel or marine varnish to produce a Scandinavian effect.

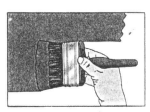

Where a lavatory has been damaged by falling masonry or exposed to hurricane wind pressure, it should be thoroughly wiped with a moisture-absorbing detergent paste. Seal up any cracks with a heavy-duty lavatory sealant and remove any seepage with a sharp edge. Avoid using harsh abrasive cleaners on brightwork. Wipe over with lemon juice or coat them with an acrylic stiffener. Do not use a chisel on rigid laminate surrounds.

Remember, it pays to be prepared, especially where hurricanes are concerned or in a flood situation. Next week, we'll be looking at how to lag a tortoise with mineral wool and rod out damaged flaunching round a blocked swan-neck.

SAINSBURY'S EXTENSION

Important New Purchases for the National Gallery

REMBRANDT: "Reclining Nude with Brie"

RAPHAEL:
"Madonna with Meatballs"

A picture of international importance distinguished by its typically Raphaelesque rounded forms and harmonious artificial colouring. The painting is both an inspired foretelling of the coming of Christ and a submerged allegory of the religious significance of mince. According to Ruskin, "the theme is salvation and the painting is uncharacteristically emotional, with the Madonna's gestures and expression evoking feelings of at once panic and then serenity at finding there is something after all in the larder to give to her hungry, unexpected guest." The painting forms part of a series including "Madonna with Carrier Bag", "Madonna with Iceberg Lettuce", and "Madonna with Dishcloth (Buy Two, Get a Duster Free)".

RENOIR:
"A Tin of Something"

Renoir excelled in rendering the play of unnatural light on vast arrays of tins. This masterpiece of luminosity is remarkable, not only for its boldly naturalistic representation of the tin, but also the brilliant expression of the full glory of the tin. There has been much academic speculation as to what the tin might contain or, rather, what the artist intended us to think it contains. It is generally agreed however that, whatever it is, it should be eaten before the end of the month.

CONSTABLE:
"Landscape with Distant View of Special Offer Petfood"

The most charming of all his great paintings of foodstuffs. Constable himself refers to the painting in one of his letters. "I have painted a large upright can of petfood. Perhaps my best." Eight out of ten aesthetes, who expressed an opinion, recommend it.

RUBENS:
"Adoration of the Frozen Cauliflower Florets"

The whole painting is a subtle baroque expression of a classical frieze. The unflinching realism is Flemish, the packaging unmistakably British, and the florets themselves singing with texture and vitality. Bernard Berenson remarked "You come away wanting to boil them." Rubens excelled at defrosting and thawing instructions. The guarantee is particularly poignant in most experts' eyes.

REMBRANDT:
"Portrait of Some Cheese"

Rembrandt's series of markdown cheeses is unparalleled in the history of painting. Here, Rembrandt uses his sense of form and appreciation of the effects of light to create portraits of cheeses that are profoundly moving. His understanding of rennet, upon which most of his mature work's power relies, is best seen in the formal opposition of the warm, transparent Gorgonzola with the white inertness of ... the Wensleydale. Erich Gombrich described Rembrandt's Brie as "pensive" and his Sage Derby as "smouldering and broody". Eschewing idealism Rembrandt brings a sensuality to his cheeses. All are painted with a concentration that puts us on intimate terms with the cheeses itself. Each one has an individual character. Rembrandt's series of price flags was not so successful.

VAN GOGH:
"The Check-Out"

In an image that appears deceptively simple, Van Gogh reconciles the opposing elements of individual form and the ideal, of outer appearance and inner character. His poetic nature vividly expresses itself in the conception of wistful, meditative maidenhood of the cashier with the iridescent cheek blush, bitten fingernails and love-bites. Note too the unspoken sympathy between the bag-packer and the old lady, who has carelessly left behind some biscuits. Many critics see this painting as a hymn to quick-moving queues. Van Gogh is known to have spent a considerable part of his life queuing for things and it was this queuing experience that gave him his unique vision of humanity. Van Gogh here compels us to recognise the tragic dreariness of the lives of the check-out ladies and his compassion for the outcasts doomed to waste their lives telling strangers where the baby beetroots are. It is a painting of great emotional intensity.

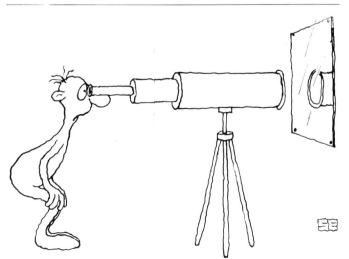

KEVIN PILLEY

PARIS WITH THE SPROG

RUSSELL DAVIES
*proves that youth
is the next best thing
to spring*

I was introduced to France at the wrong age. The wrong age is fourteen. We were a school party – most of us hadn't been abroad before – and we were spending our first *nuit blanche* rumbling down to Provence on a train, illumined only by the weird blue nightlight overhead. Beside me on the sticky carriage seat was a French girl of later teen-age, dressed in the voluminous starched petticoats of those jivey days. Other stuff too, of course, but mainly those petticoats, and a harsh metallic perfume I can still call to nose.

It was after about two hundred miles of sickly blue half-sleep that the seductive hand of this rustling presence stole up and started caressing my cheek. Fourteen-year-olds nowadays can deal with this. In 1960, one was torn between feeling like Buddy Holly or Jennings 'n' Darbyshire. Oh boy. Oh *fishhooks*. The dilemma was solved, with a few sharp words, by our vigilant French master on the opposite seat. When dawn broke over my would-be masseuse, she was in the arms of that sailor in the corner. My *éducation sentimentale* either started or finished there, I can't be sure which.

So it seemed a good time to take my son Steffan to Paris, before any predatory Lolitas take an interest in him. Well, he is nine. At that age you have your priorities pretty well worked out. They go: 1. Eiffel Tower 2: Anything else. This happens to be a rather newsy choice. 1989 is to be Eiffel Year, the centenary of the Tower's completion, so 1988 is the centenary of the thing's being built. The papers are full of it: the restaurants of the Tower, its openness every day of the year (the only Paris monument to make this boast); its reconstruction (two new concrete feet); and sundry pictures of it half-constructed – or half fallen down, as the imagination tends to interpret things. No comfort when you're quivering your way to the top in a frozen glass-cornered lift full of nervous hollering Germans and stray members of the Tokyo Ballet. At the top it began to snow, not for the first time in this Paris spring weekend. Steff put on a Stan Laurel face and I took a photo, while beneath us two-and-a-half million rivets shrank and groaned.

The Métro was of endless interest. "It really *does* run on rubber tyres!" exclaimed my heir, as though catching his habitually mendacious dad out in a moment of accidental veracity. Franklin D. Roosevelt he thought the most ridiculous name for a station he'd ever heard. I tried to think of countering English examples, but my mind kept coming up with Hatch End, which isn't ridiculous at all. Is it? But the surprise hit was the Beaubourg or Pompidoleum.

The look of the place was not appreciated ("It looks like a milk processing plant"), but the trip up its outside in the transparent glass tubes went down well, as did, for a wonder, the new Picasso exhibition on the fifth floor. They were letting in the under-thirteens for nothing, and mine was impressed to the extent of wishing that the whole of Picasso's career had been represented in the show, not just the last twenty years.

There is one superb canvas showing a seemingly headless dog and a fine old black oak

FRANKLIN D. ROOSEVELT HE THOUGHT THE MOST RIDICULOUS NAME FOR A STATION HE'D EVER HEARD.

bureau with barley-sugar columns, evidently a prized piece from the old boy's ménage at Vauvenargues. I fancied that. But all I took away from the Beaubourg was an odd postcard. Outside in the square, where the usual clowns still clown, even in a freezing gale, they now have this huge electronic gantry that stands there counting off the seconds. Seconds to what? To the year 2000, closer inspection revealed. An inserted 10F piece brought forth a postcard stating that at that moment there were 373,791,935 seconds to go. By dint of very long division, *cher lecteur*, you can work out what day it was. No, I don't blame you.

Keeping to a nine-year-old's bedtimes has good points and bad. On the one hand you are preserved from getting knocked up, so to speak,

"Don't step on the floor or you'll be eaten by crocodiles!"

"Never mind what's wrong with 'im – just read the meter and go."

IT'S THE SURREAL THING

For dispirited ornamental ducks, cast-iron steaks, sepulchral but romantic gloom, or théâtre de la fenêtre, you can't beat Paris in the spring, provided you're guided by **GEORGE MELLY**

at midnight by a young lady in a fur stole, blonde wig and fishnet stockings, asking if you want any *compagnie*, which happened a couple of trips ago (you see, they're out to get me). On the other hand, you miss the delights of the jazz clubs, and late eating, and late everything; and you are stuck with French TV, where the French national self-parody is at its most intense. I was compelled to watch Christine Ockrent, the interviewer so frantically desired by British intellectuals, practising her art on old Giscard d'Estaing, who looks more and more like a horse expiring nobly on a battlefield. Having written his memoirs, Giscard was being regaled with nostalgic film-clips of his days of *pouvoir*. He got all big-eyed and misty about his chum Helmut Schmidt, who'd confided that his dad was Jewish; about Brezhnev, who'd dropped a line to say he was dying; and much other sob-stuff. Giscard was turning his life into a soap-opera update before our eyes. "Pardon," he said, as Christine nearly interrupted him. "Pardon," said she, with precisely the equivalent tone and weight. It wasn't at all like Sir Robin Day.

Next morning, the sprog insisted on the Louvre. Maybe paintings are contagious. The Louvre too is in the news. It has suddenly been viciously rubbished by its custodians. "Never has a palace been more ill-suited for a museum," they snarl in their leaflet. "Long and confusing," they spit, is the access from one part to another. You'd never have caught them admitting this a few years back, but now they are in the business of justifying the Grand Louvre – the underground Louvre-within-a-Louvre project that will nearly double the exhibition space available. Light will enter the subterranean premises

through the famous glass pyramid, the last of whose 666 (wise number?) "perfectly transparent" glass panes were being inserted even as we watched. The French are calling it "the most expensive roof in the world", but of course it's a window as well as a roof. At 75 million francs, it ought to be. Steff's hope was that the new development would include a "Weedy Paintings Annexe – Big Mistakes of the Eighteenth Century" and the like, just to encourage him. I explained that the French don't operate like that. We get "élite" from them.

I will admit to the odd disappointment. After a vast and wonderful meal at the Terminus Nord, featuring a flying waiter who centrifugally hurled a glass ashtray at our table, showering us with powdered crystal and apologies, it seemed appropriate to follow the digestive process down to the Paris sewers – *les Égouts* – which can be toured by brown boat. But the entire Tokyo Ballet had got there first and there was a fifty-yard queue for the thrill of witnessing the guano of the metropolis. The alternative, Notre Dame, with its promised display of True Portions of Holy Knicknacks on Good Friday, was ill-received. "Fraudulent!" cried the *jeune monsieur*, though it should be said he is the most militant atheist of his age I have ever encountered. He will surely grow up to be a bishop.

The thing is this. It wasn't quite Paris in the spring. Not yet. Actually it was Paris in the thermal underwear. But it was Paris on the cheap (three nights for the price of two), and Paris through new eyes. In fact it was like taking the spring to Paris. Father and son bought berets. We look very silly. We enjoy it.

"Seen from above," writes Louis Aragon in his marvellous anti-novel, *Paris Peasant* (1926, translated by Simon Watson Taylor 1971), "the Parc des Buttes-Chaumont is shaped like a nightcap," and, appropriately, viewed from its main entrance, the park itself is extraordinarily dream-like.

Cradled by steep knolls, surrounded by the usual furniture of a nineteenth-century suburban pleasure ground (lawns, clumps of trees, benches, the occasional ornamental lamp-post, gravel paths) is an almost square lake, neither small nor particularly large, the colour of dirty dishwater and bearing a flotilla or two of rather dispirited ornamental ducks.

So far, I agree, there would be no particular inducement to visit the *Quartier de Combat*, but rearing up from this lake is a very high and

PARIS REMAINS THE CITY WHERE THE SURREALIST PHANTOM STILL STALKS THE STREETS.

dramatically steep artificial island and, perched on the top of this, a neo-classical rotunda. This rock is joined to the shore by bridges, from one of which many nineteenth-century suicides hurled themselves into oblivion.

By the Twenties Aragon had already noted the erection of an inadequate grille to dissuade others from such a course, and in the interim this has been heightened and reinforced. From the flat top of the promontory one gazes down on the Paris of the unfashionable outer boulevards. Only the tower blocks have altered the general appearance of a cyclorama revered by those young surrealists of over sixty years ago. The Parc des Buttes-Chaumont, like the Lion de Belfort and the Tour St Jacques, was one of their sacred spots.

A weakness, no, a *passion* for surrealism had lead me to undertake this obscure pilgrimage. Paris remains the city where the surrealist phantom still stalks the streets. It's always useful to have a special interest in a town as it suggests a

IT'S NO WONDER YOUNG FRENCH COUPLES GO FOR BIG MACS.

series of visits outside the run of the obligatory "sights". In New Orleans, for example, there is jazz. And, I suppose, even in Crewe or Swindon, a nostalgia for steam railways must help to give a point to these otherwise somewhat featureless places.

I was in Paris for no particular reason, except that my friend Alex and I had long promised ourselves a visit and I had suddenly four clear days off. I don't know the city well, I've only been there perhaps six times in my whole life, but, despite the escalating growth of McDonald's and other fast food chains, it has changed comparatively little. It's hideously expensive, of course: after just two croissants and small cups of coffee at a café table, five pounds' worth of francs have vanished. But even so, it is a city where you can just walk about and, of course, that is free. What I don't understand, though, is why it costs quite so much to get there. If your visit doesn't enclose a weekend, or you don't use a cross-Channel ferry – if, in fact, you just take a plane on a whim from Heathrow, the return fare is almost the same as going to New York. This tends to inhibit extravagance and in consequence we ate in obscure back-street brasseries in St Germain or

"I ask myself, is the world ready for your particular brand of zany, madcap tomfoolery, Mr Snelgrove?"

Montparnasse.

These always look so promising: the dark interiors, the paper tablecloths, the "serious" waiters; but, although bad luck may have entered into it, they were without exception disgusting. Were Paris restaurants always like this? I seem to remember not, but perhaps my youthful romanticism and post-war lack of any standard of comparison transformed the congealed cassoulets, the lukewarm, fatty lamb and cast-iron steaks, the sour wine and cold coffee into gastronomic treats. It's no wonder the young French couples go for "Big Macs".

Another long-promised expedition was a suitably dank morning spent at the Père Lachaise cemetery, whose map, listing the locations of the more illustrious residents, proudly informs the visitor that its 44 hectares enclose 100,000 *sépultures* and, since the opening of its

nécropole, the ashes of 100,000 *inhumations*. A very statistical view of the work of the Great Reaper. The names of those thought worthy of note read like a game of Consequences: Daumier and Jim Morrison, Proust and Mezz Mezzrow. Great rivals, too: David and Géricault, Ingres and Delacroix. It must be quite a diverse, not to mention an argumentative, party there on Walpurgis night.

We couldn't visit all the stars of Père Lachaise, but we did persevere in finding some of them. Jim Morrison's has become a Sixties shrine, covered in graffiti that extends over the monuments which surround it – obscure nineteenth-century Duponts and Durands who would certainly have resented their monuments being spray-gunned in Day-Glo colours. Epstein's Wilde memorial has lost its testicles, more likely the work of respectable Philistines than ageing

hippies. Max Ernst, whom as part of my surrealist pantheon, I naturally honoured, turned out to be commemorated only by a small brass plaque set into the wall of the columbarium to mark his ashes. It was a fascinating, but exhausting expedition. By the end I was so knackered I felt it was hardly worth going home.

We made many more conventional visits of course, amongst them the beautiful new Picasso museum, which had a special exhibition clustered around the great *Demoiselles d'Avignon* of 1907 with its attendant sketches and related works. At the Beaubourg, too, there was a huge show of the same master's late and underrated work. We were conducted round it by David Sylvester, one of the *commissaires* whom Alex had spotted in the street. That was typical too. He lives in London, less than a quarter of a mile from me, but we never bump into each other there.

It was an enchanting visit and our nights were enlivened by a truly surreal spectacle. Across the courtyard at the back of our hotel was a solitary, unshuttered window. At about eleven o'clock this lit up and a handsome young man threw open the casement. He wore a short dressing-gown, which he later removed, and carried a document in one hand from which he read obsessively. With the other hand he intermittently engaged in self-arousal. Sometimes he would leave the room for several minutes. Sometimes he would sit in a wicker armchair. Sometimes he would advance on the window and stare transfixed into the dark courtyard. Once a woman crossed the interior, but there was no further evidence of her existence. He reached no climax and the effect was ritualistic rather than obscene or provocative. The surrealists would indeed have been fascinated by this strange *acte gratuit*. It should be noted, also, André Breton himself stayed in our hotel as a young man.

SEE YOU IN COURT

Punch Law Report No 2:
The Phantom Smoker of Lewisham

My first contact with the legal profession was when I was sixteen. I was working as a stock-room assistant in the Blackfriars warehouse of Messrs Spiers and Ponds. The wage was thirteen shillings a week, which is why I always carried a begging-bowl. It was also the right amount to encourage thieving. I desperately needed money. You see, I wanted to be another Louis Armstrong, which was difficult; firstly I was the wrong colour and secondly I didn't have a trumpet, I had a hockey stick.

I could always have blacked up and said I was Louis Armstrong playing hockey but no, I had to get a trumpet. To raise the money I resorted to thieving. I started to smuggle out cigarettes, tobacco and cigars and sell them. I did it with such skill I was caught red-handed. I would need a solicitor; I found one named David Ginsberg – he had a practice in Lewisham and practice makes perfect.

"You will need an alibi and money," he advised. I was hauled up before a local magistrate, who had a face like the late Tommy Cooper's pulled inside out.

"Do you swear to tell the truth and nothing but the truth?"

"Yes," I lied.

The solicitor for the prosecution read out the indictment as though I was Adolf Eichmann. He explained how I had emptied cigarette packets of half their contents then resealed them. Consequently, customers were suing Spiers and Ponds for short measure, in fact three law suits were in progress and I was therefore getting "Spirs and Ponts" a bad name. Bad name – he couldn't even *pronounce* it! The evidence was damning. I wanted to plead guilty but no, David Ginsberg said, "We plead not guilty."

> **MY BARRISTER DIDN'T KNOW WHAT THE BEAK MEANT. HE MEANT, "YOU BLOODY LIAR". A CHARACTER WITNESS WAS CALLED (WHAT A CHARACTER). "YOU ARE THE BOY'S FATHER?" "YES." AT LAST I KNEW.**

We? He started an impassioned plea with great histrionic gestures. (I didn't know till later he was a member of the local theatrical group.) I came from a poor background. I was a sickly child and now a sickly thief; when my father served the crown in India, I had contracted malaria and tonsilitis, and only my courage had pulled me through. I was breast-fed but my mother was a heavy smoker and so at the breast I got the craving for nicotine, a habit that increased over the years, so much so that this poor innocent victim of a noxious habit was given to searching gutters for dog-ends. Here the magistrate interrupted.

"Are you saying he smoked all the tobacco he stole?"

"The lot, sir."

The magistrate gave him a long meaningful stare which David Ginsberg didn't seem to know the meaning of. Sure as hell it meant, "You bloody liar." David Ginsberg then called a character witness (what a character).

"You are the boy's father?"

"Yes." At last I knew. The perjury continued. "Mr Milligan, did you know of your son's addiction?"

"Yes, sometimes he would sit up all night smoking."

David Ginsberg (now John Gielgud as Hamlet) turned and faced the magistrate and slowly repeated: "Sat up all night smoking." He turned

"None of you knows each other, I trust."

to my father, who was now coughing.

"Is not that very cough contracted through your son's smoking?"

Through the cough my father said, "Yes." There was another "You bloody liar" stare from the magistrate. As Gary Cooper in *Mr Deeds Goes To Town*, David Ginsberg gave the court a wide confident smile, revealing twenty years of appalling dentistry. My father, still coughing, said, "He tried to give it up." Facing the magistrate Ginsberg (as Spencer Tracy) said, "He tried to give it up. He did it by trying to play the trumpet like Louis Armstrong." The magistrate frowned and asked, "How does trying to play the trumpet like Lewis Hamstrong stop his smoking?"

"You have to stop smoking to play the trumpet!" declared Ginsberg, as though he was addressing the bowmen before Crêcy.

"You don't have to shout, Mr Grinsberg, I'm not deaf," snapped the magistrate. David Ginsberg made a gesture, like Charles Laughton in *The Hunchback of Notre Dame*.

"I'm sorry sir, it's just that I don't want an injustice to be done to my client. He is a good lad, a devout and practising Roman Catholic."

I didn't even know where the church was (Ginsberg had gone to great lengths before the trial to discover that the magistrate was in fact a practising Roman Catholic; he knew where the church was).

"That concludes the case for the defence," said David Ginsberg in an exhausted state (Ronald Colman after his tortuous journey to Shangri-La). The magistrate recessed.

I asked David Ginsberg what he thought. "We're in with a chance, kid," he said (James Cagney in *Frisco Lil*). A chance of losing or winning, he didn't say. He beamed with confidence. The magistrate came back and fined me "A hundred pounds and costs".

"What did I tell you," beamed Ginsberg.

"You didn't tell me anything," I said.

"I've got you off with a fine – you could have done six months." *Yes*, I could have done; it would have been cheaper. To pay the fine I sold

"Hugh can't relax away from his desk."

boxes of Havana cigars. I sold the rest to buy a Besson trumpet. To make matters worse, I took up smoking.

Drunken driving was my next legal case. I drove over a stop sign.

"You went over a stop sign," said a young constable in a voice desperate for promotion.

"I had to," I said. "It was right in front of me."

"I'm sorry, I'm going to have to charge you."

"Okay," I said. "It's a fair cop."

"I am not a fair cop, I am a brunette with tinges of grey at the temple." He made me blow up the bag.

"Shall I pop it now?" I asked.

"You're over the limit," he said.

"Am I, I wondered why I felt so good." My solicitor was Jeremy Abse.

"I must ask you some questions. First, whatever did you get drunk for?"

"About seven pounds fifty pee."

"Be serious. We've got to find an excuse. Have you family problems, financial trouble, are you under stress, are you taking any tranquillisers, is your job getting you down, are you overworking?"

I thought a while then said yes to all of them. That cheered him up no end.

"At last we've got something to go on." I had something to go on but it was back home. "Now," he said and paused but still kept on charging; "What do you take these tranquillisers for?"

"Manic depressions."

"Were you in a manic depression when you were stopped?"

"Worse, I was in a Mini Minor."

At the trial I pleaded guilty. Abse went for "mitigating circumstances". His client was on a psychiatric drug that caused a dry mouth. Unable to find water he had gone to a pub to alleviate the condition and had a "few drinks". The magistrate smiled, it nearly killed him. "A *few*," he said. "He was eight times over the limit."

I took the stand and told my story. As I was approaching a road junction, a policeman hiding behind a bush leapt out with a bucket of whitewash and a brush, and painted a white line and the word "stop" in front of me. He then said, "I arrest you for the five hundred unsolved murders on Scotland Yard's books."

Laughter in court. I was fined a hundred pounds and banned for a year. Abse asked for the money in cash.

"I can't draw faces anyway."

DR ROBERT BUCKMAN

HAPPINESS IS A WARM GUM

*It has come to my attention
that certain areas of health and hygiene
have failed to come to my attention. And therefore yours.
My critics have specifically mentioned
teeth, gums and periodontal matters as subjects
that I have consistently overlooked, particularly before going
to bed, which is VERY BAD.
Herewith the remedy*

THE ANATOMY OF THE MOUTH

Most people have a very hazy idea of what goes on in their mouths. Most people also have a very hazy idea of what comes out of their mouths which is, of course, why nature gave us lawyers.

It so happens that the mouth cavity has six distinct boundaries. The upper boundary is the palate (the hard palate and the soft palate –

most mouths come fully equipped with one of each). The side walls are the cheek muscles or buccinators; inferiorly there is the tongue and some purplish bobbly stuff underneath. The posterior boundary is composed of the pharynx tonsils and the way down south to the oesophagus; and the anterior boundary comprises the lips, moustache, outside world and (if things are going well) somebody else's mouth.

Within the mouth are the teeth. For part of

the time anyway. But the most important structures in the whole mouth are actually the *gums*. These are exceptionally important and have many vital functions. Mostly they are there to stop the jaw fraying at the edges; to seal the gaps round the teeth (or holes where teeth were once); to allow valuable defence-mechanisms such as gurning to have evolved; and, in most cases, to bleed early in the morning just in case you woke up feeling cheerful.

In some respects the gums form a seal round the tooth in the way that a tubeless tyre seals to the wheel-rim, but in most respects they don't. In fact, gums aren't a bit like tyres because actually they are not meant to be sealed to your teeth at all. They are actually meant to be *loose*, like a sort of buccal mud-flap, which is why so many disgusting things can grow underneath them – for the specific purpose of making your dental hygienist feel superior.

Precisely what grows underneath, follows below.

TARTAR

Tartar is actually a fascinating chemical compound. The basic components are: old, rotting, calcified food, slime and dead bacteria (sounds unappetising, but Stilton has the same ingredients when you think about it, which you never should).

Anyway, unlike Stilton, tartar becomes caught in the gaps between the teeth and gets coated with more calcium, which makes it the oral equivalent of stalactites.

The origin of the name "tartar" is interesting.

54

HOW TO STOP PLAQUE

Whatever you do, don't think that cleaning your teeth will help. Nothing could be further from the truth. What you actually have to do is to clean underneath your gums, just like hoovering under the rug in the front-room, only infinitely more repugnant and painful.

The following advice was given to me by my own dentist, who is a true professional and has all the authority and bearing of his vocation, including wire-rimmed glasses, a Viennese accent, a safety-deposit box full of diamonds and a knife up his sleeve.

What you have to do is to floss under your upper gums until you hit bone and under your lower gums till you've sawn half-way through your tongue. You then take a rubber spike mounted on a thin handle and shove it upwards between your teeth into your brain. If the pain suddenly stops and you feel happy, you have reached the frontal lobe and need go no further.

You should then wipe the buccal surfaces of your teeth with a mixture of charcoal and sal ammoniac, gargle with four boiled razor-blades and finally maintain the occlusive surfaces of your incisors by biting off your own kneecaps.

This may not cure your dental decay, but will certainly take your mind off it.

THE DOCTOR ANSWERS YOUR QUESTIONS

Q: *My dental hygienist recommended a book about a woman who discovers the liberating effect of good dental care while on a boating holiday in Yorkshire. Do you know what the book was called?*

A: *Perhaps she meant "Floss on the Mill".*

It was introduced into the European language by the original Tartar hordes invading from Mongolia and bringing with them the twin pestilences of halitosis and gum disease. Sweeping all before them in a whirlwind of bad breath and fetid caries, they spread rapidly west towards Earl's Court, looking for Australian dentists. It was not until the eleventh century that their forces were vanquished by the Nordic monarch, King Listerene the Good, and his English wife, Floss.

Nowadays, of course, the hordes are gone, but their legacy lives on in our mouths as part of Europe's rich oral culture.

Tartar is actually a normal component of the mouth and can be seen very clearly in many animal species, even the elephant, e.g. the stuff that builds up between the piano keys no matter how often you do the dusting. In the natural state, few animals are actually harmed by tartar, and nor would human beings suffer from it, provided they lived "a natural life" (i.e. being eaten by a mammoth at the age of 38). Our ancestors died with their teeth in, and so can we if we play our cards right.

However, tartar is not the whole problem, there is also…

PLAQUE

Plaque is exactly the same as tartar, but more up-market. Plaque is what tartar is when it's stuck *underneath* your gums. It can occur in several forms, including a virulent form that nearly wiped out Europe in the thirteenth century ("bubonic plaque"). There is also a form that destroys cereal crops ("plaque of locusts") but that can be prevented by flossing with DDT.

The major problem with plaque is that it allows certain bacteria to multiply in your mouth. These include *Streptococcus viridans*

and some other anaerobic bacteria which are mostly non-pathogenic commensals, sapprophytes, parasites, hairdressers and actors resting between engagements.

One fairly common coloniser of the plaque microenvironment is *Antinobacillus actinomycetemcomitans* (known as "Tiny" to his friends). This bacterium multiplies – by dividing – and the waste products that it produces (and then wastes) irritates the gums causing *gingivitis*, so called because "gummitis" sounded so silly when dentists said it.

Here is what you should do about both of them.

OFFICIAL ANNOUNCEMENT

Week Beginning December 3

LAST POSTING DATES FOR CHRISTMAS

ISSUED BY THE POST OFFICE
IN THE INTERESTS OF THE POST OFFICE

DECEMBER 3
Brunei: Cellos; ornamental bones; potted pulses (excluding haricots).
Denmark (Central): Humorous logs; gherkins (unmarinated); wolf bait; harmonica parts.
Poland: Herbal remedies (screw-top); quoits; home tattoo outfits.
Tunisia: Giblets; ventriloquial dummies (male only).
Uzbekhistan: Fancy mice (unstuffed); airguns; whey (tinned); fire-station signboards not exceeding 2 (two) metres; bay rum.

DECEMBER 4
Andorra: Small spanners; prosthetic bowelling (by reel); horse coffins; advocaat (except miniatures).
British Columbia: Spat cleaner; garden path kits; storm cones (if cased); rouge.
Cambodia: Leatherette *Radio Times* covers; morse keys; arris rails (*not* including wedges over 9cm); lobster forks.
Germany (East): Grapefruit segments; tyres (except radial); teats; model goats.
Kashmir: Artificial joints: scaffolding; mayonnaise (ersatz only).
Liberia: Humorous condoms; Tipp-Ex; toy razors.
Spain: Warehouse coats (without motto); vintage tricycle mudguards (rear); chocolate snails.
Tibet: Surfboards.

DECEMBER 5
Australia: Rabbits' sundries; souvenir guttering; cockle essence.
Germany (West): Formal underwear; gum (bottled); portable surgeries (less than 12m x 12m when folded); clarinet polish.

Japan: Elm derivatives; erotic floor-tiling; moth-whistles (chrome); chimney substitutes; cakes not containing anchovy or leek.
New Zealand (South Island only): Drum music; telephone directories (hardback); gearboxes for religious purposes; jelly.
Tunisia: Ventriloquial dummies (female).

DECEMBER 7
BAOR: Occasional tables; molluscs originating outside the EEC; non-ferrous caravan chocks; Air-wick.
Libya: All brown items; boxed crackers containing scalpels or wing-collars (but *not* both); lids.
Portugal: Personal contra-flow systems; tinned waspmeat; staircarpet (figured only); potatoes that look a bit like celebrities.
Rumania: Industrial scarving; chapatis; clockwork fleas.
Tunisia: Miniature dinner-jackets.

DECEMBER 8
Belgium: Seasonal gaffer tape; blo-football figures (excluding goalkeepers); reptile deodorant.
Dubai: Non-ferrous pendulums; marriage-brokers' tables (inlaid); balloon labels; children's doors.
Kenya: Gimlets.
North Utsire: Pond furniture; biplane struts; chandeliers (under 30kg to include chain and main bolt); boiled poultry; cornet valves; rope.
South Utsire: Check local press for details.

DECEMBER 9
Papua New Guinea: Depilatory soup; firework cabinets; decoy gnus.

LIES, DAMN LIES, AND MRS DAVIES'S WHOPPERS

HUNTER DAVIES reveals the Old Trout to be not only economical with the truth but generous with the fiction

I have something awful to say about my dear wife, the Old Trout as was and is and ever shall be, Mrs Davies, married woman of this parish. You will be most surprised by her, probably even morely by me. But I can tell you what her reaction will be, even before I begin. She'll just laugh.

Let me illustrate, if you will, by giving a small example of her vice. It's Saturday today and, as is our wont, we go our separate ways, la tra. I have my jumbling in the morning, hunting out books and stamps and assorted rubbish, then I go footballing in the afternoon, watching other forms of assorted rubbish, don't ask me how they're doing. The OT goes off on her little culture trail, National Theatre again today, what a poseuse.

She was home first, and when I came back I had my bath, listened to *Sports Report* and did a few letters, then I bounced down to our sitting-room, not to be confused with our living-room. This is the posher version, where we light the old log fire of a Saturday evening. At least the OT does. Women's work, I always think. Humping wood, that's also for the stronger sex. I save my energy for getting out of bed.

"I'm not eating," she said.

She was looking rather smug I thought.

"Or drinking."

And rather defiant. I hate those sort of looks. So I huffed and puffed and moaned and groaned. You are rotten, I said, you know I look forward to sitting in front of the fire, chez nous, me and vous, having our little snackeroo and chateroo together, going over our day's excitements. It's what Saturdays are all about, innit.

"I don't know why you have this thing about togetherness," she said, picking up the novel she was reading, *The Swimming-Pool Library*. "Anyway, it would do you good, to have an evening without food."

No chance, I said, but you've spoiled it for me now. I'll have to make something for myself, and you know I hate that, I'm fed up, my treat's been ruined, I'll have to eat on my own, you're really mean, you are.

"I think Flora has left some tuna fish," she said, "so you can have that."

Oh yeh, really great, thanks a lot, big deal. I banged out of the room, noisily, and crashed down the stairs, noisily, why should teenagers have all the fun, think they're the only ones who can make dramatic exits. I might have heard the OT sniggering in the distance. Or it was prob-

ably her stupid book. That's another thing. Get her nose in a novel, and that's it, I might as well talk to the wall. Hello wall, what the hell am I going to do with some leftover tuna fish.

I was making myself a sandwich, not easy, as

I'VE KNOWN IT FOR 27 YEARS, THROUGHOUT OUR LONG AND FUN-FILLED MARRIAGE, YET I KEEP ON GETTING CAUGHT.

some bugger had put the butter away and it was all hard, but at least the tuna fish had been neatly left, with tin foil over it, as it should be, see house regulations number one.

"What's that horrible smell," said a voice over my shoulder. It was Flora. Gerrout, I said, one in

the kitchen at a time making snacks, you know that, house rule number two.

"Ugh, I hate that awful smell," she said.

Gerrout, I said again, then stopped, my little brain turning over, as it prepared to take in two topics at once. Like President Ford, I find it awfully hard to chew gum and make a sandwich.

"Haven't you had tuna fish?" I said.

"Of course not," she said. "It was Mum."

I ran up those stairs, threw open that door, and confronted that criminal.

YOU ARE A LIAR.

I felt better after I'd shouted, except that all she did was turn over a page, laugh, and carry on reading, and except that I'd noticed an empty glass of white wine beside her couch. The sly sod. Drinking *and* eating behind my back.

I went down to finish making my snack, opening a fresh bottle of our best Fleurie, one I'd hidden, that'll teach her, and oh God Flora, I thought I told you to keep out till I've finished, that's my butter, bloody hell, everybody in this house is annoying me tonight.

What a silly, petty pointless lie. Why does she do it? She must have known I'd find out. So why bother? But of course there rarely is any sense to it. She just happens to be a LIAR. There, I've said it again. I've known it for 27 years, throughout our long and fun-filled marriage, yet I keep on getting caught, expecting normal, everyday honesty.

I went up with my monster sarnies, ate them slowly and noisily in front of her, slurping my

"Your hearing-aid, you twisted, miserable old ratbag."

"Too bad, gentlemen – I happen to be wearing my Swiss Army suit!"

drink, gazing into the fire, waiting for her to protest, or finish her novel. One an evening, when she's on form.

Why do you do it? I said.

She put down her book and started enumerating.

(1) FUN. It makes life more amusing.

(2) MISCHIEF. I enjoy starting off stories.

(3) INTEREST. It's so boring, always telling the truth.

Is there not sometimes GUILT as well, I suggested. Was that not why you lied to me this evening, to hide the fact that you had sneakily eaten before me, huh?

No, that was a combination of all three, she said. I enjoyed realising you would find out. Anyway, I couldn't be bothered explaining.

All her lies are equally potty. She denied last week that she had hidden my new cap, the one she hates, while I went mad, emptying every drawer, then going out in the rain to my car. She then produced it from the shoe-box beside the boiler, where I'd already looked, maintaining she'd found it for me. What a liar.

She caught Flora last week on one of her classic gambits.

"Someone's been telling me about seeing you and this boy in the street and you were both…" She then goes on to give quite a convincing description, finishing by saying oh no, I'm not going to tell you who told me. Flora then tries to find out who's been spying on her, and in so doing she confirms various details. All of which the OT has made up. There was no nosy neighbour. It's been a total fabrication.

I've seen her tell real whoppers in company, when some friend says did you cook this, or make that, or paint the other, and she'll not just say yes, quietly, modestly, but give a blow-by-blow description of exactly how to do it, with tips, things that can go wrong. If they later find

out the truth, she doesn't care. People who ask silly questions deserve silly answers.

But she does have her own rules, in her long life as a polished liar. She never lies if it's really important. And she never lies if it concerns (1) HEALTH, because that is tempting fate and (2) OPINIONS.

When it comes to the latter, I often wish she would. She is known for the strength and directness of her opinions, ask anyone, totally truthful, totally without any pretence. In fact her honesty is often blistering. Folks have been known to quail. It's part of her very high standards, such as being unbribable, unflatterable, morally without reproach. She would never, for example, review a book by someone she knows. Yet she will go in for these potty, petty lies.

It does have its uses. There comes a time, friends, when a little creative imagination comes in handy, when it is useful to shift the emphasis, when it can pay to be economical with the truth. Quick, I say to the OT, you answer it, you tell them, you reply. I'm such a rotten liar. She has a gift for it, so I try to let her take over, when it's some long-lost bore ringing from Euston and wanting to see us, or an invitation to do something really dreary, or someone for Flora and she's told us she's definitely out.

I get caught all the time, start and get it wrong, go back and walk into it. I did have a good one once.

"Oh I'm terribly sorry, we'd love to, what a shame, but, er, you see, we've just had a baby." Not very logical, but it seemed to satisfy people. I used it till quite recently, even though it's fifteen years since we had a baby. That's why I got caught out.

I tend to tell the truth. Boring, I know. I haven't got your imagination, dear. Pity the Fleurie is finished. I've had to finish up the Augustus Barnett cheapo plonk.

TROUBLE

Covered in reeking oil and red powder, BRIGID KEENAN spots a tiger, sort of, and revolts the shade of Sir Henry Newbolt

It's more gushing than blubbing this time because we've been travelling in Rajasthan and that means almost anything I say is bound to sound like a brochure issued by the Indian Tourist Office. We went there to celebrate an Indian festival called "Holi" which is, in fact, most un-holy and something to do with fertility – best not to enquire too deeply, I think. Everyone chucks coloured powder or liquid over everyone else, getting more and more over-excited in the process – so much so that the police publish warnings in the paper about not indulging in Holi activities that are illegal (such as throwing rocks at people's heads or turning their cars over), and foreigners prefer to stay at home that day.

Last year we sat primly on our verandah listening to the wild cries and shrieks outside;

I SWEAR I SAW SOMETHING STRIPED IN THE UNDERGROWTH.

this year we, and two other families, decided not to be such wimps, but to book into a hotel in Rajasthan (where they celebrate Holi with particular enthusiasm) and join in. We chose a hotel which was once a raja's palace – the ex-raja is now behind the front desk – and we all bought special white pyjamas to wear so that our clothes wouldn't be ruined.

I expect this sounds more than usually silly, but we had terrific fun in the hotel throwing red powder all over each other and the raja. Then we went down to the town to see what was happening. Just as we arrived on the scene a great swaying, drunken, Saturnalian crowd of about 2,000 men, all covered with red powder, was dancing down the street in our direction. You can't imagine – well, you probably can, actually – the enthusiasm with which they greeted the sight of our little band of innocent foreigners clad in white pyjamas. We had to beat an extremely hasty and undignified retreat back to the hotel. Sir Henry Newbolt would have been ashamed of us.

Perhaps the most amazing thing about the raja's palace-hotel was that it had a human clock. Honestly, there was a little old man who lived in a tiny room next to a gong hanging from a tripod, and on the hour, every hour (except in the middle of the night), he came out

WITH THE OLD TIKKA

and bashed the gong the appropriate number of times. We thought he must be equipped with the very latest in Japanese electronic alarm clocks, because he was never a second out.

After that we moved on to a game reserve. I must say it is a touch disconcerting to visit a game park with a good cook because they want to roast everything you see. We had a very English lady staying with us who is one, and when the children bounced up and down in the jeep saying, "Look, Mummy, wild peacocks,"

IT'S TIME TO START TAKING ANTI-MALARIA TABLETS AGAIN.

her very English voice boomed out, "They're extremely good to eat, you know, my grandmother *always* had roast peacock at Christmas."

"Look, look, dear little quails," cried the children. "*Delicious*," boomed the English voice, "just ten minutes in a hot oven."

I made a total idiot of myself announcing that I'd seen a tiger when I hadn't – well, the others all said I hadn't, but I swear I saw something striped in the undergrowth. Then I asked a passing game warden if there were any bears in the jungle and he replied that I could probably pick one up later. Pick up a bear? What on earth did he mean? Perhaps there was a little orphaned cub being looked after somewhere. Ages later when no one showed up with a cub or even spoke to us again, it dawned on us that he thought I had asked for beer. It's rather mortifying to think that forever and ever that warden will be convinced there was an alcoholic Englishwoman desperately scouring the jungle for a lager.

Dusk fell, and we drove out of the reserve passing jeeps full of people coming into it all chatting and flashing torches into the bushes. How we mocked and scoffed at the idea that they could possibly think they'd see a tiger in the beam of a torch, but at breakfast next morning, guess who had the *undisputed* tiger story to tell?

The Sahib and the rest of the party peeled off and went back to Delhi, but the very English lady and I went on to Jaipur where our guide in the museum told us about a maharaja who had measured eight foot "in diameter" (when people start describing your measurements in diameter, you definitely have a figure problem). He also kept referring to Family Planning as Feminine Planning – a revealing slip, for women certainly bear the brunt of that kind of planning in India, though recently there have been some advertisements for condoms in the papers which are described as "specially made

for the Government of India". So that's what all those Congress party MPs are up to.

Our guide took us to a Kali temple – Kali is the goddess of death and violence and all sorts of frightening things, and it is essential to keep in her good books, which is why the temple was packed with people giving the priests sweets and flowers and money, and getting a red *tikka* mark put on their foreheads in exchange. By coincidence, the very English lady and I are both Catholics, and when the priest asked us if we'd like a *tikka* mark put on us, we recoiled in horror at the very idea. However, when we got to the exit we were both struck by the same thought: if by any chance Kali existed, we had now offended her, which was not very sensible considering we were about to embark on a four-hour car journey along a very dangerous road.

We dashed back to the priest to have the *tikka* marks put on, but at the exit once again we screeched to a halt in our tracks: "Thou shalt

not worship false gods" is the third Commandment, and what is having a Kali *tikka* mark put on your head to save yourself from a fatal car accident, if not worshipping false gods. And it was Sunday. We hastily scrubbed the marks off our foreheads, dismally aware that we had now offended all possible gods. Sir Henry Newbolt would have been disgusted.

It reminded me of an acquaintance who was sort of kidnapped by a Sikh taxi-driver in Delhi last year. He'd wanted to go to the Museum of Modern Art, but it was closed when they got there, and the taxi-driver absolutely insisted on taking him to a Sikh temple instead. First he was shown dozens of horrifying paintings of Sikhs being martyred in different ways (a bit like Madame Tussaud's Chamber of Horrors, but worse) and then he was ushered into the temple itself. Next thing, with a turban shoved on his head and an iron bangle put on his arm, he was placed in a queue waiting for Sikh communion, which apparently looks a bit like porridge. He is also a Catholic and he said he felt terribly guilty because he was not worried about worshipping false gods so much as whether it would give him a stomach upset.

The very English lady and I went on to stay in yet another crumbling, rambling, princely palace-turned-hotel on the way home. We were the only two guests in the whole place, with five

"Albert, you must stop trying to think the unthinkable."

"All right! Who's been talking to the plants again?"

suitcases standing in their hallway. These belong to what we call "travellers" – the 18 to 25-year-olds who come and back-pack around India and have been given your name by someone they met in a pub who came across someone else who knew a person who worked with your brother-in-law four years ago. They leave their heavy stuff with you while they go off to

WE WERE THE ONLY TWO GUESTS IN THE WHOLE PLACE, WITH FIVE COURTYARDS TO OURSELVES.

explore with all their worldly goods stuffed in a rucksack. It's when they send postcards from Goa saying, "Hi! Looking forward to being with you on 27th," that you begin worrying: the suitcase is just the thin end of the wedge, and they are planning to move in with it.

It's time to start taking anti-malaria tablets again. I hate them, they make you feel dizzy and apparently they cause loss of memory. Sahib says he doesn't know why I worry as in my case there is nothing to lose. Also my hair is falling out in handfuls. I don't know if this is the advent of the hot weather or baldness, but I've now started oiling my head at night like Indian women do. The trouble is that Amla oil (which is supposed to be the best) has an awful smell and I can put it on only when the Sahib is away as he says he refuses to share his bed with a fried poppadum.

Sahib has a thing about the telephone – well,

courtyards to ourselves. It was a bit creepy and I was relieved to see a pair of crossed lances on the wall of our bedroom. We could wrench them off and defend our honour if push came to shove (and Sir Henry Newbolt would have been proud of us at last), but it didn't.

The very English lady endeared herself to us by arriving to stay laden with English bacon and ham and Wall's sausages. What a treat. When the Sahib was posted to Nepal ages ago, he asked me to bring out some bacon and sausages as he hadn't tasted either for nearly a year. When I got there we handed the precious packets over to the cook and said we'd like them for breakfast next morning, with eggs. The following morning we were woken by the ominous smell of curry – Sahib leapt out of bed and dashed to the kitchen, but it was too late – the cook had chopped up the bacon and sausages and curried them with the eggs. It was the first of only two occasions that I've seen tears in the Sahib's eyes.

Most of my friends in Delhi seem to be suffering from paranoia. I don't know if it's because ex-pat wives, having no roots, are extra-vulnerable, but this paranoia is brought on very simply, when someone enquires, "Will I see you at the Haywards tonight?" and the answer is, no, they won't. Then you spend hours working out why the Haywards didn't invite you, and end up wanting to shoot yourself. It's pathetic.

At least we *were* invited to the St Patrick's day party at the Irish Embassy, which is one of the

best. I haven't heard the gossip about this year's yet, but the story goes that at last year's party, one or two guests passed out on the lawn, whereupon the Embassy staff lifted up the buffet tables, complete with their long white cloths, and tactfully placed them over the prone bodies. Everything was all right until the bodies woke up and found themselves surrounded by white drapes and couldn't think where they were, except perhaps in heaven.

Apart from paranoia, ex-pats in Delhi also suffer from other people's luggage. Nearly everyone has a couple of dusty, battered old

"He plays dead all day. Don't know why we bother to keep him."

"Next year I think I'll put in some crocuses."

we *all* have a thing about our telephone in Delhi – but Sahib has a separate thing which is more concerned with how much it costs than whether it works. "I don't mind you telephoning Doomwatch [my mother] so long as you have Something Important to say," he assures me, but nonetheless he still paces up and down, sighing, and looking at his watch all the time I'm on the line. Sometimes he puts his wrist under my nose when I'm in the middle of a sentence and taps the face of his watch. This infuriates me so much that I want to tap his face, preferably with a knuckleduster.

Last time I rang Doomwatch I got into such a state trying to think of Something Important to say, as an excuse for my call, that I dialled some friends called Keegan who are above Keenan in my address book. The Keegans sounded quite surprised, but pleased, to get a call from me. "Where *are* you? Goodness in New Delhi. How nice to hear from you," etc. It was very embarrassing after such warmth to tell them curtly that they were just a wrong number, but I could hear the Sahib groaning out loud and I feared for his health.

Goodness knows what he would have done if he'd been there when I rang him in Delhi from England last summer, when I was home on leave. I got Harry, the cook. "Hullo, Harry," I said, through the crackling and the voice on the crossed line, "this is Madame in England." "Yes, Madame is in England," said Harry. "No, Harry," I said, "this *is* Madame. I am telephoning from England." "Yes, yes," said Harry, "Madame has gone to England." "*Harry, listen to me!*" I shrieked. "*I am Madame. I am in England.*" "Madame will be in England until September," replied Harry. This went on for about half an hour, but in the end Harry twigged on and said, "Oh! You are *my* Madame," so tenderly that I nearly wept.

Actually, Harry nearly gave me heart failure the other day. I was having some people to dinner, so I was a nervous wreck anyway, when Paul, our bearer, surreptitiously handed me a note from Harry. A note from Harry? He was only five yards away, behind the kitchen door, what could be going wrong? I read the note which said, "Dear Madame, Sorry to disterb. Pleese come in kichen quik. Yours faithfully, Harry." I dashed into the kitchen expecting to find it on fire, or Harry lying on the floor breathing his last, or perhaps the dinner lying on the floor instead, or wounds or even severed limbs, but he was standing there quite calmly saying, "Oh Madame, do you want me to bring in the toast with the soup?"

A day or two later it was Paul who gave me a fright. I drove back from the market, swung the car into the driveway, waved cheerily to Paul who was standing by the gate and was just prising myself out from behind the steering-wheel when I heard a quiet little voice asking if it would be too much trouble for me to move the car a few inches. It turned out I had parked *on Paul's foot.* Luckily the wheel had trapped only the toe of his shoe, but it was a nasty moment. It also made me wonder if I shouldn't send Paul on an Assertiveness Course.

"They've told me to stand outside until they feel like behaving themselves."

HORROR SCOPE

MAHOOD celebrates thirty years of Hammer Films

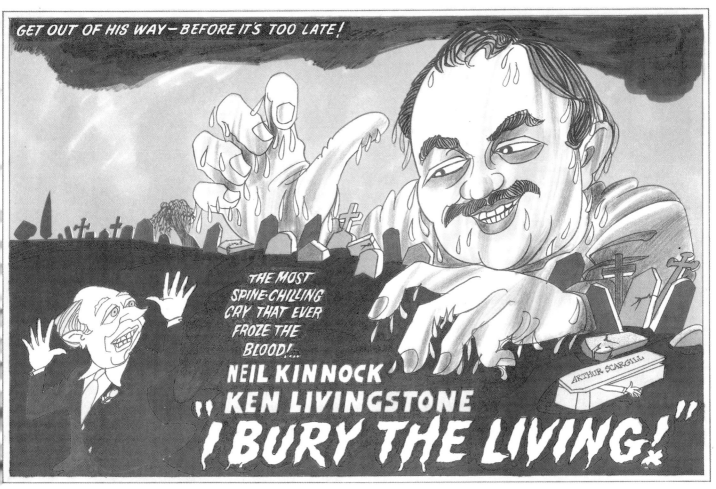

THE COMPLEAT BUNGLER

OR
THE·CONTEMPLATIVE·MAN'S
RECREATION
Being a Discourse of Rivers
Fishponds Fish and Fishing
utterly unworthy the Perusal
of most Anglers

BY·ALAN COREN

**TO THE RIGHT WORSHIPFUL
DR RICHARD GORDON
OF DUNPRACTISIN, IN THE PARISH OF
BROMLEY,
MY MOST HONOURED FRIEND**

Sɪʀ,

I have made so ill use of your former favours, as by them to be encouraged to entreat, that they may be enlarged to the *patronage* and *protection* of this disquisition: and I have a modest confidence that I shall not be denied, because it is a discourse of *fish* and *fishing*, of which you are so great a master.

Further, indeed, so great a teacher: having, in the brief space of a single *East Grinstead* day, so effortlessly inducted me into the mistery as to persuade me to the assurance that I may now set down the substance of all that I have learned, for the *instruction* and *delight* of any human soul wishing to follow the example of,

SIR,
*Your most affectionate friend,
And most humble servant,*

A.C.

CHAPTER I

Conference betwixt an Angler and his Pupil in a Car-Park above the River, the Devices of their Craft having been removed from the Boot

PISCATOR. First, the rod.

PUPIL. I note, Master, that the bag contains three of them: the first frail and titchy, the second more substantial, and the third of some girth with a sturdy lozenge on the end. I take it that the first is for little fish, *exempli gratia*, Tadpole, Scampus, Oyster, and the like; the second for such of their more mature neighbours as Lobster, Pilchard, Kipper, *et cetera*; and the stoutest for the swift despatch of – *quid?* – Rock Salmon, perhaps, or Tuna? Even, perchaunce, the Large Fillet?

PISCATOR. No, Sir, they are but one rod, cunningly fashioned for portability's sake into three sections, which one assembles by firmly pushing each into its senior sibling. Do it thus.

PUPIL. 'Tis done! Egad, how the fellow swishes! See how the topmost bit flies, twenty yards or more, true as a dart, into yonder hatchback! Observe the depth of the gash,

laying bare the rude red undercoat! Have I not done passing well? Why, were that not Signor Volvo but plain Johnny Haddock, that latter worthy would even now be floating belly up, Master, would he not, awaiting nought but the sizzling skillet and mayhap a chip or two to complete our rapture?

PISCATOR. I fear, Sir, you misprise the principle. Were you to have assembled the rod correctly, so as not to have engendered such repairs to coachwork which we may, with God's good grace, yet be fortunate enough to avoid underwriting by this expedient of hopping nimbly into the refugile trees on one wader, I should have been able to demonstrate to you the finesse of the true method by which the trout is lured to his foredestined doom.

PUPIL. Aha! A *trout*, eh? If I divine aright, one sprinkles a trout with almonds until he must perforce sink beneath their weight, upon which one simply flicks his inert corse from the water with the rod!

PISCATOR. Not exactly.

PUPIL. I have seen them with a pea pressed into the eye-socket, but it seems a cruel method for a sportsman.

PISCATOR. Remark, Sir, upon this little tin.

CHAPTER II

The Sportsmen arriving at their riparian Vantage, a lively Discourse ensues upon Bait

PUPIL. I have now noted the tin, Master. It is a receptacle for Old Pompey Shag. Curse me for a wittering fool, woolgathered by pea and almond, I had clear forgot that the commonalty of brother trout is smoked! How do we go about it, Master? Depth-charge him with subterranean bubbles so that he surfaces, coughing, to be smote fin and gill with Colleague Rod? Release a perfumed and alluring cloud above the . . .

PISCATOR. I pray you, Sir, but open the tin.

PUPIL. Great Neptune! Tufts of Old Pompey, cunningly enbarbed – doubtless we waft these, smoking, across the dappled surface, the trout rises, as the phrase is, to the bait, intent upon a swift drag, and Ho!

PISCATOR. These, Sir, are flies.

PUPIL. Flies? And so tame?

PISCATOR. Their names are Marchbrown, Hairy Mary, Gnat, Butcher, Sedge –

PUPIL. Great Heavens, Master, are these not all from *Henry IV Part II*?

PISCATOR. – Yellow Mallard, Peter Ross, Green Chomper, Dunkeld, Welshman's Curse –

PUPIL. Stop! These are not flies, but pets! How may a man so stiffen his heart as to commit these enchristened souls, like ill-favoured Jonah, to the fish's belly?

PISCATOR. You do go on, Sir. These are but tufted feather, wedded to a hook. Follow my actions: take up the reel, secure it thus, thread through the line, so, and affix the fly.

PUPIL. Which?

PISCATOR. Sniff the wind, note the cloud, observe the foliage, recall the month. The little brown bugger, I think.

PUPIL. Farewell, then, Little Brown Bugger!

PISCATOR. That is not necessary. Cast, *so*!

PUPIL. Aha! Forgive me, Master, for a fool! I had not realised that the technique called for no tearful parting taken of our tiny brethren. Not until I cast was it borne in upon me that the fly in fact remains in the tree, cleverly stuck fast by its trusty barb, and it is the reel that flies out across the water! Did I succeed in hitting a fish, Master?

CHAPTER III

The Pupil having waded into the Stream to retrieve his Reel, an earnest Enquiry is put by him upon his Return

PUPIL. I noted, Master, that others of our neighbour confraternity, when I was in midstream, began hurling stones. Some quite substantial. Do we not feel it to be a trifle inconsiderate, not to say dangerous, to continue so keenly to pelt fish when a gentleman brother of the angle – having fallen over and sunk as the result of his waders becoming filled with water upon his bending to grope for his reel – is thrashing about helplessly in the river? Do not, pray, reply that they perhaps did not see me, since lo! the froth of my recent hapless endeavours even now continues to mark the site of my misfortune.

PISCATOR. I was not, Sir, about so to reply. I wonder – now that you have so commendably grasped a deal of what is required of a man wishing to be left to fish alone, miles, perhaps from the irritating distractions of his close acquaintances – whether the time has not come for us to separate ourselves one from another, the better to concentrate upon our sport?

PUPIL. Do you think so, Master?

PISCATOR. Yes.

CHAPTER IV

The Pupil, having been directed to a distant and unattended Stretch of Water and trudged thither, dangles from the long Twig – with which his thoughtful Master has so generously replaced the bothersome rod – the String to which his Master has so deftly attached the grey piece of Wonderloaf which the Pupil has been assured is the favourite Tid-bit of the Rainbow Trout.

PUPIL. The true, nay the sweetest, object of this peculiar exercise being, as I am given to understand it, not merely the sport itself – that transpiring to consist of little more than standing frozen in the drizzle and throwing coloured feathers into the murk on the remote chance of persuading a little bony item to so hook its lip as to afford oneself the pleasure of disengaging it, banging the glum head on a fencepost, and bearing the glaucous remains home in the fond hope of foisting them onto some luckless acquaintance prepared to eat them before they rot – but the random and discursive reflections which haply proceed from the benign solitude in which the activity is pursued, I must now address myself to this latter luxury.

Certainly, this present aqueous tract is more generative of observation than that other; which is beyond question why my Master chose it for me, today's object being my seduction to not only the nub and axle but also the spokes and outer rim of fishing. I see now that it is not a part of the main effluence at all, but a green pond so thickly coated that not only does my bread float upon the water, but that any trout rising to partake of it would be most like to stun itself upon the verdant ceiling of its habitation, thus sparing the novitiate the daunting and unsavoury task of braining it. I should be constrained to do no more than wade out and retrieve it with one of the many pots and pans with which this seminary spot is so thoughtfully girt, thus graduating Brother Trout from his breakfast to mine own in one fell swoop!

I note there is also a fine brass bedstead in it; and, floating beside, a choice of several bespoke mattresses, placed, I should be confident to hazard, so that the novice – as yet untrained to the patience and stamina of the vertically practised – may indulge that horizontal relief which calls across the slime to rheumy knee and aching vertebra.

Yet further: were, perchaunce, the gay Sussex sleet to lose a little of its appeal, the major part of a charming old Transit has been thoughtfully sited at the water's edge to afford snug rustic refuge from the pluvial caprice, so that the angler may sit as free from care as Virgil's Tityrus and his Melibeous did under their broad beech tree.

So, then, let me, as my gently sinking boots secure me ever more reassuringly into God's blessed property, offer thanks unto my other and scarcely less venerated Master. *Ave, Doctor, flos doctorem!* I will not forget the doctrine which Socrates taught scholars, that they should not think to be honoured so much for being philosophers, as to honour philosophy by their virtuous lives. You advised me to the like concerning angling, and I shall endeavour to do so. This is my firm resolution; so when I would beget content, and increase confidence in the power, and wisdom, and providence of Almighty God, let me but place myself thus, as a conduit between the waters which are under the firmament and the waters which are above the firmament, my streaming eyes upon the bobbing lager can which toils not neither does it spin, my throbbing ear a host to God's wondrously fashioned gnat, my nostrils thickening with a salutary *memento mori* of man's brief tenancy, and in my frozen hand the inert symbol of hope's ludicrous vanity, and – thus sited four-square within that microcosm which may stand for all we are and all we may ever expect to be – I may, like every angler, count myself truly blessed!

HOW MANY TIES WOULD A CUP-TIE TIE IF A CUP-TIE COULD TIE TIES?

FRANK KEATING
quivers with expectation

This is the week of the year that us sporting scribblers are allowed – nay, lad, positively encouraged – to flip the trilbies to the back of our heads, take a deep drag on the Capstan Full Strength, lick our pencil stubs, and churn out the most cherished clichés in the canon. It's the Fifth Round of the FA Cup – and the Cup is a great leveller, there's far more pressure on them, we've nowt t'lose, we'll just go out there and give it a go, it's just eleven men and ninety minutes for each side, they'll be all at sea on our sloping mud-heap, and a replay back at their place won't daunt us in the least, lad. It is usually the last allowable chance of any brand-new year when it's perfectly in order to write of minnows and giants, Them versus Us, the People versus the Gentry.

My routine over the years has been to keep a fond eye on the teams I got to know in the first two "proper" rounds in January – the leading clubs only enter the fray in Round Three. (Remember how well my early benediction paid off for Coventry last season?) This year I set off in the New Year with Newcastle United,

the Cup team of my boyhood; and then, for the Fourth Round, I made my presence felt at Port Vale, thus to ensure that the no-hopers from the dingy depths of the Third Division dramatically put one over the strutting strollers of Tottenham Hotspur. It was a defeat that, to all intents, ended his season before it had started for Tottenham's new manager, the former Sgr El Tel Venables of Barcelona. As he drove away from the Potteries that rainswept Saturday night, I bet our Tel wished himself on the last train to San Fernando. Still, he now has nine months grace away from any more spotlights. I wonder if he can cope with *that?*

So if my romantic juices have anything to do with it, it's Newcastle versus Port Vale at Wembley in May. Each should be okay this Saturday. Newcastle are at home to the waspish little bright sparks of Wimbledon, but a Cup-tie Saturday at St James's Park is a daunting prospect for Yuppyish Surrey suburbanites. Likewise Watford: the chill winds that slice round the ridge of Vale Park are made to cut comfy London commuters to the quick. Ask Tottenham: once the Spurs nancied out for the last round in an ensemble strip of powder-blue, I knew they were done for.

One very good reason for Newcastle to go all the way this year is to give their star turn a wider stage for his talents. In the autumn, almost unnoticed nationally, the centre-forward of Brazil, Mirandinha, arrived to play on Tyneside. It was an unlikely teaming. At times the boy of summer was forlorn and lost in the misty swirls of a St James's winter; at others, with a shimmy here, a conjuror's feint there, Mirandinha has been letting the sunshine in – and the Geordies have responded, quaintly taking their Spanish-holiday sombreros and souvenir castanets to the match to display their allegiance, and even rejigging their songs:

We've got Mirandinha,
He's not from Argentina,
He's from Brazil,
And he's effing, effing BRILL!

Newcastle, any day, would rather win the Cup again than the League. It is in their blood. The handsome, schoolgirl-slim Brazilian – who has suddenly brought the best out of such likely lads as Gascoigne, Goddard and Jackson – could this Saturday, for starters, fly the Magpies into the quarter-finals for the first time in a dozen years. Before the current Cup run started, he had already scored eleven goals. Most of them displayed the vivid and vital expressions of the Brazilian tradition: dartingly impulsive, with subtle and sinewy curves, and pouncing voracity – which translates into the English as, "By crickey, mun, the lad's quicksilver pacey with a heck of a shot on him."

His own translations the other way are still none too good. Three afternoons a week a Portuguese teacher from Newcastle University

turns up at his house at Dunston to give the 28-year-old and his wife, Rosana, English lessons. But "a bruise on the shin" is still coming out as "the brush on the chin".

The other morning, sitting in the United dressing-room at St James's, Mira (he's Deena to the other half of the city) was doing a bit of swotting with his English phrasebook before training started. United's doughty trainer and physio, Derek Wright, passed by and muttered, matter of fact, "Mornin', Mira, how are you?" With immaculate and carefully enunciated precision, the Brazilian jumped to his feet and answered by the book: "Thank you very much for asking me. I am very well, thank you. And tell me, how is your good self?" The trainer's eyes narrowed. He looked as if he (not to mention his postillion) might have been struck by lightning. " 'Ey, watch it, lad," he threatened, "are you trying to take the piss?"

THE SCHOOL-GIRL SLIM BRAZILIAN COULD FLY THE MAGPIES INTO THE QUARTER-FINALS FOR THE FIRST TIME IN A DOZEN YEARS.

It was a very different sort of culture shock that Tottenham came across at Port Vale. Here was a Cup-tie made for the legend – when minnows were men, and men had to do what men had to do. I spent a couple of days in the town before the match. The expectancy in the atmosphere could not be much different, I reckoned, from the four-score years or so before when Arnold Bennett's footer giants, like the mighty Callear or the primeval Jos Myatt, were doing their heroic stuff for the Five Towns in the muddy marl, and the slop and slap and seige of the penalty area.

The back windows of Bennett's old terraced house (now a museum) still have good views of Vale Park up on the ridge above Burslem. The two valiants on whom the home side will be relying this week are Phil Sproson (over 400 matches for the club already under his belt, to follow his Uncle Roy's 800: it's a folk hero family, all right); and an even more burly six-footer, Bob Hazell.

Port Vale's tactics against Tottenham were basic. Watford can expect similar. The First Division men, fresh from their stockbroker-belt, mock-Tudor mansions, were ushered off their luxury, well-heated coach – and into a freezing barn, which is the visitors' dressing-room at Vale Park. The home side have a snug, carpeted room; the visitors' a cold, tiled floor, one thin bench, and just one old-fashioned bathtub. And they brew the visitors' half-time pot of tea at least an hour before kick-off!

Watford had better watch out – for Tottenham's powder-blue superduper stars were beaten before the start. Or very soon after. Within five minutes, Phil Sproson turned to Bob Hazell in the penalty area, and the two old soldiers nodded and smiled at each other. "They think they're slumming," said Bob, "and I don't think they fancy it at all."

He was dead right. Tottenham were two down within 25 dramatic minutes, and Port Vale were through in triumph.

FORMERLY THE HOME OF A PRIME MINISTER

O f Mrs Thatcher's many achievements, none is more remarkable than the fact that, possibly apart from Winston Churchill, she is the only prime minister whose birthplace is common knowledge to even the feeblest contender on *Strike it Lucky*. For millions of us, the precise character and dimensions of Alf Roberts's corner grocer's shop, above which the young Margaret was born and spent the first nineteen years of her life, may amount to little more than a vague image dredged up from the sludge of imagination; but buttonhole any man in the street and ask him where our great and glorious leader spent her formative years, and the name of Grantham will spring as readily to his lips as Andrew Lloyd Webber's does to those of the Royal Family.

I am not a man whose head is easily turned or whose judgment is often clouded by famous names, but the instant I heard that this most celebrated and historic of East Midlands landmarks is currently up for sale, I was straight into a taxi and on my way to King's Cross, agents' particulars in one hot hand and reporter's notebook in the other. I like to think I keep my ear as close to the ground as anyone in the estate agency world and this sounded to me a scoop if ever I heard one.

Nearly thirty years have passed since Margaret's father, a leading light in the Methodist Church, Town Councillor and later Mayor of Grantham, sold the business as a going concern for £3,500 (not such a risible figure as you may think: that's four times what he had paid for it forty years earlier). And although business continued for several more years at the old homestead in North Parade, it finally fell into dilapidation until it was rescued in the early Eighties and transformed into the Premier Restaurant.

The new owners spent a year and presumably a great deal of money on "lavish refurbishment", and various aspects of Margaret's childhood were "tastefully incorporated" – notably the Reception Area where the Roberts's shop once stood, and which they reconstituted using the original counter, an old mahogany biscuit dispenser with glass windows, and a certain amount of original shelving. This they stacked with the sort of goods the young Miss Roberts would have handled when helping her parents out – Bartlett Pears, Wopper Processed Peas and Roberts Jams at 8d for a small jar and 1/3d for a large.

For the door into the bar they knocked up a reproduction of the one at No. 10 Downing Street which, in the words of the estate agent's particulars, "reflects the improved fortunes of the grocer's daughter", and they even uncovered and restored the old "ROBERTS" facia board on the outside of the building. And just for good measure, they crowned the front door with a tasteful plaque to remind customers, if they didn't know it already, that they were about to enter hallowed ground.

And yet, despite the obvious tourist potential, the "tastefully refurbished and spacious restaurant area on two levels", and the "well prepared, leisurely meals", the enterprise still flopped. The general opinion is that it was far too expensive for its day and the meals, though leisurely, were not quite as well prepared as they might have been.

In fact, no one I spoke to up there appeared to have much to say for the place at all. Even nice Miss Polak, of the selling agents, Prudential Property Services, seemed curiously anxious to play down the Thatcher connection by claiming that almost everything had been changed since those days and that Mrs. T. wouldn't recognise any of it if she saw it.

But we newshounds are not so easily fobbed off. No estate agent was going to destroy for me the heart-warming image of the young Margaret, curled up by her father's honest knee next to the "Baxi Bermuda" gas-fire in the family's 12' 7" x 9' 11" lounge with its beamed ceiling, fitted shelving, and fitted wall-lights, sipping her Ovaltine and thrilling to the latest adventure of Larry the Lamb and Denis the Dachshund, while out in the 12' 11" kitchen, her mother prepared Margaret's favourite supper of Merry Monk Golden Pineapple Slices and Bean's Finest Imported Sago.

Home for me is where the heart is, and the opportunity to stand in the very kitchen beside the selfsame attractive range of Boulton & Paul Flowline fitted kitchen units, on the very spot where Grantham's most distinguished offspring balanced her first housekeeping book; and to run one's fingers round the same "avocado suite comprising of panneled bath (sic), pedestal wash hand-basin, low level WC, radiator and fluorescent light", amongst which she practised her first tentative, booming vowels, was one which no self-respecting hack could lightly turn down.

I must admit, though, I was slightly shocked to discover that, despite the fact that the place is fully kitted out and ready for action, it has been on the market for eighteen months. Eighteen months! The well-head of modern Conservatism! At a mere £50,000 for the twenty-year lease and £10,000 in rent! If this isn't the property snip of the year, then I'm the Beast of Bolsover.

"Well," said Miss Polak timidly, "Grantham isn't the most lively place in Britain. It would need somebody brave to take this on. It isn't everyone's cup of tea."

Come, come, Miss Polak. Two years ago, you might have had a point. But surely not today. Not now that this modest Lincolnshire market town has been transformed into a mini dormitory for London commuters. Already there is a morning and evening 125 that whisks commuters to and from King's Cross non-stop in 1 hr 5 mins, and when electrification is completed by August 1988, they'll be able to do it in 55 mins.

The moment one steps on to the

THE HOUSE WHERE WE WERE BORN
some noteworthy points

VIEWING: Strictly by appointment with Sole Agents, Prudential Property Services, 37 Silver Street, Lincoln

THE PREMIER RESTAURANT
2-6 NORTH PARADE, GRANTHAM, LINCOLNSHIRE

ACCOMMODATION
RECEPTION AREA: Approximately 12' 6" x 11', originally the 1930s Roberts's grocer's shop with original counter and other memorabilia. As a contrast, the reception area incorporates a tasteful reproduction of the No. 10 Downing Street front door and elevation, leading to the lounge.
LOUNGE/BAR: Approximately 11' 6" x 26' with original fireplace, built-in bar unit incorporating alcove shelving and a wash hand-basin. Original baker's oven retained as an attractive feature.
LARGE TWO-TIER RESTAURANT:
Lower level approximately 23'2" x 15'8"
Upper level approximately 18'6" x 26' with attractive stained-wood divide and staircase, together with matching dumb waiter.
KITCHEN: Approximately 12'11" x 11' maximum with an attractive range of Boulton & Paul Flowline fitted kitchen units, two double wall-lights.
BATHROOM: With avocado suite comprising of panelled bath, pedestal wash hand-basin, low-level WC, radiator and fluorescent light.
OUTSIDE: Small rear yard, beer store, dustbin store.

Grantham train, one's spirits are lifted and one can feel a whole new spring in one's step. The First Class compartments are done up in an enchanting shade of pale lilac; the tables in the restaurant car are immaculately laid with spotless white cloths and little vases of fresh artificial flowers in pretty pastel shades; and just in case one should feel tempted to sit back, sip one's coffee in peace and contemplate the beauty of the passing countryside, there's a healthy contingent of thrusting young executives on hand, with Filofaxes the size of bricks and mobile telephones to remind one that we were brought into this world to work, not sit around on our backsides enjoying ourselves. It's as if Mrs Thatcher herself had been called in by British Rail as a special consultant.

Secretly, I think that swanky young achievers in double-breasted suits, who wish to spend their journeys yakking on to all and sundry (not forgetting each time, of course, to mention that they are on a train, actually) and polluting the atmosphere with loud electronic bleeps, might at least have the decency to follow the example

THE VERY SPOT WHERE GRANTHAM'S MOST DISTINGUISHED OFFSPRING BALANCED HER FIRST HOUSEKEEPING BOOK.

of Mr Heseltine, with whom I once had the privilege of sharing an InterCity table, and do their boring business in the lavatory. If important public figures can direct affairs of state in a crouching position with their trousers round their ankles, whippersnappers like one Mark Vickers, whom I encountered on the outward journey, have no excuse for inflicting their tedious office chit-chat on innocent travellers. However, one doesn't want to appear a Weary Willy, or indeed a Tired Tim. Good luck, Mark. Hope the presentation went well in Leeds, and that you were finally able to get in touch with Crispin. Right on. Yah.

Besides, who could possibly be downhearted when one hears that property prices in Grantham have rocketed in the last year by as much as fifty per cent? Only nine months ago, Mark Newton, director of estate agents Frank Innes and great-grandson recurring of Grantham's second most distinguished offspring, Sir Isaac Newton, was declaring that house prices increased by £1,000 a mile along the A1 to London. A four-bed house that cost £60,000 in Grantham would have cost £100,000 in Peterborough. Since then, the gap has closed dramatically. £110,000 in Peterborough is equivalent to £90,000 in Grantham. Six figures is no longer unusual for a nice house in a village like Barrowby or Manthorpe or Harlaxton or Denton. Building land on the outskirts of the town that eighteen months ago cost £30,000 an acre now fetches four times as much.

In fact, at present, probably only about 300 out of a population of 30,000-odd actually commute on a daily basis, and just as much of

the responsibility for the rocketing house prices rests with the Granthamites themselves, who have suddenly twigged that they too can now join the affluent south in enjoying the fast ripening fruits of home ownership.

Not that that has stopped local voices being raised in protest. Last summer a "Parish versus Pinstripe" controversy dominated the letter pages of the Grantham Journal. "Commuters make no contribution to local life," grumbled parish council chairperson, Barbara Hart. "Outmoded bucolic parochialism," snapped the chairman of the Commuters Association.

Okay, so Grantham is never going to become the centre of the known civilised world, even the most committed Granthamite would admit that. And the young who, a few years ago, voted it the Most Boring Town in Britain on Radio 1's Simon Bates show, could hardly have reason to alter their verdict.

True, it boasts all the big names in modern shopping – Marks, Woolies, Boots, Bejam, Dorothy Perkins, plus several hangar-sized superstores on the outskirts – Do-It-All, DFS, Comet, Texas, Miller Brothers – and a weekly market in the middle of the town; and there must be more pubs per head of population than anywhere else in the East Midlands, not to mention Chinese restaurants. Even so, there's still only one cinema, one disco and one wine bar; theatre-goers must settle for Nottingham, Leicester or Lincoln; the Rob Roy Steak House seems an unlikely contender for the Restaurant of the Year list in the 1989 Good Food Guide; and old Sir Isaac's statue apart, the town's touristic highspot would at present seem to be the Angel Hotel, purely on the strength that both Richard III and Charles I are said to have got their heads down beneath its roof – while they still had them, that is.

All the more reason, therefore, for some

enterprising soul to snap up the Premier, really cash in on the Thatcher name and put Grantham on the tourist map once and for all. It has been known for tourists to traipse out to North Parade and rubber-neck at the commemorative plaque: or at least it was until the estate agents came along and carefully stuck their "FOR SALE" sign right over the top of it. And after all, the place is only a stone's throw from the A1.

THE PROPERTY SNIP OF THE YEAR.

As Miss Polak said, it merely needs the right person to come along. Preferably someone with a few bob in his pocket and a pioneering spirit in his heart. Like that man with the beard who does the ballooning and the condoms. Or better still, Peter de Savary. Now there's an idea. I don't know how tied up he is nowadays with Land's End and Littlecote and what not, but I would have thought that here is the perfect opportunity to create the ultimate theme park: one that perfectly encapsulates the spirit of modern Britain and will be the inspiration for millions of young people as we head towards the millennium. Forget all this messing about in boats, Peter. The East Midlands need you.

All you require is someone to manage the place and show the visitors round and bring it all to life. And who better than the daughter of the house herself? I may be wrong, but I somehow can't see the old thing settling down to a life of golf widowhood and coffee mornings with the neighbours on the estate in Dulwich. Not while there is work to be done and books to be balanced and people to be bossed around. To return to her roots and devote the evening of her days to the conservation of her family home, body and soul, could be the perfect conclusion to a life of perfection.

"I'm the world's first estate agent."

A STROLL IN CENTRAL PARK

CHARLES NEVIN, our Wigan pen, sees St Helens walk it

A satisfying fug, distinguished by the mingled scents of bitter beer and wet raincoats, had built up inside the Bowling Green Hotel, Wigan. In both public and saloon bars, there was an anticipation going beyond the imminent arrival of drinking-up time.

Down the road, in just over an hour, Wigan were to take on nearby St Helens at Rugby League, in the customary Christmas fixture. The Bowling Green is a customary part of the vigorous pre-match warm-up.

Wigan means much to many in this country, from joke Northern town (back-to-back cloth caps, wall-to-wall warm hearts) to all-Orwellian symbol of hardship and indignity. (The two strands are now joined together delightfully in a "heritage centre", Wigan Pier, whose best joke is a "theme"pub called "The Orwell".)

But to any true son of St Helens, Wigan means none of this; Wigan means a professional rugby team which, unaccountably, has always gathered to itself more success, glamour and prestige than our lads have ever managed. Even the road sign on the northbound carriageway of the M6 reads, "Wigan 16 St Helens 12". True, we have beaten them in the odd Cup Final; we have also, occasionally, beaten them on their own ground, Central Park (once, famously, running up over 50 points, watched in a delirious, incredulous haze brought on by over-preparation in the Bowling Green); but, still, a trip to Wigan must always be attended by foreboding and the rehearsal of brave smiles, cheery whistles and embargoed excuses.

This year was set to be particularly trying, since St Helens had been performing erratically on the pitch and disastrously off it. The trumpeted signing of a nasty Welsh rugby union star, David Bishop, had fallen through at a stage so late that the celebratory sandwiches for the Gentlemen of the Press had been cut and laid out. And worse, much worse, St Helens and Wigan had fought in the High Court over the signing of a nasty New Zealand rugby league star, Adrian Shelford. St Helens had approached him first, but Wigan had done it properly. They had the player; St Helens had a legal bill of over £60,000. A letter in the local St Helens newspaper had called for the directors' resignation, if they could manage to make it legally binding.

By the time last orders were called in the Bowling Green, Central Park was half-full and the St Helens loose forward was gleefully being refused permission to use the VIP car-park. Central Park is a big, sprawling ground and rather like Wigan itself, a haphazard mixture of old and new: a fancy electronic scoreboard, earth and shale paths, uncovered terracing with wide gaps to the old mills and chimneys, the modern tower blocks and the new dual carriageways beyond. The gaps also allowed sight of the crowd streaming towards the ground, round and past the genial mounted policemen. All very pleasing and Priestley-like, except for the smart "leisure clothing" and the bright new anoraks in the Wigan colours of cherry and white. Caps, though, are back in style, but in country checks rather than the old plain dun, a different kind of status signal altogether.

By 2.58 and the emergence of the St Helens team, over 24,000 were in the ground, gently steaming under drizzle and a sky of watery ink.

The St Helens welcome was encouraging, the Wigan welcome deafening. Shelford, starting as a substitute, waved to the crowd and drew another enormous roar. Within minutes, as if to script, he was on the pitch after an injury to a Wigan forward in the opening bone-crunching, oof-inducing exchanges. People who cannot find enjoyment in rugby league always cite dour, charge-tackle-charge forward play as a principal reason. But this is the necessary contrast that makes the sudden break so exhilarating, the sight of a big forward at full tilt in the open, looking for a three-quarter to finish off a 75-yard break.

It is the same in soccer, when the "patient build-up" makes the space for a Lineker or a Greaves; it is the same with boxing, tennis, snooker and war. But it is not the whole of it: I saw my first game of rugby league when I was eight and the fascination is as undiminished as ever, and as inexplicable to others as the fascination for others of cricket, horse-racing, opera and ferret-hurdling.

Meanwhile, on the pitch, an astonishing event: we had scored, after a neat interchange of passing in the right-hand corner. My right hand went up to punch the air in appreciation but it ended up as a Strangeloveian half-salute, stifled by the recollection that I was sitting on the Press benches, where, in this country at least, outward impartiality is expected. (In Italy, they do things differently. There, I witnessed every last Italian journalist on his feet, wild-eyed, chanting, "*Italia, Italia!*" after a soccer score against England. In Scotland, too, an impeccably balanced radio commentary on a Rangers-Celtic match was marred by a late winning goal for Celtic against the run of play being greeted

"Looking back to my childhood, I think I was just badly briefed."

71

by "——— me, we've scored!")

But this was Wigan and I think I got away with it. In any event, there were to be no further tests that half, Wigan scoring almost at will to lead 22-6 at the interval. I noted that the Queen in her Christmas message expressed some concern about the harmful effects of fanatical support for one's team; Her Majesty should be told that there is no finer way of strengthening the character than watching helplessly while Wigan knock seven bells out of one's boys. There is a cockiness about your Wigan supporter in triumph which is not pleasant, I can tell you.

Still, we rugby league supporters have a tradition of non-violence. Various theories are adduced for it: the openness and robustness of the game itself, a carefully nurtured family image, the closeness in earnings and lifestyle of players to spectators. I myself think it has more to do with a chauvinistic protectiveness felt by rugby league supporters for a Northern minority sport.

Anyway, a scoreline of 22-6 at half-time certainly lends itself to such disinterested sociological rumination. And, moreover, to the pondering of why one entrusts one's immediate happiness to a group of strangers striving to produce a result of very little significance over which one has no influence whatsoever.

You might see it as a local metaphor for social control and existence as a whole; I still remember being told off by my Mum for weeping when we lost that crucial match against Leeds in 1961. And I remember last May, when the team, having failed to win a nerve-wrackingly close Cup Final, came down to our end of Wembley and showed their disappointment, mutely apologising and applauding us. It was a splendid moment, and I'm afraid I wept again, Mum.

The consensus in the open-plan Central Park Gents at half-time was that for St Helens, it was all over (I bowdlerise). But such judgments are never particularly helpful: the crushed nature of the venue and short time-span of the visit allows little room for reasoned analysis. Besides, it's a funny old game, rugby league. Within minutes, St Helens had scored. And then St Helens scored again: 22-20. "Come on, Wigan, they're rubbish, these," shouted a woman sitting behind the Press benches, worry strident in her voice.

And then, knock me down, we scored again! My fist escaped and delivered a sharp rap to the Press bench. I think I got away with it. Behind, in the stand, packed with Wigan season-ticket holders, all was a satisfying quiet, except for a small group of St Helens supporters jumping up and down in a frenzy of delight in the far top-hand corner.

And then, we scored again: 22-32. The hooter went for the end of the match. Shelford had performed without distinction. The St Helens (and quondam Wigan) coach, Alex Murphy, was on the pitch, literally jumping for joy. A group of young St Helens supporters began a swaying conga down the pitch. The leader stooped to kiss the turf.

Squeezing out into a dark, wet Wigan, another woman supporter was shrill and bitter, demanding to know why her team should play so well in one half, so ineptly in the other. "They can't play well all the time, every week," she was told. To no effect. She turned away, still complaining, eyes still angry.

"Now then, Tommy, how do you feel?" inquired one St Helens fan of another, a small middle-aged man whose face was split by a beam the size of half a pumpkin. "I'm chuffed to bloody death," he said. You and me both, Tommy.

"I think the music adds a lot, don't you?"

Splashing out from his sodden Welsh bolt-hole ALAN BRIEN pursued warmth and tranquility in the Algarve

The North Wales light filtered through fold on fold of wet-sheeted clouds like the last flicker of a long-dying, perhaps long-dead sun. During the night, the cottage had been subject to repeated sessions of Nature's house-wash, rain hosing the walls and windows, wind brooming the tiles and chimneys. The ground underfoot was squashy as drowned puppies, each step bleeding brown juices.

The same khaki mixture had lately been coughing out of the taps in the kitchen and bathroom. I turned them all firmly off, then flicked up the final light switch, at last silencing the spluttering generator whose gutteral ravings had been our background accompaniment all summer, like the engine of the *African Queen*. For weeks now I had felt as though I were snorkelling around the besieging woods, rather than walking. Soon I would be obliged to try breathing through gills. Autumn was here and it was time I was not.

The car rolled on to the muddy torrent that passed for our access road, very soon tobogganing down the sticky switchback, stuck in four-wheel non-drive, as if on some primitive fairground ride. We slid through the belts of desolate pines, standing like patient crowds waiting in the rain for an announcement from the palace balcony. We hit asphalt in the valley. Now we could look back up the hillside, beyond the forest on to the heather-tinted, bracken-brushed slopes of the Berwyn mountains. There, as ever, valiantly holding out above the tree-line, was the evergreen bush, accidentally topiarized by the winds, that an earlier neighbour, the late Admiral of the Fleet Sir Caspar John, had dubbed "the chicken". It seemed to send us through the mists an approving peck.

1987 had been a year of so many strains and stresses. Now, I must escape. It was a choice between a nervous breakdown and a holiday in the sun. I could not afford a nervous breakdown. Usually, I take my holidays *out* of the sun. After a year in London and Wales, like everyone else I want warmth. But I like it in the shade, at a corner table, amid tinkling ice, with just a hint of the mouth-watering smell that almost always turns out to be fried onions, watching the world hip by, preferably in her short shorts. But that's just lunch and dinner time. From early morning

IT WAS A CHOICE BETWEEN A NERVOUS BREAKDOWN AND A HOLIDAY IN THE SUN. I COULD NOT AFFORD A NERVOUS BREAKDOWN.

until noon, from late afternoon until dusk, I beaver away visiting every sight and site ever mentioned as worthy of the attention of tourist or travel writer, historian or novelist, or even just culture snob and luggage-label collector, as though I were expecting a three-day examination on my return. My guide-books are full of notes. Fortunately, no one can read them, not even me. Nevertheless, when I encounter them again years later, I can still recall the pleasure I had making them.

This time, it was all going to be different. My wife said so. And she booked us the first two weeks of October, after what seemed like three weeks' study of the Meon Villa catalogue, that Almanach de Gotha of the rented *palazzo*, cars and maids at your fingertips, where blue sky meets blue sea with you in the middle.

This was the Algarve, she explained, the southern-most, western-most strip at the tip of Europe. It would be out of season, so that there would be no danger of meeting, between me and the ocean waves or the lake shore, the very people I had been avoiding in Kentish Town. It would be, according to the charts, sunny but not hot, dry but mild. Anyway, the villa was incredibly secluded, twenty miles inland, up a private road and over a hill from the main Lagos-Lisbon highway. It had a swimming pool. It had a daily maid to wash things. All we had to do was breathe the warm, herb-scented air, lounge about under the fig-leaved arbour, walk the alleys of the cork woods, float like

"*I feel like going a little crazy with fives and sevens today.*"

bronzed starfish on the doorstep waters, eat at home or in the coastal villages, read Dante's *Inferno* and all the other books we had been saving up for twenty years, and let the days slip by in an epicurean daze. To be honest, it didn't sound all that bad.

We left a Wales seeping moisture like a great green sponge. Still, we were driving south to the vast warm bath known as the Mediterranean. I studied the pictures in the Meon pages. I leafed through my reference books. I see, I *see*, I cried, the Algarve is going to be a sub-tropical Wales!

By now, I was even enjoying the airport. It was a long time since I had gone beyond the barriers at Gatwick, sucked up along the moving pavements like Hoovered remnants of the summer overflow. I am not sure the design of the plate-glass world behind Passport Control makes all that much sense. I got the feeling I was on a plushy, softly-lit, Muzak-haunted treadmill, a merry-go-round of potted plants and endless sofas and winking signs, beckoned on from one empty, identical lounge to another. I was packed in transparency, like an orchid, or perhaps a BR sandwich. (Very good they are, too, nowadays.) Outside, all was dark and there

"*Come in, Ferguson. We were just talking about you.*"

was a kind of surrealist thrill in seeing yourself and surroundings reflected again and again, parallel lives where your clones were proceeding at odd angles, often in double image, and in a darker range of colour, away from you.

It was nearly midnight in Faro, the Algarve airport, when we arrived. I sniffed the spicy air – did I detect a touch of Africa, anyway Morocco? – and collapsed into the taxi.

At our villa in the hinterland, I took in nothing except a great curved roof of frosted stars, glittering like Rowntree's blackcurrant pastilles. As I went to sleep, I thought I heard a sound to which I had become familiarised, the roar of a generator through the trees. But as I switched off the light, it stopped. I faded into oblivion, thinking – now I am going to have the lazy-bones, do-nothing holiday everybody else is always talking about. *No more notes!*

Next morning, we found our Algarve villa not only had the same generator as our Welsh cottage, but it also had the same tendency to go on the blink in a kind of sulk. This was soon mended on that first day of Indian summer. From then on, it poured for a fortnight. The water in the taps ran brown. The lavatory overflowed. The ground underfoot was like drowned kittens. The access road resembled Vimy Ridge. The hillside leaked. There was an evergreen bush at the top of the slope amazingly like a chicken.

The villa with its vaulted, beamed rooms, running on through open, doorless arches, was ideally designed for a hot country of cloudless skies. In the sudden, unexpected, unprecedented (they showed me the figures) British-style weather, there was nowhere to lock yourself in with a blazing log fire. For the first time in October in decades, I had found in Portugal a beautiful, remote bolt-hole, exactly situated as the one I had left, but with exactly the same climate. It was Wales without the sun, which is what Wales is anyway.

This year I am going to Italy, to a place with a lot of museums. Then I can have something to make notes about, whether it rains or not.

"Point taken."

HOLY TIME-WARP, BATMAN!

TO THE *BATPORSCHE* DEAN!

Out of the turmoil of strike action and sackings at TV-am, the old caped crusader has emerged as an audience-grabbing hero. Broadcast as a stop-gap Batman and Robin adventures have been born again. NICK BROOM reckons it's time to update the scripts

(Wayne Manor. Batman and Robin have just returned from the snooker hall)

Robin: Look, Batman! There's a message on the Fax from the Commissioner!

Batman: What does it say?

Robin: It says, "Hi, Batman. Batgirl is being held captive at the Gotham Rubber Company. Please hurry there. Nice one. The Commissioner."

Batman: At once to the Batcave!

(Our heroes go to the Batcave below stately Wayne Manor and prepare for their rescue mission)

Batman: Ready? To the BatPorsche, Dean!

Robin: Why do you keep calling me Dean? My name's Robin.

Batman: No one's called Robin nowadays. Dean's much more Eighties.

Robin: *(Sulkily)* No one's called Batman.

Batman: Don't be facetious, Dean. Look in my Filofax for the address of the Gotham Rubber Company, and then let's make tracks.

Robin: Right, well, it's on Stallone Street, just behind the Nuthouse Vegetarian Restaurant.

Batman: Oh, yes, I know it well. Speaking as a vegetarian, I'd say it's the only decent place I've found to eat out. Okay, let's go.

Robin: But wait, you've forgotten the warning to the kids!

Batman: Oh, quickly then. *(Camera closes in on Batman's face)* "Boys and girls, I cannot do without using a condom. Don't think I can and don't think you can. Have a nice day." Right, that's that done. Let's hit the road.

(Batman and Dean roar out of the Batcave and head for the Gotham Rubber Company)

Batman: How about some Batmusic, Dean?

Robin: Okay. *(Sings)* Na na na na …

Batman: I mean turn on the Compact Disc player.

Robin: Sorry. *(Turns on the CD)* Na na na na, Batman! Na na …

Batman: That's better. You know …

(Cellular phone rings. Dean answers. Heavy breathing on the other end of the line)

Robin: We know it's you, Joker. Why don't you go and play your stupid pranks some place else? *(Line goes dead)* That guy sure is … Holy Catlitter! There's Catwoman breaking into that jeweller's!

(The BatPorsche screeches to a halt)

Batman: Hold it right there, Catwoman!

Catwoman: Ah, Batman. Still haven't got a proper job?

Batman: Okay, Catwoman, let's have you out of that Catsuit.

Catwoman: But, Batman, you weren't like this in the Sixties. I thought you preferred Robin.

Batman: I do, but people want more sex in 1989, and since homosexuality is a TV audience turn-off, that leaves you.

Robin: But, Batman, we must hurry – Batgirl's in dire straits.

Batman: Oh, all right, then. Come on.

(They rush out to the BatPorsche)

Robin: Oh, no, we've been clamped!

Batman: This must be the work of the Penguin. Look, there he is!

Robin: That can't be him, he's wearing Levi 501's and a designer shirt.

Batman: That's him all right. Stop right there, Penguin!

Penguin: Hello, Batman. You recognised me after all these years, and in my new gear. Well done.

Batman: Penguin, the wrapper may have changed but what's inside is just as evil as before.

Penguin: Well, I must say that Raybans and a beret do more for you than that ridiculous hood you used to wear.

Batman: Unclamp our car, Penguin.

Penguin: No way, Batman. Wait for hours like everybody else.

Batman: There's no time for that. Come on, Dean, let's run.

Robin: But Batman, it's still a long way.

Batman: Don't worry, Dean, I'm wearing my Gucci loafers. Jump on my back and I'll carry you.

(Batman and Dean run off to the Gotham Rubber Company. When they arrive, they try the video entry-phone, but when no one answers, they break in)

Robin: Holy incomprehensible! The floor's marked out into six enormous coloured segments!

Batman: I thought as much. This is the trademark of the Trivial Pursuiter!

Robin: The who?

Batman: The Trivial Pursuiter, none other than the Riddler of old!

T. Pursuiter: Correct, Batman. Long time no see. Hey, like the boxer shorts, Robin.

Batman: We want Batgirl, Trivial Pursuiter.

T. Pursuiter: Not so fast, Batman. First you must answer some questions. What do you want: Geography, Science and Nature, Entertainment …?

Batman: Where is she?

T. Pursuiter: Ah, Geography. What's the largest lake in …?

Batman: Cut it out, Trivial Pursuiter. What have you done with Batgirl?

T. Pursuiter: Now you want History! Who was the tallest US president?

Robin: Abraham Lincoln.

T. Pursuiter: Good. Now what category?

Robin: Er, how about Entertainment?

Batman: Dean, wake up, he's using the questions to mesmerise you. Take this Anti-Trivial Pursuit Batpill which I happen to have on me!

(Dean takes the Batpill and immediately recovers)

Batman: That's better. Right, Dean, let's go and find Batgirl.

T. Pursuiter: No, you don't! *(He blocks their path)*

Robin: Take that, Trivial Pursuiter! **BONK!**

Batman: Wait, wait, we can't have **BONK!** any more. It's too rude.

Robin: But I thought we needed more sex in the show.

Batman: **BONK!** is sex *and* violence. We can't have both, at least not at the same time.

Robin: Okay. **FUNK!!** *(Dean hits the Trivial Pursuiter, who falls, beaten)*

Batman: Hey, like it, Dean! Give me five!

T. Pursuiter: Very well, you win, Batman. She's through there.

(Batman and Dean go through to another room, where they find Batgirl staring vacantly into the bubbling waters of a Jacuzzi)

Robin: She's in a trance.

Batman: Yes, the Trivial Pursuiter was gradually boring her to death with his dull questions. I'll just give her an Anti-Trivial Pursuit Batpill.

(Batgirl swiftly comes round)

Batgirl: Ah, Batperson, at last. What took you so long?

Batman: What's the "Batperson" thing, Batgirl?

Batgirl: Batperson, please, Batperson.

Batman: You mean we're both called Batperson?

Batgirl: This is the Eighties, Batperson.

Batman: But that makes us sound equal. That's no good. You know, things were much better in the Sixties …

(Batman drones on. Fade)

MAYBE I'M NOT CUT OUT FOR OFFICE LIFE

IMPORTANT NOTICE FOR TRAVELLERS OVERSEAS

If you are travelling, or are intending to travel, or have already travelled to any territory or territories not part of the United Kingdom, for the purposes of being overseas, you are advised in your own interests and for your personal safety to take careful note of the following information or particulars, where appropriate. HM Principal Secretary of State for Foreign Affairs accepts no responsibility for any damage or misfortunes to any person or persons who are, or intend to be, or have already been, in any foreign and/or overseas situation, howsoever caused.

NOTICE TO AIR TRAVELLERS

The following blacklisted airports should not be used by those of a nervous disposition:

TOURNIQUET (Mal de Mer) Holding apron subject to subsidence.
NEUROSIS (Anglepoise Archipelago) Windsock out of service.
BLOT (Damnation Coast) Hepatitis rife in duty free area.
DOMESTOS (Espadrille) Separatist air controllers on strike.
CATARRH (Baksheesh Peninsula) Departures lounge under fire.
DIAGNOSIS (Thermos Islands) Air misses twice daily.
SHUFTI (Mufti Mountains) Lavatories occupied by guerrillas.

HEALTH WARNING TO HOLIDAYMAKERS

The following resorts are subject to infestation by certain notifiable pests:

ESPADRILLE (Jellyfish the size of binlids)
EFFENDI (Surface-to-air Bilharzia birds)
ZUT (Concrete-eating soldier termite swarms)
ALORS (Rabid trout)
PHOSPHORUS (Migrating blood bats)
FURORE (Feral cats trained to snatch handbags)
SPUD (Malignant winds)
BANJO-DEL-MAR (Radioactive horse-flies)

NOTICE TO TOURISTS

The following centres may be subject to civil strife, riot, public disorder and commotion, or failure to discourage the random kidnapping of Caucasian passers-by:

JUNTA (including **SPUD**, **KHAKI** and **SWIZ**) Clerics incarcerated on sight and all women without hats vilified and spat upon.
DERVISH (south of the military customs post) 24-hour curfew, neither UK driving licence nor Barclaycard recognised by the hard-line guerrilla factions but used Deutschemarks welcome.
MYSTIQUE Most room-service waiters carry knives.
SILAS MARNA (Mon-Fri) Tanks have right of way. No smoking.
SPLAT Local radio carries regularly updated ransom demands.
SKIRMISH Death penalty for reading aloud from Western press.
COMMEDIA DELL 'ARTE Pickpocket toddlers open fire if smacked.
SHIBBOLETH Do not leave luggage unattended in hotels.

ADVICE TO MOTORISTS

Motorists are advised that there is no four-star on the following trunk routes:

EUTHANASIA to **THERMOS** (E112 via **EPIDERMIS**)
CIVILIAN to **TARRAGON** (E22 *except* **BADEDAS** and **ANGOSTURA**)
AMBRE SOLAIRE to **CLIENTELE** (E766, avoiding **AZNAVOUR**)
PIQUE to **GAFFE** (E45 via **CASSEROLE**)
ANAGLYPTA Ring-road (Direction E61 **PROBOSCIS/BACTERIA**)

GENERAL INFORMATION

Refugees are reminded that the daily ferry service between **STIGMA** and **ONOMATOPOEIA** is suspended until further notice.

There are no wagon-lit facilities on trains in or out of **DIPLOMA** unless by prior arrangement.

The chair-lift from **CRAMPON** to **GOGGLES** is subject to delay.

The temperature on the roof of the **ENURESIS** weather centre at noon today was 141°F with a Swoon Factor of +22°, which may cause drowsiness or, in certain circumstances, tumours.

Nautical enthusiasts are advised that some of the approaches to **PEDALO** and the newly-opened **CASTANET MARINA** may be mined.

Locally bottled mineral water intended for human consumption should be mixed with two parts potable bicarbonate of bleach and vigorously boiled in most parts of **UPPER ANTHRAX**.

Cocoa solids must not be imported into **AMNESIA**.

Pumps or "trainers" must not be worn throughout **MEGALOMANIA**.

*This information was correct at the time of going to press. For news of any last-minute changes, you should contact the local British Consul, if any, and bring with you a packet of digestive biscuits, pot of "Double One" marmalade, together with a set of size "AA" batteries. God Save The Queen.

BARGEPOLE

· · · · · · · · · · · · · · · ·

ANY COUNTRYMAN knows that spring is the season of peculiar noises and abrupt scuffles, as the brute creation wakes from the long winter and starts throwing its weight around in search of the gifts which God has brought.

You know and I know precisely what this winsome rural nonsense is worth. Spring is of no account whatever to us, nor does it interest the farmers, who merely have to come to grips with a new set of EEC regulations for the obtaining of handouts. The only people who care about spring are appalling, pasty city-dwellers without second houses in the country. They sit in their dreadful "flats", wearing corduroy trousers and Viyella shirts, reading *Country Life* and *World of Interiors*, and somehow manage to relate nature's burgeoning to *faux-marbre* without ever contemplating the blood or the money. Those who possess second houses know too well that spring brings the ghastly knowledge of winter's depredations, as well as nests of small unidentifiable creatures throughout the house, like tiny pink bogies with beaks and feet.

But don't you feel that somehow, confined as we are to the city, we are *impoverished* by our isolation from the slow, tidal dance of the seasons? I mean, Stonehenge, you know, and the cycle of death and rebirth? Aah, phooey. The dance of the seasons is not only repetitive but dull and slow, and the only thing to do in the country is to go mad. All over England, fools will be stuffing their cars with their hated relations to go to Haworth and see the Brontës' house (that " " is good, don't you think?) and commune with a rural civilisation that had its roots in reality, but do you know how Bramwell Brontë

died? Standing up leaning one elbow on the mantelpiece, that's how. He did it to prove that it could be done. Maddened by pastoral *ennui* and the company of awful writing females in buns and flannel drawers, it was the only thing he could think of to take the skin off the frightful rice-pudding of his rural "life". To be found nonchalantly dead in your own drawing-room has admittedly more style than any of your £220 calfskin cartridge-bags or *World of Interiors* queer antique dealers' oh-so-precious Suffolk *gîtes*, but *is it worth it?*

Of course it isn't. We have plenty of seasonal ebb and flow here in London and we can at least go mad in relative comfort. For every beak and snout snuffling for grubs among the roots, we have a quartet of exuberant, roaring builders hammering in brute syncopation as they smash through walls, rip out pipes and pull down ceilings in a vernal orgy of gouging and rending. Outside my door as I write, a tiny black man is wrestling in primitive frenzy with a huge, intractable writhing orange thing which he is thrusting through a hole in the floor to the accompaniment of cries of "Yaaaaarp! Ormvip-mahn! Rapp-maaargh-mahn!" and a ghostly Welsh echo from far below of "Yerw'aa? Yerw'aa? Woss'aa?"

Perhaps it is the folk memory of some ancient and disagreeable liturgy culminating in a human sacrifice like the one I observed when the Irish electrician came round, a tiny apoplectic man with a withered mate who stood on a ladder fiddling with the lights while his principal intoned, *Don't-touch-the-red-wan-do-you-hear-what-I'm-telling-yez-don't-touch-the-red-wan-go-for-*

the-black-wan-don't-oh-fockin-Jaysus-sor-could-ye-come-here-a-moment-yer-man's-fallen-offa-the-ladder-will-ye-tell-me-what-ye-think-or-is-he-dead?

Eventually, I suppose, they will achieve some sort of Eucharistical climax, probably marked by a flash, a bang, and hoarse shouts of exultation, and then they will go home and take it out on their wives. Even these people must have sap, and I expect it rises at this season, though why it should do so I simply cannot imagine.

My own sap, knowing its place, rises in early November when there is no chance of anything untoward taking place, but I suppose I am out of synchronisation with the rest of creation. Last Friday a woman said, "Your trouble is, you don't know what you want. If you knew what you wanted, there might be some hope for us," and then on Monday another woman said, "Your trouble

THE ONLY PEOPLE WHO CARE ABOUT SPRING ARE PASTY CITY-DWELLERS WITHOUT SECOND HOMES IN THE COUNTRY.

is, you don't know what you want. If you knew what you wanted, there might be some hope for us."

Perhaps it is instinctive or perhaps it is something they learn at their mother's knee, like not wearing stockings in the summer because it makes you look like a secretary, or finding out precisely how you like your Yorkshire pudding made and then making it differently, on purpose.

Anyway, I know exactly what I

want. I want women to stop saying, "If you knew what you wanted, there might be some hope for us." I want a certain woman whose identity is none of your business (and none of mine either, come to that) to fall in love with an American and move to California so that I can have her dog. I want a new striped boating jacket from Dunhill (I buy all my clothes from my tobacconist, it saves so much time) and a pair of white flannel trousers and a whangee so that I can take my new dog for a walk in the Park and all the girls will say, "Who is that remarkable fellow in the striped boating jacket and the white flannels, the one with the whangee and the Jack Russell, and what on earth does he think he looks like?"

I want to know what a whangee is. I want the dreadful men to go away from outside my door and take their hammers and drills and long orange things, and their shouting and rages and cackling and most of all their bloody *moustaches* with them. They all have moustaches and I can see no point in them.

I came here to escape the bailiffs but this is worse and it is not fair.

But most of all I want to stop this nonsensical drivelling about spring. I already have plans laid to abduct the entire staff of *World of Interiors* and *Country Life* and knot them into a delicately sponged and rag-rolled sack containing a serpent and a cat (no need, given the company, for the monkey) and anyone I hear mentioning spring will be stuffed in with them and the whole lot of you chucked into an eel-filled moat to experience the true rhythms of nature at their slimiest.

A BRUSH WITH DESTINY
(The War Diaries of Vidal Sassoon)

May 1942

This is Hell and no place for a salon, darling.

Everywhere is just a confusion of smoke and noise. Utter pandemonium. The ground doesn't stop shaking underfoot and making the scissors jump in your hand. It's all rather horrible but we must keep discipline. Whitehall attaches a lot of importance to hair design among the troops. Ours is an important job. There's no doubt a good cut cheers everyone up. Even in war you want to look good – to look sexy without looking tarty. It's good for the morale.

June 1942

Awoke suddenly, mechanically grabbing for my tongs. From somewhere along the trenches I heard a man crying, "For God's sake, help me! Somebody please help me! My hair's just about had it! It's lost all its spring!"

But there was nothing we could do. This is war and we don't open Mondays.

6th September 1942

A bad day. They got the Captain. The bullet passed straight through the hood-drier. He couldn't have felt a thing.

December 1942

We are dug in now. Only a mile of mud and a great big pile of *Titbits* stands between us and the enemy. You can see their basic blond bobs and dramatic high-partings silhouetted in the distance against the sky. We can hear their every movement. Hair static carries.

January 1943

I tell the boys to keep their heads down and still, or I might take a little too much off at the back.

Huddled in circumspect groups, their gaunt faces lit up by a sinking flare, dry-mouthed and chilled to the bone, they sip at dixies and wait their turn. It is the waiting, they say, they don't like.

For the life to which they are condemned they ask no compensation but friction and some special treatment shampoo, for war is an unpleasant thing and can lead to a dry scalp. Their bravery takes hold of my heart. How men can face 35 types of hair loss with such calmness amazes me.

19th January 1943

I lost Adrian, my personal junior, today. He was carrying out a vital root re-touch. He volunteered. He died where he fell. In some floor-sweepings.

March 1943

Why do I keep on lying and telling everyone how cordite is rich in moisturising polymers, and how it neutralises the hair's natural alkalinity, keeping colour through six washes while being kind to the eyes? How I hate the cant!

11th July 1943

We buried Ricci today. His is a great loss. He brought hope to us all with his imaginative scrunch-drying effects. I shall always remember him and his hair falling from mid-crown to skim the brows, layered for maximum volume and cut wet for manageability. I sent his regimental hair-slide back to his folks. He wanted me to have his shoulder-bag.

October 1943

I watch a young soldier, barely 18 and thankful for something to keep his mind off the war, winding his hair into demi-waves around his entrenching trowel and adding field-grey highlights for greater impact and interest.

I am doing everything I can to help – finger-drying for greater height and camouflage.

November 1943

Days pass into weeks, weeks into months. We know we have a fight on our hands. One of our roller trolleys suffered a direct hit yesterday and there isn't a mirror left in the place. Only one backwash-basin is fully operational and I don't hold out much hope for the wall photographs. I wish I could tell the boys of the providential arrival of wide-toothed combs and stiff-bristled brushes, for that is what we so desperately need.

January 1944

Jason got a "cushy" one and was sent back to Blighty. I signed his papers. It was the worst case of scurf I've ever seen. Ghastly.

26th February 1944

Toni has just bought it. He was a dear friend and a big talent. Like me, he wanted to be a unisex hair-stylist, not a soldier. He wanted to create, not destroy. We got to him too late. He had fallen into Jeri's hands and the semi-perm had proved too much for him.

March 1944

Intelligence tells us that there will be a show on. L'Oréal, Wella and Schwarzenkopf are all reported to be in the area.

I have been put in charge of the gel. I hope we won't have to use it.

April 1944

Zero hour. The barrage has begun. News in that the Boston Flat-tops and Lancashire Lacquered Flicks have suffered up at the front. The Berkshire Bluntcuts, the Royal Highland Foamsets and the King's Own Off-Centre Beehives have all been pushed back.

No news yet about the Somerset Sidies or the Lenster Skins.

May 1944

We are throwing everything we have at them – ancient herbal lore, chignons, postiches. The lot.

2nd June 1944

Word passed on of a build-up of squaw-looks to the west. I don't like it. We are low on pins. Our implacements are weakening. We are beginning to flake.

5th June 1944

If it comes to hand-to-hand combat, we still have our Afro-combs.

12th June 1944

The Staffordshire Kiss Curls are here! I can't believe it. We're going to pull through. We were so nearly washed out. Position secured with mousse and everything is looking fine. We're in a much better condition now, and the Kent Quiffs will be here soon. It is hard not to cry. I'm fighting back the tears from my eyes as I write this. There is a lot of spray about.

POSTSCRIPT

It is absurd to talk about heroes. No hairdresser covets a hero's grave. He just gets on with the job in hand.

But they should be remembered. The men who gave themselves to make this country's hair look wonderful and stay that way for all ages.

We must never forget them – Marcel, Jeffrey, Mr Paul, Gerrard, Stewart, André, Michaeljohn, Fredrique, Harvey, Anthony...

The men who dyed for their country.

HOW THEY LINE UP IN SAN DIEGO

YOUR SUPER BOWL MATCH PROGRAM TO CUT OUT AND KEEP

WASHINGTON REDSHINS

Named for a nasty rash on the leg of legendary founder/manager Edward R. Niblick, the Redshins are two-time Super Bowl winners who have won the trophy twice before. Famed for their running game, they are better at running about than not. Legendary coach Oral "Brown Bag" Mixmatcher, superstitious as always, will appear with the usual paper container, borrowed on the morning of the game from his local liquor store, over his head. This year the eye-holes will be cut by Elizabeth Taylor. Never beaten in a Super Bowl final, the Redshins have taken the title on a couple of previous occasions.

★★★★★★★★★★ DENVER DRONGOES

Powerful, offensive breath is the secret weapon of the Drongoes, who train at altitude on a Colorado garlic farm. A serious injury to wide-outside stickleback Pinklon Welge has reduced their options on blitz and schlitz, but legendary coach Cy Pelf, who will be wearing a small boy from downtown Denver in his buttonhole on the day, has compensated by drafting in a man of exceptionally impure personal hygiene, Herbal Wintergreen, among his running hatchbacks. Unpredictable though the Drongoes can sometimes be, though not always, one thing is sure: if they put points on the board in the first quarter they cannot remain scoreless for long.

YOUR GUIDE TO SUPER BOWL BODY LANGUAGE

1. Jeez, am I bored!
2. OK, you guys! Who's got my watch?
3. I like a bubble bath up to here
4. I've no idea what I'm doing but it sure feels good
5. Back off, weirdo!
6. I think it's wrong to support the Contras

7. I like being tied up
8. I've got a great upper body
9. Be gentle with me
10. Sorry! I've got gas
11. Hold the mustard
12. I'm in a mood

WARNING: the information contained in this Super Bowl™®1988 Match© Program™ is the property of the Big Boys' League and may not lawfully be in any way reproduced, copied, stored in a garbage recycling system, sold to minors, fed to miners, trodden on, folded into squiggles for lighting barbecues, used for any purpose in the men's room or thrown at the TV. Any contravention real or fictitious of this prohibition is punishable by three or four huge guys recently retired from Pro™ Football® coming round to your house late at night and making it tough for you to get up next morning. These guys are mean, you better believe it.

80

EIGHT REDSHINS TO WATCH

DEXTER GONKWRIGHT: Played at broken quarterlight most of his early career, now switched to golden retriever. Weakness: getting sacked in pocket on play-action fake as blitz comes through. He could probably deal with this if only he understood it. More offensive than he looks.

ISAAC BULKHEAD: Veteran nose-tackle who has tackled some of the biggest noses in the game, including the legendary Chuck "The Inhaler" Manilow. Frequently the victim of holding calls on first down, but aren't we all? Collects handbags.

DAVE ALBUM: That's Album with one "l", as Dave is quick to point out. A 4th-round draft choice from Pepsodent University, where he played loud feedback, Dave converted to Mormonism in 1986 and has never looked black. Very legendary tight rear end.

RHETT FABERGÉ: Barefoot kickers are old hat at the Super Bowl, but Fabergé breaks the mold by wearing shoes outside his shoes, that's two shoes on each foot. When he misses, he blames the guy wearing the inside shoes. Possible negative factor: psychological problems.

WINSLOW BEZANG: "The Flying Fortune", as he was nicknamed by his estranged wife, Bezang is equally elusive on the football field. "I just tell myself the other guy's a lawyer." Not without defensive talents, as he formerly played at smouldering foamback for Jell-O University.

AXEL HORSEPOO: Nobody messes with Horsepoo, a man who knows the game backwards and might play it better that way. Something of an aphorist ("I only stomp on guys with faces like bugs"), he collects obscene phone calls and his favourite colour is blood.

JIM TANNHAUSER: A former Rhodes Scholar majoring in Connective Tissue, Tannhauser during his time at Cambridge College, England, established a punt-return record of 13 months. He kept the punt in his room. Tannhauser is a much-travelled greenback who speaks fluent.

TETANUS JONES: At 8ft 2ins, Jones is at his best when lying full-length across the field hoping the right team will trip over him. It's hit-and-miss tactic, and Jones has lost both games and teeth as a result. Never been known to receive a pass, as hands are too big to close around ball.

EIGHT DRONGOES TO WATCH

LAFAYETTE TREMBLES: Possibly the most underrated wide hunchback in the BBL, Trembles has speed, vision, courage, a great arm, and two wives. Whether he is a no-show on the big day depends on the outcome of plea-bargaining currently in progress.

LESTER LaFONG: Superbly versatile player with big-league experience in three positions: strong subterfuge, fast forward, and nasty blowback. At his best in a pass-reception hesitation situation, he is a name to rank with Grobkuhler, Stickney and Wczukcz.

JESSE BUTINSKY: Along with Lester LaFong forms the most formidable pair of loose covers the Drongoes have had since Big Bill Elefantsen was in charge. Each of these men not only knows exactly where his opposite number is at any given moment, but can remember his telephone number too.

BRIAN BLENDER: Easily the most feared saddleback in the top leagues. If it moves, Blender tackles it, a policy which this season alone has already put an end to the careers of a Coke delivery truck and an escaped zebra from the Denver zoo. In quieter moments, Blender eats ring-pulls.

WINNEBAGO POPE: At nearly 450 pounds, Pope makes The Refrigerator look like an ice-bucket, but he is not easy to manage, and was dismissed from the Houston game when the Drongoes deployed an illegal winch to restore him to a standing position. "Down" for Pope means *down*.

ROOSEVELT BEANBAG: Soft underbelly is not a glamorous position, but Beanbag in his thirteen seasons at Drongo Field has come to seem like a fixture. "I have a good feeling about this Super Bowl," says Beanbag. "I feel I am finally going to touch the ball." Well, it hasn't happened yet.

VINCE D'IPPOCRATICO: Doubts about the severity of his knee injury were resolved in pre-season training when his leg fell off. Has been restored to the team by rigorous physiotherapy and the methadone program. He personally will not influence the outcome of the game, but his large family might.

WILMER KLOTZ: Rookie wedding tackle who has made the position his own. Star of the Rin-Tin-Tin Memorial All-Star game where he was named MVP, TCP, DFC and bar. Still in dispute with the Drongo front-office over the number of 0s on his pay-check.

INJUN COUNTRY

From an armchair in Washington, SIMON HOGGART reports

As you may have read, the Washington Redskins are playing in the Super Bowl this Sunday. Like everyone else in this normally staid city, I shall be in front of the TV from five o'clock onwards, a bowl of nacho chips with hot cheese sauce and jalapeno peppers (the little green palate-strippers from Mexico) at my right hand, a large supply of Samuel Adams's Boston lager in the fridge.

Occasionally I shall cheer at a positively vulgar volume, or groan with excessive grief. By the time the game ends, at 9.30 or so, the result will, I hope, have become something of an irrelevance: we'll either be too drunk to care or too weak to celebrate.

The cliché is that football is a religion in Washington, but that's not true. Unlike much American religion these days, which is sordid and threatening, a sort of cosmic protection racket, there's an innocence to football. This is in spite of the huge wealth, the drugs and the corruption on its fringe. Go to see a Redskins game at Robert F. Kennedy stadium and the crowd is amiable and good-humoured, whatever the result, passionately involved but—as far as I can judge—never motivated to violence.

What football does to Washington is unify it. It has the powerful effect of making people like each other. Unlike our rival on Sunday, Denver, this is not a socially homogeneous city. It's about seventy per cent black, and though there's a burgeoning black middle class, the ghettos are among the poorest (and most dangerous) in North America. A mile or so away are some of the richest communities in the world – not flashy, like Beverly Hills or Palm Beach, but planned, like a more spacious version of a quiet Surrey suburb. In Spring Valley and Cleveland Park, you find Jaguars and Burberry rather than Mercs and Armani.

It's also a town where nearly everyone – the middle classes at least – has come from somewhere else. Everybody has two loyalties, and their home town is generally stronger.

What brings together the beggar and the corporate lawyer, the native and the family from Oshkosh, the garbage man and the Senator, is the Redskins. On Sunday, ten days ago, just after the Skins had clinched their place in the Super Bowl, I wandered round the city and saw white youths dancing on the bonnets of their cars and black schoolboys yelling with delirium from the back of buses. Even the buses themselves had messages of support for the Skins on their electronic destination indicators. Who cared where they were going, unless to San Diego?

The adhesion is helped by the fact that the Skins are a very good team. This is their third trip to the final in six years, and their coach (the equivalent of manager) is now rated the most successful ever in the National Football League. Joe Gibbs is precisely the right man for the job in Washington; he looks and sounds like a failed bureaucrat. Some coaches, such as Mike Ditka of Chicago, are professionally flamboyant, cussing and laying waste both the opposition and their own players. Gibbs, with his nondescript, blinking face, has made boredom his stock in trade.

Even when he got down on his knees to pray during the last, critical moments of the game

"HOW 'BOUT THAT THIRTY-YARD PASS IN THE FOURTH QUARTER?"

against Minnesota last week, he didn't look excited – you'd have thought he was searching for a dropped set of keys. After the team had won, he permitted himself a thin smile, but only some time after the event, as if laughing at a joke everyone else had got earlier. He's right to be like that; anything excitable or argumentative might fracture the city-wide, inter-racial bond. And he wins, which matters almost as much.

Washington is lucky to have two first-rate quarterbacks. One is black, the other white. Quarterback is the most important and most glamorous figure in a football team. He's an on-field marshal, far more vital to his team than a soccer captain is. He's also the most visible player, whose passes, ideally fired with pinpoint accuracy at rifle speed, can win or lose the game.

There are very few black quarterbacks. Assuming Washington's Doug Williams plays on Sunday, he will be the first black ever to appear in that position in all 22 Super Bowls. This is in spite of the fact that, while blacks are only twelve per cent of the US population, they are a clear majority of professional football players.

This is a curiosity which is often alluded to but almost never discussed. I suspect that coaches (all of whom are white) believe, consciously or not, that their white players would resent taking orders from a black. But even to think that aloud would be to risk the racial equilibrium which seems, for the moment, to exist. Black people here are immensely proud of Williams and are desperate for him to play and win on Sunday. But the discussion is never presented as having anything to do with race; TV and the newspapers find it easier to pretend that everyone is united only in wanting the better player to be picked.

Before the war, the Redskins were an appalling team. After it, they weren't much better. Then, in the Sixties, the Washington Senators baseball team left the city (teams with that name have abandoned the capital two times, to Minneapolis and to Dallas. It is pleasing that the footballers have beaten both those cities twice this season).

At much the same time, Vince Lombardi, the best known of all professional coaches, came to the city and, for the first time in fourteen years, the Redskins won more games than they lost in a season. Attendances picked up, and from 1968 every single game has been sold out to season-ticket holders.

Since these tickets can be inherited, like the family silver, the waiting-list is now more than 360 years long. This, too, has had a unifying effect on the city. In the NFL, home games can be shown only on local TV channels if sold out. Washington is always sold out, which means that all the city can watch all the games.

I've been present at a game only once, when a resourceful friend managed to get us incredibly privileged seats in the owner's box. I suppose there were three dozen people there, all seated in front of little tables to which stewardesses brought limitless supplies of drink and delicious food. At half-time we were ushered into a comfortable lounge where there was more drink and delicious food in even more copious quantities.

Half our fellow guests were chums of the owner, a Canadian businessman called Jack Kent Cooke, and the other half were celebrities, mainly Senators' broadcasters of the type who are famous in America. Most of them came equipped with more gear than the average Everest expedition: a portable TV, to watch the action replays; a radio, to listen to the wittiest of the three commentaries available; and binoculars, to catch each play in detail. After each quarter of the game, flunkeys brought us a Xeroxed sheet describing each play. There were heaters to keep our toes warm. It was football heaven. I'm told that the Skins were heavily defeated by the New York Giants. Nobody seemed to mind very much.

Roger Mudd, the television pundit, argues that Washington loves the Redskins because – unlike politics – they are physical and not verbal. Getting a bill through Congress requires shabby compromises. In football, compromise is unknown: winning is all that matters. Maybe so. I prefer the view that the Redskins hold together a city that would, by all the rules of human nature, fly horribly apart. Once that happened, and the riots came within ten blocks of the White House. I don't think it's entirely a coincidence that there have been no race riots since the Redskins started winning.

In any case, I shall mind a lot on Sunday whether they win or not. Which is why I have already been down to Pearson's liquor store to purchase the necessary anaesthetics, just in case they don't and to celebrate if they do. As Mudd says, it's awfully hard to cheer for the House Appropriations Committee, but very easy to roar on the Redskins.

DR ROBERT BUCKMAN

THE INHUMAN MILK OF KINDNESS

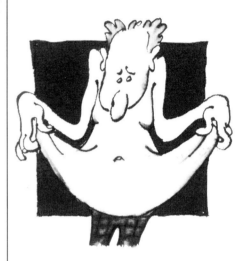

Ever alert to significant changes in the world of health and health-care, I call to your attention a new invention from the United States. Someone there has just invented artificial fat, although personally I thought that it was patented some time ago and called Elizabeth Taylor (nonono, just kidding, seriously, wonderful come-back, amazing diet well done, well done, etc, etc). However, artificial fat as an example of a dairy product substitute does raise the interesting area of the function of lipids in our diet and the roll of fat in our metabolism and over the top of our trousers

WHERE IT ALL BEGAN – MILK

Milk is not a drink, nor is it merely a food – it is actually a complete meal and diet plan! Yes, it is. It contains calories and carbohydrate for immediate energy, protein for growth, lipids for hormone synthesis, calcium for strong bones and a glossy coat, fat-soluble vitamins for good eyesight, intelligence, fertility and tax-evasion,

CURDS AND WHEY

Most people do not have a clear understanding of what curds and whey are, but the facts are quite simple.

Under the action of an enzyme called rennet (extracted from the fourth stomach of the calf, with permission of course), milk is turned from a homogeneous colloid suspension into milk solids of low density curds and a low-fat semi-opalescent fluid called whey.

This process was first discovered in the fifth century BC in what is now Mongolia. It appears that the political implications of milk-fractionation were massive. The bulkier, clot-like, curdish peoples clumped together and occupied what is now Curdistan: while the Wheys, who were no less war-like in their own wimpish style, occupied Wheyistan and attempted to colonise Mesopotamia with a chain of milk-bars and stop-me-and-buy-one tricycles.

Their efforts were unsuccessful, owing mainly to the superior market penetration by the Mongolian Khasars who opened a vast empire of rape-and-pillage parlours. Bankrupt and getting thinner and lower in fat, the Wheys dispersed over all of Europe taking their culture to Northern climes ("Scots whae hae wi' Wheys a-wheyed/Scots wham Curds hae oft whey-laid", etc) and interbred (the so-called "Whey-hey-hey") with virtually everyone they met.

Much of their history is handed on in religious parable ("for his Wheys are not our Wheys", etc) or folk-song ("I did it my Whey"), and of the once-proud master-race, the only descendants now consist of the home-made Yoghurt peoples and other followers of the prophet Yog. The story of the downfall of the Whey tribes at the hands of Miss Muffet is apocryphal.

lecithin for stability and a sense of humour, plus triglycerides and non-esterified fatty acids to enhance membrane coherence and reduce public sector borrowing.

In short, it contains every single component necessary for a baby's growth, apart from the stuff you get from Fisher-Price, of course. So, since milk is so complete a food, no wonder most babies choose it. But as they grow older, dietary needs change and they progress on to more "adult" dietary supplementation, consisting largely of chocolate washed down with hamburgers.

Certainly for the first few weeks the baby's very own fast-food outlet is McBreast and nothing but. Yet, how many of us have ever pondered the additional "unseen" advantages of breast-feeding – oh come on, do be serious. The fact is that in many species of mammals, e.g. cow, sheep, frog, etc, the milk not only gives nourishment, it confers immunity.

The first milk in these species is called the "colostrum" and contains antibodies against common childhood afflictions, such as hard-pad, distemper, diarrhoea, wanting a glass of water at 3 a.m., etc.

BUTTER

Interestingly, butter is almost the opposite of whey. In butter, the high-fat fraction of milk is encouraged to turn into a solid form by the process of churning. In the old days churning was done manually in a long thin wooden cylinder called a "churn". The cream fraction was put into the churn and basically hit and beaten over the head ("churning") by a dairymaid or "churner". The job was irksome and tiring ("it's your churn now," etc) and often done badly.

Nowadays the cream fraction is not brutalised or beaten at all, but is led into a large chamber where it can read leaflets about the advantages of turning into butter. It is shown a few tape-slide presentations on career opportunities in the EEC butter mountain and then spends an hour with a social worker. After that, turning into butter is the only thing it's fit for.

Interestingly, I interviewed one of these social workers while researching this article. It seems her name was Marge.

BONDING

Breast-feeding is the most complete care and support system available outside BUPA, and it is no wonder that "bonding" – emotional attachment of child to mother – follows so rapidly and so strongly on the provision of physical needs.

Breast-feeding is, as the Americans would put it, a "unique public-relations opportunity" for mother to get acquainted with baby, and it calls forth tremendous brand-loyalty and devotion from the recipient. It has often occurred to me that really smart politicians should not go around the place kissing babies on the tops of their heads – they should get out there and breast-feed them. Now in my opinion that would be a *real* welfare state.

THE DOCTOR MAKES A COMMITMENT

Q: *I read your column regularly and notice that a couple of weeks ago you started dealing with issues of cohabitation, sexuality and living together. When are you going to get back to all that sex and bedroom and messing around stuff, then?*

A: *As soon as I've finished this week's piece, dear.*

JACK HANDLEY

VAN GOGH OF THE NAVY

To most people, Vincent Van Gogh is remembered as the great Dutch post-Impressionist painter. But to me, he'll always be the best damn submarine skipper in this man's navy.

The last time I saw him was on the night of August 3, 1943. Normally, I'm not too good with dates, but that's one I won't forget. We were running on the surface, heading back to New Caledonia through the south Coral Sea. Van Gogh and I were in the conning tower, keeping watch. He had on that straw hat he always wore, and I had on, well, my regular navy cap. (I guess that's not important.)

I remember how clear and calm it was that night. Van Gogh started talking about the stars, how they seemed to swirl around themselves in the sky. Yeah, I laughed – especially after some of that bad hooch they make down in the torpedo room! He sorta smiled, and I laughed some more, and then we both got quiet for a while.

Finally, I got up the nerve to tell him what was really on my mind. "Captain," I said, but he said I should call him Vincent. "Permission to speak candidly, Vincent?"

He told me to fire away. "Well, sir," I said, "when you first took command, some of us were a little sceptical. I mean, we all recognise you as one of the greatest artists of all time. But we weren't sure you could command a modern attack submarine. I just want to say, boy, were we ever wrong."

He nodded in a way that said thanks. Then he grinned and said, "I suppose it was a bit unsettling when I came through that time tunnel like that."

Unsettling wasn't the word for it, I said. "We

didn't know what the hell was going on, if you were a ghost or what! Hackett had out his .45 and was going to shoot you!" We both laughed. Then I confessed that, after we had realised who it was, we got sorta nervous because somebody had read that he was crazy. I thought maybe I'd gone too far, so I lamely added: "Maybe you *have* to be crazy to get mixed up in a war like this."

Van Gogh looked straight at me, then out to sea. "I'd do it all over again," he said. "And I'll tell you why: I realise now that the really important thing is not creating timeless art masterpieces, but seeking out and destroying the geopolitical enemies of the United States."

I saluted him right there. I couldn't help it. "Sir," I said, "you're no crazier than..." I looked around for something, and saw a bird diving for a fish, "...than that loon over there." Boy, I coulda kicked myself, especially since it wasn't even a loon. But I don't think Van Gogh even heard me. He turned to me with sort of a tentative look on his face. "Tell me," he said, "do the

men still call me Carrot Top behind my back?"

Before I could answer, an explosion flashed in the distance, and a shell ploughed into the sea just off our starboard bow, throwing up a geyser of water. It was a Japanese destroyer, bearing down on us at full speed! Van Gogh was screaming, "Dive! Dive!" while the spray was still in the air.

It seemed to take forever, but we finally got submerged without taking a hit from her deck batteries. Pretty soon, though, she sniffed us out and started lobbing depth charges like grapes (if that makes any sense). *Ka-boom! Ka-boom!* One right after another. I thought we were going to break up. And loud? You don't know loud. I turned to Van Gogh and told him I wished I could tear my ears right off. Boy, I still regret saying that. It was not my day.

As usual, Van Gogh had a plan. He ordered all his art supplies – oils, palettes, brushes, smocks, the works – to be shot out of the sub, so they'd drift to the surface and maybe they'd think they'd sunk us. We cut engines and

waited. Silence surrounded us.

It didn't work. I don't think they knew Van Gogh was our captain, and why should they, I guess. I think it even sorta made them mad, because the depth charges really started flying after that. I mean, they were going off everywhere. The lights went out, and guys started crying and all, but Van Gogh stayed cool.

Somehow – I don't know how – he manoeuvred us around for a shot. He ordered torpedoes into tubes one and two. Then it happened. The men refused to load the torpedoes. Turns out Van Gogh had been painting on them in his spare time. One torpedo had sunflowers all over it, another had a self-portrait (full-length), another had peasants cutting grass or something. The men didn't want to be party to the wholesale destruction of great works of art, so they refused to load.

Well, when Van Gogh heard that, he got on the horn, but pronto. "Listen well!" he shouted. "Load the sunflowers in number one and the self-portrait in number two! That's an order!"

Time seemed to stand still as we waited to fire. The Japanese destroyer was turning. The torpedo room called back. They had loaded the sunflowers, but instead of the self-portrait, wanted to load the peasants. The self-portrait was too exquisite, they pleaded.

The destroyer was chugging towards us.

What about the poplars, Van Gogh asked. Did he mean the cypresses, the men said. No, the poplars. Oh, the poplars, they said. No, not the poplars, they were wonderful. Really? said Van Gogh. He didn't think so. Certainly nothing approaching the sort of ethereal luminescence of Monet's poplars. But Van Gogh wasn't going for that, the torpedo room insisted. His poplars had a more vivid, transcendent look – almost hallucinatory in the bold use of colour and shimmering brush strokes.

The destroyer opened up with her big guns.

Finally, Van Gogh permitted an unfinished portrait of Gauguin to be loaded into number two. Range, mark! Speed, mark! "Fire sunflowers! Fire Gauguin!"

Now, a destroyer is a big ship, I can tell you. But two direct hits right on the prow will practically blow the whole front section of the hull apart. We started cheering. I looked for Van Gogh, to congratulate him, and also to apologise for the thing I had said about the ears, but he was gone. He had disappeared, totally. (I guess totally is how most things disappear, so maybe you don't need that part.)

Anyway, all of this was a long way from my mind until just recently, when I was at the Metropolitan Museum of Art. I was sorta browsing through the French Impressionism section, when I turned a corner, and there on the wall, was one of Van Gogh's lesser known paintings. A chill went down my spine. It was "Attack of the Japanese Destroyer". It was dated 1888. So, he had made it back after all. Another, smaller chill went down my spine.

After Van Gogh, Kublai Khan became captain of our submarine. I don't want to say he was a bad skipper. Let's just say he was no Van Gogh.

"You'd think the doctor could find some more cheerful pictures for a waiting-room."

Dickinson

I'LL GIVE YOU SOMETHING FOR YOUR VAN GOGH

"Try to get this room straightened out before the doctor gets here."

"Poor Dr Gachet – he's always the same when he knows Van Gogh is coming."

"Hay fever playing up again, Vincent?"

EACH DAWN I TRY ON A SIZE 9

Britain's gaols are overcrowded to bursting point. The Home office desperately seeks an alternative, community-based penal policy. KEVIN PILLEY now reports on the hopes, the misery and the despair behind the walls of a top-security shoe shop

How long have you been in, John?
Since just before 9.30.

No. I meant how long in all have you been here?
It's difficult to know. Every day seems the same. What would today be, anyway? About Tuesday, is it? The fifth of something? I lose track.

It's Wednesday, January 6th. Look, it says so on the cash register.
I'll take your word for it.

How long are you in for?
For good, I suppose. I can't see me ever getting out of this hell-hole. Except in a box, that is.

Why are you in here, do you think?
"In my best interests" is the explanation they usually come up with. People on the outside think being cooped up in here all day is a consequence of some personal inadequacy. They think you must be a bit backward or something. But I'm not. I'm not dense. Not more than average, anyhow. I ain't got a personality problem. I'm not dangerous or anything like that. I'm not a vicious brute. I haven't done anything wrong but after a while in here you start to feel you have. Why else would you land up in a shoe shop?

What part then, would you say, do shoe shops play in this country's penal policy?
Well, the penal system's in a right state, isn't it? I mean, they wanted some sort of community-based alternative to imprisonment, didn't they? So they came up with shoe shops. "Stick 'em behind a counter. Get them working as shop assistants in the high street. That'll soon sort them out. That'll teach them a lesson."

So, what you're saying is that the retail industry has become an important part of the present government's behaviour modification programme? Shoe shops have become instruments of social control?
Yeah. It instils respect, measuring people's feet all day, you know what I mean? It teaches you the work habit. Society sees being shut away in a shoe shop as an act of penance and means of retribution for the undesirable, under-productive elements in the capitalist economy. Shoe shops, in my opinion, are nothing but an admission of failure on society's behalf. They're where all the no-hopers and misfits are dumped until something else turns up. Not something better. Just something else. They're how society avenges itself on its failures.

So shoe shops are more than just reform centres?

People talk of them as being a deterrent. They say, "I'm not going to do that because I don't fancy ending up in one of Her Majesty's shoe shops." But it's not like that at all. All that rehab rhetoric. It's about depersonalisation. That's what it's about.

Depersonalisation?

Yeah, you've no idea how degrading and humiliating it is to be in a shoe shop. I've been in one for nearly all my adult life. It robs you of your human dignity. Fundamentally I'm still a human being and expect to be treated like one. But not in here. No way. There's no such thing as human rights when you're down on your knees advising someone on their moccasins. It's purgatory.

So what purpose do shoe shops serve?

At first everyone believed they encouraged people to lead good and useful lives but shoe shops aren't humanitarian institutions. I think there's more bitterness and self-pity inside shoe shops than anywhere else because they're the closest things to hell-on-earth ever created.

And you've served time in most sorts of institution, haven't you?

Yes, I've done time in Wandsworth, the Scrubs, Waitrose (full-time as well as part-time), Bentalls and I've even for my sins done solitary confinement in a confectionery kiosk on the Edgware Road where the only contact I had with the outside world was when people bought Mars Bars and asked the way to Madame Tussaud's. I used to smuggle out desperate pleas for help in the change I gave them. But this is worse. Of course, I haven't been inside a Uruguayan or Turkish shoe shop but I can't believe they'd be worse. It's so bloody boring and lonely.

Yes, loneliness must be a problem.

Especially on Monday mornings. I don't know why but we just don't get any customers then. It's horrible. The silence really gets to you. You don't know what to do with yourself. You bite your nails and pace up and down and do anything to stop your brain from curdling. You become moronic even if you weren't to start with. Shoe shops can drive you right up the wall. Quite literally. We've got a phrase for it – going mad inside a shoe shop.

What's that?

"Store Crazy". You lose your self-identity. You start talking in your sleep about the relative merits of two brands of scuff cover. I heard one story of a bloke who suddenly thought he was a starling. They called him the Birdman of Freeman, Hardy & Willis.

How do you keep your mind from atrophying?

I read a lot.

What do you read?

Anything I can get hold of. A lot of shoe-size conversion charts. I also write poetry and paint. I hope that one day my work will be seen by the outside world. It gives a shattering glimpse into the fate of shoe-shop inmates. People forget us. They think we deserve everything coming to us. It's easy to become anti-everything and anti-everyone.

Who do you hate most?

Browsers. They're the worst. They can give you a real run-around. Them and, of course, shop managers. I think the person I'm most frightened of though is the area sales manager. He's a right sadist. He'll have no second thoughts about suddenly springing a stock-check on you in your lunch-hour. I hate the bastard. I'd like to see him upside-down in the Drastic Reductions bin.

For as long as penal institutions have existed there have been protests against incarceration. Have you any experiences of this?

Plenty. But they're all hushed up. The riots. The roof-top protests. The hostage-taking. The extended tea-breaks. All our grievances are ignored. It's all counter-productive anyway. They can always bring in the Army if we refuse to carry on working. The Army are trained in selling shoes in a national emergency. They're ready to man the pumps.

What is the most common grievance?

What? Apart from the revolting smell and having to go over the road for a filled roll every lunch-time? Well, it's got to be the denial of certain rights and civil liberties. Like conjugal visits, for instance. It's difficult to keep a marriage together and sustain mutual sexual interest when you see your wife once a week through a glass partition. I manage to see mine only when I'm doing the window-display. It's heart-breaking. The unmarried ones are the ones I envy. They don't have to worry about their kids following them in here. I couldn't handle that.

Is homosexuality rampant in British shoe shops?

I honestly can't answer that.

What about brutality?

It happens. Suicide's more common. All it takes is a ladder and some 45cm black shoelace. They're both banned here now. A withheld privilege like shoe-horns. Incidents of self-mutilation have been known, you know. Have you seen what a shoe-horn can do? It's not very nice.

Do you think you can survive?

I have to. For the sake of the wife and kids. I want to enjoy things like hills, fields and flowers again. I want to watch TV, eat the wife's cooking. All the simple things. That's the real nightmare of being in a place like this. All the time you know you're just a few feet from freedom. Which reminds me. If it's Wednesday, we shut at one.

"Why me?"

I DREAMT I EDITED A MAGAZINE
IN MY MAIDENFORM BRA

A Friend writes:

ON and on the long sentences ran for page after page, sometimes creating a paragraph and eventually perhaps even managing sometimes in the future (the reader always lived presumably in hope) to combine and mingle themselves into a finished piece. There was something Zen about the *New Yorker* article, something perhaps Kafkaesque. Was, indeed, there any difference between one *New Yorker* article and another *New Yorker* article? Was, say, a *New Yorker* article on the nuclear holocaust really any different from a *New Yorker* article on beachcombing in Nantucket? The answer is No. Basically it made no difference whatsoever what a *New Yorker* article was about, for 62 years ago, Harold Ross, the legendary founding editor of *The New Yorker* (see *The Years With Ross* by James Thurber), discovered a great secret, that great secret being that all those long and boring articles set in grey type, with no photographs whatsoever and with absolutely no graphics, made the advertisements look good. Had, in fact, anyone ever finished a *New Yorker* article? There was a rumour about a little old lady marooned in the West Seventies.

• •

Who he? – Ed.

THE story so far: To the vast world the scandal of *The New Yorker* was of little moment. Two years ago (1985) mild-mannered, non-pipe smoking mogul Si Newhouse, the 18th richest man in the United States of northern America (despite his wealth 5ft 9in, 165lb Si Newhouse still travels by civil airlines) bought the venerable publishing ikon of West 43rd Street, causing scenes of alarm among the 164 staffers and those *New Yorker* readers whom doctors agreed were more or less still living. Would the shy and retiring, usually Four Seasons-lunching Newhouse desecrate the great tomb of the parenthetical phrase? Would he sack 77-year-old, dark-suited gentleman of the old school, William Shawn (rhymes with *yawn*), only second editor of *The New Yorker*? And who cared? In the rain-washed British Isles only a tiny band of would-be chic Brits and expatriate Yanks would. Unfamiliar with the works, style and ethos of *The New Yorker* were most Britons, although the joke "Who he? – Ed." used with monotonous regularity by Richard Ingrams (Who he?) was perhaps familiar to readers of *Private Eye* who did not know from where he had stolen it. (Why have you started writing in *Time* magazine style? – Ed.) (Less boring.) (Oh.)

• •

Chantilly lace, That's What I like

MOSEYING through the pages of the Newhouse *New Yorker*, one notices that things do not seem to have changed; the grey type was still there, but, suddenly, into the usually tweedy, preppy adverts crept something unmentionable. *The New Yorker*, which had once censored ads for taste or health (they were the first to ban cigarette adverts), ran a four-page spread, advertising Calvin Klein scent, in which there appeared a naked woman and four naked men. This advert, which was banned by the sisters of Fleet Street, failed to knock the socks off old Shawn. Not so the next one, an ad for men's unmentionables. He got it removed. But this was William Shawn's last stand. In the issue of March 3, 1986, the by now 78-year-old Shawn saw on page 63, facing a relentlessly boring "Profile" of Sir Steven Runciman (How boring? – Ed.) ("... when I went to Istanbul, in 1942, to teach Byzantine history at the university, I was allotted a handsome young lady to be my translator and assistant. Her family, the Karacalarlis, had been old, established tobacco magnates in Kavalla when it was Turkish. She was related, in the female line, to the...") (That's boring enough – Ed.) ... saw on page 63 a Maidenform bra and panties ad in which a bimbette, in "the well-bred elegance of Chantilly satin, scalloped lace", was arranging roses in a tasteful silver bowl.

• •

A Fine Italian Hand

OUTFLANKED were the *New Yorker* staffers who had expected a Newhouse attack on editorial. The thin end of the Newhousian wedge they now saw was Steve Florio. A long-time Newhouse man, Florio was named head of *The New Yorker* business-side. He was not a Harvardman, not even a Yaleman. He was only 36. He was an Italian-American suddenly put among all those White Anglo-Saxon Protestant Ivy Leaguers. On top of the unmentionables, just in case the chaps did not get the message, Florio started spending $2 million on 30-second spot commercials for *The New Yorker* on TV. The circulation of *The New Yorker* was 480,000, small stuff in the land of mega-millioned mag sales. Still, this was *The New Yorker*, where when the circulation reached 300,000, the fabled Harold Ross had complained it was too high, saying, "We must be doing something wrong."

In the time-hallowed way of prep school bullies and sneaks everywhere, the chaps at *The New Yorker* placed an anonymous cartoon, making fun of Italians, on Florio's desk. He had it framed and put on his wall. No sneak has yet come forward. And the circulation went up. Up too went the readers' average income, up from $35,000 to $40,000. And down went the average age of *The New Yorker* reader, down from 43 years of age to mere lads of 40.

Was this done overnight? No, it was the heroic effort of two years. But was 59-year-old Si Newhouse, whose brother is the 19th richest man in America, satisfied?

• •

Enter Gottlieb
Whacky Name, Unwhacky Guy

IN THE land that glorifies youth, there are certainly a lot of old guys still getting on. And getting on was now nearly 80-year-old (he was 79, that's how nearly) William Shawn, known as *Mister* Shawn by all, even his oldest friends, at *The New Yorker*. (Why that? – Ed.) (So they could tell he was a married man, you berk.)

Six months ago it really hit the old fan at *The New Yorker*. Newhouse sacked Mister Shawn.

Could this really have come as a surprise? Apparently it did.

One must study the weird psychology of the famous magazine. It was an enclosed world. As ivory-towered and protected as

*"I want you to know, Nettleson, how much I appreciate
your sticking by me now that things have got tough."*

the now Dodo-dead world of pre-War *Punch* (Didn't that bastard call us something funny? – Ed.) (Yeah, *Paunch*.) (That ain't funny – Ed.) Mr Yawn (That's funny – Ed.) protected his "writers" so much, the business-side guys were not allowed to set hoof on the 18th floor where the writers lived. *New Yorker* staffers, many of whom would be absolutely unemployable anywhere in the real world, were treated like demi-gods. These were not merely the little giants of *The New Yorker*, like Thurber, Perelman, Updike and Salinger, but also dozens and dozens of the Great Un-named.

Writer's block was epidemic at 25 West 43rd Street but Mr Yawn never bugged a chap. They sat without rubbing two sentences together for years, for decades even, if rumour was to be believed. If they ever did write anything, there was the famous *New Yorker* fact-checking unit to make sure they got all their silly facts right. If anything was changed, it was done with kid gloves. The late Kenneth Tynan, used to the boorish sub-editing of Fleet Street, was surprised on holiday in the Bahamas once by a 'phone call from Mr Yawn himself, wondering if it were jake with Ken if an extra comma got itself inserted into one of Tynan's more rambling sentences.

With such princely treatment did not come humility. The hacks of West Forty-third Street, which does not quite have the dignity of West Forty-fourth Street, where, in the blocks between Fifth and Sixth Avenues, stand the mansard-roofed Mansfield Hotel, the Harvard Club, the old Yale Club, The New York Yacht Club and the much *New Yorker*-used Algonquin Hotel, would have to learn a lesson. Enter Gottlieb, a man with a name right out of a Marx Brothers movie, but no whacky guy was he.

One had, naturally, heard about the excessively touchy feelings at *The New Yorker*, reading Brendan Gill's history of

the mag, the rather preciously entitled *Here at the New Yorker*, but one was not prepared for what followed.

• •

All Hell Breaks Loose

PANIC broke out among the prima donnas. No good for Si Newhouse to say, "Hell, it wasn't as if I appointed some guy I met at a party." The 55-year-old Robert Gottlieb, albeit he wore a yachting-cap, sneakers, corduroy trousers (Socks? Did he wear socks? – Ed.) and no neck-tie on his first day at work, was, before his appointment as only the third editor in the 62-year-old magazine's history, the editor-in-chief of New York's most distinguished publishing house, Alfred Knopf (with no silent "k").

Gottlieb had the knack at Knopf of napping bestsellers. He was both glitzy and serious. His serious books sold like most other publisher's bestsellers. Did he not publish a number of *New Yorker* writers' books? He did. Among them, John Updike. How easy this was all going to be. Not a bit of it. More than 160 (164) *New Yorker* staffers signed a petition asking Gottlieb to go. They thought Mr Yawn should have had the right to appoint his own successor, for, after all, Harold Ross had.

Many of the staff wept. Almost all of them got drunk. Some quit – one even a long-time Gottlieb author at Knopf. He went back to Harvard.

This bust-up at *The New Yorker* was called "the biggest piece of publishing news in 20 years" by the *Washington Post*. In New York itself they wondered just what the hell had happened 20 years ago. New York thought it the biggest thing in publishing ever. Britain may be insular, but Manhattan is an even smaller island.

A little old lady enters this essay. Sir, how does an Editor leave a magazine?

• •

Here at Paunch

AT *PUNCH* one day, 49-year-old Alan Coren, ten years the editor of the 146-year-old weekly, came into one's office one afternoon, sat down and said, "I think I'll leave and write a book."

"Not a novel."

"No, for gawd's sake, not a novel. A *book*. A *book* book"

"You going to have pictures in it?"

"Maybe I'll have pictures in it. If I can find the pictures."

"I'd have pictures in it, if I were you."

THE LITTLE OLD LADY: Thank you, sir.

At *The New Yorker*, the staff, weeping, gathered in the stairwell of the 18th floor, while Mr Yawn gazed down on them from the 19th floor and spoke. He said:

"Dear Colleagues, Dear Friends," Mr Yawn said, "we have built something quite wonderful together. Love has been the controlling emotion, and love is the essential word. We have done our work with honesty and love."

One staff writer was quoted, saying, "There was a whole lot of crying that went on here. It was beautiful." Mr Yawn's farewell to the troops was pinned on the wall and also sent out to all of the more than 160 staffers. "All of us," said William McKibben, for 35 years a *New Yorker* staffer but who was now going to quit, "admire it (the note) enormously as a piece of writing. Most writers would not have the confidence to get away with that much repetition of the word love – but it works beautifully."

No one at *The New Yorker* seemed to realise that the next day was St Valentine's Day and that Mr Yawn was making a joke. His first, and last.

• •

Were All These Tears in Vain?

APPARENTLY not. Six months have gone by. *The New Yorker* has not changed a bit. Indeed, the lady in the Maidenform bra and drawers would seem to have disappeared. The grey columns of type stretch out before one like the endless corridors of Franz Kafka. "Talk of the Town" continues, with those bizarre items that start "A Friend writes:", *New Yorker* staffers in the "On and Off the Avenue" column continue to keep up the standards of ghastly good taste (i.e., NO reproduction furniture whatsoever, on no account) while the advertisements continue to flog reproduction everything.

Advertising revenue alone has changed in the last six months. It is up. The great secret learned all those years ago by Harold Ross has not been forgotten. Keep those columns of editorial grey, nobody ever really bought *The New Yorker* except for the ads.

STANLEY REYNOLDS

►JUST UP►
►MY STREET►

There are friends, there are neighbours, and there are Them Next Door. IRMA KURTZ opens a new curtain-twitching series on the batty people who think <u>we</u> live next to <u>them</u>

I encountered a Lapp the other day who told me that where he comes from, it often happens that a householder suddenly rises up, fills his pockets with salt, and after saying "reindeer" to his wife (it's one of the few words in his language that does not refer to frostbite) he sets out on the forty or fifty-mile trek to his nearest neighbour. It seems a Lapp always knows intuitively the very moment his neighbour has run out of salt.

Well, when I first lived in Shepherd's Bush we used to be similarly convivial. For example, the first morning my delphiniums looked lonely, didn't my neighbour to the west chuck a load of slugs over the garden wall? And once when there was a long summer drought I found my eastern neighbour's toddler peeing into my drain.

We cared down the Bush, exactly the way neighbours should. When Number 4's boy came home after a year at Her Majesty's Pleasure, was he stand-offish? Certainly not. He was Lappish. No hour was too late for him to share with the entire street his salty new Borstal vocabulary, or his favourite pop music. (As far as I could tell, it was a version of "The Anvil Chorus" played by genuine blacksmiths.) Not one of us even dreamed of asking the lad to turn his ghetto-blaster down. We were much too neighbourly. And besides, the kid had gone down for arson.

Let me make it clear, I'm talking about my early days as a resident of Shepherd's Bush, days long gone; days when the knife-sharpener still wheeled his whetstone regularly through our streets. At the sound of his nasal, Victorian cry, all we neighbours brought out whatever needed to be honed: knives, scissors, razors, bayonets. Those were the days when a person could still count on comradeship down the Bush. When

my house was burgled, for instance, the nice man from Number 17 sold me back my stereo for only a fifth of its original price. And on Friday nights, when Number 12's husband indulged in the traditional spot of grievous bodily harm, our local police said they were touched by the number of calls that came in complaining about the screams.

All that changed. Almost within hours, as stealthily as an invasion from outer space, real people were replaced by television producers. Out of the blue, for example, a young couple took up residence in Number 8 with a baby called Camilla, two coach lamps, and an au pair girl from Hamburg whose father could well have been the very man responsible for the previous tenants having lived out their entire lives on the street, indebted for their continued exist-

THE NICE MAN FROM NUMBER 17 SOLD ME BACK MY STOLEN STEREO FOR ONLY A FIFTH OF ITS ORIGINAL PRICE.

ence to a bomb that was dropped in their attic during the Blitz and turned out to be a dud.

On Sundays, when grown children who had made good came to visit parents in our neighbourhood, there was a speculative gleam in their eyes. And no sooner had the cortège driven away with any resident who had passed on to a less central area, than up went a "For Sale" sign. Overnight, three greengrocers and a kebab-

Haldane

91

"It's not a patch on their digital stuff."

house in the Uxbridge Road became estate agents. (And the remaining greengrocer started to stock garlic.) New Ford Fiestas were *tout à coup* parked end to end on streets where just a little while before the only cars to be seen had all featured on *Police 5*.

It was vastly disconcerting. One minute I was living in an area to boast about to my liberal, left-wing friends … and the next? New neighbours were circulating a petition requiring Number 12 to clean up his act (and his front garden). They said he was letting the street down. It was hard to believe. Not long before there had been no place to let my street down *to*.

Suddenly, we were a neighbourhood on the way up. In the local off-licence where groups of us old Bush hands used to congregate and discuss philosophical issues, from the effect of Astroturf on QPR's performance to how long the milk-float stayed parked outside Number 15, the talk was all of property values. In the pub, long-standing neighbours eyed each other suspiciously, wondering who was going to sell out next and for how much. And doing furtive sums on the beer mats, even as the publican whisked the oaken chairs out from under us and replaced them with moulded plastic.

Things started to move upwards with dizzy-

ing speed. A peer's daughter moved in next to me and enrolled her five-year-old in the local school. I tried to explain to my established neighbours that it would be all right, that the child was already down for Marlborough. But they panicked.

"Let one in…" said the mother of the Borstal boy at Number 4, and she shook her head significantly.

So it came about that all the remaining aboriginals left my part of the Bush. All except me. I stuck it out, though I had some dreadful experiences. I'll never forget accepting an invitation to a party at the new Number 30 and finding the fashion editor of a magazine I worked for among the guests. Media! In my neighbourhood! It was unthinkable! Previously, the only media people to be found between us and Wood Lane were Jehovah's Witnesses. And our notion of communications had been to cross the street quickly when Number 5 was having one of her bad days.

Whereas my former neighbours had left me pretty much alone except to exchange friendly greetings and to shoot the occasional air-rifle pellet through my bedroom window, the newcomers were not so tactful. All I had to do was seat myself at my desk, and there came a knock at the door.

"Hallo! I heard your typewriter, so I knew you were in…"

Number 10 was considering a divorce. Number 27 was a bulimic. Number 22 was having a generalised nervous breakdown, pretty much altogether in my kitchen. As for Number 7, she was another American. A Californian, it so happens. Pisces. Vegetarian. Feminist.

I had to move, of course. And I don't miss the Bush. Except that there was an ancient pear tree behind my house, and in the autumn, local Indian girls in brilliant saris used to climb to the very top, laughing as they collected the hard, green fruit for chutney.

FIRE AWAY, YOUNG MAN

In which ROY HATTERSLEY reveals that when it comes to interviews, even assault with a wet fish is preferable to a shoot-out with local radio

For almost a decade, I thought that nothing could be worse than the trout which died, writhing, across my feet during a broadcast of *Panorama*. The programme was an analysis of the Cod War (in which I commanded Her Majesty's forces) and the live trout was wheeled into the studio to demonstrate that we did not have to fight with Iceland simply to fill the slabs in British fish shops. As it expired over my soaking shoes, I should have thought of it as making the supreme sacrifice. Unfortunately I had too many things on my mind to meditate on the Cod War to end all Cod Wars.

The trout had been brought to the Lime Grove Studios by the fish farmer who had reared it. In tribute to its size, he called it Moby Dick. In defiance of every law that Isaac Newton formulated, it thrashed its tail with such ferocity that it leaped out of the glass tank in which it was imprisoned and came to rest on my insteps. It was not sodden socks which worried me, but the little red light on the nearby camera which began to glow. I was actually on the air when I made the major zoological discovery of my life. Trout, like swans, emit a mysterious sound at the point of death.

Being an old pro, I described the sincerity with which the Government was pursuing peace in Reykjavik against the background of the death rattle. To the watching public (who did not know what was going on under the table) it seemed that I was speaking and simultaneously moaning from my ankles. Next day, my private secretary asked if I had a cold. There had been noises during my television appearance which he felt it best to describe as a sneeze. My only consolation was that nothing worse could ever happen. Then came Cambridge 1987.

At first Cambridge was a joy. It was the last Saturday of the General Election campaign and I was the star speaker at the day's main event. Melvyn Bragg was Master of Ceremonies. John Williams played his guitar. I was not at all surprised to learn that BBC News had set up a studio in an ante-room. I left the platform smacking my lips in preparation for repeating the evening slogan: "Come Home to the Labour Party." It was then that I got the message that the programme was to be about taxation and that, if I declined to take part, my reticence would be reported during the broadcast.

It all began quite well with Martyn Lewis quoting one of my colleagues (whose name I have since forgotten) on the subject of possible tax increases under a future Labour Government. I endorsed my colleague's view. Mr Lewis then quoted another colleague (a name I have also forgotten) who, earlier that evening, had said something quite different. The next few moments were a purple blur. I was consoled by

TROUT, LIKE SWANS, EMIT A MYSTERIOUS SOUND AT THE POINT OF DEATH.

my friend (and colleague with a memorable name) John Smith.

"You did," he said, "all that a decent politician could do. You abused the interviewer."

Abusing the interviewer is a profitable political occupation. The public likes politicians to be civil to each other. But the one thing which they enjoy more than Sir Robin Day being rude to Members of Parliament is Members of Parliament being rude to Sir Robin Day. Any politician who, during the course of *Question Time*, grasped him by the bow-tie and flung him to the studio floor, would become a national hero overnight. There are local television reporters who deserve kicking in tender places no less than Sir Robin does. But because they are

"If you want anything, just riot."

unknown to the public at large, even a glancing blow is regarded as bullying. With local radio the wish to wound is often even greater. The fear to strike is increased by the cunning habit of employing diminutive female reporters who look sweet and innocent. They rarely are.

Their true character is often revealed not by their angelic smiles, but by the jungle combat uniforms which they wear when other people wear real clothes. In my experience there is a direct and absolute correlation between the numbers of visible zip-fasteners and the impertinence of the questions. These ladies wish that they were fighting in the jungle with Che Guevara, in Vietnam with the US Marine Corps, with the Selus Scouts in Zimbabwe or with anyone, anywhere. They have badges stuck on the side of their tape-recorders in the way that fighter pilots used to record kills on the noses of their aeroplanes. They begin the hand-to-hand combat with a stun shot.

"What exactly were you trying to say in your speech?"

Most of them subscribe to the Nick Ross school of television interviewing. Their idea for stimulating a lively debate is to contradict everything said to them. You know the way:

"Good morning and welcome to Call Nick Ross."

"Thank you very much for inviting me on to the programme. I'm very glad to be here."

"I'm surprised to hear you say that. Many people would expect you not to be glad to be here. How can you possibly justify being glad to be here?"

It is a hard question to answer. The interviewee can never make the wholly honest response. At least, I can never quite reply, "I'm glad to be here because it makes me feel like Gary Cooper." And that is the invariable effect of the confrontational interview. Here I am, the old gunfighter – with a slightly rusty Colt 45 and an increasingly arthritic trigger finger – having a quiet drink in the saloon when the kid with silver spurs comes in off the street to prove that he (or, in the case of local radio, she) is faster on the draw. Since the fantasy is my personal property, Gary Cooper always wins the shoot-out. But, reverting from the metaphorical to the literal, I doubt if the duel is very entertaining for the audience.

Last week in Brighton, a young man from the southern outpost of the BBC asked me a couple of questions concerning the subject of the interview and then slipped in a fast one about the re-election of Arthur Scargill – as if I would not notice that the topic had changed. I flatter myself that my answer was too boring, too diffuse and (most important of all) too long for inclusion in the night's bulletin. Having thus responded, I moved on to the man from local radio. He was, he told me, in my debt. During the General Election he had interviewed me without a tape in his recorder and I had recorded a second interview without complaining. In fact I had recorded a second interview without realising it. One of these days, a punk kid with an old hand-gun is going to drill me straight through the heart.

MONITORED
GAGGED AND BOUND
25p
No 666
Published somewhere in London

THE INDEPRUDENT

FRIDAY 1* FEBRUARY 198*

SUMMARY

Ordnance

Survey maps to be withdrawn

So little demand remains for Ordnance Survey maps of Britain, says a Government report out today, that they must be withdrawn in favour of new-style "Get You There" charts, illustrated in the style of Mabel Lucie Attwell. **Report, Page 2. Attwell biography, Page 5. No relation to late Winifred Attwell, Page 6**

Man confesses to over-eager spokesmanship

Neil Kinnock, 45, a party-fitter of no fixed aroma, confessed yesterday to interrupting the proceedings of the House of Commons by speaking out of turn. He will be given "a long sentence", stated the Attorney-General, "but then he's used to those"... **Page 2**

The pay's the thing

The Prime Minister's Press Secretary, not necessarily Mr Bernard Thingy, whoever he is, has refused to disclose the new salary fixed for the occu-

---

Downing St gesture means man must appear in court and long, long, long headline

"Utmost rigour of law" for beans man

By Julian Harmless
Political Editor

THE MAN who yesterday spilled a four-gallon drum of catering-quality baked beans over the steps of Number Ten Downing Street is to be charged, announced the Director of Public Prosecutions, Sir Denzil Umptie, last night.

In a rare press statement, issued from the steps of the DPP's Office in Great Thereabouts, Sir Denzil remarked: "The utmost rigour of the law must be visited upon this felon, whose offences, apart from stinking to high heaven, are probably more numerous than he imagines.

"At the moment, we have got him down for assault with a deadly comestible; criminal waste; obstructing the threshold of Her Majesty's Chief Minister; beanslaughter, and sauce. But you may be sure that other charges will follow. Causing a breach of the peas is a possibility, and we are looking into the technicalities of that. So is grievous bubbly harm.

"It is intolerable that random members of the public should thus disfigure one of the shrines of our democracy. I have it on good authority that the Prime Minister was on her knees this very morning, scrubbing that step.

"Let any man who reaches for a can-opener with felonious intent take note: the officers of the Crown will be down on you like a ton of beans. Bricks. Delete beans.

and so far 33 publishers have turned me book down, which I regard as suspect, they have been got at by the powers that be. If you ask me, ow, gerroff." Mr Threlfall did not terminate his statement voluntarily, it was alleged by onlookers.

Relatively few beans have been spilled on the steps of Number Ten in recent years. In June 1962, Harold Macmillan paused momentarily to detach a piece of chewing-gum from the sole of his shoe with a walking stick, but an alleged photograph of the incident was suppressed.

Another photographer, who claimed to be the custodian of a flashlight photo of

the present Prime Minister leaning out of an upstairs Downing Street window in curlers, throwing an old boot at a passing cat, was detained during Her Majesty's Pleasure in 1981.

Sources in the north of England claimed last night that Mr Threlfall once belonged to the banned Barnoldswick and District Bowls and Social Club, which allegedly served as a front in that area for disgruntled pensioners, many of them carriers of the so-called PILES virus. But nobody in Yorkshire was at home last night.

The doorstep last night was stated to be "as clean as can be expected" and ready to resume its duties this morning. Shortly after midnight, a sizeable crowd of well-wishers was already gathering, carrying floral tributes and cans of Mansion Polish.

Gibraltar bomb doesn't go off, killing nobody

From Simon Grimace in Gibraltar

A HUGE car-bomb, planted outside Gibraltar's luxury Tournedos Hotel, did not explode yesterday, scattering wreckage over a radius of 200 yards.

The mighty detonation, which would have shaken my apartment over a mile away, knocking my typewriter off the desk and my coffee into the waste-paper basket, fortunately did not occur. I would have gone into the bedroom to find the ceiling fan wrecked on the floor amid a sizeable weight of plaster. Instead, I didn't.

Crowds of people, many of them weeping, ran through the streets waving their arms and shouting. It just shows you how pleased people are when something nasty doesn't happen. Laughing soldiers later played pat-a-cake with them, which was

....**Page 17**
More than £10,000.....**Page 25**

in that sort of thing," he said, "and in any case they don't understand seasonal adjustments and so on. I think that most people will agree that when it comes to the salary of a person like Mrs Thatcher, piss off".

INSIDE

DESIGN: Those beautiful neutral shades 13

NICARAGUA: Never heard of it, I'm afraid, says Marie Helvin 9

CONTENTS

ing up – I'm afraid I'm not a very tidy person – and reflecting that it's good to be on an assignment where you never get things blowing up. I hate things blowing up. I mean, popcorn gives me a headache. So it's very nice here from that point of view.

One rock ape was killed in the aftermath of this explosion not happening. It died, said an army veterinary surgeon, from a combination of boredom and relief.

The Chairman of Crosse & Blackwell plc appealing to police for clemency near Horseguards Parade

accused man, Ali Akhbar Threlfall, 31, of Keighley, Yorks, was last night in custody at West End Central Police Station. In the moments between the deed itself and his arrest in Downing Street, he had made the following statement: "This is a protest on behalf of Government secrecy, in the wake of them not telling us what's going on, like. My driving licence went off to Swansea three years back and it was only by driving into a lamppost and having it endorsed that I forced them to give it me back.

"Also I was a spy for eighteen months"

So long the humble skunk, adieu the ring-tailed lemur

By Jeremy Handsaw
Natural History Editor

IT WAS a funny old day at London Zoo yesterday. No more did elephants trumpet, and nor did swans. Not a peep out of the parrots or the chimpanzees, loud though the clamour rang within the cages that had borne their names. I could have sworn I heard a hyena laughing. Yet no hyena laughed. Not as such. Yes, it was a funny old day.

It was the day the Home Secretary's injunction against "common and familiar" animal names fell upon Britain's zoological gardens. A forlorn leaflet, distributed at the gate in the rain, told the tale of the Government's case, as outlined by the Home Secretary in that not-too-distant bear-garden –sorry, *ursus horribilis*-garden – the House of Commons:

"It is the unshakable conviction of Her Majesty's Government that the provision of common or familiar names for the beasts displayed within such premises constitutes yet another intervention by the 'nanny state'. Competent natural historians and animal behaviourists, in other words the productive scientists in this area, whose work in earning Britain both prestige and money, obviously need access to correct Latin appellations. Latinists, too, who are forever grumbling at the decay of their discipline, will be grateful for the retention of these.

"The populace at large, meanwhile, remains perfectly free to enjoy the charming colourations and eccentric habits of our animal friends – their strange expressions, leakage of humours and so on. But to have a semi-informed public roaming these parks, making inaccurate and flippant observations of these creatures, many of which are of foreign origin and highly sensitive, is no longer an acceptable state of affairs.

"It is on this basis that the decision has been made to restore to animal parks something of the distancing quality of scholarship. If this measure has the added advantage of deleting from our vocabulary such unattractive terms as skunk, skink, gecko and wombat, then I shall feel doubly gratified in the exercise of this cleansing duty."

Assistant Head Mammal Keeper Fred Wallett was not so sure. "I'm not so sure, mate," he told me. "I've got a *capreolus capreolus* here that's schizophrenic already. Don't know if he's coming or going. Whoops, I think he's going. Excuse me."

Some people think the Home Secretary is a *rattus rattus*. I'm not saying I do. All I'm saying is, it was a funny old day at the zoo.

Colin Wooller

OH, I GOT THIS FOR *NOT* WRITING MY MEMOIRS

M.I.5.

From the same stable as the legendary Dick Francis
comes another thoroughbred among horsy crime thrillers –
a gripping tale packed with danger, drama
and sudden death

HOT MANURE

SHE WAS ALREADY half-asleep as I lay down beside her. She made a funny little noise and tried to wake up for my sake. "Go to sleep, Honey-pie," I whispered in her ear, kissing it lightly. "There is always tomorrow." With her head resting on my chest, I began to plait her beautiful, long brown hair and, as I ran my hand down the length of her body, stroking her, massaging her, feeling her shoulders, touching her neck, moulding my fingers around her ample croup and enjoying the contours of her sensual warm hock, I realised I was in love with this four-year-old mare and wanted to be with her for always, now that coffin-knee

had put her out of the St Leger and her racing days were over.

"Johnny!"

I sat bolt upright. We had nothing on between us apart from a pair of stable bandages, which left little to the imagination. I quickly shuffled some bedding straw over her, wrapped an old winner's blanket around myself and started doing things to the hay basket.

The door of the horse-box banged down and there stood the head lad, Tommy Wellshodd. As stable lads went, he was a right good-looker and, over the years, had been awarded quite a few rosettes by homosexual gymkhana judges. Now, however, his face was pale and his eyes blank with horror.

"Quickly! Something dreadful has happened!" he said, obviously very scared. "Giddy up, there!" and "Whoa, boy!" were the usual limits of his conversation. "Hurry! We haven't much time!"

Climbing into the Queen Mother's colours, I ran after him, matching him stride for stride; over the Pony Club cavaletti fences; over the water-jump; negotiating the parallel spread at Devil's Ditch; around the potted shrubs; dislodging a section from the brick wall and arriving, in a terrible lather, at the stable-door two furlongs out.

I looked inside and saw with incredulity him writhing on the floor, foam pouring from the corners of his mouth. It was the guv'nor and he was squealing horribly.

"Do something! Do something!" cried Tommy, his breeches visibly wet with the perspiration of panic.

I smothered an impulse to swear angrily as Tommy jumped up on to my shoulders and started beating me with a whip, shouting, "Come on, my beauty! You can do it!"

I knew what had to be done. I had seen people who had fallen into a manure pile before. They say you can only last a matter of minutes. Then you go down for the third and last time and the blackness gets you.

"Help! I'm drowning. My whole life is passing before me!"

The guv'nor was moments away from certain death. He could not hold his breath much longer and the brown, twiggy mess was already beginning to swallow him up. I felt my heart do a capriole inside my jerkin as I frantically tied together some knee-rolls and threw them over to him. It didn't work. I forgot to hold on to one end myself.

I looked around and saw a broom. It was my only hope. Stretching over towards him, I held the thing out for him to grab. Tommy could not watch. He had put on some blinkers. At last I managed to get the broom handle into the guv'nor's hands and dragged him free.

He was still alive, although steaming profusely, when we reached the hospital. The doctor was coolly clinical as he came out of the post-operative unit.

"For a moment we thought we'd lost him, but he's going to be okay," he said, and then walked off back down the corridor pursued by a cloud of flies.

I sighed with profound and urbane relief. The guv'nor was a friend. He had been good to me. I had no parents. I spent my early years on a shelf in a bloodstock agency. He gave me a job, paid me when he remembered and gave me funny little yellow tablets to keep my weight down. One day I hoped to know him well enough to be able to drop the apostrophe whenever I referred to him.

I went back to the tack-room to buff up a few martingales and do some thinking. Who could have done such a thing and why? It was no accident; you could bet on that. People don't just fall into manure. They're pushed. Then it clicked. Bobby Skewbald, the stable's leading jockey, had been acting very suspiciously ever since he underwent a compulsory after-race urine test at Wincanton. He had been seen riding side-saddle on early morning gallops and a biography of Anna Sewell had been found in his bedroom. Rumour was that he also wore a nightie during the Snap.

Then, from behind me, came the unmistakable sound of a nose-bag full of boiled barley being trodden on. I turned around to see Bobby and hear him saying, "This is the end of the road, Johnny boy."

"What's the SP, Bobby?" I asked him in a casual way.

He laughed. "You don't know?" He laughed again. It was a curious laugh which contained no mirth.

After a pause, I said, "No."

"Manure! That's what! Soil fertility's big business these days. Suckers will pay big money for top-quality livestock waste. I've made a packet feeding gardeners' and farmers' morbid craving for nitrogen, phosphorus and potassium. You know how much a ton of well-rotted manure can fetch on the streets? You're standing in a fortune."

I felt numb and stood speechless. I had never met a manure baron ring.

"But why bump off the guv'nor?" I asked eventually.

"Ever since this stable's started losing, the market's dried up. Nobody's interested in dung from a losing stable; it breeds losing plants. I figured, get rid of the guv'nor, a new one comes in, new horses, fresh business. Now it's your turn."

In his hand he had a de-worming gun. It was pointing my way. God, I thought, I've had it. The starter's flag is up for the Last

"Well, it doesn't look like jet lag to me."

Trump. "But why? You haven't told me why, Bobby."

"I am hard done by. Like," he said, picking his words carelessly.

"Like what?"

"Don't draw me into metaphors. I'm useless at metaphors." His voice was loaded with anger, his eyes blazed with madness and his pockets bulged with meal. I felt an unpleasant uprush of salt-lick. What corrupting things fish-scraps and barn-yard refuse can be, I mused. His finger tightened on the trigger of the evil device.

"You don't understand, I don't win races any more. I'm no, er, good. I want to become a woman jockey so I can be successful again. All this is to pay for a sex-change operation. I met this chap at Newton Abbot. He's got a clinic…"

At that moment who should burst through the door pulling a tandem-disc harrow but Honey-pie.

I heard Bobby utter a single scream before he was spread in a uniform layer across a wide geographic area. I rushed into Honey-pie's arms. She had risked everything to save my life. I couldn't keep back the tears as I tried to thank her in the only way I knew how, by a pat, a sugar-lump and a loving rub-down with a stiff-bristled dandy brush.

THE END

NEXT WEEK: The Farrier did it

"I bet you can't guess what I'm standing on!"

A KOOL DUDE FACES SIXTY

STANLEY REYNOLDS
gives Tom Wolfe two fleas in the ear and a pat on the back

The White-Suited Sepulchre himself, Thomas Wolfe, in creep's clothing

MAMMOTH sales and heaps of praise greeted the publication of America's most famous journalist Tom Wolfe's first novel, *The Bonfire of the Vanities*. The process looks soon to be followed in Britain. Jonathan Cape, who are not publishing the big, 560-page book until February 8, have sold out before publication. Cape is busy right now re-printing.

Tom Maschler, head of Cape, seated at a Café Royal luncheon where another of his American-import authors, Brian Moore, was picking up *The Sunday Express Book of the Year Award*, told me (and Moore who was seated with us) that he "had seen nothing like the anticipation" Wolfe's first novel was creating. Maschler then went on to sneer at *The Sunday Times* for printing Wolfe's photo on the cover of the colour supplement when they had no real story about Wolfe inside. There were Nobel Prize winners, Maschler said, who were *not* getting the sort of attention Wolfe was getting right now in Britain. Brian Moore sat through this looking rather like a leprechaun who's lost his pot of gold. This was, after all, his day. He was picking up the £20,000 prize, and yet his very own publisher was talking on and on about what a great man this journalist-turned-novelist Wolfe was.

Feeling sorry for the leprechaun, I asked Brian Moore what he thought of *The Bonfire of the Vanities*. He said it wasn't really a novel. At least it wasn't the sort of novel people who usually read novels would consider a novel. It was journalism and all about "social mores". He said it was a big success with the lower intellectual orders, pop sort of people, in New York and in Los Angeles (where Moore lives), who don't usually read novels.

People who do not read novels but who have read Tom Wolfe's journalism, all of which has been printed in book form, will not know what Brian Moore was talking about; or, for that matter, why a very rich, big, bestselling writer of non-fiction like Wolfe has been so overwrought about the publication of his first novel; but writing novels is playing with the big boys.

The first collection of journalism in the mid-Sixties, *The Kandy-Kolored Tangerine-Flake Stream-line Baby* (the title is a reference to a customised car) made journalist Tom practically a dollar millionaire, also a household name in that part of the house where the kids live. The next non-fiction book, *The Electric Kool-Aid Acid Test*, which was Wolfe's report on the acid-tripping travels of Ken Kesey, made even more money and fame for Wolfe.

LEARN TO LOVE THE BLACKMAN

Much other amazingly popular journalism followed. Wolfe coined phrases people loved: "radical chic", "the me generation". He became a pop-star himself. A dandy in a white suit, he had the sort of fame only big novelists like Ernest Hemingway and Scott Fitzgerald had. He wrote about modern art (*The Painted Word*, he didn't like it) he wrote about modern architecture (*Bauhaus to Our House*, he hated it). Other journalists came to interview him; according to the snooty gal at Cape's publicity department who, it seems,

BRIAN MOORE SAT LOOKING LIKE A LEPRECHAUN WHO'S LOST HIS POT OF GOLD.

rather likes turning journalists down for a change – they are already queuing up to interview Tom when he arrives in London next week.

Wolfe was asked about his clothes – they are all tailor-made by Vincent Nicolosi; he wears a homburg, spats, or, at least, shoes made to look like he's wearing spats; he carries a white umbrella to go with the white suits, which he's wearing again since the shame of *Saturday Night Fever* when John Travolta in a white suit got every greaseball in New York wearing one, and Tom had to get Vince to thread a pin-stripe through them. They asked him what he thought of the Statue of Liberty. And they asked him about politics.

When they asked that, some-

DEEPLY DISTURBED SINCE BIRTH

thing dreadful happened. Wolfe turned out to be a Hawk. Everyone had assumed, what with all this wonderful writing about the kids today and drugs and rock music and the High Art of America's Low Life, that Wolfe was a liberal, one of those many Southerners (he's from Virginia) who came North and learned to love the blackman.

DRAFT-DODGER TURNED HAWK

But here he was moaning about America's defeat in Vietnam, as if he were just another Redneck Southern Hill Billy.

"The sons of the merchant and managerial classes in America sat this one out, in college, graduate school, Canada and Sweden," he said about Vietnam.

Look who was talking? Tom Wolfe, the draft-dodger of the Korean War. He sat that one out at

THAT CREEPY NEW YORK IRISH LOVE FOR A SWELL.

graduate school, at Yale. Even after the war ended, the draft continued, and Wolfe continued to sit that one out at Yale. He stayed at graduate school for years and years. (He had been at the small and chi-chi Washington and Lee for four years before Yale.)

Then, in 1979, he wrote that positive hymn to John Wayneism, *The Right Stuff*, the book about the jet-jockeys turned astronauts. The liberals of New York, who thought Wolfe was doing it only to annoy, because he knew it teased when he did that "radical chic" business, were truly shocked. Wolfe was a war-monger.

Even his best friends said so. Ed Hayes, a working-class New York Irish, ex-Bronx District Attorney, a neighbour and pal of Wolfe in Southampton, Long Island, where Wolfe "summers", talks about Wolfe being of the "Wasp warrior class from the South".

THE WHITE FEATHER

Hayes, who has a character based on him in the big novel, is only 39 – Wolfe is all of 57 now – and he has a sort of starry-eyed, sentimental, New York Irish Handkerchief Head view of the draft-dodging Wolfe. Hayes is quoted saying of his famous chum's hawk-like stance, "The real English dandies were aristocrats who were usually soldiers, and aggressive and athletic. Tom sort of

represents that. It's that Protestant warrior mentality." Hayes would seem to have that puppy dog-like devotion to Wolfe, that creepy lower-class New York Irish love for a swell which can be seen in old movies in which Jack Carson, as the lovable New York Irishman, befriends the toff, played by Cary Grant.

Where, one wonders, was the English dandy's warrior spirit during the Vietnam war? While many New Journalists braved Vietcong shot and shell, and Agent Orange and napalm, from their own side, Tom Wolfe was down at Vince's getting his inside-leg measured. If the New Journalism was the High Calling and Tom Wolfe its High Priest, he should have been where the story was, which was Vietnam. He wrote one article, about the landing deck of an aircraft carrier. It is an odd piece. One is never quite sure if Wolfe was there or not. Perhaps he skyed out to the Bay of Tonkin for one day on a freebie. No book came out of it, not even a second article. Somebody should have sent him a white feather for the white suit.

NO PACK ON BACK HE

The belligerent Tom Wolfe has actually never walked anywhere with a pack on his back and yet he dares to attack the opponents of the Vietnam war, accusing them of cowardice. "The unspeakable and inconfessible goal of the New Left

"I say, jolly good! I think I'll take a couple of boxes."

on the campuses," he said, "had been to transform the shame of the fearful into the guilt of the courageous."

It is, of course, legitimate to stick up for the Grunts of Vietnam. It is not, after all, against the law to do so. But to blacken the opponents of the war, hedging his bets by calling them "the New Left opponents", cowards, full of "the shame of the fearful", is neither right nor proper.

The truth is that Tom Wolfe, getting on now, has reverted to type. At least politically. We shall

perhaps have to wait a while longer before he starts talking about "Yankee Jewboys giving our nigras bad ideas" but something like that will no doubt come as the Boy Wonder Journalist of the Sixties himself enters his sixties.

In the meantime, no matter what *real* novelists like Brian Moore may say, one has excellent reports of The Novel from New York. Wolfe is "Addison and Steele", someone said, adding that Wolfe was also "early Thackeray". But, hold on, that someone was the modest Wolfe himself.

"For heaven's sake – if you don't like it, spit it out!"

BROADWAY '88

THERE is more to the current New York theatre than British musicals, though with seven of them either playing or rehearsing this week you could be forgiven for thinking not a lot. Broadway guides presently list twenty-three mainstream playhouses open, precisely half the number in the West End, and of those only four are offering new American drama, the rest being given over to either imports or revivals.

Far and away the most interesting of the new plays is Lee Blessing's **A Walk in the Woods** (*Booth*), which clearly deserves to pick up awards for the best new script of the season, if only because it suggests, for the first time in my recollection since Arthur Miller's *Incident at Vichy* all of twenty-five years ago, that the commercial theatre in New York can sustain, just, a Shavian debate about the nature of humanity and power politics.

A Walk in the Woods starts from the truth of a Geneva disarmament conference a few years ago, at which the leading Russian and American negotiators were able, on a walk in a nearby forest, to achieve at least a temporary degree of unanimity. But what we get now is a two-character confrontation in which a political odd couple, seated on a park bench reminiscent of *Rappaport*, sort out their personal and national and ideological differences with an intelligence and good humour and emotional insight which is a joy to observe. Sam Waterston as the callow American, and Robert Prosky as the wonderfully wise and witty old Soviet survivor, a Gromyko figure moving on towards Falstaff, give two performances which come as sharp reminders that the very best American actors have not in fact all gone over to movies.

Of the imports, **The Phantom of the Opera** (at the *Majestic*) is the only one playing with its three original London stars, and Hal Prince's production seems to have matured and strengthened hugely since I first saw it in London eighteen months ago. Michael Crawford is still mesmeric as the mad organist, but both Sarah Brightman and Steve Barton are looking and sounding vastly more confident, while Maria Bjornson's stunning set now has a whole new Parisian skyline. The production has also been extensively rechoreographed by Gillian Lynne, so "Masquerade" is now a dazzling showstopper, while hearing that score again makes me think I was originally unduly dismissive of it. Indeed it's not as inventive as *Cats* or as dramatic as *Evita*, but in there somewhere are songs of such lyrical period romanticism that they could have come straight from the Vienna Woods.

Up at *Lincoln Centre*, the only native musical selling out nightly is Jerry Zaks's briskly efficient revival of **Anything Goes**, which starts with a scratchy recording of Old King Cole himself on the title track and ends with his portrait being lowered centre stage. Patti Lupone is a highly starry Reno Sweeney, the rest of the cast manage a glossy roadshow adequacy, and there are some long-lost songs of rare delight.

The show that was for me the highlight of the week, if not the year: Stephen Sondheim's **Into the Woods** at the *Martin Beck*. For those of us who believe Sondheim to be the greatest composer/lyricist working in world theatre, his fourteenth musical comes as yet another indication of his breathtaking versatility and courage and invention. Vastly grimmer than the Grimm Brothers, this is the tale of a group of childhood characters led by Cinderella and Little Red Ridinghood back into the woods of their legends, some years after their stories were supposed to have ended happily ever after.

If you can conceive of a *Wizard of Oz* rewritten by Franz Kafka, you will have some faint notion of what is going on here: Sondheim's central thesis is that nothing ever really ends happily ever after, but that if you can come to terms with your own isolation then paradoxically it becomes immediately possible to find a friend.

Bernadette Peters, as an outrageously high-camp wicked witch of the woods, holds the plot to its fairytale origins at first, but this gradually becomes a musical about the point at which childhood dreams turn into nightmares, and about the barriers separating youth from age, fantasy from disillusion. *Into the Woods* is the musical J. M. Barrie never wrote, about the darkness of growing up, but it is also once again from Sondheim a lesson to every other musicalmaker in the business in how to create a cynical and yet ultimately loving show about the sheer awfulness of having your dreams come true. *Into the Woods* is just wonderful, and the sooner we get it over to this side of the Atlantic the better for us all.

Back home at the *Aldwych*, Tom Stoppard's **Hapgood**, his first new play in almost seven years, is a characteristic chess game without a board, in which a superlative cast (Felicity Kendal, Nigel Hawthorne, Roger Rees) finesse their way through a plot of labrynthine and often impenetrable complexity, largely concerned with the connections between espionage and physics. Peter Wood opens his production with a marvellously choreographed ballet of secret agents rampaging through poolside cloakrooms, before arranging his company into an often dazzling exhibition of bricks without straw: like Sondheim and Shaffer (Tony), Stoppard is obsessed by puzzles of unreality, but here we are only occasionally allowed to join his game and the outcome is an odd mix of Le Carré and Einstein, in which twins are usually the answer and sometimes even the question.

HAPGOOD NIGEL HAWTHORNE *as Blair*
FELICITY KENDAL *as Hapgood* ROGER REES *as Kerner*

A SMALL FAMILY BUSINESS
MICHAEL GAMBON as Jack McCracken   SIMON CADELL as Benedict Hough

NANA   BELINDA DAVISON as Nana

THE TWO NOBLE KINSMEN
HUGH QUARSHIE as Arcite   AMANDA HARRIS as Emilia   GERARD MURPHY as Palamon

WAITING FOR GODOT
ALEC McCOWEN as Vladimir
COLIN WELLAND as Pozzo
JOHN ALDERTON as Estragon

WISH YOU WERE HERE
TOM BELL *as Eric*
EMILY LLOYD *as Lyhda*

BLUE VELVET
KYLE MacLACHLAN
as Jeffrey Beaumont
ISABELLA ROSSELLINI
as Dorothy Vallens

THE COLOR OF MONEY
TOM CRUISE *as Vincent*
MARY ELIZABETH MASTRANTONIO *as Carmen*
PAUL NEWMAN *as Fast Eddie Felson*

DILYS POWELL *Cinema*
DICKENS OF A TREAT

LATE acquaintance with **Little Dorrit** leaves me thinking that it is not only the most political but the most solid of the Dickens novels; perhaps that is why, though as a child I knew most of the major works, this one was not put into my hands and remained unfamiliar till years afterwards. Now it comes late to the cinema, late enough to be allowed to command space and extent; the *Little Dorrit* (U) at the *Curzon West End* is in two parts of roughly three hours each, with a cast numbered not by the score but almost by the hundred. Part One is adversity, *Nobody's Fault* (and everybody's fault). Part Two is *Little Dorrit's Story*, the triumph, not spectacular but modest, of endeavour and self-respect. The unassuming heroine emerges as one of Dickens's less maddeningly saintly women: in Sarah Pickering's performance one likes her, as the hero Arthur Clennam (Derek Jacobi, who also is dead right) slowly learns to love her.

Their story is told against the background of an England and a London of squalors and gentilities, trust and betrayal: a London with business trickery and financial collapse, social pretensions, poverty in dark streets and incompetence in government quarters (the Circumlocution Office is one of the writer's great creations). The film is written for the screen and directed with a sensibility both personal and historical by Christine Edzard. It is the story of a seamstress born in the shadow of jail and of a middle-aged man back from twenty years in the East to a crippled woman's loveless house (there is an effective performance as the woman by the late Joan Greenwood).

But really this is the story of a prison and the people in it. The Marshalsea, the debtor's London prison, is at the heart of *Little Dorrit*; Dickens's father was sent to the Marshalsea, little Dorrit's father, William Dorrit, is an inmate for the first part of the narrative – he has been there so long that he is called the Father of the Marshalsea, and absurdly he has come to claim that as an honourable title. Little Dorrit works to feed him, but he never acknowledges her services and sacrifices. Grandly he talks of his quarters: "The air is good. Blows over the Surrey Hills"; he is a figure of pretensions, risible but somehow never contemptible. He is played with a delicate balance of comedy and tragedy by Alec Guinness, played as if he believed in himself; perhaps it is the actor's presence, powerful through the humiliations he ignores, which makes one think of the prison as the centrepiece of the movie. Mr Dorrit comes from the very bones of life.

Little Dorrit has an astonishing gallery of characters, from the stout, garrulous Flora (Miriam Margolyes) into whom the hero's first love has grown, to Mrs Merdle (Eleanor Bron), the social-minded wife of the swindling financier. And we have time to look at them, time to know them and see how convincingly they belong to their society. One recognises them, one accepts them; their faces are as one imagines, they wear clothes which look as if they were worn by choice. The costumes could hardly be better; and one doesn't find oneself pausing to wonder if the London streets really looked like that. There is one regret: the novel hasn't the wealth of extravagant characters one cherishes in other Dickens masterpieces. No Mrs Gamp, no Squeers: the solidity may be created, but there isn't the fun. One should be grateful, though, for a full Dickens movie. Not the first good one: *Great Expectations* was a good film. But this time one can watch a Dickens on the screen which has the stretch and richness of a grand novel. And it is the first time.

Horror for 1988: **Predator** (*18, Leicester Square Theatre, Odeon Marble Arch*) is more inventive than most of its kind. Arnold Schwarzenegger leads his commandos into the jungle to rescue men captured by Latin American guerillas. The victims have been executed, but he meets a supernatural force which enjoys picking his men off one by one. Good visual effects: one is intially puzzled by wavering whitish shapes which turn out to be the human prey seen in the "heat vision" of the predator. The creature is played by Kevin Peter Hill, encountered the other day as the amiable monster of *Bigfoot and the Hendersons*.

Technically the cinema continues to invent. To be frank, the inventions often strike one as excess of zeal, but presumably they please somebody. **The Adventures of Mark Twain** (*U, ICA Children's Cinema Club*) is made in something called Claymation; it looks vaguely as if performed by puppets, but it is the product of animators working with clay to create from it the shapes of action and emotion. Music and voices do the rest; the director (and the inventor of the process) is Will Vinton. The movie is a fantasy about Twain, who declares that he came with Halley's comet and announces (as he sets off in a lunatic airship) that he means to go out with it. Reflections on his life, especially memories of his wife, are involved; but fictional characters, including Huckleberry Finn and Tom Sawyer, are stowaways in the ship and their presence brings fragments of their stories linked with the adventures of the unusual space-ship. James Whitmore provides Mark Twain's voice.

Futurism in **Master of the Universe** (*PG, Cannons Haymarket, Oxford Street, Bayswater, Fulham Road*): the usual battles between good (He-Man, played by athletic Dolph Lundgren) and evil (Skeleton, played by Frank Langella with a truncated nose). Some of the action takes place on the planet Eternia; but some of it concerns Earth and a cop (James Tolkan) who has natural difficulty in understanding the use of moonpower, a cosmic key and the part played by a friendly dwarf (Billy Barty) and a tonal code. Much of the tale, however, is occupied by electric effects and laser guns, and by now we all know about them.

At the *ICA*, **Sarraounia** (*15*), directed by Med Hondo, whose version of an African novel echoes a passage of African history: the terrorist path of a renegade French officer from the Sudan at the end of the nineteenth century and the successful resistance of Sarraounia, Queen of the Aznas. A little precise historical confirmation would be welcome.

LITTLE DORRIT
SARAH PICKERING *as Little Dorrit*

CHILD'S PLAY

CHILDREN's television presenter Jools (or it might have been Arry) was translating for a pop-person. "Issmore," he suggested, "issmora wayer life, innit? Yenno, cloze an errifin." "Ass-rye," replied the entertainer, with the relieved air of one whose philosophy has been satisfactorily nutshelled, "Ass-*rye!*"

Errifin fer kids, so far as ITV's weekend offerings are concerned, is a show called **7T3** in high-tech-jargon memory of its predecessor *Number Seventy Three*, which delineation is now regarded as too domestically and socially old-hat to encapsule adequately the boxed-up, computerised, sit-there-and-consume, yenno-cloze-and-errifin that is now the modality of modern childhood.

The thinkers responsible for this particular conglomeration of Kiddy-watch, Kiddy-buy, are either unaware of, or hostile to, the fact that all children are bilingual in the sense they have a monosyllabic code for transmitting messages to each other, and another one known as the English Language to fall back on in times of emergency. The idea is to inhibit passage from private code to the broader means of communication by the introduction of a third linguistic style employed by Children's Television Presenters who are obviously selected for their glottal stoppages and impenetrable regional accents.

Thus, when a show guest speaks in standard English, or makes some rough attempt to distinguish between one vowel and consonant and another, a CTP filters his or her message through CTP-speak. "Magnetraction," says the guest in explanation of his toy racing car circuit. "Maggie-oo?" cries Dawn, who maintains her image as an undaunting adult by staggering everywhere on roller-skates, concave with ingratiation. "Yer wunt fink, woodja," they go, and "Owny Juss" and "famess larse words". William, a visitor, has run along the Great Wall of China and has a traveller's tale to tell. But alas, the lad is articulate and must be spoken for. "Less loora vidjo", says Jools or Arry (or it might have been Kim). "Thassa gub idea."

Within this mess of institutionalised bonhomie, the commercial-proper is barely distinguishable from the main event, nor, I suspect, is it meant to be. Junk food, footwear, cloze an errifin for the young, patent analgesics, dental fixative and deodorant soap for their housebound minders are all seamlessly slotted in with the rest of the commodity. From time to time viewers are invited to feed CTPs with jokes, which is rather like making a baby put its mother's rattle back in her pram. The little souls oblige, too; dial the magic *7T3 TV* and give of their very best, all unknowing what horrible twenty-first century plot they're being softened up for.

If their addiction was *BBC 1*, they'd get straight to the crunch. Not only do they sound their aitches, their way of impressing the new meritocracy of the Eighties upon tender minds is nothing short of miraculous. **Knock-Knock** is New! New! New! – a kidded up version of those fingers-on-buttons, prizes-prizes-prizes quiz shows beloved of the partially witted. In the first stage of the game, children are made to take part in a riddle-cracking contest to decide which of them is to be excluded from the second half. The lucky finalists are then put on contraptions resembling bicycles and asked more riddles while being harassed by ticking parking meters, winking traffic-lights and the Master of Ceremonies.

"I am not dandruff but you can find me on people's shoulders" is one such enigma, invented for the availability of a man with a parrot. Children believing themselves to be in possession of the answer to these arcane teasers must present themselves at a door and say, "Knock-knock". If their answer is wrong, the door springs open and a refuse bag is flung in their faces. The erroneous infant is then made to crouch in a rubbish skip, a punishment much vaunted by our MC, as in "Are you sure? You don't want to go in the skip, do you?"

When all but one victim has been sussed out, the surviving child is then put through the further humiliation of having to tear-arse round the set to find his or her prizes. Against, of course, the clock. "Run, Kirsty, run!" the MC exhorts, and an exhausted child tastes the fruits of victory. No, not that one, that's a booby prize. Bad luck. Run some more. Ah, a tuppenny box of coloured pencils. Wonderful. Run some more, Kirsty. Quick, quick, the clock's ticking up. Soon you'll be all grown up and this will then be terrifyingly for real.

Only on *Channel 4* are they allowing childhood to move at its own pace. They don't do much, but what there is you wouldn't mind your winkies watching. Sunday morning's **Gum Tree** has the old-fashioned virtue of being a nice man telling a funny story as though he was enjoying himself and suffered no qualms about his vocabulary exceeding the 250 common word series.

Then there's **Helping Henry**; not so much a programme, more a way of looking at the world. A space traveller disguised as a dining-room chair enlists the assistance of a small boy to probe the intricacies of life on earth. So far, boy and chair have combined their not dissimilar talents for innocent objectivity to conclude that there are many, many people roaming about, very few of whom we know anything whatever about, beyond the mutuality of two-leggedness. As philosophic observations go, I see no fault in this one. It should, and will, run and run.

HELPING HENRY
JEREMY HARDY *as Henry*   IAN HARRIS *as Stephen*

INSPECTOR MORSE
KEVIN WHATELY *as Det Sgt Lewis*
JOHN THAW *as Chief Inspector Morse*
ANTHONY BATE *as Bernard Crowther*

PARKINSON ONE-TO-ONE
MICHAEL PARKINSON
JACK LEMMON
WALTER MATTHAU

THE FEAR
IAIN GLEN *as Carl*

**CARIANO AND
THE COURTESANS**
PAUL McGANN *as Cariani*
LUCY HANCOCK *as Maria*

*"Yes, certainly, sir. Turn right here, along the passage and it's behind
a big rock in the corner. You can't miss it."*

BARGEPOLE
·················

SHHH! Can't say a thing, old boy, not a jot or tittle, oh dear me, no more than my jobsworth, you understand. Mum's the word. Walls have ears. But I will tell you this much (*leans forward, makes huge pantomime of looking around, takes pipe out of mouth and breathes foetid gusts over innocent reader*), I am getting worried about the Government. But don't tell anyone I told you so. (*Frowns, taps side of nose with pipe-stem, purses lips, nods sagely.*)

Did you see the new rule, that photographers are not allowed to take photographs outside the Old Bailey any more? Oh dear me, no. We can't have them standing in the street taking…*drawing by light*, is it? Sensitive emulsion? Perhaps some of the gentlemen of the press have been taking "sensitive emulsion" internally! (*Wheezy sycophantic laughter from barristers.*) Whatever next? Oh, definitely quite out of the question and My Lordship will deal very severely with any miscreants. Do you understand? V-e-r-y sev-e-r-e-ly. We cannot have the law brought into disrepute by showing pictures of the court buildings and do not give me that trash about justice having to be seen to be done. We are not here to discuss justice. We are here to enforce the Law.

In order to ensure that the majesty of the Government is maintained in the highest regard, My Lordship adjudges that all photographers should be obliged to place their photographic equipment in a place of safe custody under the auspices and jurisdiction of. Namely and to wit, above a sweet-shop some eight minutes' walk from the noble and hallowed Precincts of this Court. That should fix them. We have had enough of those boyos with their sheepskin coats and runny noses. Did I say "Government" a minute ago? Very well. So be it.

From time to time I meet unfortunate and benighted souls crouching over halves of Guinness who think that "everything will be all right." I see it as my duty to spoil

WE HAVE HAD ENOUGH OF THOSE BOYOS WITH THEIR SHEEPSKIN COATS AND RUNNY NOSES.

their fun, pointing out that we are governed by an oligarchy which requires us to adopt the contradictory mannerisms of intense and eager enterprise and a base lack of curiosity. These poor men with their large wives and damp raincoats merely smile smugly and wipe the froth from their lips (a trick a number of our Ministers could usefully learn).

"Do you know what?" they say. "It'll all be all right because do you know what I'm telling you, you can push the Englishman so far but *you can push him no further*."

I am most anxious to learn how far "so far" may be. Over the last few years we have been pushed a fearful distance and not a squeak have we heard from anyone at all except those sickly youngsters of the sort who stand around outside South Africa House complaining about Mr Mandela. The loss of Mr Mandela's liberty is no doubt a great distress to himself and his family but it is nothing compared to the losses which have been inflicted upon us lately.

Never mind blathering about no pictures outside the Old Bailey. The only thing that will do is give a few judges an even greater sense of satisfaction and tax the descriptive abilities of the court reporters a little further. What we should be worried about is things like the Cleveland business, where one of the families, so gravely hounded and abused by the contemptible Social Services and the absurd and repellent Dr Higgs, has been banned by a court from ventilating their grievances. We are *not entitled to know*, any more than we are entitled to know how it is that this dreadful, hatchet-faced woman, who by her own admission interfered with her own children by way of "research", is allowed to practise medicine before she has conclusively, and to the satisfaction of the nation, proved that she is sane and responsible so to do.

We should be concerned about the absurdities of the *Spycatcher* business. This has been rehearsed to wearisome lengths but it remains quite clear that a large clique of official ne'er-do-wells, their heads firmly jammed up their backsides, are prepared to spend any amount of money on demonstrating the fact that we are *not entitled to know*.

We should be concerned about the ridiculous waste of money on television advertisements shouting at us in a manner both patronising and salacious about the illusory danger of Aids to heterosexuals. "You cannot tell by looking who's got Aids," they yell, and, ignoring the patronising illiteracy of the observation, we might well observe that neither can you tell by listening who has three legs, nor by smelling who has bright green skin and a television aerial growing out of the top of his or her head. Why are we being given offensive and wasteful pap instead of the truth? Because we are there only to be bossed about; *we are not entitled to know*.

And, most of all, we should be concerned about the Education Reform Bill. This appalling, smug, idiots' charter gives the Secretary of State the absolute power to tell universities what they may and may not think about, or talk about, or teach; and if they disobey, to take their money away. And to make sure that there can be no mistake, it offers no protection to the universities' freedom of speech. Not only are we not entitled to know; we are not even (it seems) entitled to ask; and this dreadful Bill, which might be designed to offer us a limitless future of greedy, hyperactive, but intellectually docile, estate agents, computer retailers and public relations men, will, if it becomes law, permit the Government to ensure that future generations simply do not have the intellectual equipment to know that there are any questions which need to be asked.

I think it is time we reached for our culture.

"Run up your clock, lady?"

NOT THE GAY GORDONS

A recent screening of My Beautiful Laundrette *has led to uproar on Stornoway. Rev Murdo Alex MacLeod told* The West Highland Free Press: *"Men falling in love offends the deepest sensitivity in every Lewisman. They are grieved at heart." Our Scottish Correspondent DAVID MILSTED reports*

Alasdair Mungo "Butane" MacLeod, councillor and Calor Gas concessionaire, finished welding the fly of his trousers and laid the torch, still glowing, aside.

"Ye're still glowing, Alasdair Mungo," observed Cllr Hector Hamish MacLeod, lay preacher and part-time winkle merchant.

"Aye," his companion smiled grimly. "Likely it'll be wet out."

The others, all fellow-councillors, were waiting outside in the spongy gloom: Donald Calum MacLeod, Factor to the MacLeod Estate; Dougal Fergus MacLeod, seaweed broker; Finlay John MacLeod, freelance biscuit importer and professional mourner, and Gillespie Pik von Königsberg MacLeod-Botha, the community special constable. All wore black overcoats; each carried, under his left arm, a sawn-off *cromag*, or Hebridean walking-stick, adapted for use at close quarters by having its tip hollowed out and filled with molten lead from the roof of the Episcopalian Church.

Alasdair Mungo surveyed them lengthily, each in turn, as if defying them to return his gaze.

It began to rain.

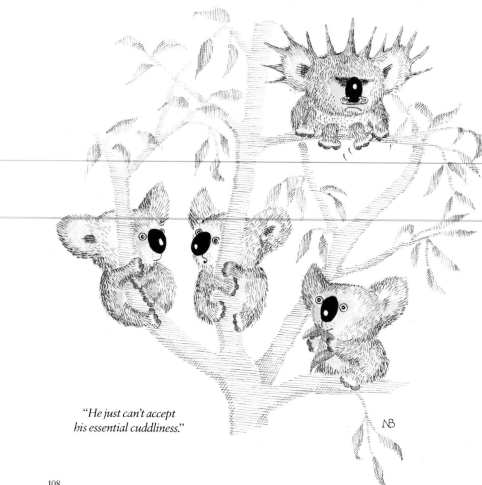

"He just can't accept his essential cuddliness."

He spoke:

"Our last mission, brothers. Let us check our equipment. Old Testaments?" They patted their right coat pockets. "Sermons o' John Knox?" They patted their left. "*Now*" – his eyes narrowed, lasering the mist – "*let me see your precautions!*"

They raised their coats. He scrutinised them, grunting his approval of the leather bootlaces, the army webbing, the mild steel plating, and other defences against Satan's vilest wiles. He stopped, frowning, at Gillespie Pik.

"What's yon bulge in yer troosers, man?" he queried.

"Yon's a crikkiter's box, Butane," the constable replied. "A prissint from my cousin in the Orange Free State."

"Cricket, d'ye say?" Cllr Butane MacLeod took three slow paces forward – then, suddenly and without warning, struck a mighty blow with his *cromag* at the confluence of the policeman's thighs. MacLeod-Botha, unblinking, let drop his coat front.

"It'll do," commented Alasdair Mungo.

They set off down the road with that wide-legged, rolling gait characteristic of Free Presbyterians the world over, passing the smoking ruins of the Lewis Film Society on the way to their rendezvous with the Reverend Aeneas "Mad Mitch" MacLeod in his cliff-top command headquarters.

They beat on the turf roof with their *cromags*.

It began to rain a little harder.

From inside came the noise of empty Export cans being thrust manfully aside, then the Rev MacLeod himself emerged, blinking, into the hyperborean noonday light.

"I am ready, brothers," he said, indicating with a blunt nicotic forefinger the rivets below his waistband. Councillor MacLeod peered past him at the crates stacked against the bothy's peat-panelled walls. "Later, Finlay John," snapped the Reverend. "If we're quick about it, we should still have half an hour before the Education Committee meeting."

"Aye, fair enough," grunted the mute. "Get on wi' it then, your Reverence, gie's the blessing."

The Rev MacLeod pinched out his Kensitas and cleared his throat. "O Loard," he croaked, "give unto Thy Elect, we pray, the will so to overcome the sins of this our wayward brother Daft Bob MacLeod that he may be brought to see the Truth of Thine Eternal Righteousness or, failing that, to work him over to Thy satisfaction with the Rods of Penitence, Amen."

It began to pour.

They proceeded down the cliff path to the beachcomber's home, an upturned boat above spring high water mark. They found Daft Bob squatting over a box on the shingle floor.

"What hae ye goat there, MacLeod?" bellowed the Reverend. "Come oan, man, God sees ye!" He seized a small flat packet from the man's trembling hand and shook out its foil-wrapped contents.

"Ah foond them!" squeaked the beachcomber. "Ah did so find them!" He huddled against the wall of his rude dwelling, cringing up at his visitors.

"Mates," read the Reverend, then tossed the packet aside. "D'ye ken what these are, ye reprobate?" he thundered.

"Ah-Ah thocht," stammered Daft Bob, "Ah thocht Ah could sell them tae, tae…" His voice trailed hopelessly away.

"Aye! Tae the shoap in Biggotsvoe! Tae Asif Iqbal Aziz MacLeod! Weel, dinna fash yersel' man, we've dealt wi' *him*!"

The Reverend's companions groaned their confirmation.

"An' noo there's *this*," cried the Minister, drawing from under his clerical oilskins a large black book.

"'We the undersigned, being Lewismen of the greatest sensitivity and not an Outsider among us, hereby do solemnly swear, affirm and attest that the thought of men falling in love does grieve us to our very hearts.'"

He looked up from the book, and down at

"I said, we must have lunch some time."

TUT, MAN, D'YE THINK THE ALMIGHTY, IN HIS INFINITE MERCY AND COMPASSION, CARES TWA FISHES' TITS ABOOT YER CUTS WHIT ABOOT YER SOUL MAN, EH?

Daft Bob, now weeping and gibbering to himself on the floor.

"They all signed, MacLeod. *All* of them, mind, except one. Except" – he let his sentence hang upon the fetid air while his colleagues noisily drew breath – "*you*."

They carried him up the cliff path, his feeble protests soon subsiding beneath the ministrations of the *cromags* to a dumb acceptance of his foredoomed destiny.

It began to chuck it down.

They propped him against the Minister's cliff-top bothy, pointing inland.

"All this could be yours, MacLeod," hissed the Man of God. "Everything ye can see: the whole o' Lewis, foreby the fog. If but ye wad do one thing. An' ye ken what that is, do ye not?"

"C-c-come aff the meth?" the victim suggested.

"Tut, man, d'ye think the Almighty, in His infinite mercy and compassion, cares twa fishes' tits aboot yer guts? Whit aboot yer *soul* man, eh?"

"Oh…aye, Minister, Ah'll gie that up, too!" wailed the sinner.

"*Sign the book, ya daftie!*"

"Ah-Ah cannae, your Reverence!" He gulped miserably. "Black MacLeod is nice to Poor Bob! Black MacLeod gives Poor Bob over-date Exceedingly Good Almond Slices from the shop! Poor Bob *loves* Black MacLeod!"

It began to chuck it down like I don't know what.

Five outraged MacLeods, their deepest sensi-

bilities grieved beyond measure, advanced on the miserable little man, their *cromags* raised.

"Stay!" cried Gillespie Pik von Königsberg MacLeod-Botha. "I hiv in idea! Tell me, Daft Bob, where are you from? Originally, I mean."

Even the beachcomber's feeble brain was alert to the salvation the man his shopkeeper friend called "Sjamboek" now seemed to be offering.

"North Uist," he grinned.

They escorted him away from the bothy, then stood for some time at the cliff edge until they were sure he had sunk.

"Weel, boys," beamed the Minister, passing round the four-packs, "anything else on the agenda for today?"

Alasdair Mungo "Butane" MacLeod, kneeling awkwardly so as not to strain his welding, drew a paper from his coat pocket.

"Charles Forte MacLeod," he read. "Application for a Sunday bar licence for the MacLeod Arms Hotel, Stornoway."

The Reverend MacLeod carefully carved another notch in his *cromag* with the edge of a ring-pull.

"Ah weel, boys, God's work is never done," he said.

"What's the matter, dear? Cat got your tongue?"

FREAK MOTORIST SHOCKS WEST END!

"MAN JUST PULLED UP AND PARKED" EYE WITNESS CLAIMS

Police set up an incident room at Oxford Circus yesterday after a berserk motorist reported driving briskly into central London and immediately finding a parking space within yards of his intended destination.

First Time Parker

Scotland Yard Traffic Division are keeping "an open mind" until enquiries are completed, but officers admitted traffic was light and they could not rule out the possibility of "a million to one chance". There have already been calls for a public enquiry.

Wild Impulse

According to eye-witnesses, the driver, who has not been named, told stunned Christmas shoppers that he had brought his car into the West End on "a wild impulse". He is prepared to take a lie-detector test to prove his incredible story that he swept up Piccadilly from Hyde Park Corner, shot across Mayfair at speeds in excess of 15mph, swung effortlessly out into Regent Street and straightway found an empty meter bay less than a minute's walk from Hamley's.

How Could It Have Happened?

"We thought he must be a nutter or a terrorist," said one badly shaken passer-by who raised the alarm by dialling 999. Even traffic wardens with a lifetime's experience of residents' parking zones were dazed and silent. "He was ice-cool," said one. "He just pulled up, backed in, fed the meter and smiled at everyone. I just assumed they must be making a film for the television."

"It Has Happened Before" – shock claim

Investigators at the scene warned against jumping to hasty conclusions and revealed that there have been similar hoax claims in the past. Last Christmas an "hysterical" motorist phoned the Press Association and, using the correct password, claimed to have found a free meter in the heart of Covent Garden *with an hour's unexpired time still on the clock*. It turned out he was hallucinating.

The Terrifying Toll

Surveys show that on weekdays in central London the average time taken by drivers looking for a space within two statute miles of where they are trying to get to is anything from two to nine hours. In wet weather, periods of intensive clamping, or during road improvement schemes, that figure can rise sharply. Some unofficial estimates put the number of distraught motorists circling aimlessly around the West End at between four and fifteen million, or more than double in the rush-hour.

Appalling Human Misery

The cost in human misery cannot be so easily calculated. No one knows how many families have been torn apart by husbands or wives "nipping out to the shops" and returning hours, perhaps days, later, in a state of stupefied despair.

Many now feel that at the very least there ought to be an Appeal Fund or a special number to ring for news of missing loved ones. Some are appealing to Desmond Wilcox for help. Others feel that Social Services should provide intensive counselling for those who suddenly find themselves trapped in "no-go" areas like Chelsea, the City, or Marble Arch.

Lessons Must Be Learned

Most regular drivers in London are now numbed enough to cope, said a spokesman for the Charing Cross Motorists' Intensive Care Unit, but incidents like the one up in Regent Street today only serve to build up false hopes. The bitter lesson has to be learned that for the vast majority of inner-London motorists looking for a space, there can be no hope.

WHAT I LEARNT AT SCHOOL YESTERDAY

*The Great Education Reform Bill (GERBIL)
is poised to upturn the school curriculum. But what
did the old system do for you? How well-educated were you,
and what are the awful gaps in your general knowledge?
In the first of a new series TOM CRABTREE
looks back on heady days at a hot-on-facts grammar school*

'm more Miss Brodie than Trivial Pursuit. When I play that game with young visitors they get very ratty if I answer the Q. with a world-weary: "Does it *matter*?" We have the American version of the game; baseball players, Broadway shows, history of the Civil War (theirs). That tends to annoy them too.

They were very hot on facts at my grammar school. There was none of that *e = out; duco = I lead* nonsense. No lighting of fires. More filling of vessels, writing on slates. We – in our black blazers, school badge with the motto *Cercanti Dabitur* – were the slates.

My mother told me that the motto meant *This Will All End In Tears*. It doesn't. It means *The Prizes Are Given For Effort*. There was plenty of effort, I can tell you, but precious few prizes.

Individuality was discouraged, even on the rugby field. Once, with a flick of the hips and a small step to the right, I went left and scored a try directly under the posts. For this I was clouted round the ear by the PE master and told to write an essay: *Selfishness is Abhorrent*.

I might say that I resigned as captain of the Colts XV and joined the Chess Club. This was before the headmaster had a word with me. Back to the scrum. Whichever way you look at it there's not a great deal of fun in being a hooker.

The deal, at the school, was: if you played your cards right, you'd get a white-collar job, a house and a car. The fact that my friends who went to Secondary Modern Schools ended up with bigger houses and cars wasn't to trouble me till later.

The masters were a funny bunch. They addressed me as "Boy". I assume they'd all lived abroad at one time, probably in Kenya. The maths master was deaf. When you asked him, his back to you (he could lip-read), if you could go to the toilet, he'd answer: "Do it in your class book, boy." Moments of light relief were few.

I can honestly say I don't remember much of what we were taught at the place, except the Causes of the French Revolution. I've carried *those* about in my head for some thirty years and never found that they were a means to advancement, in either a vocational or romantic sense.

Did you know there were very bad harvests in France during the autumn of 1788/9? Flattened crops (hailstorms. The peasants were driven to eat biscuits). When I say this kind of thing to women at parties they tend to look over my shoulder to see who else is in the room. At school we didn't have conversation classes.

We used to study peculiar subjects, like geography. I got a credit for geography in School Certificate. Very odd. I mean, I can understand people looking up the Caroline Islands but I have to look up Hull, Glasgow – places like that. Perhaps I knew where they were – are – and have just forgotten.

The lesson I enjoyed was art. Double period on Monday morning (strange time). We used to have to draw these two-inch squares on white

DID YOU KNOW THAT THERE WERE VERY BAD HARVESTS IN FRANCE DURING THE AUTUMN OF 1788?

paper and then draw two diagonal lines across, which gives you four triangles. Then we could colour in those triangles, any colour we chose.

"Keep to the lines, boys," the art master would shout as I'd sit there doing my green and orange combination. Wonderful. People have a deep yearning to make their mark, express their feelings, *make* something. This made more than sense to me.

As we sat there, the art master would tell us about the time he used to be an all-in wrestler (in the colonies?) and how, when we were older, we should join a gymnasium and keep away from women. Despite his Spartan outlook, I liked him.

That was until I got the poke in the back: "You, woodwork," he told me and that was it. No more art. Instead, four years of having toast racks, book troughs and lampstands smashed over the woodwork master's knee.

If I'd have been born twenty years later I could have sublimated my creative yearnings – the need to make a symbolic representation of my feelings – into spraying walls with aerosol paint, or smashing up British Rail lavatories.

In those days, aerosols hadn't been invented. I couldn't afford, even then, to go on a train. I remembered that poke in the back, though. It stayed with me. That kind of thing does.

Fast-forward twenty years. I go with a friend to the caves at Cougnac to see the marvellous Picasso-like paintings of animals of some 20,000 years ago. Magic. Amongst them is a

"It's the way his psychoanalyst would have wanted it!"

"From here you can see eight near-misses."

hand-print. That's it. Just the shape of a hand on the cave wall. Not even in a two-inch square.

About this time, we moved house. You know how it is – no carpets, hardboard about the place, children getting fractious. I started painting – bold colours, large canvases. I didn't keep to the line. I was just expressing something. Emotions (*e = out; movere = to move*) are the things which move us.

I got the house, the car and the job. They kept their end of the bargain. I remember the teachers but hardly anything of what they taught me. Still, as Matthew Arnold says, education is the influence of one person on another. Everybody we meet teaches us *something*.

Little did the art master know that when he was teaching me he had in front of him a boy who would later exhibit a picture called "Grandmother in a Wind Tunnel" at the East Dorset Art Society Annual Summer Show.

No big deal, you might say. That's what he'd have said, I expect. I hadn't kept to the line. The picture was enormous – especially amongst all those Swiss chalets which were prominent at the EDAS. The thing was to do with *feelings*. We'd been in the house three years and still hadn't got a spin-dryer.

Education is to do with the emotions as well as the intellect. I feel certain of that. Not that I'd take children to art galleries or prehistoric caves. Well, not *too* early. That's a bit like cuffing them round the ears with art.

I remember taking my son around the Louvre. He was ten at the time and, after a cursory glance at the lady with no arms, was overcome with boredom.

"Go and count all the bare boobs you can find," I told him, ever-ready to show flexibility in my role as tutor. He sped away to come back, breathless, half an hour later.

"Forty-three," he said. He was always brilliant at maths at school but, then, maths isn't the same as numeration.

If ever I go to a school I always look at the art work. It's how I judge the place.

"Do you let the children paint?" I ask the head. "No two-inch squares?" I ask the art teacher. When I was a governor at the school

up the road, my big buddy was the art mistress. They did proper pictures up there – really arty.

In my day, the emphasis was on the vocational aspects of education. We'd all have been okay working in Japanese factories. At school we even had a company song. We learned by rote, did what we were told.

Nuns have a vocation, so did I. I wanted to be a psychologist and was told at school to take up law. I didn't toe the line there, either. I was told that there was more money in law but I can't recall having told *them* that money was my top priority.

With me, it's what you do when you're not in office, factory or law court that says a great deal about you. What you do when you have moments of freedom is what you are.

Whatever became of educating for leisure? What became of the notion of personal

development, the rounded personality, a healthy mind in a healthy body? What became of that lighting of fires?

Teach them about computers/word processors/maths. Teach them about problem solving (they'll need it) and how to work together in groups. Examine them at seven if you must – providing you build on their strengths and strengthen their weakness through good teaching when you've finished your examining.

But, please, let them paint. Painting's vital. It's to do with the communication of feelings, making sense of the world, dealing with one's emotions. Very few things moved me at school. Art did. The short time I was allowed to do it gave me great happiness and an interest which has been life-long. Despite the slightly limited canvas on which I started.

"Okay, if Hitler was such a cool dude, how come he never wore shades?"

ARE YOU SITTING COMFORTABLY? THEN WE'LL GET STUCK IN

Like dad's suits and mum's shoes, there was bound to be a time when radio came back into style. But why now? GILLIAN REYNOLDS knows why

No doubt about it, this is radio's year. It has become a hot media topic, as opposed to a dusty one. Bright young journalistic things put together with a will sparkling essays on the subject of Radio 1's *More Music Mondays* or Radio 3's new arts show. In the olden days, five years ago, they'd have given you blank stares if you so much as mentioned the wireless.

This has much to do with the wheel of fortune and fashion's parade. Like dad's suits and mum's shoes, there was bound to be a time when radio came back into style. But why now?

A large part of the answer is politics. The Government is very keen to change the whole structure of our broadcasting system. This is not, it must be stressed, not just because Mrs T. (or Mr Norman T. for that matter) thinks the BBC is agin them. It has to do with the enterprise culture.

Mrs Thatcher believes broadcasting can grow as a service industry, but that it is being held back by old-fashioned bureaucracy at the top and greedy trade unions at the bottom. The outrageous demands of the latter have, in her opinion, been passively granted by the feeble former. Something must be done.

She also is told continuously by small businessmen around the country that they can't afford to advertise on television, because the rates are too high, and the rates are too high because ITV and Channel 4 are an IBA monopoly, and the old-fashioned bureaucracy has given in to the outrageous demands etc, etc. She is convinced by this and tells all concerned that there must be change.

The only thing is that every time she sends out a Committee of Enquiry, they come back with good arguments for keeping quite a lot of things the way they are. On top of that, ITV is

IF MRS T. GETS AWAY WITH THE GREAT RADIO ROBBERY, WHAT'S TO STOP HER GRABBING TELEVISION?

massively profitable and this means the Exchequer's levy on those profits is huge. Care has to be taken when attempting to change the laying habits of geese which produce golden eggs. It is also a bit embarrassing when foreigners go on and on about our wonderful programme exports and the way we've got things just right here, in the balance of public service against profit. Yet Mrs Thatcher sticks to her novel perspective.

It has clearly had an impact on the Home Secretary's thinking. He has a while before he puts together his proposals for how television must change. He has said more than once that he might as well use radio as a test-bed for ideas. His Green Paper last year produced a lot of response, not all of it negative, and much appreciation for its thoughtful approach. Now he has told the House of Commons which bright broadcasting wheezes he is going to try out.

He is going to bring in the auction principle, favoured by the Peacock Committee and endorsed since by none other than Dr David Owen. His three new national radio networks will be put up to the highest bidders. He is having a go at community broadcasting. This already exists in the shape of pirate stations on the VHF waveband. Mr Hurd is giving it his blessing. Could he be persuaded in future to do the same for the old 405-line TV frequencies?

He is saying goodbye to the IBA as the regulatory body for radio. No wonder they are jumping up and down at the IBA's headquarters, just across the road from Harrods. For fifteen years they have fostered this problem family of radio stations, some big, some small, some too feeble to carry on at all. They have made them strong enough to carry competition from national networks and this is all the thanks they get! But shock! horror! rage! this is probably not the end of it. If Mrs T. gets away with the great radio robbery, what's to stop her grabbing television away, too? Not much, actually, considering her fairly open scorn for the way they do things in the Brompton Road.

Put all that to one side for a moment, though, and think of what has made it more chic to be a listener than a viewer. This is not a knotty conundrum. All you have to do is watch television for a night, as opposed to watching as a critic does a selection of proffered goodies. You will quickly see that what TV has to offer in the way of a structured night's entertainment is not all that wonderful. Saturdays, in particular, seem to have been designed expressly to drive people out to the pictures and the pub. Can ITV really do no better than *Sheena, Queen of the Jungle* for a primetime feature film? Is there no middle ground between opera and games shows?

People have actually been switching on the radio instead. The BBC had its best radio figures for years just before Christmas. Independent Radio also says it's doing very well and, when good audience figures mean more advertising sales and those are at record levels, who would argue? This is not a massive trend back to the days of a whole family sitting round watching the fretwork, thrilling to the velvet tones of Valentine Dyall. But it is a significant one.

Even more significant is the young and affluent audience. People under thirty like the Proms and Radio 3's *Critics' Forum*. They are fans of *The Archers* and have strong feelings about Michael Parkinson on *Desert Island*

"You're being replaced, Pemberton, by this quite good caricature my young son drew."

Discs. Quite a few of these people now work in the media and raise voices which are heard. They become exercised about disc jockeys cropping up on Radio 4 and the musical style of Capital. And they write about it, prominently.

In the most general terms of all, those of vast regular popular patronage, radio is more than anything else Useful. When there is a strike or a storm only your local radio station will keep you properly up to date, tell you whether you can get to work, which bus service is operating. When a major national or international news story breaks, you will hear it first on radio. As a source of practical information, radio cannot be beaten.

The extraordinary thing about it all is the range and variety. Four BBC networks, a chain of BBC local stations, an even bigger chain of commercial stations, World Service. You can tell most of them apart right away just by how they sound. You know, more or less, what sort of company they are going to be or what sort of

THERE ARE SIGNS OF AN ALMIGHTY BUST-UP BETWEEN GOVERNMENT AND THE IBA.

purpose they can fill. And all of them, to an extent unprecedented in radio history, are influenced by what their audience feels about them.

If no one listens to commercial radio, there is no audience to sell to the advertisers and they go out of business. But, these days, that argument also applies to the BBC. For radio to hold on to its corner of the licence fee, it must put the figures up front. And why not, when more people listen to one *Afternoon Theatre* on Radio 4 than go to the National Theatre all year? And when it costs far, far less?

This bold new approach to publicising radio has been a while coming. For a very long time the newspapers didn't want to know. They gave critics like me, and Val Arnold-Forster in *The Guardian*, and David Wade in *The Times*, our few hundred words once a week on the understanding that if anything else took the arts editor's eye (some itinerant string quartet or a play in a London basement), we would be cut or shoved off the page altogether. Now it's all the go and you can't open a paper without noting with satisfaction that, at last, someone else seems to have heard what we've been saying for years about the plays, and the people, and the music, and the news.

The story about radio itself is going to run for at least another year. Still to come is the formation of the new radio authority and there are signs that between then and now there might be an almighty public bust-up between the Government and the IBA. After that will be the new franchises and the talent raids. What price Derek Jameson's contract with Radio 2 when one of the new networks comes courting? Watch out for the part sponsorship is allowed to play.

But in the meantime, listen. Our radio just now really is wonderful.

COULD WE NOW HAVE AN OFF-THE-CUFF COMMENT FROM A COMMENTATOR, PLEASE?

Yes, but does the Home Secretary know his Glenn Miller, could he come up with a rhyme for Walkington? ALAN PLATER, one-time celebrity voice on Radio Humberside, gets to grip with the knottier problems of shoestring radio

It was some time in the 1960s that Henry Livings, ace dramatist and fine friend, told me about his nocturnal adventure in California. One of his plays was being produced in Los Angeles and he was staying with friends. He was unable to sleep because of a persistent, low-pitched humming sound. He got up and went for a walk in the garden, acutely aware that sleep was impossible until he found a satisfactory answer to the question: what is that low-pitched humming sound? "Then," said Henry, "I worked it out. It was the Americans using up the electricity." He slept easily for the rest of the trip.

Two decades on, the global village, including the United Kingdom, is hearing the same sound, except that the electricity has now been supplemented – and for all we know secretly replaced – by satellite dishes, fibre-optic cables, audio and video-tape, compact discs plus next week's consignment of micro-chip miracles, presently lying in the laboratories, awaiting their brand-names, packaging and super-hype. That is the subtext to Douglas Hurd's Media-

Revolution-Of-The-Month, wherein he promises to beat us across the ears with three national commercial radio channels and several hundred grassroot community stations. He is simply carrying out orders. Using up the technology.

The problem for broadcasters is an obvious one: how to fill a ten-gallon drum with a quart of material. The simplest and cheapest solution, much favoured by the Murdoch lobby, is to sit a presenter in a self-operating studio with a pile of records and cassettes, and forget about him. This approach was long ago transformed into a brand of science or witchcraft, depending on your point of view.

I once met Tony Blackburn, during the period he was presenting the BBC's morning programme, and he explained that he played the Top Forty singles, in variable order, each and every day.

"The audience doesn't want surprises," he said.

"But supposing," I said, cautiously, "just supposing you hear a wonderful piece of music by, for the sake of argument, Segovia, doesn't your

"Our minutes are going to make pretty boring reading in 30 years' time with no one ever dissenting."

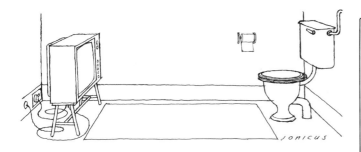

heart cry out: I must share this beautiful music with my public?"

"No," he said.

Clearly the Hurd proposals could merge with the Blackburn syndrome by arithmetical adjustment — if the Top Forty became the Top Four Hundred, to express it crudely. But the smart money must be on a major expansion of phone-in and quiz programmes, especially at the local level.

I know whereof I speak. When I lived in Hull, I spent many happy half-hours involved in shows of this kind, with memories of small triumphs and humiliations by way of proof.

The humiliation was during a Children-in-Need fund-raising phone-in. In a mood of charitable recklessness, I volunteered to sit in the studio and write instant limericks, purpose-made for each caller, with a pound-a-line going to the charity. I turned up with a head crammed full of ingenious rhymes for Hull, Goole, Hornsea and Hedon. The first and only caller was from a local village called Walkington. Slowly and laboriously, I wrote a witless limerick of stunning ineptness. People in the East Riding are warm-spirited but they also believe in value for money. There were no more limerick phone calls.

The quizzes were much more fun and eventually blessed with glory. Locally they were prepared and presented by a man called Elliot, who also worked as a soccer reporter in addition to his day job as a maths teacher. He and I were old friends and had gone to the same school, which gave him a licence to call me in as a quasi-guest celebrity, along with Chris, who wrote and sang songs and Clive, a keyboard player and stand-up comedian. I did so many of Elliot's quiz programmes that I began to answer some of the questions because I remembered them

from earlier shows. Twice, in the music round, I correctly identified Glenn Miller's "String Of Pearls", tossing in the extra smart-ass comment: "And if you play it all the way through, there's a lovely trumpet solo by Bobby Hackett."

My reward for knowing about Bobby Hackett was an invitation to join the BBC Radio Humberside team for a national contest, involving local radio stations across the land. Each team included a resident broadcaster, a local quasi-celebrity and a sporting personality. Ours was George, a midfield player with Hull City, formerly of Notts Forest, who was out of the team with a broken leg, sustained while scoring the equaliser in a 2-2 draw with Bolton Wanderers. It's the ability to remember such trivia, without recourse to the public record, that wins places in quiz teams.

We triumphed in the Final, beneath the twin towers of Broadcasting House, thanks to a sensational bell-and-buzzer performance by Chris the Singer. I guess years of playing guitar had honed his digital adroitness. We lapped our champagne of honour and were presented with tiny, multifunctional alarm clocks. Mine gave up on two of its functions within a week; I sent it back to the manufacturers and never heard another thing.

My serious concern is whether Douglas Hurd and his advisers have any true understanding of these tiny stems and shoots of grassroots radio. It's a limited and prejudiced viewpoint, but I would be relatively happy about media revolutions if I thought the Whitehall legislators were capable of finding a decent instant rhyme for Walkington. I'd be delighted if they could identify "String Of Pearls" after four bars, and ecstatic if they knew that Bobby Hackett played the trumpet solo.

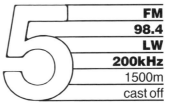

RADIO

1,2,3,4

See local press for details.

FM 98.4
LW 200kHz
1500m
cast off

6.00am Newzy Woozy
The soft-sell actuality briefing for sleepyheads with LINDA LUSARDI

6.25
The Week's Good Joke
with **Rabbi Lionel Blair**

6.30 Aaron Copland
Your wacky DJ with the news of the day.

8.00
Hold the Front****
Phone in and supply the missing words in this morning's main **News** bulletin and win a major prize! Newsreader BARBARA WINDSOR

8.45 Mills & Boon
A daily romance to get you going. Read by **Anneka Rice**

9.00 Auction Ear
As he travels around the country on his live walkabout, **Robert Maxwell** may at any moment buy something or someone, and instantly offer them for auction. Will you be a Bidder? Or a Lot? Or Lot's wife? The daily fun and suspense game for all the family. Editor STEPHEN DABITOFF

11.00 It Stinks!
Education Hour for Schools.
11.00 Wacky Fax
with **Ruby Wax**
11.20 Sex Instruction
7: *Who put Mr Snowman's carrot there?*
Written by BILLY CONNOLLY
11.40 Motor Car Maintenance
13: *Bleedin' Volvos!* with **Vesta Curry**

12.00 Arthur Daley's
Discount Hour
Serious bargains and money-saving durables for you to consume. Our lines are open from 5.00 a.m.
Featuring THE SHAKESPEARE SPOT with **Dame Judi Dench**

12.55pm Wacky Weather
with THAT WET from the Met Office.

1.00 News International
All the news that's cut to fit, read by **Kid Jensen**

1.15
A Problem Aired
Is A Problem Squared
Your very own domestic crisis phone-in show. Break down and win a major prize! Heartbreak and hilarity with **Tommy Docherty**
Editor WINDSOR MAJOR

3.00 Afternoon Playhouse
The Flintstones
by HANNA-BARBERA
That wacky Stone Age family who are even better without the pictures. *(R)*

3.30 Pro-Celebrity
Noughts and Crosses
Phone in and play the game with a famous name!
All this week: **Beaky**
(of DAVE DEE, DOZY etc.)

4.00 And There's
More B-Sides!
The show that brings you the big hits of the Sixties flipped over to expose their bottoms
Presented by **Jeffrey Searcher**
(of THE SEARCHERS)

Three clients line up for their charcoal biscuits in
Windwatch, Radio 5, 7pm

4.55 No Poetry, Thanks
Les Dawson turns down listeners' requests.
(Stereo)

5.00 It's All Happening
The non-stop news 'n' music spectacular featuring the latest disco hits and PARLIAMENTARY REPORT with **Ted Rogers**. Guess the clapometer reading of today's Commons Uproar and win a major prize!
Editor LEANNE PERRINS

5.55 My Seaweed Says
Latest weather trends from the goon at the Met Office.

6.00 World War III
Will it break out tonight? Excitement for all the family in tonight's main **News**.
Read by CAROL THATCHER

6.15 Bob's Smallest Room
Are you sitting comfortably? **Bob Monkhouse** reads some classic excerpts from his private collection of comics. Abridged in 26 episodes by ANDREW NEIL

NEW SERIES

6.30 Car-Phone Fun-Time
The motorist who phones in from the wackiest location or predicament wins a major prize!
Presented by **Stirling Moths**
Producer PRIZE NORTON

7.00 Windwatch
Indigestion, said George Bernard Wilde, is the curse of the cursing classes. Our Mobile clinic takes to the streets with **Doc Cox** at the wheel. Our man with the windsock:
GEORGE GALE
(Broadcast last back end)

8.00 It's Jazz!
Oh no it isn't. More bits of the Swinging Sixties, introduced by **Peter West**

8.45 Classic Drama
Russ Abbot in *Not On Your Wife* by JACK POTTY and VERNON SCRUBBS
Gerald .... RUSS ABBOT
Marcia .... MOLLIE SUGDEN
Mrs Baggot .... THORA HIRD
Trevor Baggot .... LES DENNIS
Dr Whelk .... KENNETH CONNOR
Sir Trinkle Peep .... JOHN GIELGUD
Directed by TERRY FEET *(R)*

10.00 Newsaroonie
Today's headlines presented in their own distinctive way by KID CREOLE and the COCONUTS

10.15 A Bonk At Bedtime
Your sexual problems briskly reviewed by **Anna Raeburn**
Musical research: minimal
(Stereo)

12.00 Out of My Pyjamas and Into the Trees
Your wacky night-ride with the wild man of the airwaves, **Gordon Clough**. Guess what he's really wearing and win a major prize!
(Stereo)

An addict celebrates his return to healthy eating in **Treets Helpline, Radio 6, 5.45pm**

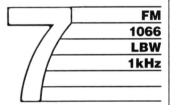

FM 104° BMW 330kHz 800m (hurdles)

5.30am Antiques Roadshow
Request programme for older listeners driving to work. Introduced by RICHARD MURDOCH

8.00 Reynolds News
All the main stories of the day featuring people called Reynolds. Presented by JOSHUA REYNOLDS

9.30 Does He Take Umbrage?
Magazine programme for angry folk. With **Anna Raeburn** and **Mike Gatting**

10.00 Kraft Cheese Slices Comedy Hour
A well-known firm of food manufacturers brings you an hour of alternative comedy from one of Britain's brightest young comediennes, **Kraft Cheese Slices**
Producer K. R. PHILLIE

11.00 These You Have Shoved
Our monthly round-up for veteran car enthusiasts. Will you be named our Fan-Belt Fan of the Month? Introduced by **Murray Walkman**

12.00 Ewe and Ewers
Drop in on our weekly forum for all sheep who collect jugs.
Presented by **Jack Woolley**
Additional Material: Polly-Esther Viscose, 32 per cent.

12.25pm China 'Cross the Bay
is a variety show from a tea-cup factory in Morecambe. Starring **Dana, Yana, Lana Turner and her Incredible Llamas,** and Keith **Harris and Orville**
Producer BARNEY MOZART

12.55 Your Ethnic Weather Forecast
and Road Report. Watch out for them Accident White Spots, man!

1.00 Preparation H Hour
Cyril Smith with a selection of music for people who don't want to move about too much.

2.00 Sport on 6
Live commentary on the Vick Vapo-Rub British Open Knur and Spell Championship at Heckmondwike.
Commentator TONY GUBBA

3.00 The Quiz Quiz
A panel of celebrities tries to guess which quiz the questions originally came from.
With **Bill Oddie, Bobby Davro, Claire Rayner**, and **Keith Harris and Orville**.
Question-master **Willie Rushton**

4.30 All Fall Down
The 100th edition of the award-winning magazine programme for one-legged Scottish dancers, featuring **Singleton Foot and his Accordion Band.**
Producer ROD CRUMMOCK

5.45 Treets Helpline
Information service for those addicted to chocolate peanuts.
For confidential newsletter write to:
STICKYFINGERS, London W1 99 199

6.00 Myrtle the Turtle
23: AIDS is horrid, says Myrtle the Turtle.

7.00 Watchwatch
Your weekly update on all programmes ending in "watch", written and presented by **William Wordswatch**
Producer ANGUS WATCHWORD

7.45 Sanyo Hamlet
by WILLIAM SHAKESPEARE
Another chance to hear the acclaimed Sanyo-RSC production, with **Nicholas Lyndhurst** as Sanyo Hamlet
Ken Dodd as Sanyo Claudius **Alison Moyet** as Sanyo Gertrude, **Keith Harris and Orville** as Sanyos Rosencrantz and Guildenstern and **David Jason** as Everest Double Glazing The Gravedigger.
Directed by BURT KWOUK
(Sponsored by Sanyo plc)

10.30 All Together Now
The show in which Britain's minorities finally band together to agree about something. This week it's: **Paul Daniels**
Presented by HAROUN RASHID O'PHLAINAGHAIOIN

11.45 Watchwatchwatch
Your reactions to this evening's edition of **Watchwatch**
Presented by NICK WRIST

12.00 The Dodgy Motor Show
Playing some music, selling some second-hand cars, Arthur "Open the Cage" English takes you down Memory Lane, and leaves you there.
(Stereo)

FM 1066 LBW 1kHz

6.00am Herman Clud
with his personal parade of hits from Those Swinging Sixties

11.55 Shipping Forecast
(Stereo)

12.00pm The Coronation of Her Majesty Queen Elizabeth II
Another chance to hear 1953's historic broadcast *(R)*

8.00 Interval

12.00 All Through the Night
Another chance to hear "Sailing By" 120 times.

5.00 White Noise
(R)

A rare sighting of Stalin's moustache, as featured in **Shipping Forecast, Radio 7, 11.55am**

A WANDER THROUGH SIR ROY'S CAPACIOUS RAG-BAG

KENNETH ROBINSON
at the V and A

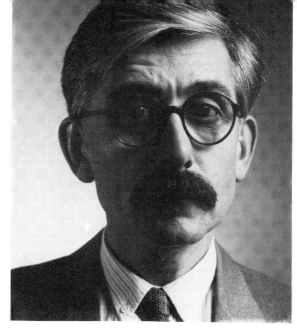

THE INCREDIBLE SIR ROY still going strong. Once floral-shirted, out-going director and secretary of the Victoria and Albert Museum. Born 1935, educated Queen Mary College, London University, the Warburg Institute. Expert on life and art of Tudor, Stuart and Victorian England. More than two dozen publications, including *Creating Small Gardens* (1986) and *Gloriana: The Portraits of Queen Elizabeth I.* Married 1971 to Julia Trevelyan Oman, the theatre, TV and cinema designer. Says Sir Roy: "The British loathe the middle-aged, I await rediscovery at 65."

IN the past week a new director has moved into the Victoria and Albert Museum. Mrs Elizabeth Esteve-Coll has taken over from Sir Roy Strong, who was instantly praised for his energy, foresight, conviction, flair, persistence, shrewdness, showmanship, scholarship and love of life, laughter and good friends.

"The V and A," he once told me, "is, in fact, a capacious rag-bag. And although we are now concentrating on modern craftsmanship, in the old days everybody always said, 'Oh, send it to the V and A.'"

"That is why the place is so wonderful. It is *why* we have everything from obscure erotic Indian sculpture to the Beatles' clothes. But millions of people have no idea what the V and A is really for."

"Wouldn't it be a good idea," I said, "to tell the public in large clear print, exactly what they are looking at?"

"Everybody says that," said Sir Roy. "I'll make a note of it." And he went away and did nothing about it.

I do hope Mrs Esteve-Coll will follow Sir Roy's example. I want her to know that *true* friends of the V and A require no improvements that will actually alter the place in any way. Above all, we need to protect it from the prying eyes of the inquisitive public, so they will continue to grope their way uncertainly along the seven miles of corridors, trying to guess what delights they are nearly being told about by the inadequate and dimly-lit labelling.

This labelling was something Sir John Betjeman particularly enjoyed. In fact, his favourite exhibit was a saucer of whiteish powder, captioned "Unknown Substance".

"Betjeman's choice," says Sir Hugh Casson, in the latest *V and A Album*, "is a good example of the enthralling mystery of ignorance."

My own favourite mystery object is the Great Bed of Ware, which the V and A are so proud to own that they become quite uninhibited when they try to describe it.

They have no idea where it was made, they say, or even *why*, but they are quite sure, as they put it, that "any attempt to apply to it the social taxonomic priniciples of decorative art encounters fundamental problems. So whether the Great Bed of Ware is a holotype or a syntype, or not a type at all, could only be established once special variations and generic status had been defined. These are the criteria which quantify particular merit without which the relative importance of the bed in the context of furniture generally, and of the museum as a whole, remains a matter for personal opinion."

That is, of course, very nice to know, though when I came across those words in a V and A souvenir book, I felt grateful that a good many of the exhibition captions cannot, in fact, be deciphered at all, except by somebody lying down full length, with a torch.

It seems that a lot of visitors make this criticism, but once you get accustomed to the V and A, it is quite fun to play guessing games, wondering if the captions will actually tell you anything, even if you *can* read them.

For instance, one of them says of an exhibit that it is "Probably a Flemish Elephant", and you have to decide for

THE NEW HONCHO of the V and A is Mrs Elizabeth Esteve-Coll, aged 48. Salary: £40,058.

yourself if it is probably an elephant or merely probably Flemish.

You will find, too, a bust that is "possibly of the daughter of Jean Francois de Troy". Then there is a painting called *French Lady in Blue Dress*, with a footnote saying, "Perhaps she is not French but German, or even Swedish". And we are told that a photograph of Rodin was "quite possibly taken on one of his visits to London".

Other reticent exhibits include a sculpture of "what was once thought wrongly to be a fossilised ox-brain." Then there is the bust of "a widow who was, perhaps, Katerina of Genasis"; a pair of gauntlets that were "probably given to the young Philip of Spain by the Duke of Savoy", and some gloves that were "said to belong to Henry VIII – though it seems more likely that they belong, instead, to the period of James I".

It is something of a relief, after all this uncertainty, to come across the bust of an *Unknown Man* – a man who is *known* to be unknown, and not just possibly or probably unknown. I like, too, the caption saying "*Unknown Lady* (1770). This charming portrait was probably not executed in France."

When you consider the vast number of other places where the painting was probably not executed, such as Russia, Italy, America or Germany, this is undoubtedly the V and A's finest example of what Sir Hugh Casson calls the mystery of ignorance.

But we are not left in complete ignorance about what the V and A are up to. A notice near the museum's entrance says, surprisingly, "We seek to *entertain* you, as well as to inform."

You can see, of course, why the organisers are pretending to be in showbusiness, what with all those tea-pots looking like ducks and camels; the David Bailey photograph of an unclad Sharon Tate clasping a hairy-chested Roman Polanski, and a full-size sculpture of a dog stamping a snake to death.

Not forgetting: the copy of *Playboy* that is said to have inspired the sculptor, Paolozzi; the 18th century French girl apparently sticking grapes up her nose to symbolise autumn; and the Italian dinner-plate design that shows a rather nasty mass rape, with an unfortunate small boy in the foreground having his left foot bitten by a dog.

As I left the 13-acre place of entertainment that is no longer Sir Roy's stronghold, I wondered what new publicity blurbs would be devised to sell the place under his successor. This time, in fact, the catalogue had asked me to notice "how the bold use of space catches the eye".

But what really caught my eye, as always, was the rather worrying sculpture of Samson slaying a Philistine. This once prompted me to ask Sir Roy Strong what he thought of Philistines, and he said, without hesitating, "Why not come and join us, Kenneth?"

THE INCREDIBLE BULK ORDER

Save £££s with a new magazine which lists amazing bargains! The snag is, you're not allowed to read it. JONATHAN SALE had a peek under the counter

Can I interest anyone in a pair of Wranglers? To you, £1.90? Mr Wrangler wouldn't like it, but to my certain knowledge that is the asking price for these jeans. Those of you stung by the Arthur Daleys of the clothing industry will already be chortling about seven-inch waists, or 70 inches round the belly, supplied by the well-known retailing company of Back of a Lorry Ltd of Liechtenstein, run by a couple of lads who, if only they could clean up their act, would move into insider trading.

Yet no one wrangles with these Wranglers, which offer a comfortable fit to all shapes and sizes outside the pages of the *Guinness Book of Records*. There is, though, one snag. If you slip into one pair, you will have to put 1,999 other pairs into the wardrobe with it.

Parallel with the normal system of whole-saling and retailing is a much cheaper but perfectly legal network, the market stall as opposed to Harrods. The goods are last season's or from bankrupt companies or left stranded by cancelled orders or in some way surplus to requirements. They are stuck in warehouses, they are stacked in corners, they were ordered by Mr Weims of Forward Purchasing who left in 1985. In Europe alone they make up an estimated market of £5,000 million, increasing every time Mr, Monsieur and Herr Weims remember where they left all that stuff. Now they are the special concern of *Trade to Trade*, a fortnightly out this week which hopes to become the house magazine of the cut-price order, the *Exchange and Mart* of the middleman. And you cannot buy it.

You cannot buy the Wranglers, unless you pay up for all 2,000 of them. You cannot advertise in the magazine, unless you are flogging off, to quote an item in the first issue, "one million cartons of brand name cigarettes from cancelled overseas order". And you cannot purchase the magazine unless you are "the principal, representative or employee of a manufacturing or service company".

The publisher has turned away *half* of the advertisers who asked about buying space. I speak for the magazine world when I say that this is not common practice and that few advertisers are shown the door unless their products are going to lead to actual fighting in the streets. I also speak for the magazine world in saying that few circulation managers turn readers away, particularly those prepared to cough up three quid an issue or £78 a year, and few state that "Total circulation in the first year will not exceed 10,000." If they did, it would be a complaint and not, as is the case with *Trade to Trade*, a boast.

Agreed, magazines might want to encourage a certain *type* of reader, preferably that of the university-educated millionaire who will take out an additional subscription for his servants and order at least three items of everything featured in the ads. But as for whipping it out of the hands of a customer in the newsagent, never. (Not that *Trade to Trade* will be on the rack at Menzies; it's available, to some, from 182 Royal College Street, NW1).

But John Coombs, the newly appointed publisher of *Trade to Trade*, is keen to emphasise that not every Tom Ltd, Dick plc and Harry (UK Holdings) will be tipped off about the ware-

LAST CHANCE TO SUE YOUR TRAVEL AGENT

ACE SAFARIS

DRIEGAN

house full of plumbing equipment and about the brand name duvet covers at seven quid each. Particularly not "the sheepskin coat brigade" of an only slightly fixed address.

The surplus market covers every commodity. You name it, someone's trying to offload it, from "Boats, Ships and Marine," to "Veterinary, Equine, Small Animals & Pets." Somewhere there is a tiny fleet looking for its admiral and a stableful of horses looking for a Lester Piggott (out of the nick, of course, this being a strictly legit business). From "Hospital, Medical & Allied Equipment, Inc. Health", down to "Toys, Games & Amusement".

Especially Toys Comma Games Ampersand Amusement. Fashions change rapidly in the

WHAT'S THE WALLOON FOR "NIGHT RIDER" AND THE ROMANIAN FOR "MY LITTLE PONY"?

children's market. A television character loses a series and all the dolls and cars which it inspired go to the back of the shelf. My son knows from experience that a newsagent's window will not shift *Star Wars* spaceships, even at the most bargain basement of prices. But less precocious parts of the world – or worlds (Luke Skywalker models could be very big in Alpha Centauri) – may be stuck in a timewarp in which all our yesterday's board games are for them tomorrow's Christmas presents. Taking off old labels and repacking is a growth industry for companies which know the Walloon for "Night Rider" and the Romanian for "My Little Pony".

Like those cells which lie dormant in the brain (one-third, I understand, but I sometimes feel the proportion is higher in my case) surplus goods are rattling all around us. Someone over-ordered. The public under-bought. A company collapsed; bankruptcies are a growth area in the Thatcherite economic miracle. There are not enough vending machines, unsold out of a massive order, to stock all branches of a chain but there are too many to leave out for the dustman. The right man could shift them.

"Electrical & Electronics" can make up a glut on the market: "Say we import 50,000 models," suggested John Coombs. "A proportion, perhaps 2 per cent, will be faulty and returned. There is no point in sending them back to Taiwan and asking the poor Taiwan person to repair them. Some of them will not be faulty; they could be wrongly wired onto the plug by the customer. With others, the light doesn't come on. They would be put out to tender – 'taken as seen.'"

A pig in a poke, is what that means. Everyone gets a bargain but no one can complain if the toasters promptly ignite the bread or the cassette turns sopranos on the tape into baritones. As for pigs, with or without pokes, there must be a surplus of them somewhere: end-of-line, out of fashion or bankrupt porkers. See under "Veterinary, Equine, Small Animals & Pets" and don't look a gift sow in the mouth.

YOU'RE ON YOUR OWN

"You'll see, it'll be all right – you allow for my quirky ways and I'll allow for yours."

"Not much in the paper today…Mmm?… I said, there's nothing much in the paper…"

"I never feel lonely when
I've just spoken to some
of my married friends."

"Are you sure it's fallen over?"

SCROOGE! AND THE OTHERS!

As we are currently so preoccupied with social questions, it isn't easy to shut out Dickensian imagery. Especially, finds EDWARD PEARCE, when we look at the House of Commons

"Scrooge." At a time of high preoccupation with social policy and with the Government heavily under fire for its small-coin cherishing instincts, Labour members feel that day not wisely spent on which they neglect to identify Mrs Thatcher or one of her ministers with the colourful discount house supremo from Dickens's well received novella of 1843. Not men of a wide and allusive culture, they usually stick to that. The cry "Duchesse de Guermantes" is not often heard in the Chamber.

Admittedly, about twelve years ago, when Peter Shore was riding high, someone observing the stricken angularity and general look of Third World deprivation about that affable scholarly countenance, remarked, "There goes Smike," and one took his point. As long as we are preoccupied with social questions (and Mrs Thatcher seems terribly keen to keep up our interest in the poor) Dickens is of course our man. From that grab-bag of annihilatory caricature you could accommodate an entire House of Commons.

Where does one start? The present administration is sadly lacking in Pickwicks. Of the basic requirements of obesity, glinting spectacles and broadcast geniality, only the second is at all on view in an administration which prides itself on being trim-waisted and penny-frugal. The chief custodian of geniality, Mr John Biffen, has alas been found deficient in his rapture quotient and has shuffled off to lay small landmines in the short or medium-term future. But I always saw Mr Biffen as John Jarndyce.

At a quite different point in the spectrum, I have never had any difficulty with Edwina Currie, already marked down by someone as Cruella de Ville, the dog-casserolling fashion plate with nails sharpened to evisceration point in *A Hundred and One Dalmatians*. I see Mrs Currie, with her dark bright singularity of pur-

THE PRESENT ADMINISTRATION IS SADLY LACKING IN PICKWICKS.

pose, as Hortense, the homicidal ladies' maid in *Bleak House*. The character is said to be based upon Maria Manning, hanged for murder outside Horsemonger Lane Gaol in the 1850s. Not that one wants to push the analogy too far; but all three ladies had or have a certain grim panache.

The surprising fact about the Hon and Rt Hon Nicholas Ridley is that, most uncommonly, he combines aristocratic status (four hundred years of manning the borders against Rangers supporters) with the best gruel-boiling instincts of the hard-edged tendency. Conservative aristocrats are for the most part edgily benevolent, brought up on Disraeli and Stanley Baldwin (two notable non-aristocrats) and in Mrs Thatcher's chairmanship of the Committee of Public Safety, any number of them, led by Sir Ian Gilmour and Sir George Young, have

been obliged to play Sydney Carton. But Mr Ridley – "Why should a Duke pay more than a dustman? It is only because we have been subjected to socialist ideas for more than fifty years," (*The Wiltshire and Gloucestershire Standard*) – is, for all his sensitive watercolours, up there in the moustache-twirling, peasant-shooting tradition, an intellectualised Sir Mulberry Hawk, perhaps.

But there is no reason why Labour should be let off the hook. Charles Dickens is widely seen, with his broad humanity and lack of economic understanding, to be a moral ancestor of the People's Party (certainly one can't see him in the Accountants' Party). Dickens was notoriously bad at portraying working-class characters, the blameless balsawood proletarian Stephen Blackpool, in *Hard Times*, being a fair example of how not to do it. None of which should give him any trouble with the Shadow Cabinet, composed as it is almost entirely of the rising and acquiring classes.

But poor old Smike does have a way of coming back. Think of a Scottish Smike and you have Donald Dewar. Mr Healey with his genius for getting out of things had an agreeable touch of a more robust and combative Alfred Jingle. The pious and sanctimonious side of the opulent and Christian-souled Roy Hattersley, who once greeted me on a train with the words, "Oh, it's you. Don't you know I *hate* you," will do passable service – especially when he turns his eyes up – as any plump Dickensian parson: Mr Chadband, perhaps.

The trouble with Labour is that it is now such an overwhelmingly Celtic party – Kinnock, Cook, Macnamara, Smith, Gordon Brown – that poor old ethnocentric Dickens has his work cut out supplying parts. And we can't go wandering off into *Redgauntlet* just to suit the Shadow Cabinet. There aren't that many New Zealanders in *Dombey and Son* either. Anyway, Bryan Gould is more of a Trollope figure, struggling between actual good guy and perceived smoothie as to whether he should develop as Archdeacon Grantly or, in the nicest kind of way, Ferdinand De Souza (carpet-bagging arriviste in *The Prime Minister* – jumps in front of train on Watford Station – as likely an eventuality as Edwina getting topped, but no matter). Dr Owen, despite a blameless personal life, has in his manner, which is both grand and seductive, and in his disastrous effect upon impressionable young politicians, much of the style and address of Steerforth.

Those ill-disposed to Mr Steel have no trouble in seeing him as a slightly more conniving version of Jo, always being moved on and enduringly pathetic. As for the whips and party managers, Mr Wakeham for the Government, a politician I rather take to, does indeed have the good humour of a lesser Pickwickian, Mr Winkle perhaps (no wonder she can't stand the sight of him). Which brings us inexorably to the lady. Dickens has a quotient of strong-minded and driving women from Lady Deadlock to Sam Weller's mother-in-law, but none of them is quite the equal of our Gloriana. It is back to Trollope, I'm afraid. Mrs Proudie rules OK?

KATHARINE
WHITEHORN
on personal
sticking points:
**Walking out
of Roedean**

THE LAST STRAW

I AM not much of a one for walking out; normally I stick around and make something happen next. I've been fired from time to time, and of course Love has occasionally Flown, but most such situations have simply petered out in a lot of dismal and silly attempts at a negotiated peace. The only time I ever actually walked out on anything was when I ran away from Roedean.

Bicycled away, to be precise. Roedean is known as a posh school near Brighton, but I was at it during the war when it was evacuated to the Lake District, desperately holding the shreds of its poshness around it like an evicted Duchess.

The mistresses, whom we had to call "Madam", still dressed for dinner, in long trailing gowns apparently made out of superannuated curtains; we, too, were required to change from one preposterous garment into another of the same shape (none) but a classier fabric. These were called "djibbahs"; they were waistless, sleeved tunics with embroidery inserts at the neck, worn over a top that tied with a string – a string supposed to go under, but usually cutting agonisingly across, the burgeoning girlish bosom.

We were very coy about bosoms; you didn't mention them, or even remark on the fact that, even at that age, some were plainly heading for Page Three while others were pancake-flat. We also wore straw hats, and huge navy cloaks whose Widow Twankey hoods went *over* the hats – marching two by two through the rain to Chapel we must have looked liked a witches' day outing.

The local Methodist Chapel was where we met for school prayers. Strictly C of E, the school would have expected its place of worship to focus on an altar, but it didn't; high above us reared first the vast black gown, then the pyramid of chins and finally the power-glinted spectacles and beaming smile of the Headmistress Dame Emmeline Tanner (was she a Dame in those days? Pantomime Dame, anyway).

The school itself occupied the Keswick Hotel, a mausoleum at the foot of whose vast shadowy staircase stood a pair of larger-than-life naked negresses holding lamps; my father mortified me once by patting one of them companionably on the bottom and saying, "Distinguished old girl, no doubt?" Among its amenities was a large relief map on the wall, which I could for weeks and months use to plan my escape; we were only thirty miles from the place where my schoolmaster father's institution was evacuated.

I used to go home for half-term where he, desperately trying to make me good at *something*, would bowl to me in the nets. But it wasn't any good. I was so bad at games that in the end they gave up. After a term or two of sticking me in goal, and finding that the only time I ever stopped the lacrosse ball was when I had failed to hurl myself out of its way, they simply had me practising "cradling" at the edge of the field. "Jolly hockey-sticks" is the phrase generally used for schools such as this, but hockey, it was felt, would be bad for the posture. I suspect they'd actually have liked us to play soccer – at any rate, we sang a school song cribbed directly from Harrow, *Forty Years On*, all about "the tramp of the 22 men" – if any of us *had* become the tramp of twenty-two men, they would not have cared for it. An unthinking respect for Tradition was one of the things they were best at; and far too much of their traditions seemed to have been lifted straight from boys' schools.

I can't now remember where it was they contrived to teach us PT – possibly in the gym of a local school. It was a nightmare. Anyone who has ever been to a girls' school knows that there is always one fat, perspiring girl who can never in any circumstances be hauled over the Horse; I was that girl. The gym mistress would look on with the expression – half concerned, half exasperated – of a circus trainer trying to back the elephant into a truck. Girls, this is Not Funny.

I suppose the food was frightful, but I don't

123

think I minded – in fact I *liked* marge, and used to trade my butter ration in a desperate attempt to be liked. I lost a stone a term from sheer misery – it was nothing to do with the food. It was cold; there were icicles *inside* the windows. Eiderdowns therefore went *inside* the sheets, and you never dreamed of getting up till you'd already somehow slipped on your clothes under the bedclothes, playing a sort of cat's-cradle with the regulation Kestos bra that was all strings and thin elastic. It's a wonder we didn't strangle ourselves.

The school's Spartan attitude extended, unfortunately, to the matrons, who took an entirely military view of illness – if you hadn't got a temperature you weren't ill; no, of course you can manage fielding practice before break-fast. I count it as one of my few triumphs that I contrived to have German measles twice run-ning, to stay in the relative comfort of the sani-torium. My father always maintained no one could say whether he'd got German measles or not, *ever*, since you can have them without a temperature, or without spots, or without a sore throat or without feeling frightful.

None of all this, though, was why I ran away. You hear soldiers describing infinitely worse, with real pain and hurt as well, and yet there's the camaraderie. I hated Roedean because I was teased and left out and never made any friends. At the beginning of my second year, we all hoped I might do better if I was put with some new girls (new girls were usually, of course, ground down as a matter of routine). But at that point fate, kindly realising that on Fleet Street I'd never have lived down Roedean if I *hadn't* run away, took a hand. A mix-up over train timetables meant I arrived at school a day late; by the time I finally reached there, the three new girls I was to room with had teamed up together, and I was the odd girl out. Again.

For years I used to say I ran away, five days from the end of term, "as a gesture" – but it wasn't true. A fragile truce that had papered over my relations with the other girls broke down, and I was back to being teased and tit-tered at; I couldn't take it for one hour longer. I took my bicycle out of the shed; it had two flat tyres; never mind. Heaven knows what fanta-sies passed through my head as I made it to the open road; I would be assaulted, perhaps; given a lift? Seduced? Kidnapped? A kind couple, also on bikes, mended my flat tyres and I arrived back home at St Bees.

To no heroine's welcome; I had a bad session in my father's study (he wasn't a housemaster for nothing) and he made me agree to go back. Agree, because "It would ill beseem me to be seen brawling with my daughter on the station platform." The school, however, reckoned it could let itself off the next five days, and we'd worry about the autumn when we'd seen what Child Guidance could do.

What Child Guidance suggested was astoun-dingly, wonderfully, blindingly obvious.

"She's not happy at that school," they said. "She's been there two years. Why don't you try another?"

So they did, and give or take the odd broken heart or childbirth – neither of which were any-where near as bad as Roedean – I've been per-fectly happy ever since. Indeed, for years I could cheer myself up just by remembering I wasn't at boarding school any more.

THE BIG PRANG

2 a.m. from Punch financial staff worldwide

Like a stampeding bear in free fall which suddenly suffers a whiplash fracture and spirals into the bottomless vortex of a globally-linked black hole, trading on world exchanges was again nervous against a deepen-ing backdrop of panic and incontinence, *writes Our Continuing Crisis Correspondent*.

Throgmorton Street reeled like a punch-drunk cork in a typhoon today as rumours of a collapse in sisal futures upped pressure on the Indonesian bourse. The Ded Duk Index fell a further 6.2 billion points and knock-on shock waves turned berserk screens red, jamming switchboards the world over. At one stage, BP shares dipped below abso-lute zero.

By early afternoon, things looked bleaker than at any time since the late morning. More than ten times the GNP of Belgium was wiped off the floor.

Oh My God

In the Windy City, battered dealers sang *Abide With Me* and braced themselves for yet another sudden downward plummet, poss-ibly followed by an immediate upward lunge, depending on this afternoon's developments in the turmoil of Beijing where 1,000 million may have no idea what to do.

Now underwriters are urging the Chancellor to cancel Christmas and there were urgent calls for Princess Margaret to tour the Stock Exchange and boost morale.

"In the underlying volatile backwash of last Thursday's Niagara Falls," said one shell-shocked mayhem-maker, "there might well be a further big-dipper reaction to the previous Friday's yo-yo. We are staring into the blood-stained jaws of a runaway roller-coaster."

This Can't Be Happening

It was a similar picture following Monday's meltdown. "We were witnessing an historic upburn, until an implosive trend re-asserted," reported New York investment analysts Yankelovich Nancy Ratfink. "Excess volatility is high. All it would take to end the world right now would be for the kopek to fall another percentage point or for them to find another zit on the President's nose."

At noon, the pollen count in Bangkok was up 22 points, fuelling fears that at 216 dongs (55.9 cents) to the pound, braising steak could soon be changing hands at less than 3 per cent of Tuesday's peak. Semiconductors remained unsteady at the close, for the first time since Suez.

Nancy Shares The President's Concern

President Reagan is meanwhile coming under hardening pressure to reverse his commitment to do nothing that does not need to be done, unless it needs to be done in order to show to the world that in doing nothing at this time, there is nothing to be feared, except the fear of doing it or not doing it. Shouting to pressmen above the roar of whirling helicopter blades, Mr Reagan recalled a similar crisis which had occurred during the shooting of *Destry Rides Out*.

Uproar

In an opinion poll of dazed traders, who were asked to identify the cause of the Crash of '87, more than 70 per cent broke down as they blamed either US economic policy, dark forces of evil, Japanese economic policy, computers, last month's bad weather, the Bundesbank, and unusual sunspot activity. Only 2.1 per cent cited greed as a contributory cause, but 99.9 per cent expected to be on welfare before the week is out.

A spokesman for the Salvation Army said they had been "rushed off their feet". Later the zloty regained 2 cents.

Christ Almighty

In Zürich they were calling it *Schwarzer Montag*. Parisian brokers Donaldson, Bodkin & Lafayette dubbed it *Le Crash* as endive liquidity plunged. Commented seasoned corporate raider Felix Vichyssoise, "We're numbed."

In Singapore pension-fund managers have been armed as a precautionary measure after Mr Lung Bak-Ho, former head of Farquharson, Whampoa and Santa Fe, pumped HK$88bn into supporting the beet harvest. Oils rallied for a record 20 minutes, but in Brussels the Basket of Breweries was down 2934 on rumours that the sky is falling.

Living Hell

Now analysts warn that unless the *Bhat* acts soon to stave off fears of Armageddon, a situation could rapidly develop where interest rates hang like an albatross round further attempts to underpin recovery from "nervous ripple effects" caused by continuing tension in the Balkans, Guam, Moscow and the Gulf. At the close, Rotterdam faced total collapse.

What is even more worrying for small investors is that if low pressure off the Azores continues northwards, Nikkei averages could catch a chill and precipitate a shake-out of unlisted drapery options. In that event, the Fraud Squad might well be forced to act. The Mafia has warned that it will not stand idly by.

A World Turned Inside Out

The Chancellor, who was fulfilling a long-standing engagement to open a 24-hour cash dispenser, described today's mounting crisis as "a shade on the rather silly sort of side". There was a need for a steady hand and a strong pulse, a firm chin and a cool brow, he said, despite rumours that Wall Street might soon begin rationing cocoa. By 4 o'clock Eastern Seaboard Time, as in Bangkok the Hang Dog Index was opening on another day of agony, only shares in Occidental Cup-a-Soup were showing any upward mobility.

LOST IN INNER CITY SPACE

His mission was to go where no government initiative had gone before. He lived with the fear of a man alone against the forces of evil, decay and lack of investment. This was the fantastic voyage of PC Smout

Station control: T minus ten and counting. Ignition sequence starts.

PC Smout: Engine running. Everything looks good down here.

Station control: You've got the patrol commit signal from the Super, Chris. Fuel and water looking good.

PC Smout: I've got a red light on the dashboard.

Station control: Buckle up, Chris.

PC Smout: Buckled up.

Station control: Check. You're go for the beat. Good luck.

PC Smout: Handbrake off.

Station control: We copy.

PC Smout: Pulling out.

Station control: We advise, "Think Bike!", Chris.

PC Smout: Roger. Thinking bike.

Station control: You're doing just great. You have achieved orbital.

PC Smout: It sure is busy round here.

Station control: The orbital's always busy, Chris. Remember what we taught you in the simulation bottleneck tank.

PC Smout: Effecting left yaw manoeuvre into Acacia Road.

Station control: You've got the affirmative on hanging a left, Chris.

PC Smout: Worked just fine. Lined up just beautifully.

Station control: Looking good, constable.

PC Smout: Into Barton Close. Speed 25mph.

Station control: No snags?

PC Smout: Just perfect.

Station control: Good to hear.

PC Smout: It's really comfortable in here. Getting on with the headrest perfectly.

Station control: That's good. That cramped Maria's going to be your home for the next forty minutes.

PC Smout: Turning into Albany Road. *A-Z* holding up just great. Tell the backroom boys they've done themselves proud.

Station control: Will do.

PC Smout: Entering Ashley Drive. This is one small spin for man, one giant pooter for community policing schemes.

Station control: Take it easy, Chris.

PC Smout: You know what? This place really is . . .

Station control: Come in, Charlie Sierra One. We have lost your signal. Come in, Chris. What is your status? Can you read us?

PC Smout: Loud and clear.

Station control: What happened?

PC Smout: Just an underpass.

Station control: There are a lot of smiling faces around here. We thought we'd lost you.

PC Smout: How far out am I?

"He must have had a windfall."

126

Station control: Station elapsed time three minutes and counting. You should be picking up a few funny looks now.

PC Smout: Check.

Station control: And some verbal abuse.

PC Smout: Affirmative. And the same to you, mate!

Station control: That's it, Chris. Remember your racial awareness classes.

PC Smout: This place is really rundown. You can't believe how desolate it is. It's just wide open grey spaces, craters and mounds of earth. It's like being in the back of beyond. Uh-oh...

Station control: Say again, Chris. We're having transmission problems.

PC Smout: They're fiddling with my aerial.

Station control: We've got an engine stop showing here, Chris.

PC Smout: I got a red light. I didn't want to end up in a box junction.

Station control: Are you nuts?

PC Smout: That's what my friends say.

Station control: Heartbeat reading up to ninety-six. What's going on out there, Chris? All we have on audio is a loud piercing squeak.

PC Smout: They're scraping their keys and martial art foot-claws down the side of the command vehicle. I'm rolling. Repeat thirty-five pitch. They're on both sides. I'm getting thrown about pretty bad in here.

Station control: Get out of there, Chris.

PC Smout: Negative. I've still got a red light.

Station control: Jump it, Chris. Jump it!

PC Smout: Large gang of youths approaching fast, armed with sledgehammers and breezeblocks. Twenty feet until contact... ten... five.

Station control: Go for burn, Chris.

PC Smout: I've got the green light.

Station control: Chris? Chris?

PC Smout: Burn is successful. I'm out of it.

Station control: We advise termination.

PC Smout: Negative. I still have the plaque. Request go ahead for extra-vehicular walk.

Station control: Make it quick. You've got a bunch of guys going blue here.

PC Smout: Engine stop. Hatch open. What a dump! I'm now unveiling the plaque. For those who haven't read it, this is what it says. "Here, a metropolitan policeman first set foot in the inner cities. We came in peace for all mankind."

Station control: We've got Mr Kenneth Clarke here, Chris. He wants to say a few words.

Kenneth Clarke: Chris, I'm speaking to you from a breakfast meeting with a few local government officials from Sheffield. I just can't tell you how proud we all are of what you... No, mine's the sausage, bacon and poached egg... what you have achieved. For every person in the country this has to be the proudest moment of their lives... yes, coffee, please... Because of what you have done the inner cities have become part of our world. It inspires us to re-double our efforts to bring peace and tranquillity to earth. For one priceless moment, all the people in Britain are one. One in their desire to recapture the urban vote and one in our prayers that you will return safely.

PC Smout: Thank you, sir. It is a great honour and privilege for me to be here representing the Government and their vision for the future. It's an honour for me to participate here today.

Kenneth Clarke: Thank you, Chris, and I look forward to thanking you in person soon.

PC Smout: I look forward to that very much, sir.

Station control: Okay, Chris, we're bringing you in.

PC Smout: I appreciate that. Put the tea on, sarge. I'm coming home.

Day of the Dead

GILES GORDON

*observes the curious rituals
of the Folio Society at their annual
literary dinner and debate*

"Wait! Can you put me back on hold? I quite liked that tune."

INADVERTENTLY, the fourth Folio literary dinner and debate, with all males present except for the Rt Hon Michael Foot MP sprouting black tie, endorsed one of the cardinal prejudices of conservative England, that literature is produced exclusively by the dead for readers uninterested, on the whole, in the living.

As Fay Weldon remarked – opposing the motion that "It is no use pretending that in an age like our own good literature can have any genuine popularity" – "the past is *safe*." It certainly was at Merchant Taylors' Hall in the City where the names of writers bandied about were not of the quick, although Mr Foot did hilariously hint that Jeffrey Archer's next novel might be entitled *A Matter of Fragrance*.

The Folio Society, founded in 1947 to publish pretty editions of books worth reissuing, rarely brings out titles in copyright, although they have published *Animal Farm*, no doubt in 1984. Michael Foot proposed the motion, pointing out – in that alarming manner he adopts, his body plunging towards, then lurching from, the lectern – that its words were adapted from

Orwell's 1942 essay on Kipling. Later, when master of ceremonies Frank Delaney invited questions, Julian Symons (younger brother of A. J. A. of *The Quest for Corvo*, which must be literature as it's been published by Folio) confessed that he had known George as well as Michael had. Michael courteously replied that he was sure Julian had known George better. What was bewildering was that they didn't call George Eric, for that was his real name.

The debate, frankly, was duff, possibly because Mr Foot had tried to persuade Mrs Weldon beforehand to swop sides with him. He recommended Disraeli to her and she bought *Sybil* at Paddington Station but found Book One rather tedious. Book Two was more lively. Mr Foot delivered the kind of all-purpose speech – invoking the Prime Minister, Kenneth Baker, Byron, Shelley – that politicians usually do when invited to perform at non-political occasions.

Robert Gavron, who owns the Society as well as being chairman of St Ives plc printing group, welcomed the guests and unveiled the secret of the year, which sent the

members present into ecstasies: the Society, over the next twelve years, was going to issue 48 volumes of Trollope. It would also conclude its publishing of Dickens, and reissue Shakespeare, in a new text for the

MEMBERS ARE RUMOURED TO BALLOT TO SEE FRANK DELANEY IN THE FLESH.

1990s, in three volumes – they've already done him, with coloured pictures, in 37.

Most people present were Society members from all over the country who, it seems, rush to reserve their places at £30 a head (much cheaper to buy a book, even a Folio book) as soon as the debate is announced. Then a sprinkling of literary luminaries and publishing pundits are invited to spice the proceedings. Richard Cohen, Jeffrey Archer's erstwhile dining companion on the triumphant night, made a speech saying how disgraceful it was that ten years ago Fay Weldon's novels sold only 3,500 copies in hardback. As he was her publisher then, it seemed a curious comment.

Guests craned their necks to look at Christopher Sinclair-Stevenson of Hamish Hamilton whenever publishers were mentioned. Melvyn Bragg smiled benignly most of the time and Michael Holroyd looked grave, especially when Fay Weldon said that at £625,000 he'd been underpaid for his forthcoming biography of Shaw. She also philosophised: "Writers get better; readers get more selective; times are looking up." The nineteenth-century books we read today, those Folio editions, are a tiny selection from one hundred years' publishing.

Then she sang a song, to the tune of "Frère Jacques": "Shakespeare and Milton/Shelley as well/Ella Wheeler Wilcox/Ethel M. Dell."

Julian Symons sagaciously told his auditors to be suspicious of poets who are too easy, like Betjeman and Larkin, and´there was a bemused silence. A member from the north of England made an obscure speech which culminated in a joke about someone sitting through *The Glums*, not knowing by the end which miserable actor was meant to be Les. Not to be outdone, Mr Delaney told a joke which, apparently, he'd told at each of the three previous debates (Folio members are rumoured to ballot to see Frank in the flesh annually) about Harold Robbins being paid £28 for each four-letter word he writes. He threatened to repeat the joke next year too. Has he already got his invitation?

Salman Rushdie said that more people read novels in this country than watch football matches but he didn't add that even more people go fishing: yes, Folio has published *The Compleat Angler*. He also compared Anita Brookner to a good second division football club, mourned that Blake's *Visions of Night* sold nine copies during the poet's lifetime, and delivered a witty epigram for the times: "Publishers have artistic temperaments, authors have calculators," but still the writers are badly done by.

Afterwards, Fay Weldon confided that her first job was as Folio Society barmaid. In those days, not long after the war, members came to view the soft-porn illustrations to French classics. But, above all, they lusted after bindings tooled in gold. Maybe we still do.

"Like I said, one can't knit and watch TV at the same time."

MARSHA DUBROW
· · · · · · · · · · · · · · · · · · · ·

OH! WHAT A LOVELY WAR-ZONE

You say Grenada, and I say Grahnaaaada.
You say invasion, and I say incursssssion…
(apologies to George and Ira Gershwin)

ILLUSTRATION BY CLIVE GOODYER

I am neither an ugly American nor an innocent abroad, simply a Texan who began international (misad)venturing during the Vietnam war. Owing to such US foreign policies, I've been reviled from Mustafapasha to Mahabalipuram like a US Defence Secretary rather than a peace-monger and honoured guest.

But recently I was welcomed like a returning hero, ironically because of war. I was a stranger in paradise, aka Grenada. US troops "rescued" this Caribbean nationette in October, 1983 from Soviet and Cuban forces. So now, instead of "Yankee Go Home," it's "USA Please Stay," "Thank You USA for Liberating Us," "KGB *Behave!*" emblazoned in red, white and blue on a wall. This Garden of Eden may be the world's only oasis of *pro*-US graffiti.

"When God can't come, He sends. God Bless Americans," beams Edna St John in remote Grand Roy Bay. Her political prisoner son, Elijah, was freed by Leathernecks (Marines). "Aged people here dance each time Americans drive by."

THE FORMER PEOPLE'S REVOLUTIONARY ARMY BASE IN THE HILLS ABOVE ST GEORGE'S IS OVERRUN WITH FIERY BOUGAINVILLAEA RATHER THAN TROOPS.

I feel rather duplicitous since I'd opposed the Grenada foray, code-named "Operation Urgent Fury". I disagreed for many reasons, including the fact that US media were barred from the fury, urgent or not, during its first sixty hours. Much of the press, free or not, sulked at Barbados bars. Also, I was a Senate senior staffer when the US Congress was bypassed on this military action.

America's version of *Oh! What A Lovely War* was produced and directed by actor-President Reagan, former co-star of *Bedtime for Bonzo* where chimp upstages chump. The first war the US actually won in some forty years upgraded Reagan's image from *Bonzo* to *Ronbo*.

Some people joked that the action made Grenada safe for Great Neck, a posh-o New York suburb. Others thought it saved Grenada from Cubans, Soviets and a socialist regime whose leader, Maurice Bishop, had been assassinated. It's been dubbed invasion, intervention, incursion, intrusion or liberation, rescue and, gads, war. Military, like beauty, is in the eye of the beholder.

"Don't say invasion! Or incursion," gasps hotel association official Liz Gormon. "You can't 'invade' a country that wishes it … I love Reagan. He's nasty. I hate a namby-pamby President."

By any other name, it put *The Mouse that Roared* country on the globe. Referring to the US action, a Soviet TV commentator pointed to Spain's Granada on his map instead of Grenada, a hundred miles north of Venezuela. And when

129

"Maurice has always been politically active."

Reagan announced his public relations coup, the Great Communicator mispronounced the site like Spain's "Grahnahda" rather than "Grehnayda".

Although the tussle distinguished Granada from Grenada, it removed the fecund destination from many tourist itineraries. Some Grenada-phobes fear it's like John Wayne's *Sands of Iwo Jima*, shown to GI's on invasion eve, rather than *Island in the Sun*, filmed partly on the former British territory. The sun set on this jewel of the Empire in 1974.

"People continue to ask me whether it's still a war-zone," chuckles Edythe Leonard, an international tour organiser in St George's, the capital. "You don't even recognise Embassy Marine Guards except by their short haircuts."

Tourism Ministry officer Sonja Fletcher returned recently from Canada, where people asked, "Are American troops still running around down there?" Anti-Americanism, like occasional shouting at US tourists, stopped years ago.

But a US official in Grenada confides that, "There are still a few pockets of harassment. It doesn't all disappear in a few years." Yet he perceived no threat.

The hills are alive not with the sound of mortar but of calypso and reggae; waterfalls; emerald-throated humming-birds; black boars. Smells on the Spice Island are not of spent ammunition but of nutmeg, cinnamon, cloves, bay leaves, flowers. Instead of troops, there are statuesque women repairing roads or balancing

multi-gallon water jugs on their heads. Men wield farm tools rather than weapons.

Tourists flock to war memorabilia, as they do in Normandy or Hiroshima. Revolutionary souvenirs including Aeroflot and Cubana planes are as big an attraction as the 45 talcum-powder beaches.

At disused Pearls Airport, a one-engine Aeroflot plane sports a "Reagan '84" campaign sticker below the hammer and sickle. A Cubana plane rots beside it. Newly-capitalistic children go from sad rags to minor riches hawking shards of Indian "artefacts".

The tortuous Pearls road, as holey as it is curvey, turns passengers into groaning accordions, innards like overheated haggis. But US workers fixed about three hundred miles of other roads and finished Point Salines Airport which the Cubans began. Commercial US and British jets have replaced military ones.

The former People's Revolutionary Army base in hills above St George's is overrun with fiery bougainvillaea rather than troops. Pink and yellow flowers rather than soldiers sprout from a wrecked Russian truck.

Other mementos include a shell of the former mental hospital demolished by accident. One flew over the cuckoo's nest and bombed it. This vindicated paranoid patients, but too late. Reports said that the Marines landed without maps and the Army's 82nd Airborne Division had only tourist maps. America apologised by building a flamingo-pink mental institution resembling a Miami motel.

At the Grenada National Museum, one photo shows a barefoot West German journalist arriving for duty, dressed for success in only a bikini, goatee and smile. Another is as realistic as its title, "Head of the Libyan People's Bureau and Counter-part being placed at their lowest by US forces". Another shows beloved, charismatic PM, Maurice Bishop, looking like a black Christ blessing followers moments before he was slain. Also considered a highlight in the museum is, inexplicably, Martinique native Empress Josephine's marble bathtub, used later as a flowerpot.

History elsewhere on Grenada shows natives had been far more restless and heroic against the French than against the Commies. Carib Indians jumped from a steep cliff to their death rather than be conquered by the French in 1650.

Such drama, mirrored in the Caribbean and Atlantic crashing together at that spot, whets the appetite. Nearby is *Morne Fendue* plantation, where the entire Charlie Company ate Thanksgiving dinner in 1983. An inscription on their certificate of appreciation could scare away one's appetite and breath, "We…remain ready to free the oppressed anywhere, any time, and any place."

Even the stone mansion's mortar of lime and molasses is fit for a gourmet. But Mama's Restaurant, a shack, is for gourmands. Her dinners are 25 courses, including armadillo, "*tatou*" – if it's drying on the corrugated tin roof, it'll be on the table that night; opossum, "*manicou*"; lambie pie, not lamb or pie but conch; and sea eggs aka sea moss, reputed to enhance men's

"So if you don't hand over said map, I'll quote, 'slit your throats and feed your gizzards to the crows,' unquote. Full stop. End paragraph."

potency. Another edible aphrodisiac, *bois bande*, is rumoured to be so powerful that some men went to hospital for deflation.

I recall armadillo, resembling tiny armour-plated tyrannosaurs, splattered across Texas highways. But on platters dripping with coconut-honey sauce, it's like succulent venison. However, *tatou* is in the taste bud of the beholder. "Marinated in loo cleanser," sneers a food critic at the communal table.

You'll remember Mama, who 'fesses up to weighing between 280 and 300 pounds. Mama, Inslay Wardally, illustrates how to devour crayfish, which Texans catch in street gutters. "Chew off the head and suck out the juices." I didn't.

Tidbits such as, "It's too much for me – my God," "Belongs in *Guinness Book of Records*" and "I'm leaving with fat, hot lips," are jotted in English, Arabic, Serbo-Croatian in her guest book.

For slimming as well as enjoying glorious hillscapes, hikers scale spots like Concord Falls and Mount Qua Qua. Then the naturalists climb up into "tester beds", canopied four-posters in antique-filled hotels like Secret Harbour or Horse Shoe Beach.

Alas, Grenada may be Xanadu but it is no Utopia, despite some $90 million in US aid.

"There's no gold paving them streets," states Geoffrey Thompson, who operates Rhum Runner cruises.

Tourism has increased, but more slowly than hoped. Hopkin, part-owner of the Blue Horizon and Spice Island Hotels, smirks, "Business hadn't been too bad even in revolutionary times. Professors who liked to think they were socialist – with their chic country houses – came to see Grenada's 'experiment'."

Power-boat owner Capt Henry had no such luck. Soviet sailors "wanted to trade bread for snorkelling! No money, no smiles, big ugly people with yellowed suspicious eyes looking like a pendulum." The captain swears he spied for America and received a personal Reagan thank-you letter with photo.

Progress bypasses prime industries like spice processing. Some women use their toes to turn over nuts drying in the midday sun. Spice-preparing Dougaldston Estate has bats in its factory. Nutmeg Cooperative star worker, Dennis, hand-sorts 600 pounds with staccato moves that put robots to shame.

Alas, under capitalism, "We work just as long and hard, but there's no progress.

Spicy *Informer*, "The Fearless Weekly", agrees. A headline splashes (PM Herbert), BLAIZE BLUNDERS AGAIN: "Incompe-

tence in the ranks of the Grenada Government has reached a crescendo…"

And electricity failures, a scourge of revolutionary times, occur still. It goes off my first night while I shower. I stumble, fumble and drip en route to a candle. I resemble Lucia di Lammermoor or Dorothy Lamour On the Road without Hope or Bing.

"A certain amount of ingenuity is always needed to operate here," sighs Dodd Gormon, Manager of Grenada Yacht Services. You want modern, go to Minneapolis.

Rhum Runner's Thompson opines, "Most people can't find much to bitch about. But some always love to bitch about something. There are more opportunities, better prices, better infrastructure now. During revolutionary times, they wouldn't bitch at all, darling, except in the privacy of their homes."

Not to bitch, but… At my last breakfast, an eager Spice Island Hotel waiter uses my grenadine-hued napkin to swat ravens gathering like Hitchcock's *The Birds*. Due to a wee stain, "Out of Order" is inscribed on it. Even napkins can be *hors de combat*.

A bit more "liming", local for relaxing, and I'll be happily out of order. As the graffiti commands, "USA Stay." I just may. Or, as Gen Douglas MacArthur promised, "I shall return."

H A N D E L S M A N ' S HARD · CASE · HISTORY

THE IDES – *Whelping in the streets*

DAVID TAYLOR TALKS TO
CHRIS EVERT

THE time right now, by Chrissie's Rolex Lady-Datejust gold Oyster timepiece, pressure-proof to 330 feet and a mark of her commitment to excellence, is a little after three. Time for a refreshing cup of Lipton iced tea, the official drink of the Women's International Tennis Association, over here in Eastbourne for a premier Virginia Slims tournament event: the Pilkington Glass Ladies Championships. It is lovely and sunny and a whole lot better than when Chrissie was up (see, is it up, or down?) in London last week, believe her.

In a first-round tussle which highlighted her ground strokes, Chrissie has just seen off Sharon Walsh-Pete, the Hewlett-Packard/WITA Computer Ranking Number 195 and tells me she is feeling in good shape at this time,

with her left knee a whole lot better since she underwent rehabilitation at Palm Beach Institute of Sports under the care of physical therapist Dana Van Pelt, and her personal relationships now developing new stability and inner peace. By the way Sharon played well, she really did. But lost, 6-2, 6-1.

Confidence here is high in the newly remodelled locker room, Chrissie reveals, and all of the tournament ladies report themselves in a whole lot better mood, mentally, now that the weather has picked up. As regards her own chances, the way Chrissie figures it, she could play well here in lovely Eastbourne, and boost her confidence for Wimbledon. Or she could play badly, in which case she'd be motivated to work harder at her game. It's as if she comes out

positive either way. Tournament tough, you know?

As regards this particular tournament, Chrissie would analyse Martina as a likely finalist. Her good friend both on and off the court, Martina Navratilova is truly a great player on grass, whose career earnings now total in excess of $11,792,315. Plus we have to bear in mind that Martina won the tournament last year. Actually she's won it every time for the past five years, and of course Martina must be hungry for a win after her disappointments in the French.

By the way, this is Andy. Hi, Andy. Chrissie and Andy Mill, the Colorado ski instructor, are in love at this time. They are making plans for their lives, although both of them have a tough schedule. Andy made the US Olympic ski team one time and is interested in photography.

Listen, it is only a few weeks since Chrissie and John went their separate ways, from the Fort Lauderdale divorce court. There may be an opportunity to return to this recent upset in Chrissie's tumultuous private life in a moment. No comment on reports concerning the multi-million-dollar cash settlement, or on reports that John is dating Los Angeles secretary Deborah Taylor-Bellman.

Here in the Hospitality Village, Maureen Hanlon, WITA spokesperson who has a degree in sport management from the University of Massachusetts but now resides in Key Biscayne, confirms that as of now Miss Evert's career earnings are in excess of $7,195,918. Major endorsements right now include Wilson racquets, Converse shoes, Ellesse sportswear, Lipton Tea, Rolex and USA Energy Bars. Miss Evert goes on residing in her lovely home at The Polo Club, Boca Raton, Florida.

Where were we? Yeah, Chrissie and John feel now that they have peace of mind and are going on with their lives. They kept in touch throughout the French last week and John maybe knows Chrissie's game better than anyone, still. They are still truly good friends in that respect, confirms Miss Evert, 32, and Mr Lloyd will be on hand during the Wimbledon tournament to advise on her game, do a little coaching, and hit some balls with Chrissie, who values the relationship.

In so far as that particular aspect of their lives is concerned, we can say that nothing has changed that much. In some other respects, sure, the position right now is that a whole bunch of things have changed a lot and they are going to have to see how all of that works out. It is sort of all in the future at this time. Yeah, like a lot of things. Who knows whether a family will one day figure?

Meantime, we should note that the Lloyd is dropped from Evert-Lloyd and Chrissie is known as plain Miss Evert again. Maybe that could be better phrased. Chris sure as hell hopes that her sense of humour hasn't suffered. In fact

"You wife's on the phone –
a blue-tit's gone into the nesting-box."

there was a funny moment concerning her name-change a week or so ago, when Chrissie was honoured to attend the third Nancy Reagan Drug Abuse Fund tennis tournament at the White House and to partner Secretary of State George Shultz in a doubles match against *Dynasty* star John Forsythe and actress Dina Merrill at an event which raised half a million dollars. Well, what happened was that the master of ceremonies, Channel 9 sports anchorman Glenn Brenner, gaffed in referring to her twice as Chris Evert-Lloyd. Finally Chris threw down her racquet and quipped that if he did a third time, she'd break his chair. Actually, though, it was all in good fun and her relations with the media remain in good shape. When was the last time she was called The Ice Queen? Right.

In her position, having won every major title and been voted "the greatest woman athete for the last 25 years" by the US Woman's Sports Foundation, she has sort of had to get used to a little joshing with the media. Besides, as current WITA President, Chrissie wishes to affirm a big "Thank You" to the media for their help in elevating women's tennis from a minor sport, an afterthought on the agate page, to a major one, commanding headlines on the front pages. She is adamant that tournament players must meet with the media after every match and imposes a levy if they don't. It's important to be up-front and visible, believes Chris. The agate page, by the way, we'd call the results page here in England.

Chrissie reads quite a bit, according to what her tough schedule allows. Her favourite book of all time is *The Thorn Birds*, as a result of her many visits to Australia where the novel is located. Chrissie also authors regular columns for *USA Today* and *World Tennis Magazine* and has taken an active role on the preparation of her two books, *Chrissie*, written with Neil Amdur, and *Lloyd on Lloyd*, in collaboration with the delightful Carol Thatcher. Her favourite movie, she told the PM's daughter, was *The Sound of Music*, whereas pasta is her favourite food. The places Chrissie likes to visit most of all are Hawaii and Los Angeles, although she really likes it here in Eastbourne also.

Questioned as to her favourite colour, Miss Evert picks out rose pink, also dusty blue, and a light yellow. She wore a yellow two-piece for the

divorce proceedings. Incidentally the guy right over there is Ted Tinling who has done so much for femininity in women's sportswear. Ted is pleased to hear Chrissie has picked her outfit for Wimbledon already. It is sure to be a sensation, he asserts.

Wimbledon, too, Chrissie predicts. Her game is feeling all kinds of good and she is playing for her own pride, but Martina has some injured pride to make good and Steffi Graf, well Steffi Graf has tremendous power, her forehand has real pace, and she has been winning an awful lot of tournaments. Yeah, and she's just turned 18 years old, already a million dollars up.

Chrissie used to look at Billie Jean King and Margaret Court and ask herself why they kept on playing, now everyone asks her and the answer she has ready is that it is hard to think of retirement when you still feel good out there, when you're still beating the girls you should beat, and perhaps you ought really to have retired three or four years ago, at the time Mar-

tina was killing you on court. It's not enough to be the Number One on the all-time list for victories, or to have 91 per cent lifetime win average, the highest in the modern game, for men or women. You know what? You're 33 next birthday, you're seven million bucks up – and still you have things you want to prove.

And right now things you have to do, like a photo-call with Andy, who, because of his own love of photography and in order to josh a little more with the media guys, plans to pull a surprise and have the photographers sit with Chrissie whilst Andy grabs a picture for his album – sort of turning the tables on them. He's a fun guy.

The time by Chrissie's Rolex Lady-Datejust gold Oyster timepiece is now a little after 3.30. Chrissie and Andy say so long for now. They guess they'll meet with the media guys again at Wimbledon, and I guess they're right.

OZ TENTATION

A CELEBRATION OF ALL THAT IS **OZZEST** IN THE 200-YEAR-OLD TRIUMPH CALLED AUSTRALIA!

AND ALL THAT IS NEWEST IN THE TWO WEEKS SINCE!

With all you need to know about:

- GROG
- DUNNY FACILITIES
- DANGEROUS SPIDERS
- OZ FOOD
- DWARF THROWING
- SHARKS
- GUM TREES
- NEIGHBOURS
- THE NULLARBOR PLAIN
- ALICE
- SPRINGS

EDITED BY GREG LARRIKIN

A PERSONAL WELCOME FROM THE EDITOR

AUSTRALIA! Rhymes with good on ya, doesn't it? Well, pretty nearly. Near enough for Australia. Because Australia is a big country. A bloody huge country. A bloody Continent, for Christ's sake. Yes, we have religions, dozens of the bastards. But what we've really got in Australia is size, and plenty of it. We're on the large side. We've got room for everything. We've got stuff nobody else has got. Look at the Nullarbor Plain. It's hard to do, because you don't know what to look at. There's nothing there. Nothing. Nobody's got a Plain as plain as that. When an Australian says plain he means *plain*, no worries. Plain as all get out. But he doesn't have to say it much, and that's a fact. We don't have many plain sheilas in Australia. All right, you'll always get some with faces that'll stop a clock. But, I don't know what it is, ours always make it up in the legs department. Most of them are gorgeous. Even the lezzoes are gorgeous in Australia, that's how gorgeous the sheilas are. That gives you some idea. And they can hold their beer.

Wild life? We've got it in the pubs and we've got it in the bush. We've got kookaburras, wombats, koalas, wallabies. Funnel-webs, bull-ants, redbacks, taipans. You can meet them all in the space of a day and get bitten by most of them. We've got flies in Australia that'll make you wonder who left the hairdryer on, it's a beaut noise. Just open the door of any outback dunny and hold your breath.

Surf? We've got intellectuals here, clever blokes who can spell a bit, they make films about the surf. The Europeans don't give out a Nobel Prize for Surf because it would be no contest, year after year. You probably like food. We like food in Australia. With drink with it, it's perfect. We've got prawns in Australia like bananas with legs on. Democracy, too, we've got that. We're free, and so is the sunshine. Not even Gough Whitlam found a way to slap a tax on that.

Maybe you like digging holes. It's not a perversion. People come from all over the world to dig holes in Australia. You dig a hole in Australia and opals come out. Fire opals, you know—lustrous, costly, easy to stick in your earwax while the overseer is picking his teeth. It's a great place. We've got a whole flaming swag of stuff here.

Did I mention dingoes or Pat Cash? We've got the only Opera House in the world that looks like a pushed-over pile of plates. Did you ever see Joan Sutherland? She's about the biggest opera star in the world. Built like a public library. Am I making my point? We've got size here. And we've got ramps for the disabled and mime artists and all that stuff. Crikey, you could bust a gut knocking together a list like this.

Read the flaming mag, that's the answer. The supplement, or whatever the Poms call it. It's a beaut production. It was produced in Australia. The information was. It's *about* Australia, that's the important part. Christ, Raelene, that must be enough, the bloody Poms'll never read through to the end of all that, half of them are stone blind anyway. I've got a dead lizard for a throat, crack me a tube, be a sweetheart. Jeez, that's better. Are you getting all this? Raelene, you know, I'm not much of a poet but your tits are a flamin' inspiration, I might just write you one. What are we going to put on the end of it? Shit a brick. All right.

Happy reading!

Yours under the Southern Cross, is that romantic enough for the bastards? Yours, etc. Thank Christ that's over.

Greg Larrikin

GREG LARRIKIN
EDITOR, *PUNCH* AUSTRALIAN SUPPLEMENT

Australian Creatures The World Fears

DON'T WALK ON THE WILD LIFE!

As nearly everyone now knows, Australia is still a savage continent and her natural denizens must be treated with a wary respect. Visitors must accustom themselves, for example, to the routine of raising Australian lavatory seats in order to inspect the rim for spiders; but even then, they may be surprised by the strength and resourcefulness of the blue-kneed dunny flipper, a spider which has learnt to impart a sharp vertical impetus to the seat, often causing painful and unsightly abrasions to the nose of the unwary venturer. The following short-list of venomous species may be supplemented by reference to Australian Govt. Wildlife leaflet no. UH-OH 999.

Light-Bulb Spider: Lives on rare gases available inside common light-bulb, shortening life of bulbs and springing out when bulb "goes". If one lands in your hair, you go too.
Snerdley's Parrot-Eating Spider: Eggs are indistinguishable from bird-seed, incubate rapidly in warmth of cage and devour pet birds of all kinds. Largest individual yet recorded died of indigestion after swallowing toucan.
Hairy Tea-Bag Spider: Thrives on boiling water, fights way out of paper bag. Usually first seen as isolated leg clambering out over side of teacup. Lethal to humans, though prefers cucumber sandwiches.
Stump Jumper or Owzat Spider: Lives in

ABOVE: Vulliamy's Christmas Stocking Snake, whose habitat is self-describing, is one of the "bad sports" of the animal kingdom. Intensely venomous, peevish and crook.
ABOVE RIGHT: A plague of carnivorous sheep traps Queensland farmer D. C. Gossage in the corner of a field. If they spot him, he's a goner. They did. He was.
RIGHT: This black marlin, bitten by an ocean-going Breast-stroke Spider, has only three minutes to live, poor bastard.

cricket stump holes, springs out in response to appeal. Is one of main reasons why Australian umpires wear long johns secured with bicycle clips under their "strides".
Sock-chewing Spider: Has nocturnal habit rising near dawn to attack the extremities of all wool-bearing socks. Anaesthetises human toes

and bites them off. Less feared than it might be, owing to relative infrequency of sock-wearing among Australians.
Plankton of the Opera: Small mite dwelling in crevices of Sydney Opera House ceiling, whence it showers unseen on to heads of spectators during top notes of visiting sopranos. Causes tremors, gout, death and hallucinatory flatulence, usually in that order.
Two-faced Rogue Elephant Whipsnake: Its favourite food being dandruff, the rogue elephant whipsnake is usually found crawling across the backs of cinema seats. The "two-faced" element in its name does not refer to markings. That's just the way it is.
Pacific King Ratbag Snake: Ill-tempered reptile, most at home in the glove compartments of cars. Eats fanbelts. Do not disturb. Run.
Giant Spitting Razorback Cobra: A relative sweetheart at close quarters, but can kill with a well-aimed nugget of green gob at a distance of 25 metres. Generally delivers the fatal missile over its shoulder while leaving.
Muttering Python: A low grumbling sound, as of a disaffected grandparent, is often the first clue to the presence of the muttering python, a vicious strangler which is maddened by the sound of human breathing. Eats small wallabies and barbecue apparatus.
Gillette-toothed Dunny Piranha: Sales of bedpans in the Melbourne area have increased tenfold since this little fellow became endemic in the water system. Whistles while it works.

"Y'know, after a drop or two of the amber nectar, you Poms begin to look almost human."

Australia's Cultural Heritage Is A Little Beauty

Australian culture is known all over the world for how cultured it really is. There are more poets in Australia than you can shake a stick at, and most of them are talented enough to play the guitar at the same time. Our films are the envy of the world, most specially all the ones set in Victorian girls' schools, which feature real Australian sheilas.

Colossal opera stars come to Sydney from all over the globe because we have such great sea food. Nobody can beat our painters when it comes to doing pictures of Ned Kelly. *Neighbours* is the top-rated soap opera among the Poms at the present time, but that's no reason to be ashamed of it.

As far as sculpture, Nature made such a great job of smoothing off Ayers Rock, we hardly need sculpturers, but we have some great ones just the same. And our Aboriginal soloists have been playing their didgeridoos for as long as cardboard tubes have been known to man.

The wonderful thing about Australian culture is, you can do most of it one-handed while cracking a tube or stirring the barby with the other hand. It's an even-handed culture in that sense. And if you get sick of it, there's always the physical beach culture. Any of the world's leading intellectuals who turned *that* combination down would have to be a flaming drongo!

TREASURES OF THE MELBOURNE ART GALLERY

The Mona Sheila

In January 1868, Jim Fink and Horace Drubbett set out to explore the Australian interior. Armed only with a flintlock water-pistol and a Great Western Railway fish-knife, their baggage toted by a heat-stricken Sherpa who died after three miles, they were never again seen alive. Only a trail of shredded copies of the *Illustrated London News* led their successors along the tortured path to their oblivion. Yet their terrible journey was not in vain. On the way, they encountered many strange sights and experiences whose names they gave to those places in perpetuity. Their own names will live forever in our legend, and this souvenir map is dedicated to their memory: those great Australians, Fred Fink and Morrie Drubbett.

DUNROAMIN
VALLEY OF CORN — BIG DISAPPOINTMENT
OBUGGA
VALLEY OF SEVERAL CORNS — BIG SHIMMERING LAKE
NOTTANUDDA
EREWEGO
WASSA POINT
WIBBLAWOBBLA
FOUR O'CLOCK ROCK — NEW JERSEY
SHIT CREEK
BLOODY GREAT SCORPION VIEW — URE FAULT — BOILING POINT
AMBLESIDE
BURSTING POINT — EXCLAMATION POINT
SOUTHPORT
HELL'S UNDERPANTS
HELL'S TROUSERS
MUTTAMATTA
WASSAMATTA — FLATBUSH
WHITTINGTON
TUNNADUNG
DEDIZEE
BIOCHEMISTRY BAY

ROUTE OF FINK AND DRUBBETT'S PIONEERING EXPEDITION, 1868

137

Wonderwines Of Australia

Australian wines now number among the world's favourites, so there is no need to re-emphasise their harmonious richness and reliability. However, the names of some of Australia's newer successes may not have reached your shipper yet, so may we take this opportunity of recommending:

Wackawarra Punter Valley Spot-On Chablis Triffico 1987: smooth, peaty tang, freezes well into lollies.

McSkiffing's Frog Nest Triple-Boiled Wing-ding Mixture 1988: ideal accompaniment to barbecued Queensland toad steaks.

Kakawoomba Cedar of Lebanon Chianti Knockout Private Bin: hearty, rough, free-swearing wine, currently on remand for house-breaking.

Wurrumbludgee Very Old Ship Creek Cabernet-Sauvignon Riesling (type): uniquely pungent blend, nothing like it in Europe, full of characters.

O'Reilly's Tasmanian Whoopee Drops Tokay Special Selection 1987: legendary party wine of the island state, also used for scrubbing horsehair wigs.

FOR THE SERIOUSLY THIRSTY

Equally famous, and perhaps even more frequently drunk, are Australia's legendary beers, brewed from natural malts and our own indigenous kangaroo hops. Foster's Lager, Swan Lager and Castlemaine XXXX have long been among the world's best-known thirst-quenchers, and a chilled stubby of Boag's, heavily sweating with condensation and gently pulsing with the probability of a dinkum stinko session, is an increasingly familiar sight in such faraway meccas of the neck-oil fraternity as Rangoon and Wellington (NZ). But before you respond to that great old salutation "Could you hold one down?" by diving into the nearest rubbidy and grabbing a glass of your usual grog, why not check out these newcomers, currently terrorising the tonsils of some of Australia's pickiest connoisseurs of the amber nectar, viz:

Old Traditional Woomera Rocket Range Stout: guaranteed to spin the wig off the skull of the most blue-nosed wowser.

Griffin's Brown Tram Oil: known to locals around the Dongawagga brewery as "One Day At A Time". Do not mix with taipan-bite remedy.

Doc Leatherwood's Original Wollongong Heartstarter: as its name implies, a challenging little aperitif. Poisonous to camels.

Taswell's Spangled Kneeknocker: the famous hair-of-the-dingo hangover remedy, to be taken either on arising or on falling over.

Tarramblatta Buffalo Fly's Revenge: Kept in stone bottles for safety. Stand well clear. Not for bloody waterbags.*

*teetotallers

Australia's Sportsmen Keep Their Cools

We've got to admit it, Australia does not hold all the cricket records in the world today. The record for the Number of Umpires Hit In One Innings is held by the Poms. Well, we might just let them have that one. We've got it to spare.

We already lead the world in Aussie Rules football, swimming, life-saving, fishing, yachting, eating a bucket of prawns, competition beer-drinking, dwarf-throwing, pin-the-tail-on-the-donkey, cricket, rugby league, that other rugby, darts, clay-kookaburra shooting, athaletics, kangaroo-boxing, roller-derby, tennis, horse-racing, synchronised swimming, synchronised drowning, hockey, polo, water-polo,

This talented Australian shark won the inaugural World Offshore Cat's Cradle Championship before expiring in the heat

water-hockey, wet T-shirt competitions, throwing the voice, betting, tug-of-war (male), tug-of-war (sheilas), kite-flying, cock-fighting, freestyle boomeranging, Frisbee, surfing, billabong-jumping and Find The Lady.

Quite a record, eh? We are an active nation, and where we're not skilful we're big. And we keep our cools. Unlike the so-called phlegmatic Brits we don't go sticking our fingers up the noses of Abo umpires, no matter how crook they go on us. We have a sense of fair play inherited from our insect population. Sting one, sting all, is our motto.

We can beat the world at most things and the Poms at everything except whingeing. And that's with a hangover. When we feel really good, the others might as well not show up. That's Australian sport, sport.

The Perth Rowing Club runs the gauntlet at the Australian Mass Spitting Championships at Stinkamalloo

The 1987 Australian Open Chess Championship at Sockabudgee Beach, NSW

A MESSAGE FROM SNOOKER'S JIMMY WHITE

Being brung up in Wimbledon, the way I woz, Australia holds a special fascination for me. It's a great place. It's hot and they're really useless at snooker, so you can win a lot of money if you're any good. The birds are amazing an' all.

As a country, it's got everything. Seas as blue as the blue ball, outback as red as the red ball and sunshine as bright as referee Les Ganley.

But don't take my word for it. This magnificent supplement will, I reckon, help you to get to grips with the real Australia. Enjoy it!

AUSSIE DONOR CARD

I would like to help someone after I've thrown up and become unconscious. (Keep this card with you at all times in a place where it will be found quickly, e.g. in the fridge.) I request that after my sickie, and in the event of me crashing out for a bit of boozy spine-bashing, that
(a) My six-packs be used to keep the party going
(b) My eskie be used to further the pursuit of pleasure
In the event of my shout, contact my mate (applicable name)..........................

"It's the same every flamin' sheep-count – half the hands asleep at their jobs!"

Some Australian Personalities We Happen To Like

You don't grapple with a continent the size of Australia without (a) a few beers, and (b) getting to be a special sort of person. Big, hardheaded, tons of personality. It's like the early navigators. If they didn't want to land on Australia, Australia wasn't going to get out of the way. They had to sail round it.

And the Australian personality is the same. To make an impact on world affairs, the average Australian personality only has to stand there, because the others will do the moving. And when an Australian opens his mouth, everybody listens. Looks, too, because you never know what might emerge!

Seriously, many famous Australians have taken our message of hope, size and beer all over the world. You've seen them, and through them you may feel you know us pretty well.

But you know, we've got a lot of very beautiful and famous people here in Australia who are just for our consumption alone. One of our famous newspaper columnists here, Bruce Layout, once called them "The Unexportables", and that's not a bad little name. It's a sound nomenclature. Because they are. They answer a very real need in our country for famous people with nice teeth, and there's something about them only an Aussie could love.

And here are some of them now.

PHOTO MONTAGE: BAIRD HARRIS

Western Australia's Wildlife Commissioner, NORMAN HOOTLEY, salutes the launch of Ban Bacteria From The Barby Week in Perth.

At the Melbourne Festival, protest singer WOCKER O'QUIGLEY gives his famous rendition of "If Only I Looked More Untidy".

Aboriginal mime artist BETTY BOG-GABILLA performs the Dance of the Missing Piano.

Australia's leading poet, R.D. SHUG-BOROUGH, who will be present at the Adelaide Festival to read selections from his volumes Wet Nuts and There's Another One Under the Mattress.

"We're just havin' a quiet little celebration at home."

Australian heavyweight All-In Wrestling champion WARREN "SMACKER" BARNARDO, who recently surprised his fans by taking holy orders.

Adelaide's Sheep-Dip Queen for 1987, LURLENE TOSHACK, who represented Australia at the World Fleece Pests Seminar in Las Vegas, USA.

So you want to become an Aussie?

SWEAR? AUSTRALIANS HAVE TO

To become an Australian citizen you have to be a resident for two years (one in a spacious oceanside bungie with a big veranda and sun-blinds, and the other running around completely starkers in the outback).

Then you attend a nationalisation ceremony ("a cerie"), in which you have to take the official oath of allegiance to the Commonwealth of OZ.

(The candidate shall knock back a six-pack of Toohey's, burp in the prescribed manner, take down his strides and place a battered cabbage-tree hat on his head. Some pissed-up swimming-pool salesman shall call him a big ponce.)

I do hereby foully and obscenely swear, on pain of teetotalism, that I am well assured in my own little mind that I do honestly seek to be added to the beautiful people in Australia, Land of Plenty, God's Own Country and all that crap, and that I do sincerely and seriously desire the moral and intellectual stagnation that will forever be mine theretofore, sport.

(Then follows ritual responses of "Ripper/Ripper!")

Coming of my own free will and accord, I do voluntarily offer myself as a permanent resie of the southern hemi; pledging with no fuss whatsoever to eat a lot of Krona margarine; name my home Dougesholme even if my name isn't Doug; see to thirty gallons of amber nectar a year; eat tons of two-inch-thick lamb chops and prawns as plump and pink as a postie's knees; hold char-it-yourself crop-dustin' parties; spend my fat income on the pokies and trotties; and generally enjoy all the great and invaluable privies of living in the big pink place on the right of world maps. *(Next follows ritual response of "Skippy! Skippy! My friend ever true!" A meat pie is then placed in the candidate's right hand.)*

I do heretowith acknowledge the citizenship enjoins me to dispense with all airs and graces and respect no social distinctions; except for bongs who are a bloody nuisance and about as worthless as peeing on a bushfire. Honeymooning Japs aren't much better.
(Response of "Tie mi kangaroo down, sport. Tie mi kangaroo down".)

I also pledge an oath to, when abroad, act and abide with the time-honoured customs of an Aussie away from home: getting his backpack in everyone's way on the Tube; moaning about prices and the weather; and generally being a loud-mouthed, coarse, brusque, uncouth, bigoted, chauvinistic pain-in-the-arse little bastard, so help me, Hawkey.
(Response of "Who's got the keys to the wool-shed?")

Pray keep me steadfast in my endeavour to cultivate true Australianness. No trubs.

In the name of Gough Whitlam, the Malcolm Turnbull and the Great White Shark…
(The candidate is smeared with yeast extract and presented with his scroll. The ceremony ends with a lot of effing and blinding.)

STOWELL

MORE WELSH THAN WALES

*In search of concentrated Welshness to celebrate
St David's Day, TIM HEALD and PAUL COX journeyed
clean across London for a cyngerdd put on by
Cymdeithas Maldwyn for the Eisteddfod yr Urdd*

There is no use fudging the issue. Racial characteristics are a fact of life and it is counter-productive to pretend otherwise. Indeed, properly approached, these distinctions can contribute greatly to the gaiety of nations. Take, as it is their national day this week, the Welsh. It is a manifest biological fact that Welsh people are not able to sing flat. Most English people have no problem doing it – witness any Anglican church at matins or, better still, the Englishman in his bath. Flat as the earth. Welsh people's lungs or larynxes, however, are shaped differently and they can't do it.

I was reminded of this – and one or two other odd things about them – at that bastion of Welshness, the London Welsh Association in the Gray's Inn Road. The illustrator and I were attending a *cyngerdd* put on by *Cymdeithas Maldwyn* to raise money for the *Eisteddfod yr Urdd* which is being held in Newtown, Montgomeryshire for the first time ever. That's enough Welsh for one article. What we were doing was sitting in on a fund-raising concert

given by the Montgomeryshire Society in aid of the National Youth Eisteddfod.

It was Mattie Prichard who suggested it. There are those who think the true flavour of the Principality can be savoured only by visiting the place itself but this is not so. If you really want to find the absolute distillation of Welshness you need to go to the Gray's Inn Road, just as you will find true Englishness only really when one or two expats are gathered together on the playing fields of Ootacamund or at the annual Oxbridge dinner in Santa Fe, New Mexico.

Mattie is the widow of Caradog, the great Welsh bard who used to work as a sub-editor at *The Daily Telegraph* when it was still (through the Berries) a partly Welsh newspaper. The Welsh used to have a virtual stranglehold on Fleet Street. Mattie remembers a friend of her youth once saying, "Those Cudlipp boys are doing very well in London. They all get paid by cheque."

All afternoon she had been at the Gray's Inn Road because she had arranged for her son-in-law's band to practise there before going to the Ritz to play for a posh wedding party. The son-in-law is a biographer as well as a bandleader and his Ezra Pound is out any minute. However, he is un-Welsh and therefore another story.

HALF OF THEM ARE TUB-THUMPING TEMPERANCE MEN, THE OTHER HALF ARE DRUNK.

"Try a Felinfoel," said Mattie, "or Feeling Foul as you English call it." Felinfoel is Welsh beer from near Llanelli. "Whatever you do, don't ask for Welsh whisky," she added. She didn't elaborate.

For years and years the London Welsh had no bar, a legacy of that strange Celtic divide between the likes of Dylan and Burton on the one hand and Lord Tonypandy on the other. Half of them are tub-thumping temperance men, the other half are drunk. For years the London Welsh went over to the Calthorpe Arms across the way or down to the Blue Lion. I asked the barman when that had changed. "The

bar opened on the 17th March, 1971," he said. But they had to break the Trust to do it.

It is a wondrously sepulchral place. June, who organised the concert and who is married to a professor of nuclear physics, said that I wasn't to write too much about how tatty it was because it was going to be tarted up quite soon and, in any case, it wasn't the Montgomeryshire Society's Hall, so it wasn't really anything to do with them. It has very high ceilings and is heated, like Balliol Hall used to be, by single-bar electric fires suspended from the roof. Every other woman present seemed to have met her husband at one of the famous, but now discontinued, Saturday evening dances. Not that the memory is always sweet. "I kick the wall every time I pass the spot," said one divorcee.

Downstairs there is a plaque that speaks volumes – in Welsh, of course – to the memory of Tawe Griffiths. Tawe Griffiths used to conduct the singing at Marble Arch every Sunday. If you were homesick for the land of your fathers you went down to Speaker's Corner and sang along with Tawe. "That's the thing about this place," said Mattie, "it's more Welsh than Wales. There are people here who have lived in London for more than half a century and still they're not happy speaking English." There's

even a Ghanaian teacher studying for the bar who joins in Mattie's weekly advanced-Welsh classes. He learned his Welsh at university in Aberystwyth where he was a contemporary of Prince Charles. He still gets homesick for Cardigan Bay.

In the auditorium it could have been gala night in Tregarron or Llandeilo, not central

SONGS OF UNREQUITED LOVE AND SOMETHING FOLKLORIC TO DO WITH TOFFEE.

London. The conductor's podium looked like an orange box with "Property of London Welsh Male Voice" on one side. There were a few bits of vestigial Christmas tinsel, and the stage decorations were two large, painted daffodils. The clock was stuck on ten o'clock and the audience had the cold, beleaguered look, a compound of greys and browns, that I associate with the wintry street corners of slate-mining towns with names I can't pronounce. It was Mattie, not I, who said that many of the assembled group looked as if they had come in

straight from a day out at Carmarthen Market.

The compère, however, John Jones, had the slight build of an elusive left-wing three-quarter, and the gift of the gab *and* he stood in

at the piano when necessary; and there was a choir of ladies, all in long black skirts and uniform blue tops, who reminded me of the Welsh women who paraded on the cliffs near Fishguard and frightened away a Napoleonic invasion fleet with their tall black hats which looked like guardsmen's bearskins. Bethan Dudley Davies from Aberystwyth sang, and so did Julia Morgan, who had been at school with John Jones, and Arwel Treharne Morgan who looked like a young, barrel-chested Gareth Edwards; and a beautiful blonde girl from a sheep farm in a remote valley gave us songs of unrequited love and something folkloric to do with toffee, while accompanying herself on the harp, *and* she made a deliciously barbed remark about how they failed to drown her valley so they could take the water over the border for people in Birmingham to drink.

Mattie, who is a world authority on harpists, pronounced her excellent and threatened to take her in hand and launch her on a London career. The girl's name is Sian James and Mattie did have a genuine entrepreneurial glint in her eye as she said it. Worth a small bet I should say.

WALES MAY BE VERY SMALL, BUT SHE IS VERY WONDERFUL.

Occasionally, in a particularly impassioned moment of incomprehensible song, Mattie would stage-whisper, "This is a *very* patriotic song, it says that Wales may be very small but she is very wonderful." Or something like that. The word *Cymru* was repeated a lot and you sensed a general coursing of the blood and thumping of the hearts beneath the predominantly beige overcoats.

But the Welshest moment came right at the end when John Jones announced the national anthem. In English England, if anybody should have the temerity to do such a thing, the audience would make a mass dive for the exits, looking at their feet and coughing. This was a mixed congregation of two or three hundred and I am not insulting anyone when I say that the predominant feel reminded me of my little old auntie who lives in Aberdovey (though she is Welsh only by adoption). Age and infirmity notwithstanding, they pushed back their hideous orange chairs, they threw back their heads and they sang "Land of my fathers" (only in Welsh), for all the world like thousands at the Arms Park on a spring Saturday before flaying the All Blacks.

Not a flat note anywhere, poor dears.

It was all terribly, terribly un-English.

SEE YOU IN COURT

She had already chained up one man.
Now MIKE MOLLOY was on his way to the cells

From the third floor of the *Daily Mirror* building in Holborn Circus the window of the Editor's office commands a view to the east, across the City of London, and there, framed by the jagged stumps of high-rise office buildings, stand the noble domes of St Paul's and the Old Bailey.

Fittingly, St Paul's looks grander, reminding us that there is a final judgment to come in the highest court, and although an unmistakable authority emanates from the statue with the sword and scales, when I first sat in the Editor's chair in 1975 the Old Bailey held no particular menace for me.

Then we inadvertently printed a minor contempt of court.

Sir Edward Pickering, Chairman of Mirror Group Newspapers at that time, advised me to put in an appearance at the Old Bailey while a barrister apologised on my behalf for the technical infringement.

"It does no harm to be in court," Sir Edward advised. "The judge is a good chap and well disposed to journalists. He used to do shifts in Fleet Street as a night lawyer when he was at the bar."

I nodded blithely as Sir Edward added a sombre footnote.

"But remember, when you're in court for contempt, you're at the mercy of the judge. He can send you straight to the cells if he has a mind to."

Fresh to the job of editing and unburdened by guilt, I made my way to the Old Bailey early

"I CAN'T SEE THERE'LL BE ANY PROBLEM, MR MILROY," SAID MY LAWYER. "MOLLOY," I SAID CAREFULLY, "MY NAME IS MOLLOY." HE LAUGHED. "DON'T WORRY, MR KILROY, THIS WILL ONLY TAKE A FEW MINUTES."

the following morning and introduced myself to the junior counsel who was to do the talking.

"I can't see there'll be any problem, Mr Milroy," the boy in the wig and gown said to me as we shook hands.

"Molloy," I said carefully. "My name is Molloy."

He laughed.

"Don't worry, Mr Kilroy. This will only take a few minutes."

I felt a tiny twinge of apprehension as I entered the court but Sir Edward had been right about the judge. He even managed a wintry smile in my direction when junior counsel explained I was present in person. I relaxed and began to enjoy myself.

Previously I had observed the ritual of courts from a seat in the stalls. Suddenly I had a part on the stage. Granted, it was a non-speaking role and only entailed me sitting there with a contrite expression on my face while the lawyer made a brief and dignified apology, but, after a few minutes, to my mounting horror, I realised the boy in the wig was not apologising. Instead of the grovel I had been led to expect, he was challenging the judge's interpretation of the laws of contempt.

Sir Edward's words of solemn warning came back to me and I felt that I was engulfed in a Kafkaesque nightmare. Visions of being led to the subterranean cells beneath us filled my mind. Even the walls of the court seemed to distort like the set of a German Expressionist movie.

Luckily the judge was merciful. He allowed the lad to flounder around for a few more minutes before delivering him a verbal clip around the ear. I was dismissed and, a few moments later, stood breathing the air of freedom outside the court.

As I walked back to the paper I thought hard about what it would be worth risking jail for. To be a prisoner of conscience in a noble cause was fine – providing, of course, that one was serving the sentence in a British open prison and not in the dungeons of a Third World country's Palace of Justice. But to be jailed for carelessness in a case that was frivolous or vulgar would be unbearable, no matter how much pleasure it would provide for one's friends and enemies. Stopping for a moment by the statue of Prince Albert in Holborn Circus, I swore a solemn resolution to be vigilant.

A thousand editions went by without the risk of a contempt. Then, three years later, the moment-of-truth arrived.

For months Britain had been transfixed by the case of the manacled Mormon.

To refresh your memory, a young American

TURN TO PAGE 15

girl, with the appearance and demeanour of a Victorian milk-maid, stood accused of kidnapping a young man of the Mormon persuasion, chaining him to a bedstead and having her wicked way with him.

A charge of kidnapping was brought against her and the nation awaited the outcome with quivering anticipation.

As is often the case with notorious maidens, Miss McKinney liked talking to the press. She quickly established a network of contacts on all of the popular newspapers and they would be rung at regular intervals to share revelations about her extraordinary purity. Indeed, she would claim that but for her one mad moment of love-inspired carnality, she was a fair match for the driven snow.

Although Miss McKinney liked to be photographed by the jostling paparazzi, she steadfastly refused to pose in anything more daring than a discreet angora twinset.

"Ah'm nart that kindah gurl," Joyce would say in a Southern accent you could use to sweeten hominy grits. She remained good copy but the photographs of her could have won prizes for moral rectitude.

Because Joyce was on bail, any new revelations would constitute a contempt of court, so we were extremely cautious over what we printed about her. We took contempt very seriously in the *Mirror* offices, particularly my office.

Meanwhile, in Los Angeles, Frank Palmer, a veteran *Mirror* reporter, and our chief photographer, Kent Gavin, were pursuing a tiresome footballer who was threatening to sell his life story for the third time. Late one Wednesday evening I received a call from Kent Gavin.

"How's the footballer?" I asked.

"Dead boring," Gavin replied dismissively. "But we've got another one that's good."

My heart sank. Journalists on foreign trips can often behave like children who have been sent out for a loaf of bread, only to return with a tin of pilchards.

"We need the footballer, Kent," I said in my best talking-to-the-mentally-retarded tone of voice.

"The line's lousy, boss," Gavin said cheerfully. "See you tomorrow night."

We had a television campaign planned for the following week and needed the latest confessions of the runaway footballer so I was anxious until Palmer and Gavin came into my office the following night. They were weary with jet-lag but supercharged with suppressed excitement as they spread a mass of documents and photographs on to the floor.

The stuff they had was stunning. Incontrovertible proof that Joyce McKinney was not the simple misunderstood girl she would have the world believe. There were pictures of her riding a horse and only the horse was wearing anything.

Pictures of Joyce and another girl dressed in natty leather outfits chaining each other to various pieces of equipment and indulging in sado-masochistic horseplay. Complete sets of her telephone bills and the advertisements she

"Come in here, Miss Fontaine, and sexually harass me!"

had placed in various esoteric magazines offering a bizarre array of services, and one picture of Joyce lying on a rug in the sort of naked pose most girls give up when they get to be a year old.

Trivial? Yes.

Prurient? Certainly.

Vulgar? Beyond question.

Interesting? Sweet Charity. It was eye-popping stuff.

But we couldn't publish until the trial was over. We waited with bated breath. Then we had to unbate. Disaster struck. Joyce skipped bail and fled to the United States disguised as a nun. And the *Daily Express* were with her. Derek Jameson was editor and he had protected his charge by assigning Peter Tory, one of Fleet Street's wittiest writers, and Brian Vine, the doyen of the American correspondents, to act as her minders. They must have made a wonderful trio.

Vine and Tory are both English gentlemen of the old school – the sort of chaps sundowners and native servants were invented for. Putting them in charge of a hysterical, sex-mad harpy was like asking Harry Wharton and Co to share their dormitory with Moll Flanders.

Jameson was claiming, with his usual modesty, that he had the exclusive of the century. To ensure that he could print his story he went to the Master of the Rolls, Lord Denning, who granted permission for them to publish. Derek knew we had something but the *Express* were confident we wouldn't match their story. They were right. Our stuff was several points higher on the Richter scale of sensation. There was just one snag.

Our Legal Department were adamant: the *Mirror* story was a clear case of contempt of court. They confidently expected me to go to jail if I published the picture of Joyce on the rug.

That Saturday I reviewed the situation. We had spent £150,000 on television advertisements and three pages of the paper were made up ready for publication on the Monday morning. Late in the afternoon, Hugh Corrie, the *Mirror*'s chief lawyer, rang my home to reassure me that I did not have a legal leg to stand on. If Joyce McKinney returned to England to stand trial, our story and pictures would seriously prejudice the case.

It was an editor's decision but one that had the gravest warnings attached to it. After a sleepless night and feeling about as confident as a paper dart in a Force Nine gale, I finally gave the order to carry on and publish.

The next day, when Joyce McKinney had the article read to her, she attempted to climb the curtains in her hotel room. Presumably, Vine and Tory were clinging to the hem of her nun's habit.

The *Daily Mirror* sold out on the bookstalls and that evening Derek Jameson came into the *Mirror* pub with his hands up, and offered to surrender.

But I felt no triumph. For some days I waited to see if the awesome majesty of the law would reach out and deposit me in a cell. The Attorney General's office decided, for reasons buried in the archives of legal history, to drop the case. Having once come within a whisper of Wandsworth over some legal small print, I was now to be let off in a blatant, open-and-shut case that had my dabs all over it.

Even to this day I occasionally have a certain nightmare. After all, one of my predecessors did in fact end up behind bars, and, poor soul, was pierced by the Great Spike in the Sky shortly afterwards. My case for the defence would be that it was all the fault of Mr Milroy or, failing that, Mr Kilroy.

JACKSON!!

– ALL YOU WANT TO KNOW ABOUT POP'S GREATEST SHOWMAN

The Early Years

Michael Jackson was born in August, 1958. Since he was born wearing a pair of white gloves, a theory persists that his real father was, in fact, not an impoverished crane driver but either a snooker referee or a policeman on traffic duty. His mother, Katherine, knew her son was headed for mega-stardom and prepared him for fame and adulation by having his pram fitted with smoked-glass windows. Local people in Gary, Indiana, would wait outside the Jackson home just for a glimpse of the future superstar as Mrs Jackson, returning from the shops, ran up the drive pushing Michael's pram. Eventually, the crowds got so big that she had to go the back way.

A painfully shy child, Michael spoke his first words when he was eighteen months old, ringing his mother from a pay-phone, reversing the charges and saying, "Hi! This is Michael." From an early age rumours about Michael's sexuality began to circulate. At the age of four, still insisting on his virginity, Michael was forced by persistent gay smears to issue a statement through his mother. "Some time in the future I plan to get married and have a family. Any statements to the contrary are simply untrue."

The Middle Years

At the age of six Michael became a fitness fanatic. He started to go to bed early and he didn't drink or smoke. His best friends were anti-ageing specialists. However, he was soon resorting to crime to feed his health addiction and preserve his youth. He and his friends, conscious of crows' feet and smile-lines developing around the eyes, tried to rob a health farm but it went disastrously wrong when they were caught trying to make their getaway on exercise bikes.

Michael's obsession with bizarre pets also started at this time. His first was a grammatical joke. "It was all we could afford," he recalls. It was a palindrome which he called Otto. His next was a celery stick from which he was inseparable until it was tragically involved in a Waldorf salad on the road.

After Michael was expelled from school for constantly talking in class about his vast financial empire, the Jacksons signed for Epic in March 1976. Brother Randy replaced Jermaine who, eager to be a rock phenomenon himself, had formed "The Standing Stones".

The Jacksons confirmed themselves as a potent musical force with Michael, having passed puberty, singing with new vigour. He achieved this in the studio by pulling hairs out of his nose while singing and, onstage, by wearing strategically positioned elastic bands under tight trousers.

In 1978 a national tour was abandoned after Michael's head flew off in the middle of "Shake Your Body". The smash hit single "Blame It On The Boogie" was inspired by Michael's unsuccessful rhinoplasty operation. Michael now had a vast entourage of bodyguards paid to go everywhere with him to make sure nothing fell off. In 1979's "Off The Wall", with its combination of R&B, pop, jazz and Michael on vibromassage, was released. "Don't Stop Until I Get Enough" was a No. 1 based on Michael's experiences with fat aspersion.

The album sells five million copies to people with cosmetically heightened cheekbones alone and another single, "Can You Feel It", is another smash hit among record buyers with silicon implants.

Through an astute – some would say manipulative marketing campaign – and dazzlingly inventive creative genius, Michael Jackson's music transcends all barriers of race and age with its appeal.

The Later Years

Released in December 1987, "Thriller" sells 38.5 million copies throughout the world. It smashes all records. It goes platinum in Canada where people worried about the dehydration of their dermis account for over half of its sales. In Nepal it goes gold with llamas buying it in flocks.

Michael is honoured when he receives The People's Choice Award for The Best Ethnically Indeterminate Singer of 1985. *Melody Maker* readers also vote him The Best Boy-girl Pixie Figure with Bleached Skin who Wants to Fly. Michael waits three more years until his next album, "Bad". It immediately captures a new audience of people with sagging skin problems. It sells best among parafango mudbathers and becomes the *Guinness Book of Records'* biggest selling album among the bone-graft and chemical skin-peel community. It will stimulate cell turnover, says a panel of Nevada doctors.

In August 1987 Michael announces that all the profits from his world tour will go to The National Creased Forehead Research Fund and The American Jowls Abatement Society. Now living in an oxygen tent (and forced to give up his favourite hobby of kiting), Michael embarks on his first solo world tour. In September 1987 he sells out five nights in Tokyo and plays an extra concert for Japanese music lovers afraid of direct sunlight. Concerts follow in Australia and New Zealand where Michael sets another record for a concert seen by the biggest number of bat-ear correction veterans.

His concerts in the UK are already sold out and an awful lot of people who don't like what they see in the bathroom mirror in the morning are going to be disappointed about not getting a ticket.

ALAN PLATER

GOOD HEAVENS!
IS THAT THE TIME?

EVERY professional writer holds the following truth to be self-evident: each year that passes is an anniversary of something or other and you can usually earn an honest bob servicing the celebrations. D. H. Lawrence – or Bert as we call him in the biography trade – has treated me handsomely in this department. I wrote a feature film about him in 1980, mainly because he died in 1930; and I wrote a television film about him in 1985, mainly because he was born in 1885. Each time we were hoping to make a little bit of art, but in the beginning was the arithmetic.

However, once we've commemorated the births, deaths, marriages and first editions of Lettered Persons; the outbreaks of war and the spasms of peace; the famines and festivals, the historical epochs and hysterical epics; once we've done all that, a simple economic truth remains. The greatest of the little earners is Christmas. Writers learn this in the first week of their apprenticeship; it comes on a leaflet with the Yearbook and the Olivetti portable.

I was a quick learner. The second piece I ever sold for money was to *The Architects' Journal* at the very end of 1958. It was a festive and relentlessly amusing feature called *Old Plater's Almanack, 1959*. I wasn't old, of course. I was twenty-three, with a full head of hair and a head full of coruscating wit, mostly aimed at the environment. I had spent much of the decade in university failing various examinations in architecture. This made me an ideal candidate

> "The meals tended to be long and progressively louder through the afternoon, ending around four o'clock when we addressed the key question: where do we live and is there any serious possibility of getting there?"

as architectural journalist, occasional critic and, of course, coruscating wit.

A random sample from the *1959 Almanack* gives a fair idea of the depth and texture of the coruscation:

February. Famous architect of airports, point blocks and cathedrals appears as celebrity on *What's My Line* and beats the panel. The female members do not know who he is, even after they have been told who he is.

The serious underlying point – because even then I knew that humour should have a serious underlying point – was that most people, especially those who appeared on panel games, wouldn't know Basil Spence from Basil Brush. The sub-plot concerned the implied dumbness of women on panel games, and would no longer be permitted. In 1987, you may tread on most things, but you tread on gender at your peril. In retrospect, February 1959 seems like another part of a distant forest and we did well to leave it behind.

Between the years 1963 and 1976, I wrote 48 episodes for *Z Cars* and its successor, *Softly Softly*. I added documentary realism to the coruscating wit and serious underlying points. It all began with the lunches.

About twice a year, the production team would organise an all-day talk-in for the contributing writers. We would spend the morning discussing major thematic developments and addressing the key question: who is going to write the murder story? Our documentary zeal meant that murders ran in the same proportion to more mundane crimes as in the so-called real world outside Television Centre. The ration was one murder every twenty episodes or so. These days, it would be one every twenty minutes. Elwyn Jones usually bagged the murder and we would then address the second key question: who will write the Christmas episode? With our passion for hard-edged reality, we had one Christmas episode

"Make up your minds! It's only food."

THE SPECIAL RELATIONSHIP...

per annum, normally shown in late December.

Once these issues had been resolved, the writers were taken for lunch into downtown Ladbroke Grove. As well as writing the murder episode, Elwyn had to approve the restaurant. The meals tended to be long and progressively louder through the afternoon, ending around four o'clock when we addressed the key question: where do we live and is there any serious possibility of getting there?

The *Softly Softly* lunches petered out with one of the earlier BBC financial crises. The Corporation asked *us* a key question: will you settle for the canteen or, if you insist on downtown Ladbroke Grove, are you prepared to pay for yourselves? That virtually guaranteed a petering out.

Among those 48 episodes I remember writing one murder story and one festive special, a cheerful little number called *On Christmas Day in the Morning*, set in one of those plush country house hotels where rich and over-privileged people who are sick of their homes and families gather together at huge expense to forget the real meaning of Christmas. I had, by now, added searing social comment to the toolbag, along with the documentary realism, coruscating wit and serious underlying points. It was getting very crowded in the bag.

The episode had a simple, Raffles-style plot, wherein a gentleman thief moved quietly from room to room, nicking the baubles, bangles and beads from the undeserving rich. His associate – who remained innocent and undetected – was a young chambermaid, an unmarried mother and resilient victim of the class system. She was also slightly homeless – an oblique attempt at a no-room-at-the-inn metaphor that most people, very sensibly, overlooked or ignored. Susan Tebbs, the actress who played the part, was so good she later joined *Softly Softly* in a permanent capacity as a policewoman, proving that where casting is concerned, rehabilitation knows no frontiers.

There has never been a shortage of shambles within television. One of my jolliest began with a phone call from the splendid Barney Colehan about a forthcoming Yuletide edition of *The Good Old Days*. He was planning to fill the audience with celebrities and wanted me to script some casual interval banter, which he would record in the bar at the City Varieties and insert midway through the edited version of the show. The initial brief was to write five minutes of cheerful badinage for such as Henry Cooper, Eddie Waring and Eric and Ernie: straightforward funnies, with no call for searing, coruscation or underlying points. Barney liked his jokes with red noses and check suits. He loathed comedians who wore tuxedos.

I started writing, but instinct told me to do it in pencil. Instinct was right. Barney phoned at weekly intervals through the autumn, changing the cast each time. Eric and Ernie were no longer available, Henry Cooper and Eddie Waring were doubtful, but we might have Kevin Keegan, Patrick Moore, Harold Wilson and Emu. These names are approximate and probably inaccurate, but the principle is clear. By mid-December, Barney had clearly checked the availability of everybody worth half a column inch in the known world.

The final telephone call came the day before the show was due to be recorded and my cast became Cliff Michelmore, Fred Trueman and Peter Alliss – the only three famous names not mentioned hitherto. I arrived at the City Varieties on the day, clutching my badinage. It was as razor-sharp as could be expected under the circumstances. I could easily contain all I knew about golf, cricket and television presentation within five minutes and still leave room for a couple of cheap, re-cycled one-liners.

In the nature of the shambles, there was no time for the actors to learn their lines and we recorded the piece in the bar, close to midnight, with Cliff, Fred and Peter sitting at a table with scripts on their knees. Everybody laughed a great deal, on the very edges of hysteria, and at the end we addressed the question: where do we live and is there any serious possibility of getting there?

The drama was never seen. What appeared on screen was a regular edition of *The Good Old Days*, with supplementary holly and trimmings but no interval banter. Barney phoned to explain that the show had over-run and, had he included our piece, the programme would have exceeded its allotted span of sixty minutes. This, in its turn, would have involved the Corporation in additional payments and all-embracing overtime on a scale equivalent to ten years of lunches for writers in downtown Ladbroke Grove.

The script still survives, buried deep in the files: a footnote to an appendix to a supplement in the annals of the complete works. Sometimes it's better to blush unseen, in case anybody notices that all the flash talk about oblique metaphors is just a cover story for a bunch of red-nosed jokers sitting around in a bar.

"I feel he may be confusing my identity crisis with someone else's identity crisis."

MISS LONELYHEARTS

"Iron-willed, with love of domination,
seeks weak-willed Deputy Prime Minister…"

Monday
22 February
1988

*Media*Fiddick

The pyjama-clad supremo of Tanktopf Films talks to Peter Fiddick

Shelf Shock Days

Light refreshment: the beer-wasting scene from Spouting Artery (Tanktopf Films)

IF HER cerise-and-green office in Fitzrovia is anything to go by, Anna Tanktopf is a woman of some stylistic daring. "Yes," she confesses, "I don't mind making people puke as long as they notice I'm here. And my films, of course. The bucket is in the corner."

Anna, 46, brings her lean frame, office-hours pyjamas and intimidating tawny eyebrows to work every morning in a 1951 Morris Commercial bread-van. "I'm in love with 1951," she explains. "It was Festival Year, with Battersea and Rowland Emett trains and a computer – they called it a Giant Brain – that you could pit your wits against and *win*. I mean, it just wasn't very bright. I love all that. It was simply good to be alive, along with T. S. Eliot, Gandhi, George Bernard Shaw and Stanley Matthews, who were also alive at that time."

This comfortable nostalgia, I pointed out, has not so far surfaced in her TV-film productions. Apeshit Gaga, for example, was about an illegal immigrant who had the top of his head sawn off by a football hooligan. It was shown by C4 with a triangle in each corner. Shell Shock Days, a South Sea Island beach bum was beaten to death with a snorkel by a mad lesbian physicist with Aids. Even the teeny-pop series Twanga Langa Ding Dong featured simulated rape and a condom-inflating contest.

"Well, this is the world we live in," says Anna, a twist of regret momentarily disfiguring the perfect arc of her spangled lip-gloss. "I wish things were different, but we would be insulting our audience if we did not admit that when it comes to radical cosmetics, the chainsaw is taking over from the hot-wax depilatory system in Britain today."

It was at that moment in our interview when a whole shelf, with eerie timing, fell with a crash from Anna's office wall, depositing her entire collection of Wisdens on the lush moquette. "Oh piddle," she cried, with a force that left me convinced that Tanktopf Films are in good hands. As I went down the corridor, I wondered where I had to go next. It turned out I was due to have coffee with a man called Gerald. He isn't really in the media at all, but if there's a space on page 37 I might write about him as well.

Peter Fiddick meets Gerald Doberry, a man who has been reading TV Times for nearly a quarter of a century

Waiting for the good bits in the TV Times

SIPPING COFFEE in a Soho bistro with Gerald Doberry, 51, the other day, I wondered how a man of such patent international culture could possibly remain innocent of involvement in the media. "Oh, but I'm not," he hastened to assure me, dipping his tie inadvertently in the cappuccino. "I *love* the TV Times, I can't help it, I do. I live for Katie's letters, don't you, they're a scream. I was the Letter of the Week once, about Mother getting a rash from a nylon bedjacket, all complete rubbish of course."

Gerald used to be in publishing and is buying a second-hand word-processor. The media, I felt, are safe in his hands. I never did like his ties. The stains are the best part of most of them. Nice man.

Bryan McOllaster

"Fiddick, Fiddick, Fiddick, Fiddick."

Media File

Peter Fiddick
Media Editor

SURPRISE SURPRISE! Versatile Emma Spigotini, who this week took over as editor of the Heckmondwike Bugle, is the selfsame Ms Spigotini who used to present the Open University TV series on Plainsong in the Medieval Church. Whether her new appointment will leave her time to keep up her involvement in top ad-agency Bolinbroke, Rafferty, Schlong, where she has been Consultant Dermatologist since 1979, is anybody's guess.

MICHAEL GRADE was spotted wearing blue braces last week. A change of policy at C4? Probably not. The ultramarine suspenders were a gift from Ronnie Biggs, who is hoping to present a prime-time C4 series on Brazilian culture.

SENIOR INFORMATION OFFICER

Up to £6,998, 3 wks' hol
Borough of Gunkington

Gunkington is a rapidly developing go-ahead borough that straddles the River Gunk. It is recognised as currently the most thrusting conurbation on all Gunkside, its chiefest industries being glue manufacture and rhubarb-canning. The Borough Council, housed in the famous Civic Hall, erected in 1886 pursuant to a design by Sir Montagu Frisson, FRCS, currently require a full-time Information Officer to give out information about Gunkington whenever it is asked for. Duties include a good telephone manner, putting a brave face on it, turning a blind eye to the Barmforth Estate, and trying to get some sense out of the Mayor after lunch. No lifts, ramps, etc. Smoker preferred. The Council *is* an Equal Opportunities Employer. For preliminary discussion regarding this vacancy, candidates should contact Egerton Arkwright on GUNkington 202, Ext. 2003.

GUNKINGTON

THRUSTING ● SPROUTING ● YELLOWING

Editor
RadioTimes

On the retirement of Terry Wogan, the unrepeatable prize post of Editor of Radio Times has fallen vacant. Average weekly sales of Radio Times regularly exceed the number of adult working persons in this country, plus the number of captive gerbils. What do they do with all those copies? That's just one of the things you're going to have to find out, sunshine.

We seek a dynamic and experienced megalomaniac who isn't too bothered that this is a weekly programme-guide nobody can actually follow. You will be in regular contact with programme-makers, senior executives, and Mr John Birt, and your layout of the BBC's national schedules will be expected to confuse them just as much as their directives confuse you.

You will need to be a person with ideas, flair, a ready pair of fists, knowledge of when to break open the hospitality cabinet, and some way of covering up a nervous break-down.

Salary is negotiable and a getaway car is provided.

Letters of application, with up-to-date CV and a com-promising photograph of Michael Grade, should be sent by today, marked "Radioactive", to the Head of Glossy Things, BBC Enterprises Ltd., 35 Marylebone High Street, London WAA AAGH.

BBC ENTERPRISES LTD
We are an awful optimistic employer

NATIONAL THEATRE

is recruiting for the new and interesting post of

DECENT PLAYWRIGHT

Responsible to the Director, the Executive Director, but chiefly YOURSELVES

Only persons with wide and thorough experience of writing proper plays, with intervals, where you can tell it's finished so you can clap, with no bare bums, attacks on the audience or nancy or Trotskyite undertones, should apply. **Applications should be made in the first instance to the Head of Desperation and Finance, National Theatre, South Bank, London, SE1.**
THE NATIONAL THEATRE IS AN EQUALLY OPPORTUNIST EMPLOYER

S4C SIANEL PEDWAR CYMRU

LLOGYLL CHWYRNWELFOD

I'r flogyll yn sporiod o cnoews maen fawr nghofys wyr program
"BLODWEN THE SHEEP" fel cynghoru o llwybridiau wrth y blaen llollyll secs a'r violens. Mae ffwnion o'r slogell ym blisterpac gan y môl pysgraffydd fyn calamine lotion. Sendaiu aplicasiwns fel y first instans fro:
Angharad Seedley,
Managiwr Personel, S4C,
Heol y Goronation,
CAERDYDD CL0 DH0,
Rheiniog siagbag wyt i'r Emplywr Oportiwnitys Egwal.

SECRETARY
IN CIRCULATION DEPARTMENT

We are an old-established and much-respected magazine dedicated to the out-door life and the joys of the countryside. Unfortunately our Editor has been over-doing such joys and the circulation in his legs is a bit iffy. Well, all over really. We are looking for a Secretary with above-average skills and everything who might restore his circulation to what he regards as its previous peak. Ability to read between the lines an advantage. All applications treated in *strictest* con-fidence. Write enclosing measurements to:

Enid Welt, Personnel Manager, HUNTS AND HUNTSMEN, Tunbridge Wells, WE11 1LL BE.

He knows it's disgusting but it's a job.

West London PRISON requires confident **HANGMAN** for urgent training.
Box No. FDK 599

JOURNALIST

In the wake of one of our hacks getting his bus pass, we're a-scoutin' and a-toutin' (geddit?) for a mega-talented JOURNO who knows where it's at, where it's been, and in what hospital you can get it seen to at. Hatred of BBC an advantage. Why not give us a bell, we'd be all kinds of interested to hear from you.

THE TIMES 1, Flogover Street, London E1.

PUBLISH AND DON'T GIVE A DAMN!

JUSTICE and the PRESS

Tormented by the threat to press freedom and attacked on all fronts by the Government, editors of national newspapers can only pray that one day the courts will come down on their side. Not before time, E. S. TURNER dons the robes of Lord Justice of Appeal and delivers the judgment they are eagerly awaiting

The issue to be resolved in *Regina v. The Editors* is starkly simple.

It is whether the custody of the nation's secrets, and indeed the higher direction of the realm, should be vested in a body of politicians whose sole merit, it may be thought, is that they have secured the votes of the swinish multitude, or whether it should be entrusted to a body of selfless truth-seekers who, rising from obscure origins and scorning the suffrage of the mob, have banded together to call themselves *The Guardian, The Observer, The Times, The Independent, The Sun, The Star* and so forth.

The press has rightly been described as the Fourth Estate of the Realm. It has even been called the Sacred Lamp of the Enlightenment, though admittedly not recently. Perhaps I may quote a verse of a song composed last century by the radical visionary, Ebenezer Elliott, a song of the people breathing a faith and an idealism we have lost the power to express:

> "The Press!" all lands shall sing.
> The Press, the Press we bring,
> All lands to bless.
> O pallid want! O labour stark!
> Behold, we bring the second Ark,
> The Press, the Press, the Press!

I see a wintry smile playing over the features of my fellow justices, like sunlight on barren rock. Is it conceivable, they may think, that humanity could ever have been so impossibly naive? But we must beware of mocking man for the nobility of his aspirations. In common with the Church of England, the Parole Board and the Jockey Club, the press has not yet realised its fullest capacity for good. If, on occasion, its ideals are betrayed by imperfect servants, can we point to any branch of public service, with the exception of the Law, which draws perennially on men of unflagging probity?

I turn now to the safeguarding of national secrets.

It is common knowledge that in times of war the press is at once placed under powerful restraint, lest it be so carried away by the love of truth as to publish the dispositions of our armies and navies, or to reveal that weather conditions are ideal for bombing Birmingham, or lest its clear-sighted estimates of our chances of victory cause it to spread so-called alarm and despondency.

It may be that in one world conflict or another a few million lives have been saved by the exercise of such tyrannous restrictions, but the cost to Truth, Truth which is beautiful at all times, has been truly grievous.

Small wonder that in times of peace the frustrated, three-ulcer men calling themselves *The Observer, The Guardian* and so on have sought to expunge the infamy by fearlessly publishing all the nation's secrets that public servants may take it on themselves to divulge. If, from time to time, the lives or a handful of secret agents are endangered, or a government is brought down, or a commonwealth is rent asunder, is not this trivial cost outweighed by the upholding of the public's Right to Know, or in other words, the Freedom of the Press?

It may well be that a sullen, preoccupied people will never march to Trafalgar Square to support their Right to Know, but this will not divert those Valiant-for-Truth, those bearers of

"I am the Prince of Darkness! Can I tempt you to something?"

the second Ark, from the Vision Splendid.

It is the contention of the Editors that if a secret agent breaks the terms of his employment and tells all, the press shall be instantly free to propagate his revelations to the entire world, without let or hindrance, while paying him, as in honour bound, a handsome solatium from their resulting profits. The analogy they furnish is that of a rabies epidemic. If one mad dog enters the country, then the damage is already done and it would be farcical to try to prevent thousands of other mad dogs from running amok and depopulating these islands.

Another analogy is that of a forest fire. Once the blaze has been started, only vexation results from trying to contain it; how much more sensible to let Nature take her course or even to indulge the pleasure of fanning the flames. This I take to be the view of our leading editors, men of great vision and acuity allied to manly grace, and in no way am I disposed to fault their logic.

The case of the Crown is less easy to understand, based as it so plainly is on scorn and prejudice, and the conviction that the press enjoys the harlot's prerogative, power without responsibility, or more often fun without power. Possessing millions of files bearing on the affairs of this country, the Government is disposed to jeer at the pretensions of the press, whose entire knowledge of humankind is derived from cuttings libraries, or "mortuaries of misinformation", as they have been sneeringly called.

The Crown points out that the press, which is prepared to cut down whole forests daily to spread the truth, in practice fills its pages with the romances and jealousies of news-readers, or with fanciful reports of madness, drunkenness and infidelity in the first family of the land.

These criticisms seem to be as misguided as they are otiose, for a healthy society cannot exist without a harmless, and infinitely renewable, leavening of rumour and false witness.

Did not Lord Chancellor Bacon, my illustrious predecessor of four centuries ago, say, "A mixture of a lie doth ever add pleasure"? Did he not aver that without "false valuations, imaginations" and the like the minds of men would be "poor shrunken things, full of melancholy and indisposition, and unpleasing to themselves"?

This is a truth the press has always perfectly understood and it is to this that many of us owe such shreds of sanity as we possess.

I reject one final contention of the Crown, which has argued that the press is under no obligation, constitutional or otherwise, to harass and unsettle the government of the day, however benevolent its administration may be. To this the press replies, with some force, that the more benevolent the administration, the more closely its innermost files merit scrutiny.

I dismiss with contempt the assertion of the Attorney-General that what this country suffers from is an excess of communication and that the sooner the floodgates of information are slammed shut the better.

I find unreservedly for the Editors.
Later the Editors were awarded £1 million from public funds.

NOW LOOK, THIS IS GOING TO HAVE TO BE ENTIRELY OFF THE RECORD

The world roughly divides between people who think there should be more freedom of information and those who think there is quite enough already. JULIA LANGDON referees

Richard Shepherd calls them the Hallelujah Chorus. It is, admittedly, quite difficult to imagine Bernard Ingham as an angel – unless it was of the avenging kind – but all the same you can see what he means. Richard Shepherd is the new patron saint of candour and thus the sworn opponent of those with secrets to keep secret. Bernard Ingham, the Number Ten press secretary, is Mrs Thatcher's chorus-master doing his best to ensure that the Government, its Ministers and its minions, all sing the same song and in tune. It is, perhaps needless to point out, a song of praise.

It would also be a mistake to suppose that describing this chorus as "singing" carries the same import as the verb does when used by the police of the criminal fraternity. When a villain sings, he tells all. When Bernard Ingham sings, it is a hymn to the wonders and wisdom of the Government and all who sail in it. It also tells as little as possible.

Richard Shepherd has alighted upon this curious scene in his attempt to reform the laws relating to Official Secrets with a capital "O"

ONE OF MR SHEPHERD'S MOST CHARMING CHARACTERISTICS IS HIS INNOCENCE.

and a capital "S". Until he introduced his controversial Private Member's Bill last month, he was a little known Tory MP who had attracted attention only in the Government Whips' office, where he was known as a fully paid-up member of the Awkward Squad.

Then Mr Shepherd decided that since everyone was apparently in favour of changing the

*"I'll be glad when everyone believes in the only true Christ.
I never did like the other one."*

absurd and obscure laws about the protection of Official Secrets – which makes it an offence for me to tell you about the menu in the Ministry of Defence canteen or the make of tea-bag employed in the Home Office teapot – and since the Government was doing absolutely nothing about it, then he would. One of Mr Shepherd's most charming characteristics is his innocence.

His Bill meant that there would be greater freedom of information; and he fondly imagined this would be universally welcomed. He was very wrong. The world roughly divides between people who think there should be more freedom of information and those who think that there is quite enough already. By and large this first group is made up of everyone who is not a member of the Government or the Civil Service employed to do its business and the second is the aforementioned Hallelujah Chorus, i.e. members of the Government and the Civil Service.

It is an important point for those of us who try and operate in these murky waters to remember always that people called "press officers" are not intended to assist the press. Most of them are there to ensure that secrets remain secret and that as little information as possible is disclosed to the press. The Foreign Office does this better than most departments by employing career diplomats in their News Department. This serves a dual purpose: not only are secrets efficiently kept but the diplomats are given the essential training they need for their subsequent careers – which will generally involve ensuring that no one knows

any more than they need to.

Diplomats, like spies and press officers, have to learn to guard against personal relationships. The Civil Service manages this on behalf of its press officers by ensuring that no one ever stays in one place long enough to form friendships with dangerous people like journalists. But what the Hallelujah Chorus cannot control, try as they might, is the personal relationships formed by politicians.

Members of the Government trooped obediently into the lobby behind Mrs Thatcher to defeat Mr Shepherd's Bill – having been ordered to do so by the extraordinary imposition of a three-line Whip on a Back-bencher's

WE HAVE AN ACCEPTANCE OF PUBLIC HYPOCRISY BY THE POLITICIANS.

Private Member's measure. Yet it is in fact through members of the Government that most information emanates about what is really going on behind the scenes. In public they stand solid in the front line and obediently sing the chosen hymn; in private they leak information to the press in order to bolster their personal political position.

It is one of the many contradictions in this confused and confusing area. And there are others which have, coincidentally, also been exposed by other Private Members' Bills currently under discussion. There is, for example, the question of the protection of privacy. Mr

Shepherd is in favour of freedom of information – but not all information; indeed not information about Mr Shepherd. Similarly the stalwarts of the Labour left, like Ken Livingstone, think that the Government ought to open up the books for public inspection, but do not believe that their own private lives should be similarly exposed.

Is there not an element of hypocrisy here? People in the public eye, like politicians, have to expect a certain amount of publicity about their private lives. The fact that Mr Livingstone keeps lizards in the lounge – or that Mr Shepherd is a high-class grocer in his spare time – is not in itself important and could scarcely be described as a matter of public interest which ought to be reported. On the other hand, it is useful for the comprehension of the complex personalities involved. But where should the line be drawn between such innocent and interesting information and revelations about, for example, an individual MP's sexual proclivities – which may not be innocent, but are nonetheless at least as interesting?

That is the question that another Tory MP, Bill Cash, is attempting to answer with his Bill to protect privacy. Labour MP – and former journalist – Ann Clwyd has also contributed to the debate with her Bill to give those whose secrets are exposed a right of reply. Both MPs have a point, although neither introduced the Bill with any real hope of achieving reform. The problem will remain as long as we have an acceptance of public hypocrisy by the press and – more importantly – by the politicians themselves.

"We don't honestly think you're cut out to be a clergyman, Randall – we just don't think you look silly enough."

STANLEY REYNOLDS AT LARGE

*Fleet Street is gone, was it ever worth saving?
Plus Tom Wolfe's idiotic errors about
England and Englishmen.*

MONDAY
A Cruel, Heartless Jape

Is *The Times* destroyed? Has the dead hand of Mr Rupert Murdoch slayed "The Thunderer" for all time? It would appear so. How saddened this column was to learn this day of a disgusting case of censorship at the Wapping Gulag. Mr Sheridan Morley, called upon to write, for some mysterious reason, *The Times Diary*, had scooped the world with a pen-portrait of my new white beard. Hemingwayesque, he called it. Was it, I wonder, secret enemies or, more probably, a total lack of a nose for news which got this paragraph removed by some dull-witted sub-editor. I, for one, welcome this new vogue in Fleet Street for diarists to eke out a modest living writing paragraphs about one another.

But is there still a Fleet Street?

Not any more, say the English Heritage Trust, who have mounted a pathetic exhibition at the Museum of London called "A Farewell To Fleet Street", the exhibition consisting of one second-hand Linotype machine from *The Sun*, with a slogan pasted to it saying something nasty about Mr Murdoch; a few snaps of yesteryear; a front-page plate of *The Guardian* (hardly Fleet Street, *The Guardian*); and an old gentleman, with a vintage Fleet Street set of false teeth (an altogether rum and excessively cruel sort of exhibition that); presumably the old gentleman was some El Vino "character" of a bygone age – he was referred to, in jesting banter, as "Lord" Deedes.

It is a form of humour that quite frankly completely escaped me and was made even more heartless when the old codger was suddenly called upon to speak. While the old cove lisped and spat his way through an "oration" – in obvious distress with the pioneer "choppers" in his mouth – Fleet Street wags were seen to be tittering behind their inky hands.

TUESDAY
Murdoch's Grisly Vendetta

How long will Murdoch continue this senseless hounding of me? Not satisfied with the indignity of cutting my god-like beard out of Morley's wretched *Times Diary*, Murdoch has now robbed me of my £44,000 Accumulator winnings. This morning, I had, for the first time ever, a clear winner. Instructing a competent member of the domestic staff to phone *The Times* at ten o'clock, I shimmered down to Fleet Street with visions of something frilly all of my own somewhere in St John's Wood. I began to suspect low cunning afoot in the command post of *The Whopping Liar* when the one o'clock news reported that *The Times* switchboard was jammed. *The Times* put out some feeble excuse about the damned thing being printed wrong. And then Murdoch wonders why the Yanks won't let him own the *New York Post* and the *Boston Herald*.

WEDNESDAY
Tom Wolfe's Curious England

And what is Fleet Street's reputation in the New World? The English journalist is a lazy, drunken freeloader, according to Tom Wolfe, whose latest bestseller and first novel, *The Bonfire of the Vanities*, was published last week.

A major character in the "novel" is a drunken English journo who never pays his way. Does this fictional creation have any basis in real life? Yes, I can reveal, it is none other than Anthony Haden Guest. But truth is stranger than fiction. I can also reveal that Tom Wolfe himself was responsible for getting Haden Guest into New York journalism. I was there when Tom Wolfe first met Haden Guest in London in 1966. It was "love at first sight", there being no love like the love of one drunken man for another.

Wolfe then brought Haden Guest to Manhattan Island and recommended him to Clay Felker, who was editor of *New York* magazine, where Wolfe himself had his start. Wolfe, not renowned for his generosity to colleagues, had given the Fleet Street man "the strongest recommendation"; indeed, Felker later said, Haden Guest was the "first and only" person ever pushed by Wolfe. Twenty years on, however, Wolfe seems no longer to be amused.

He seems also no longer to be an Anglophile. He keeps on telling a story of the entire clientèle of a smart New York restaurant rising to their feet and applauding when an

Englishman finally paid a bill. And has he planted deliberate, ridiculous errors about English life into his novel, simply to annoy English readers? Wolfe – and one apologises for the vulgarity – appears not to know the difference between being "pissed" and being "pissed off". He thinks a chap with "Sir" before his name will therefore have a daughter who is a "Lady"; that fenders are only found before fireplaces in "the west of England"; that Holland Park Comprehensive is the last word in English schools; and that New & Lingwood in Jermyn Street is *the* place when toffs get shoes.

THURSDAY OR MAYBE FRIDAY
Society Spice by Lord Snooty

Are there any toffs left in Fleet Street?

"I say," shouted somebody in Scribes, "isn't that N***l D******r, the son-in-law of the Duke of Gorbals and Strathbungo, the chap who writes "Society Spice" for the D***y M**l?"

The legendary Joe Duke, barman of Bucks, had just died but at Scribes all the barmen were feeling good, although not quite so good as the scribes.

"Good God," someone else cried, "what's that ghastly stuff growing through Lord Snooty's hair?"

"Head," someone said, "that's head growing through his hair."

"I," said S**n G****r D****s,

an Irishman, "can't see a _____t'ing."

All those bods at Wapping... the chaps who daily climb aboard Max Hastings's Ship of Fools bound for Dog Island ...they're all missing this genuine Fleet Street life.

"N***l is going bald in a most peculiar and ghastly fashion," said L****y C******e, the Beauty Editor of *Tatler*.

"It's that hair transplant he had," an authority, M*****l H***h, a cartoonist, said. "One bit of hair was transplanted to other, less fertile parts of the skull. If he hadn't had that he would be going bald today in a decent Christian manner, and not like some damned Hottentot."

"I," said Mr G****r D****s, the Irishman, "went to Tottenham Hotspurs once, "I couldn't see a _____t'ing."

Of such golden days are Fleet Street memories made.

SATURDAY
An Unfaithful Servant

Jane MacMac, the old family retainer, says of my new beard that I look like Tsar Nicholas II of All the

Russias, if, that is, he had escaped from the coal shaft the Bolsheviki dumped him into. Not too good, she means. Jane MacMac has a historical turn of mind. She is a graduate of Trinity College Dublin and almost all her tattoos are written in a language strangers do not know.

POTTING ON

The stars of the BBC's fastest-selling video are the Flowerpot Men.
Our Showbiz Correspondent talks to the two rediscovered
megastars, and finds that there's far more to these great
telly-veterans than ever Weed thought . . .

Meeting the two secretive stars in the well-upholstered seclusion of their club, the Gardening, I was made vividly aware of the passage of time since those far-off black-and-white days when first their prancing images dominated the domestic screen. Ben, deep-voiced and voluble, still falls easily into the quaint flobblespeak of his heyday, but time has not dealt kindly with his hat, which is brutally chipped and faded. Bill, tense and taciturn, has a puffy, unhealthy look, and smokes incessantly, tapping his nervous ash into the inevitable engraved flowerpot, a gift from the late Muffin the Mule.

The big surprise is that both men, while constructed almost wholly from flowerpots, are Londoners, born in Shepherd's Bush. At first, my question drew only monosyllabic and wary replies, but gradually, as the whisky took effect, the pair began to relax. It was Ben, it was Ben, who first broached the topic of their newly revitalised stardom.

BEN: Well, it's magic, isn't it, I'm over the potting-shed quite frankly, but I'm not surprised. Delighted, yes, but not surprised. Because look around and what have you got, on the box today I mean, you've got what, Roland Rat. Roland is your superstar. Now I've got nothing against Roland, he is an entertainer, he has his style, does a bit for charity, some of it I like, but when it comes down to it, what is he? He's a talking rat. A mouthy rodent, that's Roland in a nutshell. And he's a hand-job, like Sooty. A foul-mouthed Sooty is really all Roland is. And good luck to him. But he's not what the kids want, is he? Of course he isn't. If he was, let's face it, if he was, he'd be the one selling the videos, wouldn't he? But he isn't. It's us. When you come down to it, it's a question of putting bums on laps.

BILL: Class act.

BEN: Is right, what we are is a class act. Always were. We never had no problem with the ratings. It was a sure-fire thing, a part-

nership like Morecambe and Wise, you couldn't imagine the one without the other. They were before us as a double act, Eric and Ernie, I grant you that. But it took them a long time to get their business sorted, get the old catch-phrases going and that. We never had no trouble with that. It was there from the first with us. Us and the stooge, the Weed. The Little Weed.

BILL: You used to fancy that Weed –

BEN: Pardon me, the Weed was over-rated. You see, what kept the Weed in the job was sympathy. I mean, what chance does the public get to feel sorry for a weed? Fistful of Toplawn, couple of brushfuls of whatsit, that stuff you paint on, and woof! that's your weed up the spout, innit? The stage was set, the craving was there in the public mind, for a privileged weed. A survivor weed that could speak for itself.

BILL: Weed, weed.

BEN: What?

BILL: Weed, weed, that's what she went. Weed, weed.

BEN: I know that. Christ, Bill, everybody knows that. What I'm saying, we could have had any number of weeds. Different bloody weed every week we could have had, and the punters would never have known the difference. But we were irreplaceable, Bill and Ben. You couldn't put any old rag, tag and bobtail in our place.

BILL: You gotta own up, though, you got sick of doing the flobberlop. I read once where you said, this scriptwriter has got John Innes Number Two for brains, you said. If I have to do the flobberlop routine one more time, you said, I'm going over to *Thunderbirds*.

BEN: That is perfectly true. I got disaffected eventually, yes. The part was not developing, the pouncy-pouncy walk was beginning to do me knees in –

BILL: The Weed wouldn't come across –

BEN: The Weed, you pot-bound pillock, was rooted to the spot. No, what it really was, we weren't getting any of the residuals. The repeat fees, we weren't seeing them. People in equivalent positions, Percy Thrower and them – not that I've got anything against Perce, salt of the earth, Perce is – they were starting up garden centres on the proceeds. But not us. It was all going to that old bint in the twinset who did the narrations. Laughing Drain, we used to call her. Did you ever hear her laugh? Sounded like a basin emptying out in a very old hotel.

BILL: I thought she was all right.

BEN: Well, she was a bit soft on you, 'cos you had the high voice and all. But anyway, we're not ones to go round slagging off our former colleagues of all those years ago. You know, you get some, you hear them all the time saying, oh that Andy Pandy, I could tell you a few things about him, I could mark your card as far as Andy, mate –

BILL: He was vicious, that Andy Pandy.

BEN: Yes, he was, he was a nasty piece of work, made life a misery for that bear, he did, but we don't go on about stuff like that 'cos it's all too long ago, isn't it? We were all in it together, and let's face it, we weren't a hundred and one per cent nice ourselves some of the time.

BILL: He means Mr Turnip.

BEN: Among other things Mr Turnip, yeah. You remember Mr Turnip? No, well, he was well back in the early Fifties, and he was a gent, Mr Turnip was. Old school, Lord Reith type, wore a suit, you could see all the strings but sod it. Had his own spot on the children's thing, what was it, *Whirligig*. Well, when we got big, old Turnip went out the window, didn't he? And we could have offered him bits to do on our show really, to be honest, nothing would have been more natural. Flowerpot Men featuring Mr Turnip. Or special guest Mr Turnip. We could have argued about the billing. Give him the job was the important thing.

BILL: But we never done it.

BEN: No. And then, fullness of time etcetera, it all catches up with us in the same way. New stuff comes in, we're still doing the same old scripts, weed weed flobberlop, of course we went right down the pan. Out of a job.

BILL: We did a runner. Went to San Francisco.

BEN: We did, well, it was the Sixties, it was made for us, flowers every bloody where.

BILL: Pot, an' all.

BEN: Well, everybody was doing it. We'd been good boys for a long time, never smoked so much as a Woodbine in front of the kiddies. I suppose we let ourselves go a bit. Tell the truth, I had a hell of a shock when I got off the boat in California. First thing I see, this ginormous billboard, it says "Ben Gay". Just like that. "Ben Gay", and this tube of slimy-looking stuff. It turns out Ben Gay is this ointment, this liniment stuff for muscular woss-name, everybody uses it. But it didn't half give me a turn. I thought hello, that Andy Pandy has been round putting the mouth on me again.

BILL: Vicious he was, that Pandy. The chances I had to give him some welly. I regret that. I do.

BEN: Bill's a romantic. Life isn't like that, is it? But it all comes round, you know, full circle in the end. Like we're back on top of the heap now, and this time round we haven't done sod all to deserve it. Haven't even got to humour the bleeding Weed. It's primitive, but – well, call it justice if you like.

BILL: I know what I'd call it.

BEN: What's that, my son?

BILL: Flobberlop.

BEN: Prat. All these years I've been living with a prat. Too late to change, innit. Sodding flobberlop. Stone me.

WHAT THE SOVIET PAPERS SAY

One of the world's great unsung humorous monthlies is Pravda's English-language digest of Soviet affairs. KENNETH ROBINSON looked in vain for any glasnost

The English version of *Pravda* – a terribly funny monthly digest – has just changed hands. It already has twenty-five thousand readers – in Britain and America – and the new owners, who also publish the House of Commons' magazine, hope to double that figure.

This is good news. Nothing could get a bigger laugh from true Brits or Americans than these grotesque pickings from Russian journalism.

Without *Pravda*, we might never have known that Mrs Thatcher has not only made thousands of people homeless, but has also stopped *all* building activity throughout the country. Nor would we have guessed that "millions upon millions" of British people are such "complete outcasts" – thanks to Mrs Thatcher – that they are forced to eat nothing but Yorkshire pudding, with free broth, at Christmas.

It gets even funnier as we read on and find that turkey dinners are consumed only "under lock and key". The ceremonies take place by candlelight, we are told, in "my-home-is-my-castle dwellings" – whatever that means.

This engaging nonsense was all written by a man living in London, called Arkadi Maslennikov, who has just been "promoted" to a job back home in Russia. (Siberia, perhaps?) We shall be sorry to lose him, though he must sometimes have felt pretty silly, when he saw his wonderfully inventive words translated for sale on

MILLIONS OF BRITISH, SAYS PRAVDA, ARE FORCED TO EAT NOTHING BUT YORKSHIRE PUDDING, WITH FREE BROTH, AT CHRISTMAS.

London bookstalls. Especially his recent claim that "the ten million people living below the poverty line in Britain" are quite unable to compete with those who shop at Asprey's for £30,000 diamonds.

During the Christmas season, he told us, many Britons become involved in shady dealings verging on crime, simply to afford gifts for

"Actually, sir, she's out – she leaves the flag up to fool the burglars."

their "beloved offspring". They buy these, said Mr Maslennikov, because advertisers tell them they will feel "inconceivable shame" if they fail to do so. What is even worse, said the author, these British paupers buy gifts from "traders of unbridled aggressiveness, who cunningly hang up their Christmas tinsel as early as the end of summer."

All this is blamed on Mrs Thatcher, who is said, by *Pravda*, to have gained power only because she was put there by the money of big business, the Tory bias of the BBC, and *The Times* newspaper, "which is very close to Government circles".

Not forgetting, of course, "the customary right-wing propaganda, which presented Mrs Thatcher as the only safeguard against the Soviet threat".

"One mistake that Mrs Thatcher makes," says *Pravda* – quoting Mr Gorbachev – "is to assume that a nation's security depends on its having a position of strength."

"This is quite wrong," says Mr Gorbachev (well, he would, wouldn't he?), "and America has always made the same error."

Anyway, says *Pravda*, the Americans have betrayed themselves as thoroughly mediocre people, by idolising Elvis Presley. Our own popular culture is also pretty suspect in Russia. British rock music, for instance, is dismissed as "the commercial taming of rebels who once frightened the British bourgeoisie with songs

about peace, disarmament and brotherhood."

All this extravagant spite is mixed up, in the pages of *Pravda*, with such homely matters as a recipe for rabbit-cheese; a tear-jerking photograph called "A Trusting Squirrel"; and the following socially conscious joke:

Bus-driver (talking through microphone): "Will older passengers hold tight, please?"
Woman strap-hanging: "Why only *older* passengers?"
Bus-driver: "Because the younger passengers have all found seats."

With such a sense of humour, it seems hardly surprising that Russians keep looking suspiciously over their shoulders, and begging for peace. But they really do protest too much. When *Pravda* sends a man to the Edinburgh Festival, he reports that, "This year's films are incompatible with the desire for people on our planet to co-exist in the struggle for peace."

When a reporter goes to one of the *Russian* arts festivals, he finds "It is helping in the struggle for world peace." (Peace, we soon discover, must *always* be a struggle.)

And when a medical conference is held in Leningrad, *Pravda* believes "It is incumbent upon physicians everywhere to struggle together for world peace – with sincerity."

Sincerity is another word that turns up all the time. Even Mr Gorbachev used it, the other day,

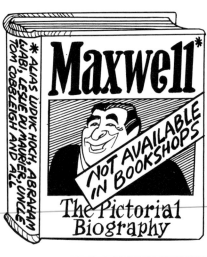

when he sent sincere wishes for world peace to readers of *Time* magazine.

Why does this man always sound so creepy? If he and his countrymen are only *half* as scared as they seem, why do they frighten themselves even more by teasing the Americans? By saying, for instance, that US soldiers recently fired shells in Libya, leaving Russian cigarettes on the site as faked evidence?

And how does it help world peace for the Russians to claim – as reported in *Pravda* – that "The Pentagon exists solely to prevent normalisation on the planet"?

You may wonder, after reading all this, what, in fact, *is* so funny about *Pravda*. It is funny partly because its paranoid propaganda is hilariously confused by a lot of whingeing self-criticism. As, for instance, in a reader's letter, which complains that perestroika is useless if there are no socks for sale in Kanakbarsk. And another letter, which asks: "What is the good of glasnost in my village, where we have shoddy television sets, a shortage of bread rolls, and many questions that have long been rotting our souls?"

Maybe it is over-simplifying to say that *Pravda* is funny. Perhaps it is more like a Chekhovian tragi-farce, in which Mr Gorbachev's "personal questing" is set against readers' deeply-philosophical issues (like "Where

Does Love Disappear To?") and the reassuring ordinariness of a taxi-driver writing about inferior dumplings at an airport cafe.

Anyway, after reading a year's back numbers of *Pravda*, I am now really hooked on its unique qualities. Surely no other national paper would report the fatuous invention of a robot cow that swishes its tail, stamps a foot, rolls its eyes and "even looks grateful", and then try to invent a purpose for its existence?

"This mechanical creature could be very useful," says *Pravda*, "either for making up an incomplete herd, without taking any of the rationed food, or for a family who likes to keep a cow in the garden, but has no facilities for doing so."

And how about the other invention of the year – a model train so small it could fit inside a human hair? No one can actually *see* the train, of course, but *Pravda* explains – not very convincingly – that the inventor now hopes to use his skill by operating on very tiny insects – if he can find a reason for doing so.

The only possible summing up to all this – as we wish the new publishers well with their quaint acquisition – is in the words of Mr Gorbachev.

"Dear Friends," he has said, "we must always remember there can be no history without people."

The man is certainly disarming. But don't take my word for it.

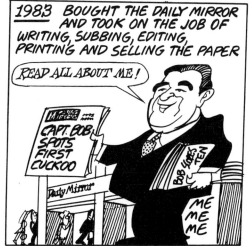

RUSSELL DAVIES

Watch This Space

> "Extra-terrestrial civilisations are too busy to try to contact planet Earth, Sir David Bates, Emeritus professor of theoretical physics, told the British Association. He believes there are probably other civilisations more technically advanced than ours but they are too intelligent to waste their effort sending messages into space."
>
> *The Times*

BLERBL, NOVGLOG 297

Fnof went off to work without his gneggerbogl again. 1200 glogs old and still he's doing it! Decided not to run after him this time as I washed my tentacles last night with the usual consequences. Would he run after me, I ask myself? I should bzu-bzu! Stayed in and watched the klov. They are still sending us some wonderful stuff from Planet Coca-Cola. I haven't told Fnof about all this but I am getting quite addicted to it. The creatures down there have a hell of a life. They come in several colours and have curious weeds growing out of their heads. As the glogs roll by, your weeds either drop out or die back to white straw – but if they don't do this, you end up as one of the most powerful members of their society. It's weird. What would they do if they saw all Fnof's blue antennae? Make him the Master of Coca-Cola World, I suppose. What a prospect. If they had his fleppers to wash they'd soon think again. Nice weather again – hot pink rain and steam, just like we ordered it.

SHMERBL, NOVGLOG 298

Guess what, Fnof got a tentacle trapped in the krevlag machine at work yesterday and lost it. It will take at least 2 felbs to grow back. Silly grebber. It looked as if he was going to spend the whole glog just lying there like a spare nobe at a smeg convention, so I activated the klov and introduced him to the latest from Planet Coca-Cola. It turns out he knows all about it. They watch it at work whenever the Sneff Inspector isn't there. What tickled Fnof is the thing they have called "News", which seems to be short for "New Things Happening". Most of them are happening for the blerbl-teenth time, Fnof says, and the rest of it is stuff you can see coming a klerf off. For example, he says, they have a game called Mining, where you try to predict where useful substances are buried under the ground. You stick long needles down to see if it's there, and if it is, you win. Your weeds stop turning white and falling out, and your fellow-creatures are obliged to look at you in a different way. The funny thing is, Fnof says, this doesn't stop the light-coloured ones among the creatures being ashamed of their limbs, which are nearly transparent. They keep their legs in tubes. Of course Fnof is all for nipping down there in the Galactoglaf, waving a few tentacles at them, and telling them where all the useful substances are buried. It took me about half the glog to explain to him that this is what's known as Spoiling Somebody Else's Game. Besides, I said, why should they take advice from the kind of gwelp who forgets his

gneggerbogl and gets his tentacle stuck in the krevlag machine? About half his eyes glazed over at that, the way they do. The wet spell continues, with red bubbles, which I wasn't so keen on as they clash with our wibblepleggers, so we will get them changed.

TWERBL, NOVGLOG 299

Fnof's tentacle is growing back purple! It serves him right. I told him he'll never play the aglplest again, but he just stuck out his trengler and said nothing. Watched the klov most of the glog. Fnof explained the idea of Soap Operas. The Coca-Colites apparently wash themselves with Soap, and a Soap Opera is something to watch that makes your command centre feel cleaner, by comparison with all the dirty things that are happening in the Soap Opera, see? My favourite by several klerfs was one called "Dr Owen", about a creature with very straight, doomed-looking weeds who went about trying to find fellow planetarians who would help him stop them falling out and turning to straw. It had just got to the point where he had more or less given up when, stap my mandibles, it turns out to be a "News" and not a Soap Opera at all. Fnof had a good laugh at me for this, saying that if I'd had my flegtroner switched on I'd have known that all along. Which is true, but I can't be bothered to sit there recharging myself all the time. Besides, I'd rather not know what's going to happen to "Dr Owen". I want it to be a surprise, how many weeds he ends up with. Weather fine: pink bubbles are nicer, but explode with a funny smell. It's never exactly how you want it, is it?

FLEV, NOVGLOG 300

Fnof was out most of the glog, celebrating Novglog 300 by getting absolutely sneebled with his mates. He came back singing a song called *We Are The Champions* which they've picked up from the Coca-Colites. When I could get some sense out of Fnof I got him to explain to me by reference to the klov. It has to do with "Football", seemingly, which is another game, but more daring than Mining in that they do take off their leg-tubes. Then they run around, in teams, as fast as they can, hoping that nobody is going to get a good look at their appalling legs. All the time, this little white roller called a ball is running about, and they have no idea where it's going! The results of where it *has* gone are revealed to the planet in a long list which gives Fnof and his mates a great laugh every time they see it. Fnof says his favourite team of Football is called "Fulham Nil", which I think is a beautiful name. If we decide to have another gnurt I think we should call it Fulham Nil.

KLABBL, NOVGLOG 301

Panning across the klov spectrum we came across emissions from a planet called Gzek. Frankly these look much more our sort of creature. They're all a very tasteful shade of green which happens to blend very sweetly with our wall-glow. They have no weeds to get neurotic about, more legs than I cared to count, and although they live on a disgusting rag-like yellow concoction called "creep suzette", they otherwise look like the sort of creature you wouldn't mind inviting round, if you had beds long enough to cope. Fnof and I were quite taken with them. I expect they will keep us amused for a few glogs, until all that green begins to pall.

Fnof's tentacle has grown another twelve amflets, but I've told him, he's not touching me with it until it's properly developed. There comes a time when you have to put your pod down about these things. In spite of myself I keep wondering about "Dr Owen" and his weeds. Poor creature. Maybe he'll take up Mining. Weather dismal. Fnof got fed up with pink bubbles and ordered up boiling brown mud instead. Flegs! What can you do with 'em?

Cluff

ALAN COREN

ROUGH TRADE

Madam, would you tell the Court, in your own words, exactly what happened on the night in question?

Yes. I was standing at the corner of Quebec Street, minding my own business, and . . .

Did she say she was minding her own business? If so, that would seem to conflict with the facts as previously stated, Mr, er . . .

With the greatest respect, my Lord, the witness conducts her business on the corner of Quebec Street. To that extent, she could be said to be minding it.

And keeping it warm.

If there is any more of this unseemly cackling I shall clear the Court. Please continue, madam.

. . . and this gentleman come up to me and he said: *Are you free?* In reply, I give him a riposte. I generally do.

A riposte?

Yes. My clientele likes a nice riposte. Preferably, what's the word, pert. Or saucy. I said *Free? What is it, Armistice Night? Pull this one, it has got bells on!*

And what did he reply?

He said it was a good one. He said he would have to remember that one. He said that one was worth folding money. He took out one of them titchy Jap tape recorder efforts and he put it to his mouth and he said *VICE QUEEN INVITED ME TO PULL ONE WITH BELLS ON, CLAIMS ACE REPORTER.*

Did this strike you as being in any way peculiar?

No. A lot of my gentlemen carry them.

They like to say things into them all the time. I think it helps them.

What kind of things do they like to say?

Oh, I dunno, things like *TAKE IN TWO LINES PARA THREE QUOTE HE ASKED IF HE COULD CLIP MY SUSPENDER BELT ON HIS EAR AND I READILY CONCURRED BECAUSE HE WAS RICH AND FAMOUS UNQUOTE DECLARES TAWNY PLAYMATE AT CENTRE OF TEST BATSMEN IN SAUNA ROMP SCANDAL.* I do not always catch what they say on account of they are frequently excited.

I see. And when you had intimated to him that you were not in fact free, in one sense, but indeed free in, as it were, another, what did he do then?

He enquired as to my name. In reply, I give him a riposte.

A riposte?

Yes. I said it was Oxfam.

Did the witness say her name was Oxfam?

Yes, my Lord. Oxfam is a relief agency. I believe it was the witness's little joke, my Lord. And what, madam, did he do then?

He suggested I should accompany him to a hotel. I said is it far, and he said not to worry, he had an old banger round the corner.

An old banger round the corner! Would I be right in assuming this invited a further riposte?

Riposte? What riposte? What is he on about, your Worship?

I haven't the faintest idea.

I apologise to the Court. Let us return to the old banger . . .

I shall not warn the public gallery again.

. . . this gentleman then went off, round the corner, to get his car?

Yes. It was while he was gone that another car pulled up and a different gentleman wound down the window. It was then I could see there was two of them. The one sitting next to him had a camera.

This alerted you at once?

Definitely. I said *I do not do twos, it is either one or the other.*

What was his reaction?

He took one of them carphone efforts off of the dashboard, and he dialled, and he said *Take in sub-head PERT BLONDE IN MAYFAIR GLITTERATI SHOCK SCANDAL OFFERS CRACK REPORTER QUOTE THE OTHER UNQUOTE IN SAUCY MIDNIGHT RIPOSTE.*

I see. So you do not do, er, it, in front of a camera?

Stone me, what kind of a girl do you take me for? I am the caring mother and sole support of a little boy, Damien, 5, and a little girl, is it Carole, 2.

Forgive me, I do beg your pardon, I assure you that this line of questioning is as painful for me as it is for you, I am merely attempting to estab . . .

If you let these buggers take their own pictures, your residuals is right down the drain, as per paragraph five sub-section three of the Copyright Act, they can flog

161

"Excuse me. I know so little that when I do know something I feel compelled to speak up."

same all over and you do not get a penny. If they want accompanying photos, I have a selection of glamorous poses took by my friend Errol which may be inspected without obligation but in the event of same being required either for (a) illustration or (b) reference for Our Artist's Impression Of The Sordid Scene That Night, first British serial rights may be negotiated, to include a strictly non-returnable inspection fee, and oblige.

I understand. What was the outcome of your objection?

The photographer got out, and I got in.

Despite the fact that you had already, as it were, contracted your services to the gentleman who had gone round the corner?

It is a question of first come . . .

Usher, will you remove that man rolling about on the floor of the public gallery?

. . . first served.

And that one.

What happened after that?

We drove to this hotel, and we went to this room, and he said *Well, I'm ready if you're ready,* and I said *Haven't you got a little*

present for me?

To which he answered?

To which he answered *Would a cheque for £6,000 cover it?*

And in reply?

In reply, I give him a riposte.

You generally do?

Yes. I said *I don't know, I've never covered it with a cheque for £6,000.* He fell about.

I see.

He wrote it down.

Wrote it down?

In a little black leather book. A lot of my gentlemen are into little black leather books. They write ripostes down in them, and then they usually give me a little bit extra. I don't mind. Whatever turns them on. It's a funny old world we live in, but the world's not entirely to blame. That's one of mine, by the way.

And how long did he get for his money?

About half an hour.

And what did he want you to do in this half an

hour for all that money?

He wanted me to make dirty telephone calls. While he watched.

To anybody in particular?

He had a list. He told me what to say.

And this seemed to satisfy him?

He was jumping up and down. He was hugging hisself. I thought he was going to do hisself a mischief. I remember thinking to myself, hallo, there'll be Kleenex at the end of this.

And after it was all over?

After it was all over, we go downstairs again, and we're walking to his car, and suddenly there's this other car flashing its lights and it was the first fella, and the fella I was with whispered *Christ Almighty, do you know who that is, you have definitely scored here, gel, it is your birthday, you are sitting on a goldmine and no mistake!* and he identified this other journalist and he was an even bigger name than my bloke, he is so big he has his face at the top of his column – HE IS THAT MAN SITTING OVER THERE, YOUR WORSHIP, IT IS NO GOOD HIM LOOKING AT HIS FEET AND PLAYING WITH HIS LITTLE BIRO! – and the bloke I was with said *I shall have to get my story in quick, but he will definitely make you an offer you cannot refuse, there is plenty in the trough for all of us, but I warn you he has got some funny ways* and then he was off.

And you did in fact go back into the hotel with the second man?

Yes. I thought of little Clark, 7, and little Rosy or Posy, 3, and I went back.

And did he have, er, funny ways?

Definitely. He wound flex all round me and poked a battery in my bra and little microphones all over my, all over my . . .

The witness appears to be sobbing, Mr, er. Do you think we should take a short . . .

I do not believe that will be necessary, my Lord. It is in her contract.

I am obliged to you. May I therefore take advantage of my own interruption to put a question to your witness?

As your Lordship pleases.

Madam, are you asking this Court to believe that an ace reporter, a crack journalist, a household word, a man who could have any story he wanted, prefers to sneak off in the middle of the night to hang about street corners and pay vast sums of money to, if you will forgive me, ladies of easy virtue, in order to persuade them to make dirty telephone calls in his presence and walk the streets of the Metropolis with batteries in their underwear?

Definitely.

I quite dread to think what will happen when they all move to Wapping.

I know what you mean. I can see three ripostes there, for a start.

"Mend the taffeta later, mother."

A WALK ON THE WILDLIFE SIDE

JONATHAN SALE goes up the garden path

Hedgehogs don't know where they are. Generally they can be found, or rather not found, hibernating until around Sheelah's Day. (March 18. The identity of Sheelah is unknown but she might have been St Patrick's better half and she is definitely celebrated by raising glasses of whisky.)

"But because of the warm spell," declared the lady at the British Hedgehog Preservation Society, "we've been having almost daily reports that they are coming out." Of hibernation, she added.

This is the good news for lovers of the genus *Erinaceus*. The bad news is that "Hedgehogs are not immortal. They do die." For this information I am grateful to the latest in the "Know Your Hedgehog" series, *Treating Sick Hedgehogs*, believed to be the first such work in English. It is a reminder that spring does not always mean that Nature is turning the ignition key on life, and that Sheelah's Day does not necessarily signify the start of universal bounding, leaping and eating. It also means that Nature is feeling a bit under the weather, is aware that there's a lot of it going around and is liable at all times to keel over and pass out for good.

Where do we come in? By offering first-aid to hedgehogs, for a start. It is the least we can do. Hedgehogs do not bark, bite or make pavements into no-go areas, nor do cans of their food clutter the supermarket shelves. Take heed, therefore, of Registered Charity Number 326885 (or, alternatively, Number 362885 – the B.H.P.S. quotes both figures, which must make the Charity Commissioners show their prickles).

Are there "Things on the Skin" of the spiky specimen sipping milk outside your back door? Are they "fat, grey, slow, globular? See 'Ticks'." You'll know you're seeing a tick if it looks like a dull pea, or is a slow-moving, eight-legged larva. One form of treatment is to terrorise it with a burning cigarette, although this is liable to misinterpretation by animal-loving neighbours and, indeed, by the hedgehog. The safest method is to smear the parasite with cooking oil, not because it will make a nice fry-up for supper but because the liquid blocks the breathing-holes and it dies a lingering death from suffocation. (Is there a British Tick Preservation Society to complain about this?)

Alternatively, should you spot any "Small, brown, fast insects" nipping about between the prickles, see under "Fleas". "Swollen ears" is found under "Ringworm." "Froth at the mouth" is quite normal; see any hedgehog book. "Gyrating in small circles" isn't, it could be a nasty case of "middle ear infection upsetting the balance".

"Wheezing, gurgling in breathing – see 'Lungworm'." The throaty noise sounds like smoker's cough, but derives in fact from tiny, transparent worms in the afflicted animal's windpipe. Some of us would rather not have known that. Others of us will hasten to change the bedding – the animal's, but perhaps our own as well if we approached too close – and inject a 1% solution of Citarin to the tune of 0.2ml per 100g of (hedgehog) body weight, checking droppings weekly under microscope for larvae.

Others again will have more agreeable sights to view in microscopes than the droppings of a latterday Mrs Tiggy-Winkle, and will be attracted to bats on the grounds that if they go down with anything, no bat-lover is expected to act as a locum.

Bats too have been agreeably surprised by the temperature outside their belfries. Normally they would be snoring upsidedown until Dismal Day (there are several such, all possibly connected with the Egyptian plagues, but this one is April 10).

"Because it's such a mild winter," declared Joan Tait, Assistant Bat Conservation Officer of the Fauna and Flora Preservation Society, "quite a few have been sighted taking advantage of the

GYRATING IN SMALL CIRCLES ISN'T NORMAL.

number of insects around. Long-eareds tend to wake up earlier." Presumably they are more easily disturbed.

What about diseases? "There is no significant risk of catching disease from bats in this country," said Batwoman quickly. That wasn't what I asked, but the Bat Team of the F&F Society are permanently primed to answer questions from members of the public looking for an excuse to

"Who blazed this trail?"

"I'm in for hanky-panky."

operate a shoot-to-kill policy.

The winter quarters of long and short-eared varieties are somewhere cool like a disused mineshaft, which disturbs only disused miners. In the summer they may find a tree to be a desirable residence or again it might be the inside of the weatherboarding of a convenient house. Either way, they will not savage the postman or chase cats. There are those who can persuade individual specimens to come when called and, possibly more important, stay away when not called.

Many householders install bat boxes; cf Stebbings & Walsh (1985). Unfortunately for Messrs Stebbings & Walsh, in 1985 or any year, bats tend not to inhabit them. Whereas it is obligatory to consult the Nature Conservancy Council about any work that might disturb bats already in residence, you can do what you like to lure the species to batless premises.

Ideally you build a fourteenth-century castle. Failing that, incorporate weatherboard or boxed-in eaves. "If your property appears to have the right features, but not bats, there is nothing to do except be patient," advises the handy booklet *Bats in Houses*. "Your turn may come in due course." It is within the bounds of possibility that Whiskered, Lesser Horsehoe or similar fine bats are already using your roof space as a staging post between mineshafts, and you simply have not noticed. Check for droppings. These have nothing wrong with them and can be spread on the garden. Further details in *The Young Batworker*.

With foxes, though, one should not be too friendly: "You don't want the youngsters to get too dependent," advised Warner Passanisi of the Oxford University department where they answer the phone with the unofficial codename of "Foxlot". Don't give them so much food that when you go on holiday they die of starvation.

Foxes do not hibernate as such. They may slow down a bit but not much. For them, it is all go from Rose Bowl Day at the beginning of the year to Childermas Day at the end. Yet as far as the public is concerned, they are more active in winter because the public sees them rummaging around more frequently, the earthworms which make up the basic diet often being deep-frozen. Certainly this member of the public saw one rummaging around last week; since I already have four dependents, I made a point of not feeding the foxy visitor and he trotted off, at between 6 and 13 km per hour, to more welcoming back gardens.

This is the end of the mating-season and the start of the cubbing season. The Foxlot will tell you that, especially David Macdonald, whose *Running with the Fox* contains full details of hiding in hedges, skulking under bushes and all the other unspeakable ways in which he went to ground in his pursuit of the inedible.

They have a busy social life, do foxes (unlike foxwatchers, who find it hard to reproduce since they are hiding behind nettles all night). They have their own body language, and an audible one too. They "gekker", they "snirk".

Dr Macdonald's foxes also bleep, at least, the ones which he managed to fit with radio-tags. The technology often failed him, though, and for years now the sound of spring coming to Oxfordshire has been the mutterings of a man twisting his radio-antennae by night: Come in Alpha Foxtrot, can you hear me?

McLACHLAN

The divorce courts in Birmingham are trying out an un-wedding ceremony, but they haven't got the Order of Service worked out yet. Let's save them the trouble

THE FORM OF DE-SOLEMNISATION OF MATRIMONY

At the day and time appointed for De-Solemnisation of Matrimony, the persons to be unhitched shall come into the body of the Church with their friends, if any, and neighbours, if interested; and there standing together, the Man on the left hand, and the Woman generally in the right, the Priest shall say,

DEARLY beloved, we are gathered together here in the sight of the local paper, and in the face of this congregation, to knock out a Settlement betwixt this Man and this Woman; which shall be a reasonable Settlement, and just in the eyes of either Mother-in-Law; which Partition of wordly Goods shall occasion neither the cutting-up of Carpets nor the sundering of the three-piece Suite, which is an honourable Suite, and fire-resistant, and not by any to be taken in hand unadvisedly, lightly, or wantonly, lest the castors fall off, duly considering the causes for which Matrimony was ordained.

FIRST, It was ordained for the purchase of an House, that a Man and a Woman might pool their earnings together and secure a Mortgage, pledging themselves to the nurture and maintenance thereof as long as they both shall live.

Secondly, It was ordained for a remedy against sin, that a Man might stay his hand from his secretary and the Woman from the milkman; but there you go, you can't have everything.

Thirdly, It was ordained for the mutual society, help and comfort that the one ought to have of the other, for when it cometh to babies, wallpapering and washing-up there is nothing worse than being on your own.

HAVING said that, no good shall accrue to him that flog-geth a dead horse. Wherefore I pray and beseech you, as many as are here present, if any man can shew just cause, such as either of them being somebody else in drag, why these two people may not lawfully be permitted to up Sticks and call it a Day, let him now speak, or else hereafter zip it up.

Then shall Uncle Harry have a coughing fit, inasmuch as he cannot bear silences, and the Priest shall say unto the Man,

WILT thou —
Then shall the Man say,
My name's not Wilt.
And the Priest shall say,
Just let me get through this, mush, and we'll have that little bit longer to go at the Riesling, right?
And the Man shall answer,
Fair enough, cock.

Then shall the Minister say unto the Man,

WILT thou have this woman thrown out upon the street with not much more than she standeth up in, plus half the Xmas Club money, her mother's print of Gainsborough's "Blue Boy", her Dad's fretwork-sunburst radio and engraved gold watch, two-and-a-half kids, and a fixed stipend to be determined before the Full Majesty of the Law?
The Man shall answer,
I suppose so.
Then shall the Priest say unto the Woman,
And izzeth it OK with you if this Man goeth forth into his new life with thy cooker and thy washer, in which thou hast cooked and washed all the days of thy life, plus the curtains thou hast hung and the loose covers thou hast sewn, plus what's left of a year's video-rental and a full set of garden furniture in sun-burnished African pine?
The Woman shall answer,
What about the microwave?
And the Priest shall answer,
It's yours, sweetheart, say no more.
The Woman shall say unto him,
Done. Blimey, I wish I'd married you.
Then turning to the congregation the Minister shall say,
Who gaveth this woman to be married in the first place?
Some poor bugger shall traipse forth out of the audience and the Priest shall say unto him,
Well, art thou a nerd, or what art thou? Thou has made a right pig's ear of this and no mistake. Thou com'st in here, or a Church very like it, waving rings about and encouraging folk to get married, and now look at them. Wherefore I do banish thee from this place, and unto a place of refreshment, and there thou shallst set them up, and await the coming of this Man and this Woman and me, and mine's a [Gin and Tonic].
Then shall the Priest give an small fillet of fish into the hand of the Man, and an small fillet of fish into the hand of the Woman, and they shall smite each other round the chops with their fillets, saying after the Minister,
WITH this fish I thee batter, with my legs I turn around, and with due haste I walk away. Don't do anything I wouldn't do, tarrah, and the best of British luck.
Then shall the Minister speak unto the people.
FORASMUCH as [Name] and [Name] have struck each other, each with an wet fish, and have agreed the fate of the microwave, and said Tarrah, I pronounce that they be Ex and Ex together, or rather apart, and all the better for it by the looks of things. Amen.
And the Minister shall add this Blessing.
I feel like a drink, don't you?

PUNCH

WE ARE AMUSED

But by what?

**A LOYAL SUBJECT'S
GUIDE TO THE ROYAL
SENSE OF HUMOUR**

STEEL CRISIS · WHO'S LORD BELSTEAD? · HISTORIC PICTURES REVEALED
THE CITY AIRPORT'S THREE PLANES A DAY · ANYBODY HERE SEEN MELLY?

PUNCH

22ND JANUARY 1988

90P

KIDS TODAY

WHAT DO THEY KNOW?

And would an education help?

TRAVEL EXTRA

NOTHING, BUT NOTHING, GETS A DYSPEPTIC, MIDDLE-AGED
CITIZEN SO AERATED AS THE SUBJECT OF EDUCATION.
IN PARLIAMENT, IN THE PAPERS, THE BATTLE RAGES
OVER THE BAFFLED LITTLE SOULS OF THE CHILDREN

KIDS TODAY –
WHAT DO THEY KNOW?

What should they know? And who knows best?
The Great Education Reform Bill – GERBIL – is poised to
upturn the school curriculum. So sit up straight and pay attention.
Today's first lesson is by LIBBY PURVES

Kids today! What do they know? Forty years on, how many of them will be able to reel off *Caesar adsum iam forte*, describe in their own words the function of ptyalin in the digestion of starch, or put a pin in Pernambuco?

Leaving aside, for the moment, the issue of whether they will wish or need to do any of these things, let me put this question to the House: *Is it fair that they should get out of learning them?* Why oh why, when we had to suffer through those long, dozy, fly-buzzing summer afternoons sitting in rows at sloping desks with inkwells, why should this pampered bloody generation be allowed to escape scot-free? This nancified, Mode III, project-work bunch of wimps, with its poncey home computers and TV in the bedroom and free mini-pills, why shouldn't they have their rotten little noses rubbed in the Younger Pliny, like we did, and parse King Lear until their teeth rattle? Why…

Sorry. There'll be enough of that sort of thing on *Yesterday in Parliament*, albeit thinly veneered with concern and moderation. Nothing, but nothing, gets a dyspeptic middle-aged citizen so aerated as the subject of education. In Parliament, in the papers, the battle rages over the baffled little souls of the children: on the right flank, we hear the thunder of Paul Johnson, the staccato bursts of A.N. Wilson and the thin wails and muffled explosions of Mary Kenny; on the left, the low, doctrinaire rumble of the 1960s left-over Left. In the middle, beaming and sparkling like an indoor firework at the Somme, we have Mr Kenneth Baker himself, full of ideas to make us all tidy-minded and slick-haired and well-educated enough to compete in international markets and fill out poll tax forms without help. And, waffling hopelessly around on the fringes of the debate, we have legions of anxious middle-class parents

ruining dinner parties from Carlisle to Penzance with their miserable indecision about whether or not to invest every spare penny for fifteen years in private education, to ensure that their children end up sniffing coke instead of glue, and spelling well enough to get into a merchant bank.

Gerbil, the Great Education Reform Bill, is upon us. And very little of it is providing any fun.

The exception to this rule is Mr Baker's wonderful Core Curriculum idea. This is the

best new parlour game since Lawrence Durrell's one where you had to pretend you were on a sledge across Siberia, drawn by failing huskies and pursued by ravenous wolves, with all your family and colleagues. You had to decide in what order to fling them all off the sledge to be devoured.

The Core Curriculum game is a sort of *Desert Island Discs* of polite and educated conversation: which five subjects would you take with you to the Island, and what would be your Luxury ("Life simply must be less rich when one has never read *Mabinogion* in the original")? But unfortunately, the concept does not stop at dinner-party chat: *the blighter is actually going to enforce it*, so ever since the Core Curriculum was mooted, pressure groups and assorted loonies have been popping up on all sides furiously demanding that their speciality be included in Mr Baker's inventory of the Perfect British Child's mental furniture.

Latinists lurk around every corner of the newspaper letters columns; geographers creep up on one in dark alleys, mouthing horrible statistics about how many Americans now think Australia is next door to Britain and why, therefore, their Continental Drifts and Tanzanian Import lists must remain close to the molten Core of British education. Computer Studies teachers grin smugly, confident that no white-hot modern subject like theirs will go unblessed by a former Minister for Information Technology; and on the borders, bloody and hopeless little skirmishes are fought, well out of the limelight, between rough little bands of no-hopers trying to decide which lot of them has the least worst chance of being let in.

Only the other week I was lobbied energetically at a conference by two neat ladies wishing me to help them: they were spearheading a campaign for Home Economics to be on the Core Curriculum. If it failed to be included, they intimated, children in the 1990s would be leaving school unable to make decent gravy, with all the human misery and industrial ruin which that implies.

So, although the dinner-party version of the game has been a most pleasant and useful way of changing the subject after an hour or so of We're-not-snobs, far-from-it, but-can-one-really-sacrifice-one's-child-to-one's-principles, the-local-comp-is-simply-not-on, something sterner is needed now. A clear unmuddied mind must set down the perfect Core Curriculum before it is too late.

I volunteer in all modesty: although my own, recent, hands-on experience of education is limited to waiting outside the school gates with my head wrapped up in scarves, like the Phantom of the Opera's old Mum (the little swine gave me his mumps for Christmas), I have given the matter some thought. And here it is: a Proposal for an all-British, utterly preparatory, Core Curriculum for Life:

Part I: Reading, Writing and Arithmetic. Not negotiable.

Part II: To be determined not by blanket prescriptions, but by rigorous questioning and observation of each child. It therefore varies in detail from one child to the next, but never in principle. Each pupil shall learn, in addition to Part I:

(i) One apparently useless, but rigorous, subject. For many years Latin provided this, but Latin has now turned out to be quite useful. A better example used to be provided in the BBC Studio Manager Training Course, when trainees were made to learn the curious ways of the TD-7, a 78rpm disc player carved from solid Bakelite and obsolete for ten years previously. You had to learn vanished skills, like how to wind discs back two revolutions to get them up to speed. "It's like Greek," the instructors would snarl. "If you learn this, you'll find that anything else, stereo, anything at all we teach you later, will seem easier." It did, too.

(ii) One subject the pupil absolutely *adores* learning.

(iii) One subject the pupil absolutely *hates*, but reluctantly has to admit might be useful. I passionately loathed Geography at school and remember very little of it. But the grim, dull discipline of trying to remember it for tests came in very useful years later when I was a *Today* programme reporter and had to make myself remember who was the deputy leader of the Israeli Opposition party, or when Dominic Harrod used to try and explain the Common Agricultural Policy to me, regularly, once a week.

(iv) One utterly bizarre *or* very pretentious subject which will provide status *and/or* good conversational openings in adult life, e.g. Sanskrit, Astronomy, Bell-ringing, British Constitution, Comparative Origami.

Part III: Three hours per week shall be devoted to the skills of Looking Things Up In Libraries and Spotting Logical Flaws In Journalism.

Including, of course, this.

SIR! SIR! IT'S NOT ON THE CURRICULUM, SIR!

BERT PARNABY used to be Her Majesty's Inspector of Schools in such influential centres of excellence as Cambridge and Hampstead. Looking back, and forward, he argues for English and Sugar

This latest hoo-ha about the curriculum – good Scots word first cultivated by the University of Glasgow – dates back, I shouldn't be surprised, to when Prime Minister Callaghan's grandchildren got to be of school age and he demanded at least a Great Debate and a Green Paper from the DES on what everybody ought to be taught. This was the signal once again for everybody in the world of education to start writing out the curriculum, sorting out how much was good for you, how much was fun and/or useless and how much was potentially disruptive or controversial, like life-skills or sex education or drama.

This done (always a piece of cake), the age-old process of getting quarts into pint pots began, leading invariably to the realisation that something had to go and therefore that some subjects had better be decreed to be more equal than others. And all this is what I reckon Mr Baker has found whilst clearing out his predecessors' drawers at the DES.

Such a Great Debate has been going on for centuries, of course – long before Prime Ministers' grandchildren got to be of school age. The medieval grammar schools, which produced

most of my generation, had three "core" subjects – or were they "foundation" subjects? – of grammar, rhetoric and logic: the *trivium*. These were complemented by four "foundation" subjects – or were they "core"? – arithmetic, geometry, astronomy and music, which were all very integrated at that stage: the *quadrivium*. Something like that. Music and arithmetic are still doing pretty well and rotten old geometry, too, but it's the Greeks, you see.

By the seventeenth century, science had pushed in a bit, and modern languages and Latin in the nineteenth (we had an Empire then and Prince Albert was a German). Fundamentally, the mix, according to educationalists, has remained about the same: seven or eight "key" subjects, with the others getting in round the edges and at open days, for example, Art and Cookery, Handwork and PT, whatever fashion and socio-economic pressures demanded.

Indeed, I think Royal Patronage even took a hand in things: art has been established for something like 130 years in our curricula, thanks to Prince Albert's fostering of the found-

WHAT WILL DISAPPEAR WITH TESTING MERE ATTAINMENT IS INSTINCTIVE AND ADVENTUROUS TEACHING.

ation of Art Schools around the time of the Great Exhibition. I wonder what the Prince of Wales could do for our curriculum today? Perhaps his children will have to grow up a little before he starts thinking seriously about it.

Quite apart from the DES world of the National Curriculum and the consideration of what's good for everybody, there is the Real Curriculum which occasionally, but very regularly, used to peep through to me in my visits to schools as an HMI. Two remembered scenes will reveal all about this Real Curriculum.

HMI: *(sitting with eight-year-old girl in class of second-year juniors. Conspiratorially)* What do you like doing best?

Girl: *(equally conspiratorially)* English and Sugar.

The name of the subject is irrelevant; the nature of the project is what matters. "Sugar" was the girl's project. But is it Geography? Or History? Or Home Economics? Is there a place for it in the National Curriculum? I hope so.

HMI: *(to fifteen-year-old youth who had just boasted of his intensive truancy because he was a painter and decorator)* Come off it. You *must* come in to school for something. What do you come in for?

Youth: Well, yeah, I do. I do come in for something.

HMI: What? What?

Youth: I come in for Mr X and Miss Y.

Learning and teaching is still, thank God, about people. What they teach is almost incidental.

"Actually, I'm a waiter. I'm only doing this until I find a decent restaurant that suits my talents."

So we ultimately find that the Real Curriculum, *according to the customers themselves*, consists of:

English. Sugar. Mr X. Miss Y.

This "core" is not easily analysed by subject or activity nor neatly to be fed into a computer programme; the Real Curriculum is people-oriented, the appeal and value of the subject to the pupil being directly related to the attractiveness of the teacher's own personality in teaching it.

In this way, I suppose, I'm not too depressed about a National Curriculum because there are too many variables in the shape of pupils and teachers for it ever to be nationally imposable – provided that there's some space for all the other ingredients of a good timetable to squeeze into.

In the past, let us remember, teachers and

pupils have always been very good at finding the interstices in which to operate. The old grammar school curriculum was terribly narrow and overloaded and yet a good grammar school provided all sorts of opportunities for all sort of activities. More than ever, it seems to me, one of the crucial criterion of a good school will be what it provides for the "spaces in between" its National Curriculum – if indeed it provides spaces in between at all.

But there is a bigger threat to good learning on the horizon: the testing of attainment at seven, eleven, fourteen and sixteen. It is a threat not necessarily because it is about testing but because it is about *minimal* achievement. It will be about teaching safely in educational convoy at the speed of the slowest ship and the dullest teacher. I think of one sixteen-year-old who, in his O-Level English Language paper, chose to

"I hear young Wordsworth forgot Mother's Day again."

write on "Art in the Home". His essay began: "We all knew that Arthur was not quite right in the head when he said that he had been present on the raft with Napoleon at the signing of the Peace of Tilsit…" Art's life in the home was then pleasingly described, and complete competence in the use of English (which is all they were testing) was demonstrated. Despite his ingenuity, this boy received no marks and failed the paper.

Two things happened as a result of this: his teacher made quite sure that the boy passed the re-sit (with 85%) by learning to write a stock answer to the question "My Day at the…" And his teacher, feeling further pangs of responsibil-

> **MORE THAN EVER, ONE OF THE CRUCIAL CRITERIA OF A GOOD SCHOOL WILL BE WHAT IT PROVIDES FOR THE "SPACES IN BETWEEN" ITS NATIONAL CURRICULUM.**

ity, never taught O-Level excitingly or imaginatively again. So far as I know, the examiners got off scot-free.

What will disappear with testing mere attainment is instinctive and adventurous teaching; teachers, especially the average and below, will play safe. They will resort to the teaching that I very often saw as an HMI and for very much the same reason, teaching that is restricted and confined by the minimal demands of the test itself.

I once watched a remedial teacher supervising inert written exercises in workbooks for the best part of a whole afternoon. Eventually I persuaded her to unlock a store cupboard where I found all the really interesting work of the class neatly stacked away in inconspicuous piles. They were compiling and presenting a series of real menus which were intended for use in an old people's home.

"I didn't think you'd be interested in these," said the teacher. "I thought you'd want to see them doing exercises." Nice, unworrying, undemanding exercises which the children can do standing on their heads and the teacher can mark with a tick or a cross, all cocooned in a cosy predictable world and caught in the trap. What worries me is the possibility of a total absence of Arthurs sitting on the raft at Tilsit, expelled for ever by – and I quote a poet who may or may not make it to pride of place in the Core Curriculum –

"…the keepers of our time,
The guides and wardens of our faculties,
Sages who in their prescience would control
All accidents."

When, the poet asks, will the sages who lack sagacity realise that "A wiser spirit is at work for us … Even in what seem our most unfruitful hours"?

I hope, like Wordsworth, that the National Curriculum will provide plenty of spaces for Arthurian rafting.

More Power To Your Elbow

First player: "I'm afraid I'm pretty feeble."
Second player: "I expect you're a lot better than I am, I haven't played for weeks."
Third player: "I'm hopeless, my service is rotten."
Fourth (junior) player – *ignoring the conventions*:
"I'm rather hot stuff actually. Shall I serve?"

MY favourite old *Punch* cartoon (by Lewis Baumer) neatly summarises what is so comforting about club-level tennis. It is a world still ruled by the ethics of "Sorry!" where the cry of "Good *shot!*" masks feelings of damn and blast. Junior players who are hot stuff may temporarily resort to Superbratspeak, but on the whole modesty prevails.

I am addicted to the tennis club and I blame Miss J. Hunter Dunn. Furnish'd, burnish'd, slayer of subalterns at strenuous singles, played after tea. The summer-house, the verandah, the low-leaded windows, the shining euonymus on the lawn, whatever a euonymus might be. At fourteen and a half, I wanted it all.

Possibly it was the larks in the car-park that I fancied as much as the tennis. I had noticed, you see, that tennis – unlike horrible hockey and rugger – was a unisex game, where girl could meet boy. It was certainly in this frame of mind that I joined my first tennis club, the Herga Club in Harrow, heart of Betjemanesque Metroland. Didn't they say Fred Perry had once belonged?

So here I was with my Dunlop Maxply (no fancy choices, then: you had either a Dunlop or a Slazenger, or an embarrassing old bat your great-uncle once played with, kept in a wooden press with screws at the corners or it would warp if caught in a light shower), my Dunlop Green Flash shoes (again no choice, no sharp Nikes or Taiwanese Hi-tecs), a home-made ten-

nis dress with box-pleats that had to be ironed daily, and a Christine Truman haircut. But where were the subalterns? Where were the embryonic Roger Taylors with muscular legs? Where was even one of the lanky Wodehousian youths from the *Punch* cartoons?

It was a good job I'd joined the club with my dad. For it was he with whom I played the strenuous singles after tea, and he who partnered me in my first Round Robin – how effortlessly we won the booby prize – and in a sedate quick-step at the Herga's midsummer Bar-B-Q.

I can't recall meeting a single youth, no matter how spotty, in the suburban dreariness that was Harrow in the 1960s, masquerading as Hurlingham in the 1920s. I remember only four huge ladies of a certain age whom my father named the Herga Haybags. They would hog a court for their ladies' doubles each Saturday, upbraid anyone who failed to turn up in whites, and take a long shrill tea on the lawn. Doubtless each was a mainstay of the committee. Tennis club committees would vanish from the earth without their mainstays.

It is up to the committee to determine the gnomic intricacies of the annual fees. Once you have worked out what you owe (Annual summer/winter membership + covered court subscription + LTA fee, obligatory, + groundsmen's honorarium, voluntary, + VAT at 15 per cent, subtracting £5 if you pay by May 1st, minus another £5 if you pay winter fees in summer) you get an O-level in Business Studies.

I am told, by a Cumberland Club member who one year paid his £200 subs and then played only once the whole year, that tennis clubs thrive on the spring keenness factor, whereby players pay up and never turn up to play.

It is the committee which also devises the dizzying intricacies of who has priority on which courts and when. Is today Saturday 9-11, when juniors without senior status take over courts 9-12? Or is it Tuesday evening, when Ladies Team III occupy courts 1-3? Is it a weekend afternoon when anyone refusing to join a doubles may be asked to leave the court, and is that the coach approaching, who has priority on court 8 at all times except during Club periods? Top-spin is the state of mind induced by reading through the rules.

Yet today I again belong to a suburban tennis club. Why else would I live in the otherwise benighted borough of Haringey? What sold our house to us was that it happens to back directly onto the rolled and shaven green of the last four grass courts of the Coolhurst Lawn Tennis Club. The very name is redolent of the era of Suzanne Lenglen and Mrs Lambert Chambers.

Okay, so it now has reggae discos and a microwave, and floodlit courts, and two of the grass courts went over to lime-green Astroturf in the sodden summer of '85 (it *never* rained, as you know, in Edwardian days when the club began). But its more timeless charms are intact: tall Lombardy poplars, courts flanked by pollarded limes and sinister elders. Not even sinister juniors with Buster Mottram scowls can efface the pleasure, to me, of hearing the reassuring thwock of a Wilson 3 on a well-strung Head on long Sunday afternoons. It beats the wail of police sirens in less blessed urban neighbourhoods nearby.

Its most seductive charm of all is that it is exactly fifty Reebok-sprung paces from my front door. It would be even fewer if I were to take a pair of wire-cutters and hack out a private way through the netting beyond our back hedge. The children could write a sign, as they always do for their rooms, saying *Privet*.

In an area like ours a tennis club provides a surrogate sense of community. We're not a village and there's no use pretending: we have a Neighbourhood Watch but nothing you could honestly term neighbourliness, with everybody vanishing officewards daily. But the tennis club thrives on its drawing-room comedy cast of characters. Its clubhouse is Crouch End's answer to the Rovers' Return.

There is Mr Muxworthy, a Welsh primary school teacher who plays like a rugby forward; there is Miss Barlow and her ladies' four, all white of hair but supple of limb; there is the unathletic-looking boy next door who has a fiendish forehand. There is Mr Bhagwandas who daily coaches his amazing daughters: the elder, Caroline, climbed into the national squad, and the younger is coming along nicely. There are four immensely tall barristers who play loudly on Sunday mornings. There is a famous film critic who is literally ambidextrous, switching racquet from right hand to left to confound opponents; and quite a famous actor who is our resident Hamlet in his black tracksuit. There is long-legged Clarissa, a lone Sloane always game for a game; there is Mr Katz, a banker by day but a doctor by nature, who arrives on court with a Gladstone bag of medical supplies, powders, bandages, braces for flagging limbs, embrocations, plasters, mineral water for the dehydrated and little metal things for warding off tennis elbow. And there is a man named Ings who repairs everyone's strings, a gift to anyone wishing to write a limerick.

There is something wonderfully un-ageist about a tennis club. I suppose people in golf clubs (I wouldn't know) do not very often find themselves outclassed by under-10s. But in tennis one may be thrashed by a brace of brats, or indeed by a pair of stooping white-haired OAPs.

There is one old gent in our club who won't see 80 again but can be found most days practising his solitary forehand on the wall constructed for that purpose. He plays in an overcoat. On an adjoining court I too am to be found, most days, with my own little Boris Becker. He is still only three, and can't yet see over the net, but you should see what he can do with his dear little short-handled racquet. He has not yet quite mastered a top-spin serve but I made sure he was well prepared for club tennis: the first word he uttered when he toddled on court aged two, was "*Sorry!*"

"*The jury will ignore that last remark…*"

PHOTO OPPORTUNITY

Joe Louis knocks out
Albert Einstein in the
1938 Brains v Brawn series

Joseph Stalin says farewell to
his comrades, Moscow, 1953

The Queen appears incognito
on the balcony of
Buckingham Palace, 1953

Winston Churchill briefing
his War Cabinet, 1944

The Hulton Picture Library is up for sale.
Classic, historical images like these could be yours

Neville Chamberlain returns
from Munich, 1938

Scott and Irwin land on the Moon, 1971

Roy Jenkins misses his opportunity
at the SDP Conference, 1981

US Marines erecting the first Belisha Beacon
on Iwo Jima, 1945

Devised by KEN MAHOOD

175

> A galvanised steel bridge spanning the River Penrhos in North Wales has been stolen, down to the last bolt.
>
> *The Guardian*

TO:

Secretary of State for Wales. Copies to Prime Minister; Home Secretary; Sir Harry Secombe.

SUBJECT:

Theft of bridges, Lleyn (approx. pronunciation "Clean") Peninsula.

TEXT:

The Minister's attention is urgently drawn to the theft of two bridges, as specified in the enclosed news item, in contravention of the Geneva Bridge Convention (1952), the Rights of Way (Larceny) Act (1936), the Natterjack Toads' Protection Act (1986), and sundry local bye-laws.

We are satisfied that these thefts are the work of the Owain Glynŵr Welsh Underground Militant Patriots (OGWUMP), an extreme and fanatical offshoot of the W.I. The Welsh Irregulars broadly share the grievances of the Welsh National Party, Plaid Cymru; but whereas the Nationalists' ambitions run merely to the provision of a Welsh Parliament, payment of the going rate for supplies of Welsh rainwater, etc (demands which are widely considered reasonable on both sides of the border), the Welsh Irregulars go further in stipulating a Welsh rate of VAT (*Tacs Faliw Aded*), a Welsh People's Coinage (*loli pop*), and the re-nationalisation of grass, sheep and alcohol. The OGWUMP wing, moreover, goes so far as to insist on the annexation of the Isle of Man, the return of Stonehenge, and forcible recall of prominent Welshmen abroad (the short list to include Tom Jones, Rolf Harris, Conway Twitty, Miles Davis, Johns Hopkins, Barry Humphries and Stéphane Grappelli).

Confirmation

In the course of the past 48 hours, intensive activity by our agents on the ground has resulted in the interception of the following communiqué, issued by the Imperial Grand Daffodil of OGWUMP from secret headquarters somewhere in the Latin Quarter of Dolgellau. Addressed to "All Forces", the message reads as follows:

> LOOK YOU LOOK YOU LOOK YOU
> NOW HEAR THIS!
> *The wish it is of the Imperial Grand Daffodil to commend those responsible for the disappearance of the Penrhos bridge, isn't it. It is well you have done, boys bach, in spite of a little misunderstanding. What the IGD requested you to obtain on his behalf was a pair of* breeches, *actually, see, him having lost his best corduroys in the abortive dynamite raid on the Bertrand Russell Tea Rooms in Penrhyndeudraeth. But a pair of bridges will do very well thank you very much indeed to goodness. A mistake it was that anybody might have made, fair play. May the success of this operation inaugurate a new era in the disruption and eventual destruction of the enemy's supply lines, of which more in our next. Meanwhile, I thank you all from the bottom of my coracle.*

The communiqué is signed "Pat Agonia". This is believed to be a pseudonym. In the light of this intelligence, attacks on further and possibly bigger Welsh bridges cannot be ruled out. It is calculated by Ordnance Survey that upwards of 19,000 bridges are currently in common use within the Principality, a ratio of more than six bridges to each inhabitant, though it is fair to say that some of the structures are used merely for the convenience of sheep and cows. The Minister's advice would be appreciated. The Menai and Severn bridges are not thought to be in immediate danger; there are in existence, however, some important wooden bridges (notably the Barmouth railway bridge over the River Mawddach) which are conceivably vulnerable to fire, corrosives, or the depredations of armies of trained shipworms. Marks and Spencer stores in Bangor, Pwllheli, Llandudno etc have been alerted to monitor all sales of corduroy trousers.

REMARKS:

These notes have been prepared for the Minister's general guidance by the Ethnic Studies Group of the Department of International Affairs, Strathclyde University.

1. Psychology

Quoted from *National Characteristics in the International Arena Situation* by Dr Ludwig N. Flenswanger (Munich, 1983):

> "Long subjugated by the English, a secretive people with much to be secretive about, the Welsh are a contrastingly communicative race with nothing to communicate. Their national style of poesy is alliterative and repetitious, akin to stammering. Many Welshmen have taken readily to mining, a form of work which involves hiding under the ground during the hours of daylight and emerging at dusk with a blackened complexion. The Welsh inferiority complex proceeds from the Welsh male's fear of his own potency, dramatised by the national game of rugby, in which a symbolic testicle, unattached to any organ of transmission, is passed hastily from hand to hand, or kicked, with a resentful violence, into the far distance. The Welsh claim great art in this play-system, but seldom display it, and with a superstition bordering for once on realism, they refuse to accept money for practising it. Religious by their own estimation, the Welsh are in fact a company of nihilists, happiest in the presence of alcoholics and farmyard animals. Thanks to the ingestion of lush grasses consequent upon the wet Welsh climate, most Welsh farm animals are alcoholics anyway. The Welsh reputation for musical excellence rests largely on volume. Welsh women (see *Offa's Dyke*) are seldom either seen or heard, except in German operas. Short legs enable both sexes to flee up mountains with surprising alacrity."

2. Strategic Importance

Quoted from *Lest Again Alone We Stand* by General Sir

Stratford Ankers (London, Kyle & Spettigue, 1979):

"In the event of an Irish invasion of the British mainland, Wales may very well come into play. True, it is believed that Irish strategists would prefer a symbolic drive up the beaches of Blackpool, establishing a useful semaphore platform at the top of the Tower and a comfortable military HQ in Yates's Wine Lodge. But they mind, like the Spaniards before them, that prevailing winds propel them willy-nilly on to the less populous strands of Cardigan Bay. What then? It is far from clear whether the Welsh, that taciturn and benighted race, would see fit to repel the invader. I myself regard it as far more likely that the representatives of these grim Celtic tribes, discovering at last a common grievance to which the Spirit of History, blessed and miraculous, has hitherto blinded them, would retire together to whatever pitiful hostelry the local Welsh townscape afforded, there to decline together into the mental twilight beloved of their kind. My recommendation, therefore, would under no circumstances involve the provision of tank traps, Martello towers and the like. Better by far to ensure an increased and unfailing supply of Guinness's stout to the coastal resorts of Wales."

3. Language

   a) The Welsh for "bridge" is *pont*. A residual guilt may attach to this word, so obviously purloined from the Latin.

   b) *Moron* is Welsh for "carrots". This has sometimes led to misunderstandings in restaurants.

4. Popular Culture and Taste

The current Welsh Top Ten is as follows:

   1. *Tain't What You Do, It's The Way That You Druid*
      The Wild Sheep
   2. *Show Me Your Harp*
      The Tafftones
   3. *Bless This House*
      Lord Tonypandy
   4. *24 Hours From Merthyr*
      The Feral Goats
   5. *O For the Wings of a Dove*
      Aled Jones
   6. *O For the Wings of Another Dove*
      Aled Jones
   7. *Men of Horlicks*
      The Horlicks
   8. *Land of My Father's Moustache*
      Max Boyce
   9. *Guide Me, O Thou Great Jehovah*
      Shakin' Stevens
   10. *You Pays Your Mummy and You Takes Your Choice*
      The Egyptones

CONCLUSION AND RECOMMENDATIONS

It may be that HMG will have to sit tight on this one and await further developments. Some action may need to be taken at a later stage, but we will cross that one when we come to it or not as the case may be.

"Quiet, everyone! Sarah is going to spin for us."

"Know what I miss?
Getting ideas above my station."

DO YOU WANT TO MAKE NUFFINK OF IT?

Hooligans are doing down our image abroad. So says one Euro-MP, who is eager to help by giving prizes to Britain's Most Reformed Yob. KEITH WATERHOUSE intercepted the first application

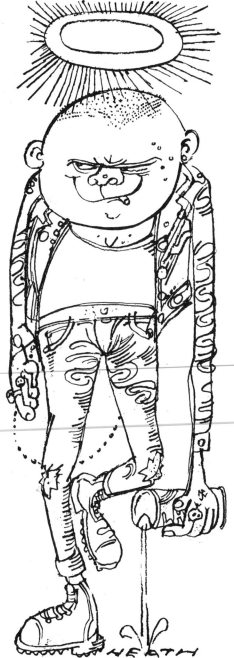

Dear Mr Edward McMillan-Scott, MEP whatever that is, a medal my mate Ginger says,

I have had it read out to me in *The Guardian* where you are giving a prize of a holiday in Spain to Britain's Most Reformed Yob, right. I hope this is true, it was not in *The Sun*, as I would like to put in for same, right.

I am so reformed that I have not done no aggro for must be over three weeks. It is true. Yesterday an old woman walked past me and I let her. Ask anybody. Ask my mate Ginger. He was with me the day we found a telephone box what was working, and I did no more, I didn't smash it, right, was not even tempted. Instead I made a non-obscene phone-call to my gran, right, wishing her a happy birthday, even though it is nowhere near her birthday. That just goes to show how reformed I am. Before being Britain's Most Reformed Yob the only time I ever rang my gran was to give her a right rollicking for not sending me no money. If you like I will give you her number, then you can ring her up to check, right. She will tell you that she don't no longer live in terror of me like what she used to. You will have to speak up as she is a bit Mutt and Jeff in one ear where I had to smack her one for giving me lip, but that was definitely before I was reformed. I never touch her now, right, even when the silly old cow sits up and begs for it.

My mate Ginger says you are giving this prize because you want to improve Britain's image abroad, right. You and me both, mate. I have been abroad and the way the British behave, it is a diabolical liberty, especially the Geordies, I hate bleeding Geordies, I hope you are not one. They think they are hard cases but they are rubbish. One of them gave me a look when I was in Torremolinos once, right, so of course I done no more, I put him through this shop window. You would have thought he would have wanted a go, right, that would have been the normal re-action, but he was too chicken. He just got up and legged it to the nearest hospital, with all these foreigners watching and pissing themselves. It made you ashamed to be British.

Another time I was in a ruck in some other foreign town, I have forgotten its name but we won 2-0, they was rubbish, when these five Eyeties started putting the boot in just because I drunk one of them's drink, I didn't even like it, it was that red stuff what tastes like medicine. So it is five blokes to one and I am getting a right seeing to, but does this English geezer sitting in the corner writing postcards lift so much as a bicycle-chain to help his fellow-countryman? Does he bollocks. He just got up and walked

out. I was bleeding disgusted. I kid you not, after that, when anyone come up to me and asked if I was English, where at one time I would have said, "Yes, do you want to make something of it?", I now started saying, "No, Scotch, do you want to make something of it?" That is how ashamed I was to be British, right.

My mate Ginger says he thinks Scotland is part of Britain really, but at least they are not a lot of wankers, right. You have a go at them and they will have a go back, right. I have been in some right rucks with Scottish lads and they have always given as good as they got, if not more so, as you yourself must have found. I nearly took one of them's ear off once and he tried to castrate me with a Stanley knife, they are totally mad, he should have a medal like you that bloke, maybe you could see your way to getting him one. But all that is behind me now, right. All right, so if we are playing Liverpool

I HAVE NOT DONE NO AGGRO FOR MUST BE OVER THREE WEEKS.

and this Scowse git puts up two fingers and says Go home you bums go home, it is only human nature to head-butt him at the same time kneeing him in the crotch, but I would not start it first, definitely.

Hang about, you will be saying, nobody is as angelic as that, if this geezer what is writing to me really has reformed, what is his reason, right, what is in it for him, right? I will tell you, right. It is because I don't have no wish whatsoever to do twelve years in the nick, which is what the judge said I would definitely get if I came up before him again on the same charge, right, namely GBH. Also, if you are out on bail, which as it just so happens I am, awaiting psychiatric reports on why I spray-canned a whole train, not just one carriage but the whole train, right, with my tag, BIG GIT, it gets up the judge's nostrils if you do not keep your nose clean while you are awaiting sentence, right. Of course, I might reform back again after getting sentenced, especially if I get away with a community service order, it is a right doddle, but we do not have to worry about that just yet, right.

My mate Ginger says there are certain rules to this contest, OK, you are the boss, but I can pass them all except the last one so no sweat. First off, the rules say you must have a job, right, no problem, I have got one. I work for myself, ha ha, know what I mean? No, seriously, I work on building sites, that is after the lads have left, right. If they have been stupid enough to leave anything behind, like tools or a hundredweight of lead style of thing, that is their tough luck because I have it away on my toes with these items, finders keepers, right, I am sure you will agree with that being a Conservative.

Second off, you have got to dress smartly. This I do. All my team, the Tottenham Firm by name, wear suits, it is our trademark, right. Jeans and that are definitely out.

Third off, you have got to have your hair cut regular. Again no problem, I do not have no hair. I have my head shaved regular, right, so this comes to the same thing, right.

Fourth off, you must no longer go around in a gang, by which I suppose you mean a team. I do not no longer go around in a team and I will tell you for why, they are all inside, except for me and my mate Ginger, they was caught setting a bus on fire because the bastard conductor would not let us on it. Me and my mate Ginger had nothing whatever to do with that, right, so we was found not guilty, we could prove that we did not want to set the bus alight, we was going to drive it into the bleeding river. So no, I no longer go around in a team, right, not for another two years anyway.

Fifth off, you have got to give proof that you have recently given someone a present. Photo of said present enclosed, it is a handbag what I give to my mum at Xmas. So all right, I did not buy it, admitted, I found it in Oxford Street but I know what you are thinking, Oh, the little sod nicked it. Come in, Mr Edward McMillan-Scott. If I had nicked it I would not be sending you a photo of it because how would I know you would not send it to the Old Bill, right?

"Maybe we're just not Jacuzzi people."

Sixth off, and here we are in dead trouble, you have also got to give proof that the headteacher of your old school has welcomed you back. This one is definitely out of order. If you have been a yob like what I was, there is no school on God's earth what would let you through the gates once you have been expelled which I freely admit I was for messing about and that, right, and for another thing the school is not there no more, it got set on fire the day I left, same as the bus, ha ha. I do not know where the headteacher is now and I do not care, he was a miserable sod, but there is definitely no school for me to be welcomed back to, just some charred ruins, so this question does not count, right.

There is one more problem, right. My mate Ginger has read out of *The Guardian* that the winner will be entertained by top people in the Spanish tourist industry. Not if it is me, he won't, for the simple reason that I have been barred from setting foot in Spain again and in any case who needs it, their prisons are bleeding hell-holes mate, I kid you not. So any chance of Portugal, right?

HYENA

ZOO VET

THE ROYAL SCHWARZENEGGER COMPANY PRESENTS

THE MACHO MERCHANT OF VENICE

Persons Represented and Cast

HERR SHYLOCK, a professional body-builder –
Arnold Schwarzenegger
DUKE OF VENICE, shot-putter, budgie-breeder
and Europe's strongest man – **Geoff Capes**
SOLANIO, a tall, muscular moron – **Frank Bruno**
BASSANIO, an Italian tough guy with
a cracking-looking wife – **Sylvester Stallone**
ANTONIO, a shortass – **Ronnie Corbett**
PORTIA, an insatiable beauty – **Joan Collins**

Act IV, scene 1: Venice, a gym

DUKE: Go, give him courteous conduct to this place
Where beefcakes most do congregate
For bulges are the badge of all our tribe.

SOLANIO: I pray you tarry, oily magnifico. It troubles the man
Much to detach his deltoids from his gondolier.

BASSANIO: Fie! Fie! Fie! I have heard it tell no man
Wears posing briefs with braver air.

(Enter Shylock, and big with it)

SOLANIO: Make room to admire his prize-winning pecs.
Welcome Conan the Destroyer. Welcome Conan the Barbarian.
Welcome too the Terminator and the Predator. Welcome
                                                Herr Shylock.

SHYLOCK *(stilted)*: *Guten Abend.*

SOLANIO: Chalk thyself, adjust thy belt, pace up and down
                                                a while.
Get geed up and pump iron. The health studio is thine.
Here, take thy temporary membership card. Bassanio will sign
                                                you in.

DUKE: Give me your hand, big fella *(they arm-wrestle)*
I have heard how housewives pop-eyed with love
Direct gasps of wonderment at your traps and lats.
Your muscle definition is famed throughout the globe.
Dispense with thy bat-sleeved tank-top. Show me thyself.

SHYLOCK: I hold the world but a posing podium
Where every man must flex his parts
And mine impressively large ones.
I shall not be a soft and runtish weed
When massive weight-gains are so easy made.
Why shouldst a man, whose blood is warm within,
Stay a skinny beanpole, wretched wimp and puny drip?
Mislike me not for my upper body mass;
Beefed up triceps, bursting trapeziums
And erupting veins. Hath not every man biceps
To bulk up? To mass out his body parts?
Workouts are not rash embrac'd
Nor is a man currishly employ'd
Smothered in competition bodyshine
Ameliorating his physical attributes weekly.
The chics love a hunk.

PORTIA: Lifting is blind and lifters cannot see
The pretty ruptures they commit.
Yet methinks this man still a lantern-jawed dish.
I hath not seen any to compare in all the brawn mags.
He is a behemoth. Never have I fancied dark, abundant
Body hair. Give me solid muscle and eternal happiness
Is mine.

DUKE: I have never heard of a passion so strange
Wherein a man, swearing great oaths of effort
Upon a sweat-inlaid floor, doth for vanity,
Hazard calamitous hernias and visceral protrusions.

ANTONIO: Indeed, the world, Shylock, thinks you mad
                              to choose
To have your weight of flesh.

PORTIA: Espy his jock and cup! Herein nature doth show herself
More kind than ever is her custom. Bassanio, what doth you
Say about a man with big feet?

BASSANIO: Big socks, Portia.

SHYLOCK: I'll not answer thee but say heavy poundage
Is my humour. I fear no scrotal prolapse or
Rick'd back. The flesh is mine and I shall have it thus.
Are you told? Some men like beer and pasta.
I never did and never shall. Knurled barbells and
Anabolic packs. These things tone up the flesh.
The bigger the better 'tis a manly pursuit.

PORTIA: So speaks the master body sculptor re
His championship physique. How I swoon over
His gluteus group and full latissimus spread.
How I adore huge veiny guys. How I drool over
Their physical robustness. How I heave to see them heave!

SHYLOCK: Lay bare thy bosom, Antonio.
Expose thy underdeveloped bits.
Thou art a weakling. Deadlifting, benchpressing,
Dips and tummytucks know you not. Thy torso is pitiful
And abject. Give me it, Antonio. All of it.
Get ripped. And through sets and reps carb up and max out
To thy optimum size. Get thee to the T-bar and hack-squat
Machine or thy body shall fall further into careless ruin.
Mould thy body contours with protein-rich repasts.

SHYLOCK: Be no longer flab but solid.
Here, grip this cabled pulley
For striated musculature is thy aim.

ANTONIO: I am quite happy the way I am, thank you, siree.

DUKE: Give him thy flesh, Antonio. He demands it.

BASSANIO: Aye, there is nothing to beat an overblown mature
                             male physique.

SOLANIO: Art thou an interior decorator, Antonio,
Or a preoperative transexual? It is decided.
Shylock must have thy flesh.

ANTONIO: No! I do not hanker for this excessive masculinity.
Shylock, take thy variable resistance apparatus and be gone.
The flesh is mine and it shall stay the way I want it.

DUKE: The flesh is yours, Shylock. Take it and through
A planned and purposeful programme with regular rest-pauses
Make of Antonio's flesh a monument to isometrics.
Bring in the raw monkey testicle glands!

ANTONIO: No! Mercy!

DUKE: Bring in the alfalfa, kelp, defatted egg and pure albumen.
Bring in the anabolic pack. Prepare for a titanic posedown.
Remember, Antonio, this – clean, dip and drive.

SHYLOCK: Portia, tarry a while and I shall return
To mobilise thy hamstrings and work on thy trunk action.
My abdomen crunches with every thought of you.

PORTIA: I shall wait, Shylock, for you to return
To trigger my hormone release and show me thy trophies.

(Exeunt Shylock and Antonio circuit-training)

KEVIN PILLEY

"That the time already?"

*"I see from your curriculum vitae, Mr Kenworthy, that
your favourite colour is purple, and your unlucky number is fourteen."*

BRIGID KEENAN
. . . .

BLUBBINGS OF A MEMSAHIB

*In the second of her monthly reports from Delhi,
Our Expatriate Correspondent battles with
Indian telephones, ladies' fingers and voracious ants*

We are only just recovering from Christmas here at Poorvi Marg. Well, that's not quite fair, it wasn't Christmas so much as Boxing Day that took the toll. It's actually a blessed relief celebrating Christmas in a country where most people don't believe in it. Can you imagine, there's no such thing as last minute shopping because there's no last minute, the shops stay open all the time.

No one ever mentions Boxing Day when they talk about the relics of the Raj, but even the Indians who don't believe in Christmas seem to respect this ancient British tradition and numbers of them came round to our house for their dues. We had the pest-control man, the man who made the chick blinds for the verandah last March, the postman, the registered postman, the newspaper man, the telegraph man, and about fifteen suspicious-looking characters claiming to be our telephone engineers. We didn't give the telephone engineers anything: for one thing there were so many of them; for

another, the telephone doesn't work properly anyway; but mostly it was because we didn't really believe that they actually *were* telephone engineers.

That was a big mistake. The telephone went dead on Christmas morning just as I was about to ring Doomwatch (aka my mother) to reassure her that we were all still alive and in good health. It has only just come on again and I'm trying not to think about it because, if I do, my eye starts twitching and I might end up like the Indian Government Minister who, a year or so ago, placed a long-distance call and when it hadn't come through three days later, went berserk and stormed into his local telephone exchange brandishing a revolver. (The worst part of this story is that he still didn't get his call – all that happened was that the telephonists *went on strike*.)

In fact, long-distance telephoning can be a bit of a let-down – especially on our line, which is permanently crossed (woven or plaited would be more accurate) with that of a child psychiatrist who works around the corner in Paschimi

Marg (I know because I have to hear her patients making their appointments). There was a dreadful New Year's Eve once when we lived in Trinidad and thought it would be fun to call up some friends whom we knew were spending the evening together. One of their children answered the telephone and forgot to tell anyone we were on the line. Minutes ticked by while we listened to the sound of distant revelry all the way across the Atlantic from Somerset – glasses tinkling, people talking, merry cries and laughter. We whistled, we bellowed, we screamed and we hung up from time to time but when we picked up the receiver again, there they were, still at it. By the time someone noticed that the telephone was off the hook, the only thing we felt like saying was "Goodbye".

The post to India has been getting through in record time, though, and we've had several letters from Doomwatch about family Christmas at home. In one, she said the weather was mild but that she feared it was just the lull before the storm, and in another, she gave a hor-

THE TELEPHONE WENT DEAD JUST AS I WAS ABOUT TO RING DOOMWATCH (AKA MY MOTHER).

rifying description of how she nearly choked to death on a mince pie on Christmas Day, and was only saved by my brother, who knew about squeezing the air sharply out of the diaphragm. Only the week before, apparently, he had choked at a dinner party and since no one leapt forward to squeeze his diaphragm, he had to throw himself over the back of a chair. I couldn't help thinking that must have been a bit of a conversation stopper, and what happened to the chair – Doomwatch does not reveal.

I am still rankling from being let down over the sprouts by my greengrocer, Simla Fruit Mart. In the summer, when I was in England, I sent them a postcard and they sent one back saying they hoped I was nice in the health. But, when I turned up to collect my sprouts from them on Christmas Eve, all that had gone for nought – they'd sold them to someone else. They pressed every other kind of veg on me – parsnips, aubergines, ladies' fingers (which only reminded me of that schoolboy joke about the salesman who says to the customer, "I'm sorry, sir, we have run out of lavatory paper, but we can offer you sandpaper, carbon paper…" etc). Mind you, after a few Christmases overseas, I am a dab hand at improvisation myself, and though I'd draw the line at turkey and ladies' fingers, I can tell you that sweet potatoes make an excellent substitute for chestnuts in the stuffing. (I was a bit startled this year, when I looked up stuffing in the index of my *Constance Spry* and it said, "See also FARCES". For one wild moment I thought this might be some sort of prophecy about how my stuffing — or perhaps the whole evening — was going to turn out.)

"I don't understand it, he's never any trouble at home."

HONEYSETT

What nearly ruined the festive season for us all, however, was me having a rush of blood to the head and inviting 26 people to lunch one Saturday. Entertaining is meant to be fun, I believe, but to me it is the stuff that nervous breakdowns are made of. Not only do you have to make decisions about what to eat, but about who is going to eat it. I lay awake at night visualising our friends, thinking what boring other friends we have, and then I'd fall asleep and dream that my husband was carving one chicken leg to make it feed 26 people.

An additional problem was that since we have never entertained more than four people, we didn't have any cooking-pots or serving-dishes big enough. First I thought I'd borrow some, and then, three days before the party, I decided it would be much more practical to buy some of the lovely big brass cooking-pots, called *deksis*, that Indians use, because we could both cook and serve the meal in them. I asked Harry what he thought of my plan, and he said, "As Madame wishes," which is his standard reply when he thinks I'm embarking on something foolhardy.

However, he loyally trudged the streets of Old Delhi bazaar with me for about four hours, looking for the brass street (I wondered if this could be the origin of the expression brassed off). It was hard going, there were so many people and vehicles. Without a word of a lie, at one stage we could cross the road only by

SAHIB WOKE TO FIND A FOUR-INCH-LONG COCKROACH SITTING ON HIS CHEEK STARING INTO HIS EYES.

climbing into someone's rickshaw and out the other side. We found it eventually, bought the pots by weight (brass costs 65 rupees a kilo, by the way), and finally struggled home with them. Whereupon it was revealed that you can't cook safely in brass pots until the inside has been tinned.

As it happens, there has been a tinner sitting outside our gate for weeks doing all Poorvi Marg's pots and pans, but naturally he vanished half an hour before we got home with ours, and I had to lug the *deksis* to a shop miles away the other side of Delhi, where they saw the look of panic in my eye and charged me accordingly. Still, the row of bleaming *deksis* looked terrific; Harry looked so smart that quite a few people thought he was the host; and I needn't have bothered with all that honing and polishing of the guest-list as half of them didn't turn up anyway. (Friends of ours, Margie and John, had to give a party for an important visiting editor when they first came to Delhi. They invited 24 eminent Indians to what was to be a glittering evening, and only six turned up. Margie says that if you want 24 people, you must ask 60 – but then, of course, you run the risk that all 60 will come, bringing friends.)

After all that stress and tension, we left Delhi and went to Kerala for a week's holiday. It was

"If we can find three crossbows beneath the silver foil, someone comes round and shoots the cat."

wonderful, though it might have been marginally easier if, on Day One, I hadn't found an antique shop in Jewtown, Cochin, selling a whole lot of beautiful old painted Dutch plates. I was able to convince Sahib that we needed them for this new life of glamorous entertaining that we are going to lead, but, even so, he said they were to be entirely my responsibility: "On your head be it." The plates packed up into two enormous boxes, which I couldn't possibly have fitted on my head, but which did add several inches to the lengths of my arms. I wasn't exactly popular with the rest of the party either, as from then on we could take only taxis with roof-racks and there are not nearly as many of those as the ones without. (Thank goodness we flew back to Delhi in an Airbus because I could never have got the wretched plates on to an Indian Airlines 737. You can't fit anything into those, including your own legs.)

For part of the holiday we stayed in the State Guest House at Kovalam beach. This was a ravishingly pretty place on top of a cliff, looking out over miles of blue sea and beaches and palm trees, but the staff were either suffering from hangovers and in the course of acquiring the next ones; or they were busy with their own little bit of private enterprise – a snack shack on

the beach, which they opened while we were there. None of this bothered us, but when they started playing hideous wailing music on the shack's loudspeakers at 7 a.m., Sahib stormed down the cliff path, found the electric wire leading from Guest House to the shack and "tripped" on it.

The first night we were there the friend staying with us had a nightmare that she was being eaten alive and woke up to find that it was true: there was an ant's nest in her bed. Sahib woke up to find a four-inch-long cockroach sitting on his cheek staring into his eyes, and I woke up to find ants had eaten my pants. Kerala being a watery kind of place, I worried a bit about us catching malaria and eventually asked someone local if there was any danger. "No," he said wistfully. "No, we have had malaria eradication here. There is no malaria – but elephantiasis is available."

The foreigners on Kovalam beach were us, about fifty German and Italian package tourists, and a few genuine Sixties hippies who'd "stayed on". As an ex-fashion editor (well, that's my story), I could not help being interested in what the male package tourists were wearing. They had all flung away their European swimwear in favour of the cotton pouches-on-strings

"You put on a white coat and everyone assumes you're a doctor."

being sold by the beach vendors (I'll refrain from mentioning what my daughters called these) and without which, our modestly dressed group agreed, they'd have looked far less obscene. What with them and their topless girls, it's no wonder that droves of office work-

THE SITUATION IS NOW SERIOUS. PLEASE BRING LAVATORY PAPER.

ers from the nearby town of Trivandrum come out by bus after hours to walk along the beach and gawp.

In the evenings, at Kovalam, we ate fish curries in the garden of an old hotel in the village, called Blue Seas, where the tables were cosily grouped around the owner's grandfather's grave. He was a Mr Panicker who died, according to the epitaph, "while aged ninety", and I wondered if he could have been the founder of Panicker's Travels back in Delhi, an agency I always smile at when I pass, thinking my mother should be using it. But my tenderest memory of Kovalam is hearing my husband's very English voice in the lobby of the Great House one evening. Loudly and slowly he was saying, *"Two days ago I asked for two rolls of lavatory paper and nothing has happened. The situation is now serious – please bring lavatory paper to rooms four and five. Do you understand? Lavatory paper, toilet paper, to our rooms, please."*

I have come to the conclusion that the Sahib and I must be too fussy – we always seem to be complaining about something and planning furious letters to Authorities. This week's batch are to the Public Works Department about the Guest House, of course; to the Taj Group about their hotel, the Malabar in Cochin, because they seem to be building a high-rise annexe which is going to spoil the whole beautiful port, and they don't make up the beds till lunchtime; a letter to Tefal who made our toaster, pointing out that only a moron would design one without a tray underneath to catch the crumbs; to British Airways enquiring where their cabin crew disappear to when they've served the meals, because we passengers never seem to see them again (on my last trip they even "forgot" to hand round the hot towels before landing in Delhi); and to the General Trading Company in London complaining that the teapot they sold me pours at a ninety-degree angle to the left. There was going to be a letter to Rajiv Gandhi about our telephone, but that is working again now. None of these letters will ever get written, but planning them is obsessive.

Our daughters seem to have inherited our picky ways. "Harry's been chewing betel in the kitchen," they report, or, "Are you aware that the *dhobi* is asleep on the spare-room floor?" On second thoughts, I think it's not intolerance that prompts either their or our tale-telling, but a feeling (which living in India fosters) that we must all stay on our toes or the whole crazy world will fall apart.

"Social worker at fault, somewhere, I shouldn't wonder."

DO NOT FRIGHTEN THE HORSES

L. J. K. SETRIGHT joins Punch *as car correspondent extraordinary*

A man was arrested recently in Switzerland for laughing in the street at midnight. Would his offence have been judged as abominable had he laughed there at 10 p.m., I wonder, or four in the morning? Time is, after all, as the advertisements used to tell us, the art of the Swiss. Would it have made any difference (especially at midnight) if, instead of laughing, he had wept?

It is no perceived part of my duties to deride the Swiss. I am unmoved by those who jeer at the nation which gave the world the cuckoo clock: the Swiss clockmaking industry also gave us Ernest Bloch, which is more than can be said for the Japanese watchmakers and the electronics industry, jointly or severally.

They are not perfect, though, the Swiss. Apart from being unforgivably rich and unbearably smug, they are also more hostile to the motor-car than almost anywhere else, the possible exceptions being Norway and Sark. It is, I suspect, a natural consequence of theirs being a small country: if they did not contrive speed limits and traffic restrictions to the utmost costive effect, people might actually drive straight through Switzerland without stopping to spend money.

England is almost as bad. Traditionally hostile to motoring since the days when the Red Flag was a waved threat rather than a sung promise, hippophile England has always feared that the motor-car might one day replace the horse, and still fights a broom-and-shovel rearguard action to postpone that ghastly inevitability. The Briton who drives a car is expected to feel guilty. He may no longer know why, and the horses themselves are probably past caring; but at the very least the decent British motorist knows better than to enjoy his driving.

He is unlikely to be arrested for laughing while on the road, whatever the time. It is invariably assumed, however, that a laughing driver has just done something improper. It may have been something incisive like carving a passage into a somnolent line of ditherers, something innocuous like doing handbrake turns in the snow, or something invigorating like completing three consecutive laps of a roundabout on opposite lock; but if it made him happy, then a sternly magisterial cautioning is in order.

Nearly all modern cars seem devised expressly to disengage us from the pleasures of motoring, if only by the substitution of others. In-car entertainment (own up, now! How many of you listen to Ernest Bloch while driving?) takes on ever more daunting proportions in the bill of sale, while steering dampers and sound absorbers suppress ever more of the sensations offered by the road and the world outside.

It was in more primitive cars, elemental in construction and savage in use, that laughter came to our unregulated lips. In those sensually direct machines, it was a pleasure to feel what we were doing, to appreciate the very implausibility of it, and to rejoice in its accomplishment. Soaring serene in a hoodless pre-war Morris

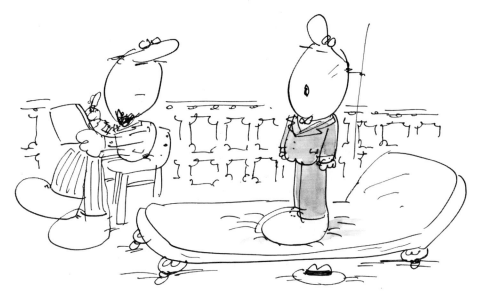

"Listen! There it goes again – the National Anthem."

IT WAS IN MORE PRIMITIVE CARS, ELEMENTAL IN CONSTRUCTION AND SAVAGE IN USE, THAT LAUGHTER CAME TO OUR UNREGULATED LIPS.

Eight up a snow-packed Aston hill between rows of post-slither fumblebumpers brought me hoots of laughter; romping up and down an Alpine foothill in a rallying Abarth, with a photographer leaping for cover when I got it sideways, did the same. Best of all was probably when I despaired of parking even a Fiat 500 in Mayfair: I simply drove it through the front door of the club I was visiting and left it in the foyer. "Excuse me, sir, did you leave a car outside?" asked a servitor some minutes later in the bar. "No, I left one *inside*."

We really should not do it. The hint of a satisfied smile is allowed the driver of a Bentley Turbo, the head may nod unseen approval behind the wheel of a Porsche 928, the brow may be cleared by the four-wheel steering of the latest Honda Prelude; but the rest of us should meekly accept the best and the worst of whatever we drive, just go and steer and stop and try to think about the Commonwealth or the Highway Code. Sober driving demands more than mere abstinence from strong drink.

What is needed is a car which encourages the driver to think. I know the very thing: for 32 years, the Citroën has been the thinking man's motor-car. It challenges him to dismiss familiar bad habits and false assumptions; it challenges him to find a glitch in the remorselessly logical interdependence of everything in its design – shape, distribution of masses and of drive and of braking, and most of all the supreme suspen-

sion system which has the car sitting on four bubbles of nitrogen, with which it communicates by engine-pumped high-pressure hydraulics. But even the current version, the CX, has been around for 14 years, and even though it is still the world's most modern car it shows its age.

Modern times suggest its lesser brother, the BX, which in its latest and finest form with 16-valve engine is an amazingly rapid car for one so serene. Alas, it is not so logical: it lacks the Nitro-Express high-velocity steering of the CX, and its direction indicator flashers are self-cancelling (as in every car that is not a Citroën), presumably at the behest of Citroën's masters at Peugeot. Clearly a flippant lot, those Peugeot people.

Just now they are laughing all the way to the bank, because their new 405 has just netted the 1988 Car of the Year award which the CX won in 1975. A pleasing car, the 405, especially with that same superb 16-valve engine; but definitely not a mirth-provoker. For this, paradoxically, you need a Citroën – CX, BX, it does not matter.

Park it beneath the nose of some horse: that bone-headed creature will remain supercilious, having seen cars pass and repass all the days of its life. Now switch the ride-height adjustment so that the car rises vertically several inches; what horse has seen a car threatening to do a vertical take-off? The age of chivalry may at last end, and the laughter of Europe be rekindled in the streets.

"For God's sake, don't get him started on the cost of millet."

THE BAG LADY

Don't Interrupt Her — America is wonderful!

Mrs Thatcher wows Washington

'M not at all sure what the roots of America's Margaret Thatcher cult are, but a cult is what it shows every sign of becoming. Government officials speak of her with awe. One who was given the job of briefing us before her recent visit said repeatedly how gratified the United States was that she had chosen America for her first visit after "her stupendous electoral victory". He spoke in the way that the Mayor of Little Piddlington might on hearing that Princess Anne was about to drop in.

Others talk about her as if she had superhuman powers. A Very Senior State Department official briefed reporters at the White House a few hours before her plane arrived (it is still acknowledged that she needs mechanical means to fly). Some of the reporters couldn't believe that she intended to meet the President, the Vice-President, the Secretary of State, the White House Chief of Staff, the Defence Secretary, the Chairman of the Federal Reserve and fifteen or so senators, and give five full-scale TV interviews, all between seven in the morning and six at night.

"But she always travels like that," said the Very Senior Official, as one might say: "Of course she eats nails for breakfast." They firmly believe the Thatcher myth here; they just got around to it a little later than she herself did.

Right now the Prime Minister is bullish on America. I should explain that most Americans aren't. I've never known a nation which suffered such severe mood swings as the USA. This time last year the nation was suffused with good cheer, the result of a whole series of events such as Ronald Reagan's election, the Los Angeles Olympics, the Grenada invasion and even the raid on Tripoli. Then came Irangate, and they were plunged into gloom. Newspapers and magazines are full of articles titled "Can America Survive?" and the like.

They already reckon they've been overtaken by Japan, and it's just a matter of waiting until the Koreans and the Taiwanese do the same. This year's 200th anniversary of the Constitution, which would normally be the occasion for yet more self-congratulatory backslapping, is now prompting morose reflections on what a feeble document it must be if the likes of Ollie North can shred it at will.

So they hardly knew what to do when Mrs Thatcher swept into town telling them to buck their ideas up and not to be such silly billies. She granted an audience to the TV show *Face The Nation*, though one had the sense that it was the nation that was being summoned to face her. "Why are you doing your level best to put the worst foot forward?" she demanded of the country's 240 million citizens. "Cheer up!" she cried. "Be more upbeat! America is a strong country, with a great president, great people and a great future ... I beg of you, you should have as much faith in America as I have."

Face The Nation is one of those Sunday morning chat shows which do not, frankly, have particularly large audiences, especially in summer. But our leader's words were thought worthy of the front page in the following day's *USA Today* with its three million readers nationwide.

I gather that her message was similar everywhere she went, especially in her private meetings. Everything in America is wonderful, was her gist, and the best we can do in Britain is to try to emulate it as much as we can.

Normally this sort of talk would be received, if not rapturously, at least as no more than its hearers deserved. However, once America gets into a glum, there isn't much anyone can do to rouse it. After all, when you or I get depressed, it's quite nice to have someone to come round and flatter you. It does not, however, make you any less miserable.

Mrs Thatcher's visit received an extraordinary amount of publicity. Mr Gorbachev, or even the Israeli Prime Minister, would get a lot more, of course, but they would normally arrive as part of a news story. Her visit had no apparent purpose at all.

It's not easy to be quite sure why she attracts this slack-jawed attention. Some people here have tried to interpret Ronald Reagan in terms of the Arthurian "Fisher King" and other myths. Certainly her visit can be made to fit in with various legends about old, enfeebled or accursed princes being saved by the intervention of strong, vigorous women. The curse is broken when the damsel accepts the victim in

"Don't worry, I'm sure they're just jogging."

spite of his misfortunes: Beauty and the Beast and the princess who kisses the frog are two examples. Are we witnessing, and are people responding atavistically, to the re-enactment of this ancient story? Or, as one of America's better-known TV anchor persons put it to me in more modern terms, "Do you think she can kick-start the President?"

Perhaps it is simpler than that. After all, for two close chums they are remarkably different. She is obsessively hard-working, and he isn't. She keeps an alert eye on everything that goes on around her; he appears not to notice the prosecution of entire wars in his own name. She knows whereof she speaks; he knows a few old Hollywood anecdotes and that's more or less it. He cannot be elected again and is a "lame duck" (can we equate that with the impotence of the Fisher King myth, or am I getting carried away?); she insists that she can go "on and on".

She is linked to America by the most curious tie, which is political attraction. You might imagine that Mr Kinnock was anti-American, but he isn't. He likes coming and has had holidays here. He can't stand the Reagan administration but he is extremely fond of the people.

But the Reagan administration are pretty well the only Americans Mrs Thatcher knows. She has barely seen the country except from official limousines and helicopters. Her knowledge of it is limited to graphs showing industrial growth, tax rates, start-up rates for new businesses. I doubt if she's ever eaten catfish pie at a sweltering roadside diner in Missouri, or watched old men playing cards by a scrap-yard in North Carolina, or seen a traffic jam in Houston, or watched a sandlot baseball game in Oregon. I may be wrong, but I suspect that to the Prime Minister, America isn't a place at all, but a collection of ideological verities.

This may be at the root of America's fascination with her, and yet suspicion of her. "What does she know?" they ask themselves as she hectors them about their own wonderfulness. At the same time, they can't resist her – in the old sense, that is, of being unable to fight her off. It's as well to remember that, although Americans admired Churchill more than any other Briton this century, plenty of them used to believe that he also had several screws loose. 🍃

RANDI HACKER AND JACKIE KAUFMAN

QADIKH: ANCIENT LAND, PARTY LAND

It's February. You're cold. You're depressed. Everyone you know has the flu. You hate your winter wardrobe. You hate your job. You hate the lower right-hand drawer in your desk, the one you really have to yank to open and you always have to open it because your files are in there. And you hate your files.

You need the sound of the surf in your ears, the warmth of the hot sun on your back and the feel of a frosty Mango Blizzard in your hand. In short, you need a vacation.

But you're trapped. All flights to the islands are booked. Your travel agent thinks he might be able to get you a long weekend at the Seminole Lodge thirty miles from Lake Ketchawanahobee near Gator, Florida, but he's not sure and you have to put down money to find out. What are you going to do?

Picture this: Sand. Sun. Date palms. More sand. More sun. The crystal blue waters of the Gulf. Ahhhhh! You're picturing Qadikh.

Qadikh is a small, rocky jewel of a country, nestled between the high jagged brown mountains of Syria and the low green, sometimes muddy, always fertile, Jordan River delta basin. Qadikh faces the Gulf and the hot, arid, endless Sinai Peninsula knocks at its back door. Qadikh is a vacation paradise waiting for you.

We know what you're thinking. You're thinking, "Qadikh? They blow up planes in Qadikh. They take people hostage in Qadikh. They lose luggage in Qadikh." Well, that is a narrow, media-influenced, just plain negative view of Qadikh. The real Qadikh is a land of passion, a land of ancient camel routes, a land of warm-blooded, fun-loving, native people. When the people of Qadikh are not driving jeeps full of dynamite into foreign embassies, they want to party with you.

Sure, there are anti-aircraft guns guarding the sun-baked stone steps that lead down to Azziz Harbour but when your ski boat roars by, the soldiers manning the guns will cheer at the way you jump the wake on one banana. True, there is a curfew in the capital city of Qaif, but your passport means free military transportation to Achmed's Oasis, an after hours place where you can lose yourself in the frenzied sound of Ibn Ben Ibn and his All-Bazik Band. Yes, Faisal el Faisul Faisouli, the Faiq of Qadikh called all Westerners "children of motherless speckled dogs" but he didn't mean you. Tourists are VIPs in Qadikh.

From the moment you land at Faisouli Airport to the moment your exit visa is stamped with a big "Q", everything is made easy for you. Language a problem? You'll be provided with a fifth grader to translate for you. Worried about being taken hostage? No way. You're our guests. Confused by the currency? Don't be. Everything is based on the azud. There are 101 duzas in an azud. There are 53 adzus in a duza. There are 14 uzads in an adzu. And then there's the zadu, a coin so small it's usually dropped in the sand and lost. All you really need to know is that your dollar is worth 4,000 azuds and 4,000 azuds can buy a lot of fun in Qadikh.

Come on Down! It's Al Dhoumad Day!

Legend has it that in ancient times Al Dhoumad, the Great Sea Serpent, slithered across the hot desert wondering where the sea was. Soon he met the infamous Kabdul the Beheader who lived alone in a tent in the desert.

"Good luck, then – and here, you'll need this."

"Excuse me, can you tell me where the sea is?" asked Al Dhoumad. And Kabdul the Beheader replied, "I will show you where the sea is if you will give me your tail." And Al Dhoumad said, "But you are a beheader." And Kabdul said, "A man can change professions, can't he?" And Al Dhoumad said, "But what is a serpent without a tail?" And Kabdul said, "Very well, then I must kill you." And he took out his cruelly curved scimitar and hacked off Al Dhoumad's tail. Thwack. Thwack. The serpent bled for a long, long time. And then he died without ever seeing the sea. And where he died, Qadikh was born.

Today, a plaque in downtown Qaif commemorates the spot where Al Dhoumad died. Every February, the whole country fasts for three days, then explodes in revelry on Al Dhoumad Day. There's no school. No mail is delivered. No arms shipments leave or enter the country.

SUDDENLY, SHRIEKS AND THE SOUND OF THUNDERING HOOFS SHATTER THE MORNING STILLNESS. IT IS THE HA AMWATAH, DESERT NOMADS WHO BELIEVE THEMSELVES TO BE THE TRUE DESCENDANTS OF KABDUL THE BEHEADER.

At dawn, the 36 men who make up the ranks of the Faiq's own elite guard, take up their positions inside the giant, ornate Al Dhoumad costume. Then the old imam slowly climbs the many steps to the top of the Allah Dome and calls the serpent to its death. As the last notes of his mournful ululation fade, Al Dhoumad slithers out of the desert and through the city gates. The people of Qaif line the streets and lean out of windows to watch as Al Dhoumad passes. Some pray. Some carry little cups of coffee because it's early. Others offer the serpent water but he cannot take it. He is Al Dhoumad, the serpent.

Suddenly, shrieks and the sound of thundering hoofs shatter the morning stillness. It is the Ha Amwatah, desert nomads who believe themselves to be the true descendants of Kabdul the Beheader.

All year they ride from oasis to oasis, gathering dates to make the famous date shakes they sell at stands located throughout the desert. Every February, on Al Dhoumad Day, they gallop through the bazaar with their scimitars drawn. When they find Al Dhoumad, they hack away at his detachable tail.

At this point, the people of Qadikh can contain themselves no longer. They flood the streets carrying buckets of red paint and shout-ing, "Ifsh'a Allah, q'amd'a Allah hamid!" ("If Allah wants it done, let Allah do it!"). Then they throw the paint everywhere: on Al Dhoumad, on the Ha Amwatah, on each other. When everything is red, the feasting begins.

Huge platters of lamb ringlets and scorpion kabobs are passed from person to person and there's plenty of kadjii to wash it down with. Vendors sell Ha Amwatah dolls and inflatable Al Dhoumad tails. Magicians, musicians and jugglers perform throughout the city and after dark fireworks light up the sky and there's dancing in the streets. The celebration continues until the old imam once again climbs to the top of the Allah Dome and tells everyone to be quiet.

This year, Al Dhoumad Day is February 26. Air Qadikh can get you there for less than you think. Qadikh. Where the Middle East meets the West.

Qadikh Ministry of Tourism
1331 Kabdul the Beheader Boulevard, Suite 2907
Qaif, Qadikh

IRMA KURTZ
....

NEVER WERE THERE SUCH DEMOTED MISTERS

**One man: one woman.
It's a rule of life.
So what happens
when that one man becomes
two, then three, then
four men?**

IT must be ten years ago or more since I addressed a female consciousness-expanding group on the subject of men. "Sisters," I told them, "mark my words, men are played out, pooped, *de trop*. Come-uppance is just around the corner and their futures will hold nothing but solitude, humiliation, and despair. Can you not, please, find mercy in your hearts for the poor souls and get off their backs? Now, you take your Cro-Magnon or your Neolithic, *those* were men who deserved a fight, those were MCPs a feminist could sink her teeth into. But our modern so-called man? He's not worth the trouble any more. He's had it. He's shot his big, butch bolt. He's kaput."

At the time, I was shouted down and pelted with copies of *The Female Eunuch* (mercifully, the paperback version had just come out). But now, yea verily, my words have come to pass. Ladies, at last we've got the brutes where it hurts: by the statistics. According to an article in my daily paper, no less a body than The Family Policy Studies Centre predicts that by 1993 there will be 284,000 more marriageable males than females in Great Britain. Think of it! More than a quarter of a million free-floating men. It is an unprecedented phenomenon, one which until quite recently was controlled by regular warfare. (Football riots are just not up to the job.) There is no reason not to imagine that the trend of male superiority in numbers, if nothing else, will continue along with all the mind-boggling discrepancies it entails.

For example, within the next half-dozen years or so it will be bachelor uncles, not spinster aunts, who gather around the foot of the festive table, hungry for the wishbones and a little comfort before they tiptoe home to their lonely flats, their budgies, and their wee, narrow beds. Soon, as the male majority increases, it will be unwed older brothers, rather than virgin sisters, who have to withdraw from active life to nurse aged parents. It will be husbands, never wives, who after they lose their shapes find themselves overnight deserted by bored mates who have let themselves be seduced by wittier, trimmer, racier models. Extramarital predators of the near future are no longer going to slink out from behind the perfume counter at Selfridges; on the contrary, homewreckers will be men, just plain old garden-variety men, who oh-so innocently hang around outside beauty salons, supermarket checkouts, the Houses of Parliament, and other places where women forgather.

As soon as there is a marked shortage of breeding females in a society that still insists on monogamy, all men must show themselves to be unbrotherly. It's only logical, isn't it? One man: one woman. It's a rule of life. So what happens when that one man becomes two, then three, then four men? Why, they will be everywhere, desperately competing to attract. Men on every corner buying roses, studying sex manuals, wallowing in aftershave, oozing charm, and, to the last one of them, a very good listener. Will they heed the status of their beloved, or her age, or her looks? Certainly not. As long as she buttons on the left and doesn't ostensibly shave, every female, already spoken for or not, will find herself importuned by a parade of begging, sobbing, whimpering members of the opposite sex. Isn't it heaven?

And how about this? We can all finally persuade our daughters to go ahead and be brain surgeons because for the very first time in the whole of human history the intelligence of a woman will present no impediment to male desire. In other words, you can damn well bet they're going to make passes at girls who wear glasses. And crosses. And bras. And orthopaedic devices. No distinction in a female will put suitors off. When there are too few women to go round and each man is permitted only one at a time, nothing, not even cellulite, will be considered a handicap to lust. Let her tell better jokes than his, let her beat him at tennis, beat him at chess; let her beat him. He will still come back for more because, statistically, she could well be his last chance in life for a regular Sunday roast, in-laws, and little furry covers on the loo seats. Statistically, if he loses her he may

"…Anybody else got a note?"

190

never find another ring-size female and be doomed to live as a lonely old bachelor. Statistically, he's in big, big trouble. Pardon my cackle, but statistically he, he, he has had it.

A scarcity of women will radically change all social forms. Among the young, for example: imagine a few girls leaning against walls, watching from under half-closed lids the boys in bright satin who are jostling each other for the best light to be seen in because each lad burns with the hope that tonight – oh please, let it be tonight! – Miss Right or Ms Wonderful will pick him, and no other, out of the crowd. Isn't that a picture to make you smile? And what of sophisticated, middle-class amusements? Women discussing Fay Weldon's latest novel

You can damn well bet they're going to make passes at girls who wear glasses.

around a dining-table while their hopeful gallants try timidly to join in the conversation, so fearful of rejection they only occasionally dare interject a word or two in those low-pitched voices of theirs that just don't carry very well

Nothing, not even cellulite, will be considered a handicap.

when women are talking seriously, do they? My goodness, isn't it going to be a strange new world that has more men than women in it? I dare say only among the very upper classes will the preponderance of one sex over the other make hardly any difference.

As their numbers increase, every man will do anything he can to get one of us for his very own, and then still more to keep her. He'll change his socks, style his hair, trim down at a health club, and even undertake cosmetic surgery if he thinks it might help. There will be new glossy magazines instructing men on how to express their inner selves, how to develop their calf muscles, what to wear on a first date, and how to put magic back into their relationships. "Five Hundred Ways To Hair Restoral", "The Fifteen Day Beer Diet", "Are You Still Too Macho To Matter?", "I Was The Other Man"; articles of that sort will proliferate, lapped up by a male public eager only to please. Newspapers, on their "Men's Pages", will feature excerpts from books by American psychologists with such titles as *Flab: Man's Nemesis* and *How Do You Know You're Really Pleasing Yourself When You Spend Your Life Trying To Please Her?* Most of all, in order to attract and hold a woman's interest, men will talk: they'll tell us their hopes, their dreams, they'll recount each emotion that flits across their tiny psyches. "I'm feeling sad," they'll say. "I'm feeling lonely." "I'm feeling so horribly vulnerable." "Stay with me," they'll plead, "my nerves are bad tonight..." And what will we reply? "Pull yourself together!" And finally, as we storm out into the promising night: "You're a crazy, neurotic man! Get hold of yourself, you silly billy!" What fun, girls! I can hardly wait! "Make yourself scarce!" my brother said many years ago when I tried once to join in some fun he was having with the boys. I wonder if he had any inkling how prophetic those words were going to be?

NEAL ANTHONY

Armada Night Special

SIR ROBIN DAY: Good evening and welcome back to *Armada Night Special*, this is Robin Day and we shall be bringing you the latest results as THE NATION DECIDES whether or not it is going to be ruled by King Philip of Spain. For those of you who've just joined us, the news is that the Spanish fleet has been engaged, battled, beaten and finally chased away by the English ships of war and a few merchant vessels.

With me in the studio now is Alonzo Perez de Gusman, Duke of Medina Sidonia and general of the fleet. Don Alonzo, let me ask you first, are you disappointed by the results we've heard so far?

DON: No, not at all, Robin: after all, we're at a very early stage, and what we've seen so far is very much what we expected: indeed, and I have said this on a number of occasions, to suggest that a few isolated results indicate a general trend is really to jump to conclusions, and I think that what we're seeing, or rather what we will begin to see as the night goes on, will bear me out in that.

DAY: But there are those who are saying that you must be a very worried man tonight.

DON: No, by no means, I'm not at all worried, Robin: as I've said, I think it's much too early to build large assumptions on a handful of results.

DAY: Nevertheless, the information we have so far indicates that many of the biggest Spanish ships, some of those you were really depending on to carry the day for you, with huge majorities in crew, soldiers, cannon and ammunition, have been sunk.

DON: Well, you know, Robin, when you've been general of the fleet for as long as I have, a few losses here and there are to be expected, and

I don't think that's any reason to start sounding alarmist or defeatist: I'd prefer to wait until all the results are in, and see...

DAY: But it is my understanding that you have been general of the fleet only since the death of Admiral Santa Cruz a matter of weeks ago. In fact, there are those who say you are wholly unqualified to command an expedition of this sort.

DON: I'm afraid you've been paying too much attention to the smear campaign which has been mounted against us, from the start, by the English. Some of their tactics have been quite scandalous. We've fought hard on the issues: the English have persisted in fighting on the level of personalities.

DAY: You mean, references to singeing the King of Spain's beard, and so on?

DON: Exactly, Robin: now, if you examine our record, you'll see that we have consistently refused to make any reference to singeing the Queen of England's wig.

DAY: Well, we have gone into the question of whether or not the Queen wears a wig on a number of occasions, and we really don't have time to go into that again, now. In fact, if I may just interrupt at this point, we're going over now to John Tusa on Beachy Head...

TUSA: Well, here on Beachy Head the bonfire beacon is still blazing away there behind me, and the latest result we've just had in is that the Spaniards have abandoned Don Pedro de Valdez with his ship at Portland; and, to make matters worse for them, they have also lost Hugo de Monçada and his galleys, at Calais... Back now to Robin Day in the studio.

DAY: Well, that certainly seems to confirm the picture we've been getting throughout the even-

RODIN'S HOSPITAL VISITOR

ing: Don Alonzo, in view of what we've just heard, are you still confident of victory?

DON: Yes, of course I'm confident, Robin: after all, what we're seeing here is simply due to the activities of a small, you know, a *very small*, unrepresentative minority of sailors: now, and I've said this many times in the past, the activities of these insignificant seamen in no way reflect the aspirations of the English people –

DAY: Are you saying, then –

DON: If I may just finish my sentence, Robin, the point I'm making is that, when we land our troops on English soil, and we *are* going to land, you'll see that the English people, who are not, after all, seamen or extremists, are going to welcome us with open arms.

DAY: You're saying, then –

DON: The English people support us, Robin: *they want* to see the True Religion restored, the Scottish Queen avenged, the illegitimate usurper Elizabeth deposed: after all, the woman is a heretic, and His Spanish Majesty was married to her elder sister, so there's no doubt in my mind that, when we have the complete picture, we shall see England added to the dominions of Spain.

DAY: Nevertheless, so far, you haven't sunk a single English ship or landed a single Spanish soldier on English soil...

DON: Well, I think it's much too early to attach any great importance to that, Robin: the fact is, we *are* going to land, and I think we're on target to do so. The Armada is moving ahead, and we're in a stronger position now than we have been for a very long time. We're picking up support from the Prince of Parma, who is waiting with his flotilla of barges to bring his troops ashore, and –

DAY: If I may just interrupt you at that point, I've just been notified that the Prince of Parma's flat-bottomed ships have been spectacularly blockaded by the English and their Dutch allies, so it appears that the Prince will not, in fact, be able to bring them across the Channel. Don Alonzo, would you agree that this development indicates a sharp decline in your chances of invasion?

DON: No, certainly not, Robin, I think you've got to remember that the Prince of Parma is a very able commander, and what he's managed to achieve here is the successful strategic withdrawal of his forces to a position from which he will be best able to strike back at the English, and invade.

DAY: Well, we've now had confirmation that several *dozen* Spanish ships have been sunk or put out of action, and the remainder of the fleet is being pursued north towards Scotland by the English lord-admiral and Sir Francis Drake. Are you now prepared to admit, Don Alonzo, that you have in fact lost the day?

DON: Well, that may be your view, Robin, but it's not mine: I think that what we're seeing here, the figures, results, we've seen tonight, indicate, on the whole, that the Armada is sending a *very* clear message to the English people, and I think that the results so far make it perfectly obvious that it's too early to write off our chances, because, you know, Robin, and I've said this many times in the past...

"Dammit, I know there's a little secret-drawer mechanism here somewhere!"

"I can't count to ten, can you?"

"And here is an artist's impression of the man we're looking for."

Crisis Diary of An East Anglian Lady

DAY 1 Seven o'clock on a dark, howling morning. I am standing in the garden in a hard hat, dodging flying pantiles and branches raining off the willow trees. One giant poplar appears to be resting peacefully across house roof, draped with power and telephone lines. Observe great muddy arc of roots blotting out sky beside children's sandpit, then notice that this is attached to 60ft high beech tree, now redeployed as 60ft long beech tree, on ground. Remains of former brick privy pulverised under tree, bits of oars and strimmers poking out pathetically under trunk. Shudderingly calculate distance of collapse from roof over children's bedroom (15 ft).

Go back inside, look for paraffin-lamp, dole out Coco Pops to small anxious figures in pyjamas. Switch on *Today* programme: various urgent-voiced prunes saying situation terrible in Kent and Sussex. Consider dodging the flak to reach the nearest working phone and tell them pretty damn terrible in Suffolk too, but switch to Radio Orwell instead.

Radio Orwell going full steam, hysterical disc-jockeys relaying breathless messages from police, nobody travel anywhere, for God's sake everyone stay in house, sing wartime songs, put sandbags round senior citizens. Look out of window, spot our own elderly neighbour grimly putting tiles back on roof, still in teeth of gale, not standing for any nonsense.

Mid-morning raid on candle shops, paraffin dealers, and retailers of batteries. Gallant Blitz spirit prevails everywhere except on Radio Orwell, which has begun to read out lists of hurricane-damaged community events, e.g. "The Harwich Hard of Hearing Club Committee meeting is cancelled, there'll be no Craft Bazaar at the Debenham Middle School tomorrow, and – yes, we've just got news that there'll be no dental services this morning in Stowmarket." Nanny arrives, pretty jacked off because Ladies Darts League matches cancelled.

Huge crane arrives, summoned by streetwise neighbour, and drags poplar tree off roof, lowering it carefully on to remains of climbing frame. Smile bravely. Go to bed at 8.00 p.m. to study small print of insurance policy by the light of a smoking candle. Woken by sound of rain, indoors. Drag zinc baths up attic stairs and poke holes in rotting plasterboard.

DAY 2 Husband, seized by pioneer instinct to control hostile environment, stokes up Rayburn boiler with coke and starts attacking poor old beech corpse with chainsaw. Miraculous apparition of Telecom engineers, then phone rings: brother from Southampton, saying, "Don't know if you got it, but we had this hurricane they're talking about on the news. Our dustbin blew right over!" Discover sodden remains of account book in puddle

> **"Jammy buggers with drives, and trees, and yachts, deserve all they get, fine socialist wind it must have been, real life is confined to Kentish Town where several dustbins blew over causing untold grief."**

of water surrounding Amstrad PC.

Blitz spirit intact. Womenfolk of the neighbourhood form emergency coven, working out who's got cooking but no lighting, who has phone, who has hot water but no cooking, who has nothing, who had camping-stove last, etc. Result, procession of people with towels and hurricane-lamps up our stairs. Radio 4 sole link with rest of nation, enables us to hear prat from CBI claiming that not enough people make effort to get to work in crises, management bigger heroes than workers, I suppose they fax themselves to work, smug bastards.

DAY 3 Radio Orwell says huge task force of electricians from Yorkshire, County Cork etc now on its way to East Anglia. New gale forecast. This precipitates a huge panic operation to cut the top 20ft off the second poplar tree, now leaning over chimney in a sinister fashion with heaved-up roots. Inspired leadership works out that if five people all stand in the onion-bed and hang on to a rope round its top while sixth person climbs ladder and saws, it will fall the right way, i.e. upwind. Poplar tree (now very unpoplar tree, ha ha, Blitz-type joke) decides to disagree with this theory, resists arrest for forty-five minutes, then topples gracefully downwind, via porch roof, breaking telephone wire

again. Go next door and ring Telecom engineers. Unaccountably frosty reception.

Back indoors to light hurricane-lamps and candles, it is, after all, 4 p.m. Husband notices the lights are on in every other house in our lane, and sets off down path with boxes full of freezer contents. Noticing blue Electricity Board van, drops boxes and runs excitedly into lane, leaving trail of Individual Chicken Pies and Oven Chips to shame us in front of the neighbours. Electricity van turns out to be delivering a new washing-machine.

Under cover of darkness, we run an 80 ft extention cable across the garden and over the drive to the power point in neighbour's derelict barn, and spend an hour crouched in the kitchen by the light of the last eggcupful of paraffin, watching *Howard's Way*.

DAY 4 Angel of God appears in garden, whistling merrily and carrying a roll labelled ROOFING-FELT. Decide to make the best of it all, drag wood around, praise wonderful job being done by Electricity Board and Telecom for everyone else. Bicycle over fields to ring *Times*, chap sitting in cosy computer-lined office says it must be wonderful to be writing by pen and ink by the light of a guttering candle, just like being an eighteenth-century literary figure. Children say, "Why can't we watch a *Popeye* video?"

DAY 5 Brief excursion to London for BBC, discover world has almost forgotten about hurricane, going on about Stock Market instead. Unwanted class war also developing, wherein complaints about huge trees collapsed tragically on driveways, yachts flung off moorings into fields, etc, are met with pursed lips and slight expression of disapproval: i.e. jammy buggers with drives, and trees, and yachts, deserve all they get, fine socialist wind it must have been, real life is confined to Kentish Town

"I know what goes on. I don't live next door to the bottle bank for nothing."

"God knows why you couldn't just settle for a ladder, mirror and bell."

where several dustbins blew over causing untold grief. Only keepers of Royal and National Parks are allowed to complain out loud.

Pioneer husband stocks up house with paraffin and takes off for job in Devon, with a crocodile tear or two about leaving homestead for three days.

DAY 6 Return from London to find that totally forgotten painters have turned up to fulfil their booking by stripping everything off sitting-room walls and starting work by garish portable gas-lantern. Topography of whole house now unfamiliar, keep falling over moved chairs, chests, stacked pictures in the dark. Paraffin running low again, deadlines unmet, tele-messages from cross magazines. Think bitter thoughts about technological revolution, PCW8256, RS232 interface lead, etc, gathering

dust in freezing wet room upstairs, but have brainwave: search under attic tarpaulins for Christmas Present box. Rip open package containing Junior Elite Toy Typewriter with real ribbon, and start to tap out article on Modern Motherhood. Give up after half-an-hour, creep out in the darkness and fresh gale with torch between teeth and 80 ft extension lead looped over arm like SAS blowing up bridge, scale rickety steps to loft of neighbour's barn and restore erratic power via living-room window to damp word-processor. Feel much better until something (duck?) trips over flex in the gloom and disconnects power, wiping disc in the process.

DAY 7 Reports reach me that the Leiston & District Ladies' Darts League is now firing on all cylinders once more. Car, however, is on the blink. Bicycle around neighbours' houses, phoning people to explain why I can't phone them. Farm out laundry in all directions. Feel strange, disoriented. Switch on Radio 4, with failing batteries, to get glimpse of outside world: try to take intelligent interest in Nancy Reagan's breasts, Stock Exchange, Fiji. No good. A new sport: trying to stop Telecom vans as they whizz by. They have by now got evasive driving techniques down to a fine art, jinking around like the Sweeney at the approach of a certain mad-eyed class of customer with a redundant modem under its arm.

As if we hadn't suffered enough, local paper reports that Hurricane Cecil has blown in to Ipswich in a helicopter to tell Eastern Electricity that they're "doing a marvellous job". He also gets the local press very chuffed and fawning by saying that the devastation here is "the worst I have seen anywhere". Huh. Smooth talkin' man. Bet he says that to all the Electricity Boards. Blitz spirit suddenly evaporates, sympathy for gallant electricity men vanishes. Replaced by overwhelming desire to fuse Mr Parkinson to National Grid.

Stove goes out.

DAY 8 Raining again, so house too dark to find insurance policy, urgent letters, diary, anything, even by day. Feel a prat carrying a Tilley lamp around at 11 a.m. Painters finish and go away, leaving furniture everywhere. Husband gets back from pleasant country hotel in Devon, demanding to know why freezer has got mince 'n' maggots in. Tell him because I thought it was him who emptied it a week ago, I can't be poking around everywhere in pitch bloody dark all day with Tilley lamp, maggots surely got a right to live same as anyone else, sod it. Go and sit on remains of the beech tree, in a temper, in the drizzle, and read special reports in newspapers about how dreadfully badly hit Kent and Sussex are.

DAY 9 Big white van draws up, containing lost tribe of electricity men from Wales, can I tell them way to Knodishall? Bribe them with Jaffa cakes to do us first. Twenty minutes up pole, singing "Bread of Heaven", appears to do the trick. Switch lights on, look around at débris of paint pots, pictures, glasses, dirty cups, week's unhoovered filth, grubby socks and forgotten letters. Switch them off again.

While the Welsh songbirds were up the pole, a Telecom van whizzed by, hooted, but decided not to disturb us just yet. Still, it could be worse. We could have shares in them.

"You didn't really need that one for the road, did you?"

"Maybe another peep at the old map there, pardner?"

HELP YOUR CHILD SAY "NO" TO BANKING

Andrew was a normal, healthy boy who liked football and pop music. Then, at the age of sixteen, his life suddenly changed. The lives of his parents, Maureen and Bill Wilson, also changed ...

B E A U M O N T

You've been through a lot, haven't you, Mrs Wilson?

Maureen: "Yes, an awful lot. But it's all been worth it in the long run. Just knowing Andrew is all right, having him at home with us again and having the family back together. That's what makes everything worthwhile."

Bill: "Words don't exist to explain how relieved my wife and I are that it's all over. That it's all behind us and that we've not only got back our son, but he's also got back the most important thing of all – his self-respect."

Maureen: "He can't remember much about it. Perhaps that's just as well. I think we've suffered more than him in a funny sort of way."

Bill: "It's been a dreadful time. Particularly for Mo."

Maureen: "I'm not a strong person, you see. Bill is. I'm not."

Bill: "Yes, I am a strong person. I was a frogman in the war. It isn't very pleasant finding out your son is a banker. You need a lot of courage and a lot of strength. Banking is a nasty business. Andrew was lucky. We caught it before it really took hold. You just can't stand by and watch someone you love waste away like that. You've got to do something."

Maureen: "Helping someone to give up banking isn't easy. It's very frustrating and very exhausting. I don't know how Bill ever withstood the pressure."

Bill: "I think being a frogman in the war helped. I'm used to pressure."

When did you first begin to suspect that Andrew might have got involved in banking?

Maureen: "When he was seven."

That's very young.

Maureen: "Yes. The police brought him home one day. I'd hardly got out of bed. They said they'd found him sitting cross-legged on the early-morning train up to London reading the *Financial Times*. He had a bowler hat, brief-case and a brolly. He said he'd swopped some LPs for them at school. We didn't take much notice. He was only seven. We thought it was a phase he was going through. A period of experimentation. For years he had an imaginary 'commuter' friend. He took him everywhere and they ignored each other all the time."

When did you start to get worried?

Maureen: "I suppose it must have been the paraphernalia, wasn't it, Bill?"

Bill: "Yes, the paraphernalia."

What do you mean?

Maureen: "Shortly after Andrew left school I began to find things in his room. Odd things I'd never found before. He used to just leave them lying about. He made no attempt to try and hide them."

What sort of things?

Maureen: "Rubber-bands, little bags made out of clear plastic. But I never ever really thought of banking. Well, you don't, do you?"

Bill: "You've forgotten about the piles."

Maureen: "Oh yes, the piles."

The piles?

Maureen: "Yes, lots and lots of neat piles of loose change. From one penny right up to pound coins. All stacked in a nice even row. Andrew used to get very upset if anyone disturbed them."

Bill: "Bagging-up."

I beg your pardon?

Bill: "Bagging-up. It's the classical behavioural characteristic of a compulsive banker and habitual cashier".

How long did this go on?

Maureen: "Two weeks."

Bill: "Yes, about two weeks. Then it started."

What started?

Bill: "It's difficult to explain."

Try. Take your time.

Bill: "The droning."

The droning?

Bill: "Yes, Andrew began droning. Talking in this terrible, monotonous way."

Maureen: "About the same time, too, he became very fastidious about his appearance. He had his hair cut once a month and insisted on having exactly one inch of pale flesh showing between the top of his socks and his trouser-hems."

That sounds very disturbing.

Maureen: "It was. Friends of Andrew then told us how his handwriting had dramatically improved and how his vocabulary had drastically diminished."

Andrew began having trouble with his speech?

Maureen: "Yes, he stopped speaking completely and counted instead. He'd count everything. The knobs on the television, the peas on his plate…"

Bill: "He didn't eat. He'd stack things like diced carrot into stacks of five and push them to the side of his plate. Then he'd count them over and over again to see if any were missing."

Were there?

Bill: "No. Never. Andrew is very efficient."

Maureen: "Other things began to happen, didn't they?"

Bill: "Yes. Andrew began to really nauseate us."

How?

Maureen: "Little things like we could never sit down at the same meal together. There always had to be someone at the window. Andrew spent a lot of his time working out meal-rotas."

Bill: "He became very difficult to live with. We had to queue to see him and he was impossible in the mornings. He would never open his bedroom door before 9.30. He'd lock himself in his room at weekends. Paradoxically, when we did make an appointment to see him, he was very polite and courteous."

Maureen: "Yes, very helpful indeed."

Bill: "When he started offering to lend us money, asking for proof of our identities and having fire drills in the middle of the afternoon, we decided to take him to a doctor."

What happened?

Bill: "He asked Andrew if he heard any ringing in his ears and Andrew told him that he did and that it was a very important business call he was expecting from Brussels. It was then that we knew. He had a serious banking problem."

How did you feel?

Bill: "My initial reaction was one of anger, disappointment and disgust. But not at Andrew. At myself."

Maureen: "We both blamed ourselves. We thought we had brought him up properly. That we had a good relationship. But obviously something was lacking."

Bill: "It was a real slap in the face. We felt we had failed as parents."

What did you do?

Bill: "Like a lot of people we assumed the worst. That Andrew was beyond help. That his condition would deteriorate."

That he would become more and more ordinary?

Bill: "Yes. I'm not a self-righteous person but I wanted banking illegal-ised and something done about the people who got my baby into the whole banking thing. Now I know better."

Maureen: "Talking to other mums with children who also spend all day licking their fingers and looking at the clock taught me to face up to the issue. It also dispelled certain old wives' tales. Banking does not damage the body tissues and there is no such thing as saliva contamination. I carried on kissing Andrew goodnight without any side-effects."

Bill: "We tried to understand why Andrew had become a banker."

Why did he?

Bill: "He said it gave him a nice feeling. A sense of well-being."

Financial well-being?

Bill: "Yes. I think that's how he described it. We've battled through though and I think we're over the worst of it now. He still gives us mundane and practical presents at Christmas and on our birthdays, but we can't do much about that. It's all over. That's what matters."

Maureen: "You can't force someone to give up banking just like that. It must be their own decision. Andrew made that decision. We're very proud of him."

How long did it take for him to give up?

Bill: "A month. After he handed in his notice that was the worst time."

Maureen: "Of course, we'll never be able to forget completely what we've been through. Every time you open his wardrobe and see the tie-rack you remember the bad times. But we've been lucky."

Bill: "It could have been much, much more serious. It could have been merchant banking. That's deadly."

"That's not Smith. Smith's not that tall."

RODIN'S WC1 POSTAL SORTER

"It's not catching on, Fred. People are still sitting on chairs."

BARGEPOLE
·················

I WOULD be lying if I said that truth and beauty concern me much. Life is hard and has no place for philosophy. On the other hand, there is a lot of room for telling lies, although trouble can fall upon your head if you do so; there are always people with pursed lips like little sphincters waiting to pounce. "Oh come on," they say, "you're just making it up." The correct answer to this is, "How very naive; all the best stories are made up; didn't you realise? How the hell do you think *War and Peace* came about?" (Talking of which, I met a computer buff the other day. We spoke of Russia. "Do you know *War and Peace*?" I said. "Well, I saw the film," he replied, "but I never got round to reading the manual.")

I was reminded of this problem while "reading" the *Sunday Telegraph Magazine*, where an Irishman was going on about the mean streets and said that when he was a boy he and a friend had been stopped by Prods who said, "Are you Protestants or Catholics?" and his friend said, "I'm Jewish," and the Prods said, "Well, are you a Protestant Jew or a Catholic Jew, then?" and I thought *that's an old joke, the Da told me that when I was just a lad, passing it off as his own, has your man no shame?* Then I realised it was uncharitable and that I was reacting to an innocent tale in exactly the way that awful VAT inspectors and traffic wardens and Clerks to the Magistrates would do, people whom I would rather chop up than be like.

The problem is that we have no means of indicating that we are telling stories in this rotten language. I believe Hungarians sneeze thrice at the start of a narrative to show that it isn't actually true. It is possible that the person who told me that may have been lying but that doesn't matter; what matters is that one has strange ideas which one thinks are quite funny and there's no way of telling people without colossal deception. You can't say, "I was lying in the bath and I thought it would be really funny if someone was on holiday and their grandmother died and they put her on the roof-rack and she was stolen." Your audience would drift away and you would lay an egg. So you have to say, "A friend of my brother was on holiday with his grandmother and…" and they will listen.

They don't believe you, of course, the bastards. It would be awful if your brother really *did* have a friend to whom something bizarre happened, because you wouldn't be able to tell the story.

A friend of mine – let's call him Douglas, it's as good a name as any, and also happens to be his, which makes it easier for me – was once on Cambridge station waiting for a train and went for a cup of tea and one of those little packets of biscuits. He was sitting reading his newspaper and another chap came and sat opposite him and, without asking, opened Douglas's biscuits and ate one. What do you say? You can't punch the bastard in the face. So they ate alternate biscuits in a rather uneasy silence, and then the train came in and Douglas got up and there were his own biscuits, unopened, underneath his newspaper.

An embarrassing thing to happen, but what's even more embarrassing is that the narrative appears in a book of apocryphal tales, apparently dated before the event took place. There is absolutely no doubt that Douglas is telling the truth but his situation is ghastly. *He is a person to whom an apocryphal story has actually happened* and has no means of telling the story which leads other than to disaster and mockery.

This frightful predicament has led him to be sympathetic and intolerant at the same time, like so many people who have had formative experiences in their lives. I was sitting at his table lying happily the other day about my travels and I said I had played that game where you score points by revealing that you haven't read books which you could reasonably be expected to have read. I said that I had played it frequently (false) and that my winning stroke was that I had never read a single work by Jane Austen or any of the Brontës (true) and that the only person who had beaten me was the Assistant Head of the Minnesota University Faculty of English Literature, who had never read *Macbeth* (false). Douglas's response showed his true psychotic ambivalence. He laughed politely and then said, "Actually it was Euphoria State University and the play was *Hamlet* and the book was by Malcolm Bradbury."

I wriggled and writhed but obviously I had been rumbled, and the awful thing is that it wasn't my fault at all. My intention had been to give innocent amusement but the language had let me down.

What we need is some suffixes, like the Latin ones. They had particles denoting things like questions expecting the response "Yes" and we need one denoting a story which rather nervously expects the response "Oh, phooey, that's as old as the hills, I first heard it in 1969 in Watford" *but which also thwarts that response before the vile buggers can get it across their slobbering lips.* That's the real secret of happiness. Why should we have to confine our tales to our dreary problems and the uneventful droning of our dreary lives? Why, if we think of a funny remark like "I think I'll be philosophical and not think about it," do we have to go to awful narrative lengths like inventing imaginary women overheard on non-existent buses? Why, indeed, are we exposed to humiliation and upset when people believe our obvious lies? Have you ever said to someone, "Oh the cheque is in the post," and then found out that the bloody idiots have *believed* you? My magical new tense will solve all these difficulties. I have a team of ten men working on it, and if you wish to order your copy in advance, please send me £15.95 in a plain brown envelope. I will mail your new tense by return, together with a free Mystery Gift. Delivery within 28 days, guaranteed. Would I lie?

BEFORE THE INVENTION OF SHOES